Conspiracy
Who Killed JFK?

by
James R. Duffy

SPI
BOOKS
A division of Shapolsky Publishers, Inc.

Conspiracy: Who Killed JFK?

S.P.I. BOOKS

A division of Shapolsky Publishers, Inc.

Copyright © 1992 by James R. Duffy

Parts of this book were previously published by Shapolsky Publishers, Inc., as *Who Killed JFK?* by James R. Duffy, copyright © 1989.

For any additional information, contact:

S.P.I. BOOKS/Shapolsky Publishers, Inc.
136 West 22nd Street
New York, NY 10011
(212) 633-2022
FAX (212) 633-2123

ISBN: 1-56171-190-X

10 9 8 7 6 5 4 3 2 1

Printed and bound in the United States of America

CONTENTS

EXCERPT FROM

The Report of the President's Commission on the Assassination of President Kennedy (THE WARREN COMMISSION)

'[T]o determine the motives for the assassination of President Kennedy, one must look to the assassin himself.

'Clues to Oswald's motives can be found in his family history, his education or lack of it, his acts, his writings, and the recollections of those who had close contacts with him throughout his life . . .

'[O]thers may study Lee Harvey Oswald's life and arrive at their own conclusions as to his possible motives.'

EXCERPTS FROM

The Report of the Select Committee on Assassinations

US HOUSE OF REPRESENTATIVES

'The Committee believes, on the basis of the evidence available to it, that President John F. Kennedy was probably assassinated as a result of a conspiracy . . .

'Supreme Court Justice Oliver Wendell Holmes once simply defined conspiracy as "a partnership in criminal purposes". That definition is adequate. Nevertheless, it may be helpful to set out a more precise definition. If two or more individuals agreed to take action to kill President Kennedy, and at least one of them took action in furtherance of the plan, and it resulted in President Kennedy's death, the President would have been assassinated as a result of a conspiracy . . .

'Even without physical evidence of conspiracy at the scene of the assassination, there would, of course, be a conspiracy if others assisted Oswald in his efforts. Accordingly, an examination of Oswald's associates is necessary . . .

'It is important to realize, too, that the term "associate" may connote widely varying meanings to different people. A person's associate may be his next door neighbor and vacation companion, or it may be an individual he has met only once for the purpose of discussing a contract for a murder.'

'I think the CIA deliberately deceived the Warren Commission, based on the evidence that I have seen. I think the answer that they have given that they didn't provide the information because nobody asked them is the kind of statement I get from criminal defendants time in and time out . . .'
(House Committee testimony by Judge Burt W. Griffin, formerly Assistant Counsel for the Warren Commission)

INTRODUCTION
by Senator Alfonse M. D'Amato

On the twenty-fifth anniversary of the assassination of President John F. Kennedy, many unanswered questions persist in the collective mind of Americans.

The events of that fateful day have been thoroughly examined, researched and investigated, to the conclusion that Lee Harvey Oswald was the sole triggerman in Dallas. Still, there is a lingering sense that certain facts about Oswald's motivations have eluded us.

Clearly, the national tragedy of the cold-blooded murder of an American President draws us to search for the truth. But our efforts to understand the assassination are magnified by the recognition that the world of 1963 was a very different one from today's.

There was a genuine sense that a grand future of hope and idealism lay ahead of us. With his words, his ideas and, in the age of television, his personal grace, President Kennedy offered his youthful optimism to an eager American public.

In two minutes, one man's actions shattererd those ideals and changed the course of American history.

What drove Lee Harvey Oswald to load his rifle and take aim at the symbol of America's future?

James Duffy's "The Web" studies Oswald's life, associations, and the world in which he immersed himself. It was a contradictory world of Marxist studies, a Marine tour of duty, and defection to the Soviet Union. Oswald allegedly consorted with a wide spectrum of individuals, such as Communists, American patriots, organized crime families, anti-Castro Cuban exiles and the intelligence community.

His bizarre life has been broken down into many parts and studied at length by authors, investigators, and Congressional committees. However, a single, all-encompassing analysis of the numerous and contradictory factors which influenced Lee Harvey Oswald has not yet been adequately addressed.

In a thought-provoking reevaluation of Oswald, Duffy uses his experience as a respected trial lawyer to piece together the reams of information in U.S. Government investigations and reports as the sole basis for his penetrating analysis of the man whose bullets changed America.

"The Web" begins with the emotional instability of Oswald's childhood, and continues through his years of military service, where his strange behavior patterns became more pronounced. As a Marine at a key Air Force base, Oswald flaunted his love for things Russian, exhorting Marxist philosophy and learning and speaking the Russian language. Later, upon his defection to the Soviet Union, Oswald openly alerted U.S. Embassy personnel in Moscow of his intention to disclose sensitive intelligence to the KGB.

Duffy delves into those circumstances and events in Oswald's life which have never been fully explained. We are forced to think about the relative ease with which Oswald entered the Soviet Union, was employed at a Soviet radio factory of great militray interest to the United States, and yet, according to a Soviet defector, was never interrogated by the KGB. Duffy describes Oswald's connections with the henchmen of Fidel Castro, who had his own personal reasons for wanting President Kennedy dead, as well as with organized crime families and anti-Castro Cuban exiles in the U.S.

After his own thorough study of the key individuals and events surrounding Oswald, Duffy readily acknowledges the inability to reach a definitive conclusion. After all, the key answers to the comprehensive truth are buried forever with Oswald.

All that James Duffy asks is that the facts, the contradictions, and the widespread network of Lee Harvey Oswald's associations, which encompass this critical event in our nation's history, be further examined.

A quarter of a century after his assassination, we owe the memory of President John F. Kennedy no less.

Alfonse M. D'Amato
United States Senator

PREFACE

There have been many – perhaps too many – books purporting to solve the myriad of technical questions which have been raised regarding the tragic events in Dealey Plaza on 22 November 1963 (the number of shots, the angle of fire, the grassy knoll, the Zapruder film, the various wounds, the 'magic bullet', etc.), most of them having as their objective either proving or disproving that Lee Harvey Oswald was the assassin.

This is *not* such a book.

There have been a number of books wherein the writers purport – on the basis of their own personal research and interviews – to reveal some new information about the assassination. Interesting, but in the end totally dependent upon accepting the credibility and impartiality of the authors, who may in fact be merely setting forth their own pet theories.

This is not *that* type of book, either.

What, then, is this book? Or, perhaps more to the point: Why yet another assassination book?

As the introductory quotes suggest, this is a book about Lee Harvey Oswald, his background and his 'associates' – a word not ordinarily employed when discussing this man.

Oswald has, from the time of the assassination, been widely perceived as a somewhat one-dimensional, almost sub-human figure: non-conforming, anti-social, a malcontent, anti-American, an avowed Marxist and Communist, isolated, profoundly alienated, frustrated, resentful, hostile, presumably possessed of less than ordinary intelligence and – perhaps most important of all – he has consistently been portrayed as a 'loner'. To be sure, there is evidence to suggest that he was all of these things.

Yet, scattered through various official US Government documents, there are bits and pieces of information which, when brought together, constitute a substantial body of evidence which permits some rather strikingly different conclusions to be drawn about this notorious but 'unknown' man.

This book, derived wholly and solely from United States Government investigations and reports, narrates all the relevant evidence about Lee Harvey Oswald, points out and discusses the areas of conflict, and leaves the conclusions to the reader.

It tells the arresting story of one of history's most bewildering characters, and the threads seemingly linking him to remarkably diverse groups of people: threads of a web which included intelligence agents and underworld bosses, communists and anti-communists, patriots and spies, big shots and bimbos – a web of bizarre, indeed shocking, activities ranging from infiltration and subversion to assassination plots against the leaders of a number of countries.

It proves once again the old adage that 'Truth is stranger than fiction'.

A WORD AS TO FORMAT

The underlying premise of this book is that within official government reports there is abundant credible evidence to seriously question the accepted wisdom regarding Lee Harvey Oswald. To underscore this assertion, whenever it is consistent with maintaining a readable flow, the text of this work consists of direct quotes from these reports.

A compromise has been attempted as to attribution. On the one hand, this is not a history book and numerous footnotes can prove burdensome and distracting to the person reading for enjoyment. On the other hand, the reader can be confident as to the authenticity of the material only if the sources are specified and can be checked.

Therefore, at the end of the book is a chapter-by-chapter breakdown wherein the source(s) for each topic in that chapter is specifically cited.

Meanwhile, the reader is advised that each and every fact set forth in this book — whether in quotes or not — is drawn directly and exclusively from the following sources:

Report of the President's Commission on the Assassination of President John F. Kennedy, published by the US Government Printing Office in 1964 (known as the Warren Report).

Alleged Assassination Plots Involving Foreign Leaders, conducted by the Select Committee to Study Governmental Operations with respect to Intelligence Activities, United States Senate, published by the US Government Printing Office in 1975.

The Investigation of the Assassination of President John F. Kennedy, conducted by the Senate Select Committee to study Governmental Operations, published by the US Government Printing Office in 1976.

Investigation of the Assassination of President John F. Kennedy, conducted by the Select Committee on Assassinations of the US House of Representatives, published by the US Government Printing Office in 1979.

BOOK 1

CHAPTER

1

The Family

Exchange Alley, on the outskirts of the French Quarter, was a rough area. It was the hub of some of the most notorious, openly conducted underworld joints in New Orleans. This narrow bleak street was the location of various gambling operations affiliated to the organization of Carlos Marcello, the city's crime boss. Sordid bars also operated there, including some in which aggressive homosexuals and prostitutes were frequenters.

At 126 Exchange Alley, over the pool hall which was a hangout for gamblers, was a dingy little apartment where, during 1955 and 1956, a teenager named Lee Harvey Oswald lived with his once-widowed, twice-divorced mother.

Marguerite Claverie, born in New Orleans in 1907, had first married one Edward John Pic, jun. in August 1929. By the summer of 1931, she and Pic were separated, though she was then three months pregnant with a son who would be named John Edward Pic.

On 20 July 1933, having obtained a divorce from Pic, Marguerite married Robert Edward Lee Oswald, an insurance premium collector whom she had been seeing during her separation. Mr Oswald's offer to adopt his wife's young son was objected to by Marguerite since that might cut off her support payments from Edward Pic.

A son born to the Oswalds on 7 April 1934 was named Robert Oswald, jun. On 18 October 1939, two months after her husband died suddenly of a heart attack, Marguerite gave birth to the second son of this marriage, naming him Lee after his father and Harvey which was his paternal grandmother's maiden name.

The two older boys, John Pic and Robert Oswald, were soon sent to a Catholic boarding school in Algiers, Louisiana, where they remained for about a year. They then returned home for a while, but on 3 January 1942 their mother placed them in an orphan asylum, known as Bethlehem Children's Home. Marguerite had actually inquired about placing all three boys in the orphanage, but Lee was not accepted because at two years of age he was too young to be admitted.

Marguerite returned to work, leaving Lee for much of the next year with her sister, Mrs Lillian Murret, and at other times with a sitter.

Then, on the day after Christmas, 1942, three-year-old Lee Harvey Oswald was sent to the orphanage.

During the year 1943, Marguerite was dating Edwin A. Ekdahl, and by January 1944 they had decided to marry. Marguerite withdrew Lee from the orphanage and moved with him to Dallas, where Ekdahl expected to be working. John and Robert were thereafter withdrawn from the home and went to live with their mother in Dallas. Marguerite then decided she did not want to marry Ekdahl, though she continued to see him. Finally, however, she and Ekdahl were married in May 1945.

Several months before this, in February 1945, Marguerite had stated that she expected to travel a great deal, and tried to return the older boys to the home. Though she failed in that endeavor, in the fall of that year she succeeded in sending John and Robert away to a military academy where they would live until the summer of 1948.

Concurrent with sending the older boys off to the military academy, the Ekdahls moved to Benbrook, a suburb of Fort Worth, Texas. Lee was immediately entered into the first grade at the Benbrook Common School (whose records show his birth date as 9 July 1939, an incorrect date presumably given by his mother to satisfy the age requirement).

Lee became quite attached to Ekdahl, finding in him the father he never had. But this father-son relationship was to be short-lived, for the marriage between his mother and Ekdahl soon became stormy. Marguerite separated from Ekdahl, and moved with Lee to Covington, Louisiana.

Since Lee had not completed the first grade at Benbrook, in September 1946 he was again entered into the first grade, this time at the Covington Elementary School. He was withdrawn from the Covington School on 23 January 1947 because the Ekdahls, having reconciled, were now moving to Fort Worth. He finally completed first grade in the Clayton Public School and entered second grade at that school the following September. However, relations between the Ekdahls having deteriorated again, Marguerite moved to another location in Fort Worth and Lee completed second grade at the Clark Elementary School.

The Ekdahls were finally divorced in June, 1948, after a bitter trial in which the jury found that Marguerite was guilty of 'excesses, cruel treatment, or outrages' unprovoked by Ekdahl's conduct. The divorce restored to Marguerite her former name, Marguerite C. Oswald.

Mrs Oswald then purchased a small, one-bedroom house in Benbrook and moved in with her three sons. John and Robert slept on the porch, and Lee slept with his mother (a practice which continued until he was almost eleven years old). By the end of the summer, she had sold this house and moved once again into Fort Worth. Lee attended third grade at the Arlington Heights Elementary School, but the following year he was transferred to his sixth school, Ridglea West Elementary School, which he attended for the next three years.

After the divorce, Marguerite complained considerably about how unfairly she was treated, dwelling on the fact that she was a widow with three children. She overstated her financial problems, was unduly concerned about money, and Lee was brought up in an atmosphere of constant money problems.

Marguerite worked in miscellaneous jobs after her divorce from Ekdahl. When she worked during the school year, Lee not only left an empty house in the morning, but returned to it at lunch and then again at night, his mother having trained him to do that rather than to play with other children. Lee seemed to enjoy being by himself and to resent discipline.

In 1950, John entered the Coast Guard, and in July 1952 Robert joined the Marines.

In August 1952, Marguerite and Lee moved to New York City. They lived for a time with John (who was stationed there) and his wife and baby. Marguerite did not get along with John's wife, with whom she quarrelled frequently. In late September, Marguerite and Lee moved to their own apartment.

Lee's truancy soon became a severe problem, and after several unsuccessful attempts were made to resolve the situation, on 12 March 1953 the attendance officer filed a petition in court which ultimately resulted in Lee being remanded to Youth House from 16 April to 7 May for psychiatric study.

The Chief Psychiatrist at Youth House, Dr Renatus Hartogs, summarized his report on Lee by stating: 'This 13-year-old well-built boy has superior mental resources and functions only slightly below his capacity level in spite of chronic truancy from school which brought him into Youth House. No findings of neurological impairment or psychotic mental changes could be made. Lee has to be diagnosed as "personality pattern disturbance with schizoid features and passive-aggressive tendencies". Lee has to be seen as an emotionally, quite disturbed youngster who suffers under the impact of really existing emotional isolation and deprivation, lack of affection, absences of family life and rejection by a self-involved and conflicted mother.'

Mrs Evelyn Strickman Siegel, a social worker who interviewed both Lee and his mother while Lee was confined in Youth House, described him as a 'seriously detached, withdrawn youngster'. She also noted that there was 'a rather pleasant, appealing quality about this emotionally starved, affectionless youngster which grows as one speaks to him'. She thought he had detached himself from the world around him because 'no one in it ever met any of his needs for love'.

Irving Sokolow, a Youth House psychologist, reported that: 'The Human Figure Drawings are empty, poor characterizations of persons approximately the same age as the subject. They reflect a considerable amount of impoverishment in the social and emotional areas. He appears to be a somewhat insecure youngster exhibiting much inclination for warm and satisfying relationships to others. There is some indication that he may relate to men more easily than to women in view of the more mature conceptualization. He appears slightly withdrawn and in view of the lack of detail within the drawings that may assume a more significant characteristic. He exhibits some difficulty in relationship to the maternal figure suggesting more anxiety in this area than in any other.'

Lee scored an IQ of 118 on the Wechsler Intelligence Scale for Children. According to Sokolow, this indicated a 'present intellectual functioning in the upper range of bright normal intelligence'. Sokolow said that although Lee was 'presumably disinterested in school subjects he operates on a much higher than average level'. On the Monroe Silent Reading Test, Lee's score indicated no retardation in reading speed or comprehension; he had better than average ability in arithmetical reasoning for his age group.

On the basis of all the test results, Dr Hartogs recommended that Lee be placed on probation with a requirement that he be provided help and guidance during the probation. However, such help and guidance was never provided, the basic problem being that the few facilities which provided the necessary services already had full case-loads.

On 24 September, the day the probation had originally been scheduled to end, Mrs Oswald phoned the probation officer and said that she could not appear in court, adding that there was no need to do so, as Lee was attending school regularly and was now well adjusted. The probation was extended until 29 October, before which date the school was to submit a progress report. Mrs Oswald's assurances to the contrary notwithstanding, the report, when it was submitted, was a highly unfavorable one.

On 29 October, Mrs Oswald again telephoned to say she would be unable to appear. The probation was continued until 19 November, on which date Lee and his mother appeared. But, despite Mrs Oswald's request that Lee be discharged, Justice Sicher stated his belief that Lee needed treatment, and he continued his probation until 29 January 1954. The probation officer was directed to contact the Big Brothers counseling service in the meantime. On 4 January a caseworker from Big Brothers visited the Oswald home, where he was cordially received, but was told by Mrs Oswald that further counseling was unnecessary.

Mrs Oswald informed the Big Brother caseworker that she intended to return to New Orleans. The caseworker advised her that she must obtain Lee's release from the court's jurisdiction before she left. The next day she called the probation officer. In his absence (he was away on vacation) his office advised Mrs

Oswald not to take Lee out of the jurisdiction without the court's consent. The same advice was repeated to her by the Big Brother caseworker on 6 January. Without further communication to the court (and without him ever getting any of the help or treatment deemed necessary for him) Mrs Oswald took Lee to New Orleans sometime before 10 January.

BOOK 1

CHAPTER

2

Another Kind of 'Family'

Back in New Orleans, Lee and his mother stayed with her sister and brother-in-law, Mr and Mrs Charles Murret, until they got an apartment of their own. Lee had developed a close relationship with the Murrets during his numerous stays with them over the years. Now that he was back in New Orleans, he visited with them regularly, eating dinner with them on Friday evenings and spending his Saturdays there. His uncle Charles Murret was a father figure of sorts. The Murrets served as the closest thing to a real family he had been exposed to up to that point. This special relationship would continue throughout Oswald's life.

Years earlier, Charles Murret (commonly called 'Dutz'), who had been involved in promoting several prize-fighters in New Orleans, had served as the manager of a boxer named Tony Sciambra. After his boxing days, Sciambra had gone on to become a lieutenant to a local organized crime leader named Sam Saia.

'Dutz' Murret later became involved with Saia in an underworld gambling syndicate affiliated to the Carlos Marcello crime family. Saia, who had made his money by dope peddling in the early years, was one of the largest bookmakers in New Orleans, and the financial backer of numerous underworld clubs throughout the New Orleans area. Saia was known to be 'very close' to Carlos Marcello, and it was through the gambling wire service controlled by Marcello that Saia and his associates such as 'Dutz' Murret conducted their betting operations.

Prior to her first marriage, Lee's mother had been working as a secretary for a New Orleans lawyer named Raoul Sere. They became friendly enough that when that marriage failed, Sere re-hired her and helped her pay some debts she had acquired for furniture and other items. This friendship continued into 1960 at the earliest, when Sere took her out to dinner on at least one occasion. In the interim Sere, who was politically active as an attorney, had for a period of time become an assistant district attorney for the city of New Orleans.

Aaron Kohn, chairman of the Metropolitan Crime Commission of New Orleans, has testified that 'Sere played a key role in running the DA's office during the period in which that office was later proven to be highly corrupt' and, 'The DA's office was then under the corrupt influence of the gambling syndicate – Carlos Marcello and various others – to a very significant degree'.

Marguerite had been friends from childhood with another New Orleans attorney, Clem Sehrt, whose law partner counted Carlos Marcello among his clients. Sehrt, a former state banking official, had risen to prominence in Louisiana through his close relationship with Louis J. Rousell, a New Orleans banking executive who was an old and close associate of Carlos Marcello. During the 1950s, when Sehrt's relationship to him was the closest, Rousell had become involved in a political scandal concerning reported cash pay-offs to two Louisiana Supreme Court justices from an unreported corporate payroll of Rousell plus the provision of a new Cadillac each year to the Chief Judge of the Louisiana Supreme Court.

Another of Marguerite's friends (as well as of 'Dutz' Murret and Sam Saia) was Sam Termine, who, according to the New Orleans Metropolitan Crime Commission, was a Louisiana crime figure involved in a number of illicit operations including syndicate gambling and prostitution, as well as in the operation of a motel used for underworld activities. Termine was particularly close to Carlos Marcello, whom he had once served as a chauffeur and bodyguard.

Of the ubiquitous Carlos Marcello, more later.

BOOK 1

CHAPTER

3

Svengali

Upon returning to New Orleans, Lee had been enrolled in the eighth grade at Beauregard Junior High School on 13 January 1954, and he continued there in the ninth grade that September. In September 1955 he entered the tenth grade at Warren Eastern High School.

Meanwhile, in the early summer of 1955, Lee Harvey Oswald had begun attending meetings of the Civil Air Patrol, a student aviation organization which met twice a week. The first unit he was involved with was located at the Lakefront Airport. The commander of that group, who also participated in the training of recruits, was a man named David Ferrie. There was another CAP unit over at Moisant Airport, and by late summer both Lee Oswald and David Ferrie had become attached to that unit. For at least the next few months Lee Harvey Oswald had continued involvement at the Moisant Airport unit of the CAP with David Ferrie.

Born in Cleveland, Ohio in 1918, David Ferrie was 'a complex, even bizarre individual . . . His unusual personal appearance was partially a result of the loss of his body hair induced by a rare disease. He wore a makeshift toupee and exaggerated fake eyebrows affixed crudely with glue as compensation [for his missing hair] . . . Persons who knew him considered him sloppy and unkempt, with a proclivity for foul language . . .

'Although his formal education was not extensive, Ferrie was considered highly intelligent, even brilliant. He had originally studied theology in the hope of becoming an ordained priest, but he left seminary school before graduation because of "emotional instability". Later, in 1941, he received a bachelor of arts degree from Baldwin-Wallace College, majoring in philosophy. He also received, through a correspondence course, a doctorate degree in psychology from an uncredited school, Phoenix University, Bari, Italy . . .

'Ferrie spent considerable time studying medicine and psychology, especially the techniques of hypnosis which he frequently practiced on his young associates.

'Ferrie's major avocation and occupation was flying. Even associates who were critical of Ferrie's character considered him an excellent pilot . . . He took flying lessons at Sky Tech Airway Service in Cleveland, Ohio, between 1942 and 1945, following his failure at the seminary. He then worked as a pilot for an oil drilling firm which had jobs in South America. When the company went out of business, Ferrie tried teaching at Rocky River High School, but was fired in 1948 for psychoanalyzing his students instead of teaching them. Although his exact movements [thereafter] are not known, it appears he had gone to Tampa, Florida, where he received his instrument rating at Sunnyside Flying School. In 1950, Ferrie returned to Cleveland [where] he worked as an insurance inspector . . . In 1951, he submitted an application to Eastern Airlines, omitting details of his past emotional and occupational difficulties. Eastern Airlines hired him in Miami, and soon transferred him to New Orleans.'

David Ferrie was a homosexual and misogynist whose sexual exploitation of younger men was at about this time becoming more and more flagrant. 'He often gave parties at his residence where liquor flowed freely.' On at least one occasion some CAP cadets became drunk at his home and engaged in various activities in the nude. Such incidents led to Ferrie being expelled from the CAP in late 1955.

Over the next few years, a number of different complaints involving his activities with a variety of boys of about fifteen years of age resulted in charges such as 'crimes against nature', 'indecent behavior', and 'contributing to the delinquency of a juvenile'. These ultimately led to his discharge from Eastern Airlines for moral turpitude.

'Many of Ferrie's cadets became involved in Ferrie's wide spectrum of other activities.'

'Ferrie's tremendous influence and close association with these young men eventually became a controversial subject with many parents.'

'He was able to exert tremendous influence over his close associates, including many young men in his Civil Air Patrol squadron.'

'He was rabidly anti-Communist . . . frequently critical of each Presidential administration for what he perceived to be sell-outs to communism.'

'He urged several boys to join the armed forces.'

In October 1955, Lee Harvey Oswald, who had just turned sixteen, dropped out of school and tried to enlist in the Marines, using a false affidavit from his mother stating that he was seventeen. Lee was by all accounts particularly susceptible to the thought of entering the service. His older brothers had both done so, perhaps as a way of escaping from their mother, and Lee himself had seen the service as a way to be on his own, according to Evelyn Strickman, the social worker who had seen him in New York.

The attempted enlistment failed, and according to his mother, Lee spent the next year reading and memorizing the Marine Manual which he had obtained from Robert, and 'living to when he is age 17 to join the Marines'.

Anticipating that Lee would join the Marines as soon as he was seventeen, Mrs Oswald moved in July 1956 to Fort Worth, where Lee was enrolled in the tenth grade at the Arlington Heights High School. Lee became seventeen on 18 October and enlisted in the Marines on 24 October 1956.

At some later date, according to one of Ferrie's colleagues, Jack S. Martin, David Ferrie told him 'about a young friend who had witnessed an alleged "crime against nature" that Ferrie had committed, a young man who had left New Orleans and "subsequently joined the US Marine Corps"'.

The eccentric David Ferrie will reappear later in our story.

BOOK 1

CHAPTER

4

The Chameleon

The period of time, beginning in mid-1955, when he first came into contact with David Ferrie, until October, 1956 when he entered the Marines, marks the emergence of the first in a long series of what appear to be striking inconsistencies in the conduct of Lee Harvey Oswald. Careful evaluation of these seemingly incongruous actions is essential if we can ever hope to discern who or what this chameleonic figure really was like.

At some point during this period, Lee had begun – and had openly flaunted – the reading of Communist literature, surely a curious choice of reading material for one so intent on joining the United States Marine Corps.

The Warren Commission speculated that 'his study of Communist literature, which might appear to be inconsistent with his desire to join the Marines, could have been another manifestation of Oswald's rejection of his environment'. Perhaps so.

But that theory did not take into account that this was an even more curious, more inconsistent activity for someone involved with such a fanatical anti-Communist as David Ferrie. It is indisputable that it did not take this into account because the Warren Commission was not even aware of the Ferrie connection, which came to light many years later.

Therefore, without in any way dismissing the Warren Commission's explanation, which may be completely correct, any rational analysis of this incongruity should, at the very least, consider the relationship between the emotionally-starved, fatherless, young Lee Harvey Oswald, and the Svengali-like David Ferrie.

Though perhaps somewhat more extreme than others, Ferrie's anti-Communism was not unique for the time. Since the end of World War II, the fear of Godless Communism had been a major concern of many Americans. It was the era of the House Unamerican Activities Committee, Senator Joseph McCarthy, the Smith Act, the Internal Security Act of 1950, and the Communist Control Act of 1954.

It was also the era of covert action programs run by the FBI. While the FBI by no means had a monopoly on such anti-Communist covert action programs, they did initiate a new one in 1956, an operation called COINTELPRO, which was their acronym for 'counter-intelligence program'.

Counter-intelligence, an art-form practiced as well by the CIA as the various military intelligence groups, can be defined as those actions by an intelligence agency intended to protect its own security including affirmative action taken to undermine or neutralize hostile intelligence operations.

One contemporaneous example of counter-intelligence (and of the public obsession with Communism) was the highly-popular television series, *I Led Three Lives*, a program which purported to relate the clandestine adventures and triumphs of Herb Philbrick, an FBI undercover agent who had been surreptitiously infiltrated into the Communist Party. According to Lee's mother, *I Led Three Lives* was a steady part of his TV viewing diet.

****

Reading and flaunting Communist literature, while at the same time avidly studying, and wishing his life away until he could join the Marines, was not his only contradictory trait during this time.

On 3 October 1956, just two weeks before the birthday on which he had long planned to leave the Fort Worth area in order to enter the Marines Corps, Lee wrote the following letter to the Socialist Party of America:

Dear Sirs:
I am sixteen years of age and would like more information about your Youth League, I would like to know if there is a branch in my area, how to join, etc. I am a Marxist, and have been studying socialist principles for well over fifteen months. I am very interested in your YPSL.

Sincerely
Lee Oswald

BOOK 1

CHAPTER

5

The Unique Marine

On 26 October 1956, Lee Harvey Oswald reported for duty at the Marine Corps Recruit Depot in San Diego, California. His preference of duty was recorded as Aircraft Maintenance and Repair, the duty assignment for which he was recommended.

Following basic training at San Diego and then at Camp Pendelton, California, Oswald was assigned for additional training, first to the Naval Air Technical Training Center at the Naval Air Station in Jacksonville, Florida, then to Kessler Air Force Base in Biloxi, Mississippi, and then to the Marine Corps Air Station at El Toro, California.

While at San Diego, Oswald was trained in the use of the M-1 rifle. His practice scores were not very good, but somehow when his company fired for record on 21 December, he scored 212, two points above the score necessary to qualify as a 'sharpshooter' on a marksman/ sharpshooter/expert scale. (He did not do nearly as well when he fired for record again shortly before he left the Marines.)

It may just have been another case of the service

assigning an Eskimo to the tropics, but it has been perhaps too facilely passed over that the additional training Oswald received at these military locations was as a radar operator; and it was in that capacity that he ultimately came to be assigned to the Marine Air Control Squadron at Atsugi Air Base, 20 miles west of Tokyo, Japan.

Radar, by definition, is 'a method of detecting distant objects and determining their position, velocity, or other characteristics by analysis of very high frequency radio waves reflected from their surfaces'. The training, in addition to radar theory and use, included aircraft surveillance, map reading and air traffic control procedures.

On his aptitude tests, taken on 30 October – which are presumably what would have prompted someone to assign him to this specialty – although Oswald had scored significantly above the Marine Corps averages in reading and vocabularly, significantly *below* the average in arithmetic and pattern analysis, and near the bottom of the lowest group in the radio code test, his composite general classification score was 105, two points below the Corps average. Indeed, he finished the six-week course at Jacksonville forty-sixth in a class of fifty-four students.

Then a most surprising thing happened. At Kessler, following a six-week course during which none of his fellow Marines knew where he spent his free time, except that it was thought to be away from the base, Lee was placed seventh in a class of thirty.

We shall in a subsequent chapter consider whether there could have been some purpose in taking Oswald, despite his aptitude test scores, and qualifying him to be a radar operator.

The specialty of radar operator, even from the training stage, required dealing with confidential material. On 3 May 1957, this young man who had been flaunting an apparent interest in Communist literature was granted a 'confidential' clearance.

Oswald retained his clearance throughout his

enlistment despite the fact that he became more and more blatant in overtly showcasing his interest in Russia – a fact which is rather curious considering that Atsugi Air Base was home to the super-secret U-2 spy plane which took off and landed there.

Most of those who knew him in the Marines, at Atsugi and at the other bases, were able to recount anecdotes which suggested to the Warren Commission that Oswald was anxious to publicize his liking for things Russian, sometimes in good humor and sometimes seriously. Some of his colleagues called him 'Oswaldskovich', apparently to his pleasure. He was said to have had his name written in Russian on one of his jackets; to have played records of Russian songs 'so loud that one could hear them outside the barracks'; frequently to have made remarks in Russian or used expressions like 'da' or 'nyet' or addressed others (and been addressed) as 'Comrade'; to have come over and said jokingly, 'You called?' when one of the marines played a particular record of Russian music. When he played chess, according to one of his opponents he chose the red pieces, expressing a preference for the 'Red Army'. He regularly and openly read a Russian language newspaper; Lieutenant John Donovan thought it was a Communist newspaper and believed Oswald had a subscription to it.

It appeared to most observers that connected with this Russophilia was an interest in and acceptance of Russian political views and Communist ideology. Indeed, Kerry Thornley, a marine who described himself as a close acquaintance but not a good friend of Oswald, thought he definitely believed that 'the Marxist morality was the most rational morality to follow', and Communism 'the best system in the world'.

Oswald the political heretic received even more endorsement as a malcontent with his two court martials in 1957, one for possession of an unauthorized .22 caliber derringer pistol, and the other for verbally assaulting and pouring a drink on a non-commissioned officer. For these offenses his combined punishments cost him $105, a reduction in rank to the grade of private and confinement to hard labor for 48 days.

Most of the marines who knew Lee Oswald were aware that he was studying the Russian language. By 25 February 1959 his studying had progressed to the point that he attempted a foreign language qualification test; his rating of 'poor' on this exam must be evaluated in light of the fact that he was apparently studying on his own. One observer with some knowledge of Russian, Rosaleen Quinn, thought he spoke the language well in view of his lack of formal training.

Oswald's fellow marines at his various units can provide little if any information as to his activities when not actually on the base and in the unit. Throughout his tour of duty, Oswald invariably tended to disappear from the view of his fellow marines during off-hours, weekends and leaves.

In November 1958 Oswald finished his overseas tour of duty, and was shipped back to California; after travel time and thirty-day leave, he was assigned to a Marine Air Control Squadron at the Marine Corps Air Station at El Toro, where he had been based briefly before he went overseas.

In March 1959, Oswald took a series of high-school level general level educational development tests, and received an overall rating of 'satisfactory'. In the same month, he applied to Albert Schweitzer College in Churwalden, Switzerland, for admission to the spring term in 1960. This application was approved by the college, and by letter dated 19 June, Oswald sent his registration fee of $25.

Lee was obligated to serve on active duty until 7 December 1959 (the date having been adjusted to compensate for the period of confinement). But then, in August, he made a voluntary allotment of $40 to his mother, applied for a dependant's quarters ('Q') allotment on her behalf, and on 17 August he submitted a request for a dependency discharge on the ground that his mother needed his support due to an injury she had sustained at work (there had been an injury the previous December). Within two weeks, the application had been approved.

This is one of a number of occasions when Lee Harvey Oswald appeared to be remarkably expeditious in cutting through red tape, ostensibly because this unintelligent non-conformist somehow seemed to always have his papers complete and in order.

But it so happens that this particular application was not truly complete. Although the requisite preconditions of a voluntary allotment and request for 'Q' allotment had been made, and although the application was accompanied by an affidavit of Mrs Oswald and corroborating affidavits from an attorney, a doctor, and two friends, all the supporting affidavits for the quarters allotment had not been submitted at the time the hardship discharge application was filed. Nonetheless, the application was quickly forwarded, with merely an endorsement that the reviewing officers were aware that both the requisite voluntary contribution and the application for a quarters allotment had been made.

However, under the applicable procedures, Oswald's requisite application for a quarters allowance for his mother should have been disallowed because he had not contributed any money to her during the preceding year. Moreover, the reviewing officer in his endorsement, dated 19 August (only two days after it was submitted), stated 'A genuine hardship exists in this case, and in my opinion approval of the "Q" allotment will not sufficiently alleviate this situation.'

This is a puzzling statement in light of the fact that the Fort Worth Red Cross office indicated that only a quarters allotment was necessary for Marguerite Oswald, rather than a hardship discharge for Lee. On 28 August, the Wing Hardship or Dependency Discharge Board recommended that Oswald's request for a discharge be approved, which was done shortly thereafter.

On 4 September, pending his hardship discharge so he could go home and support his injured mother, Lee Oswald applied for a passport. His application stated that he planned to leave the United States on 21 September to attend the Albert Schweitzer College and the University of Turku in Finland, as well as to travel in Cuba, the Dominican Republic, England, France, Germany, and Russia. The passport was issued six days later.

Oswald received his hardship discharge on 11 September. He arrived in Fort Worth by 14 September, gave his mother $100, and departed three days later for New Orleans.

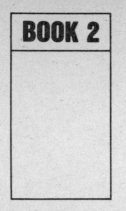

BOOK 2

DEFECTOR ?

BOOK 2

CHAPTER 6

Destination Golub

The Warren Commission, utilizing Oswald's own 'Historic Diary' together with various documents and testimony from Russian and American sources, reconstructed a rather detailed account of his defection to, and life in, the Soviet Union.

In summary, according to this account, Lee Harvey Oswald sought to defect to Russia; was rejected; became despondent, and attempted suicide, which resulted in the Russians accepting him; was sent to an obscure job in an obscure city; grew dissatisfied with Russian life; and thereupon re-defected to the United States, having in the meantime acquired a Russian wife.

Information has subsequently emerged which demonstrates that there are significant problems with each of the sources for this account, and which therefore suggests that the above scenario may be totally untrue.

Indeed, one of the questions which arise is: Could it be that Lee Harvey Oswald was actually an agent of the United States, and that his defection to Russia was for some mission of the US?

What follows below is the Warren Commission reconstruction supplemented by the more recent evidence and observations.

According to the Warren Report: 'On 17 September, Oswald spoke with a representative of Travel Consultants, Inc., a New Orleans travel bureau; he filled out a "Passenger Immigration Questionnaire" on which he gave his occupation as "shipping export agent", and said that he would be abroad for 2 months on a pleasure trip. He booked passage from New Orleans to Le Havre, France, on a freighter, the SS *Marion Lykes*, scheduled to sail on 18 September, for which he paid $220.75. On the evening of 17 September, he registered at the Liberty Hotel.

'The *Marion Lykes* did not sail until the early morning of 20 September . . . [It] carried only four passengers. Oswald shared his cabin with Billy Joe Lord, a young man who had just graduated from high school and was going to France to continue his education . . . The other two passengers were Lieutenant Colonel and Mrs George B. Church : . ..

'Oswald disembarked at Le Havre on 8 October. He left for England that same day, and arrived on 9 October. He told English customs officials in Southampton that he had $700 and planned to remain in the United Kingdom for 1 week before proceeding to a school in Switzerland. But on the same day he flew to Helsinki, Finland, where he registered at the Torni Hotel; on the following day, he moved to the Klaus Kurki Hotel. Oswald probably applied for a visa at the Russian Consulate on 12 October, his first business day in Helsinki. The visa was issued on 14 October . . . He left Helsinki by train on the following day, crossed the Finnish-Russian border at Vainikkala, and arrived in Moscow on 16 October . . . He was met at the Moscow railroad station by a representative of "Intourist", the state tourist agency, and taken to the Hotel Berlin, where he registered as a student '

There are noteworthy difficulties with the above scenario.

The circumstances surrounding Oswald's trip from London to Helsinki are most suspicious and mysterious. Oswald's passport indicates he arrived in Finland on 10 October, 1959, and the Torni Hotel in Helsinki has him registered as a guest on that same date.

However, unless Oswald received some well-placed help, there was no way that he could have been registered at the Torni on the same day he arrived in Finland. That is true because of two immutable facts, which no investigation has found to be in error or in dispute:

(1) the only direct flight from London to Helsinki landed at 11.33 p.m. on that date; and,

(2) as conceded in a memorandum by the then CIA Deputy Director, Richard M. Helms, '[i]f Oswald had taken this flight, he could not normally have cleared customs and landing formalities and reached the Torni Hotel downtown by 24.00 (midnight) on the same day'.

Louis Hopkins, the travel agent who arranged for Oswald's passage from the United States, was not aware of Oswald's ultimate destination and so had nothing to do with the London–Helsinki trip. Moreover, Hopkins has testified, had he known Oswald's ultimate destination, his advice would have been to sail not on the *Marion Lykes*, but on a different ship to a port more convenient for Russia.

The mystery is enhanced by Louis Hopkins' observation that Oswald did not appear to be particularly well-informed about travel in Europe.

Further questions arise from Oswald's obtaining a Soviet entry visa within only two days of having applied for it on 12 October, 1959 (10 October, the date of arrival, having been a Saturday, the first opportunity to apply for a visa would have been on Monday, 12 October).

Normally at least a week would elapse between the time of a tourist's application and the issuance of a visa.

This minimum time was, if anything, all the more necessary if, in addition to the processing of the visa application, lodgings were to be arranged through Soviet Intourist, as appears to have been the case with Oswald, inasmuch as he was met at the Moscow railroad station by an Intourist representative and taken to the Hotel Berlin.

However, the Soviet Consul in Helsinki, Gregory Golub, was suspected by American intelligence of also being an officer in the Soviet KGB. Golub had once disclosed in a luncheon conversation that Moscow had given him authority to give Americans visas without prior approval from Moscow, and that 'as long as he was convinced the American was "all right", he could give him a visa in a matter of minutes'.

An American Embassy dispatch, dated 9 October 1959, the day before Oswald arrived in Helsinki, illustrates that Golub indeed had such authority (while at the same time, it prompts some intriguing questions). The dispatch, which had been referring to an earlier telephone contact between Golub and the American Embassy in Helsinki, goes on to state: '. . . Since that evening [4 September 1959] Golub has only phoned [the US consul] once and this was on a business matter. Two Americans were in the Soviet Consulate at the time and were applying for Soviet visas thru Golub. They had previously been in the American consulate inquiring about the possiblilty of obtaining a Soviet visa in 1 or 2 days. [The US Consul] advised them to go directly to Golub and make their request, which they did. Golub phoned [the US Consul] to state that he would give them their visas as soon as they made advance Intourist reservations. When they did this, Golub immediately gave them their visas . . .'

The House Select Committee, which developed this evidence about Golub, concluded: 'Thus, based upon these two factors, (1) Golub's authority to issue visas to

Americans without prior approval from Moscow, and (2) a demonstration of this authority, as reported in an embassy dispatch approximately 1 month prior to Oswald's appearance at the Soviet Embassy, the Committee found that the available evidence tends to support the conclusion that the issuance of Oswald's tourist visa within 2 days after his appearance at the Soviet Consulate was not indicative of an American intelligence agency connection.' And, in a footnote, they observed: 'If anything, Oswald's ability to receive a Soviet entry visa so quickly was more indicative of a Soviet interest in him.'

This footnote is puzzling in the extreme, since it appears to be inconsistent with the very conclusion it footnotes. That conclusion makes crystal-clear that Oswald's ability to receive a Soviet entry visa so quickly had absolutely nothing to do with a Soviet interest in him; that, in fact, its speedy issuance would indicate that it was not cleared in Moscow (a presumption which the reader might find even more compelling when we discuss the less-than-enthusiastic reception Oswald received in Moscow).

However, the conclusion itself is, if anything, more puzzling than the footnote. What the conclusion really amounts to is a statement that there is no American intelligence agency connection, since we have evidence that the expedited visa was issued by Golub.

But the premise does not support the conclusion. The probable involvement of Golub in the issuance of Oswald's expedited – and uninvestigated – visa does not eliminate the possibility of American intelligence agency involvement; it may, in fact, make such involvement more likely.

Logically, it should be the beginning of a line of inquiry that asks the simple question: Why Golub?

The above cited evidence would seem to justify the following speculative queries on that score:

(1) If the United States wished to infiltrate someone into the Soviet Union, would it be helpful if the

necessity of prior clearance from Moscow for his visa could be circumvented?

(2) Did the United States know that the necessity of prior visa clearance from Moscow could be circumvented via Gregory Golub?

(3) If (hypothetically) the United States wished to infiltrate a Lee Harvey Oswald into the Soviet Union, would it make sense to steer him to Gregory Golub?

(4) Might 'Destination Golub' explain Oswald's odyssey from New Orleans to Le Havre to London to Helsinki, instead of proceeding to a port more convenient for Russia?

(5) If the answers to the last four questions appear to be in the affirmative, may it be that the Committee has actually proven the exact opposite of the conclusion it has stated?

In other words, might 'Destination Golub' point to involvement of the US intelligence community in Oswald's defection?

BOOK 2

CHAPTER

7

Russia

The Warren Commission reconstruction indicates that on the day after his arrival in Moscow, Oswald told Rima Shirokova, the young woman assigned by Intourist as his guide during his stay in Russia, that he wanted to leave the United States and become a citizen of the Soviet Union. He then sent a letter to the Supreme Soviet requesting that he be granted citizenship.

On 21 October, an official of the Passport and Visa Department notified Oswald that his visa had expired and that he had to leave Moscow within two hours. Oswald responded to this unfavorable decision by cutting himself above the left wrist in an apparent suicide attempt which resulted in his being taken to the Botkinskaya Hospital where he was confined for three days in the psychiatric ward before being transferred to the 'somatic' ward. He was released from the hospital on 28 October.

Oswald now checked out of the Hotel Berlin and registered at the Metropole. His visa had expired while he was in the hospital, and his presence in Russia was technically illegal; he had received no word that the decision that he must leave had been reversed. Later that day, however, an official at the Pass and Registration Office sent for him, and asked whether he still wanted to become a Soviet citizen. Oswald replied in the affirmative, and provided his Marine Corps discharge papers for identification. He was told that he could not expect a decision soon, and was dismissed. For the next three days, he remained in his room, near the phone, fully dressed and ready to leave immediately if summoned.

Then, on the afternoon of 31 October, he apparently decided to act. He took a taxi to the American Embassy, where he asked to see the consul. When the receptionist asked him first to sign the tourist register, he laid his passport on the desk and said that he had come to 'dissolve his American citizenship'.

Richard E. Snyder, the second secretary and senior consular official, was summoned, and he invited Oswald into his office. There, with Snyder's assistant John A. McVickar also present, Oswald declared that he wanted to renounce his American citizenship; he denounced the United States and praised the Government of the Soviet Union. Over Oswald's objections, Snyder sought to learn something of Oswald's motives and background and to forestall immediate action. Oswald stated his admiration for the system and policies of the Soviet Union and his desire to serve the Soviet State; and at one point alluded to hardships endured by his mother as a 'worker', saying he did not intend to let this happen to him.

Oswald informed Snyder that he had been a radar operator in the Marine Corps, intimating that he might know something of special interest, and that he had informed a Soviet official that he would give the Soviets any information he possessed.

Oswald handed to Snyder a note which suggests that he had studied and sought to comply with section 349 of the Immigration and Nationality Act (which provides for the loss of American citizenship) since the note attempts to cast off citizenship in three of the ways specified by the statute.

The interview ended when Snyder told Oswald that he could renounce his citizenship on the following Monday, two days later, if he would appear personally. Snyder has testified that he was attempting to delay Oswald's decision so as to give him a chance to reconsider before making such a step.

Oswald returned to the hotel angry about the delay, but 'elated' by the 'showdown' and sure that he would be permitted to remain after his 'sign of faith' in the Russians.

His sign of faith in the Russians was not to remain a secret for very long. No sooner had he left these closed offices (it being Saturday), than the Embassy – which supposedly was giving Oswald time for cool reflection – sought out and notified the press of the defection.

Soon after he returned to the hotel, he was approached by A. I. Goldberg, a reporter for the Associated Press,. and later that day by two other reporters, R. J. Korengold and Aline Mosby. He answered a few questions for the latter two, but refused to be interviewed at this time (though a few weeks later he did give an interview to Miss Mosby of United Press International in which among other things he referred again to his mother's poverty).

A few days after his Saturday visit, the Embassy received a letter from Oswald dated 3 November which requested that his citizenship be revoked. The Embassy replied on 9 November that he could renounce his citizenship by appearing at the Embassy and executing the necessary papers.

Both on 8 November, in a letter to his brother Robert, and on 13 November, in the interview with Aline Mosby, Oswald stated that he had been told that he could remain in the Soviet Union. This conflicts with his diary which states that he was not told until later that he could even remain temporarily. Indeed, according to his diary it was this 'comforting news' that prompted him to grant a second interview on 16 November, this time with Priscilla Johnson of the North American Newspaper Alliance.

When, during this interview, Miss Johnson suggested that if Oswald really wished to renounce his American citizenship he could do so by returning to the Embassy, he said he would 'never set foot in the Embassy again', since he was sure he would be given the 'same run-around' as before.

Miss Johnson's seemingly curious advice from one American to another was followed by her reporting to the Embassy on the next day that she thought that Oswald 'may have purposely not carried through his original intent to renounce in order to leave a crack open'.

Apparently Miss Johnson was not the only reporter to get strange vibes about this attempted renunciation of American citizenship. The Warren Commission related that 'reporters noticed Oswald's apparent ambivalence in regard to renouncing his citizenship – stormily demanding that he be permitted to renounce while failing to follow through by completing the necessary papers. [. . .] He seemed to be avoiding effective renunciation, consciously or unconsciously, in order to preserve his right to re-enter the United States. [. . .] . . . if he had expatriated himself his eventual return to the United States would have been much more difficult and perhaps impossible'.

On 4 January, Oswald was summoned to the Soviet Passport Office and given Identity Document for Stateless Persons No. 311479. He was told that he was being sent to Minsk, an industrial city located about 450 miles southwest of Moscow, with a population at that time of about 510,000. On the following day, he went to a Government agency which the Russians call the 'Red Cross'; it gave him 5,000 rubles (about $500). He used 2,200 rubles to pay his hotel bill and 150 rubles to purchase a railroad ticket to Minsk, where he arrived on 7 January. On the following day he met the 'Mayor', who welcomed him to Minsk and promised him a rent-free apartment.

Oswald reported for work at the Belorussian Radio and Television Factory on 13 January. The factory, a major producer of electronic parts and systems, employed about 5,000 persons. His salary varied from 700 to perhaps as high as 900 rubles per month ($70 – $90), a salary which was normal for his type of work. It was supplemented, however, by 700 rubles per month which he received from the 'Red Cross', and, according to Oswald, his total income was about equal to that of the director of the factory. In August he applied for membership of the union; he became a dues-paying member in September.

Undoubtedly more noteworthy to most Russians than his extra income was the attractive apartment which Oswald was given in March 1959. It was a small flat with a balcony overlooking the river, for which he paid only 60 rubles a month. Oswald describes it in his diary as 'a Russian dream'. Had Oswald been a Russian worker, he would probably have had to wait for several years for a comparable apartment, and would have been given one then only if he had a family. The 'Red Cross' subsidy and the apartment were typical of the favorable treatment which the Soviet Union has given defectors.

Oswald's diary records that he enjoyed his first months in Minsk. His work at the factory was easy and his co-workers were friendly and curious about life in the United States. He dated frequently, attending the theater, a movie, or an opera almost every night. He wrote in his diary 'I'm living big and am very satisfied'.

The spring and summer passed easily and uneventfully. There were picnics and drives in the country, which Oswald described as 'green beauty'. On 18 June, he obtained a hunting licence and soon afterwards he purchased a 16 gauge single-barrel shotgun. He joined a local chapter of the Belorussian Society of Hunters and Fishermen, a hunting club sponsored by his factory, and hunted for small game in the farm regions around Minsk about half a dozen times in the summer and fall, spending the night in small villages. (Parenthetically, Russian records contain statements from fellow hunters that Oswald was an extremely poor shot and it was necessary for persons who accompanied him on hunts to provide him with game.) According to his diary, at about this period of time he felt 'uneasy inside' after a friend took him aside at a party and advised him to return to the United States. In another entry he writes, 'I have become habituated to a small cafe which is where I dine in the evening. The food is generally poor and always exactly the same menu in any cafe at any point in the city. The food is cheap and I don't really care about quality after three years in the USMC.' (Note: Oswald's numerous spelling errors are omitted throughout this book.)

According to Russian records, on 4 January 1961, one year after he had been issued his 'stateless' residence permit, Oswald was summoned to the passport office in Minsk; was asked if he still wanted to become a Soviet citizen; replied that he did not, but asked that his residence permit be extended for another year.

The entry in his diary for 4–31 January reads, 'I am starting to reconsider my desire about staying. The work is drab. The money I get has nowhere to be spent. No nightclubs or bowling alleys, no places of recreation except the trade-union dances. I have had enough.'

On 25 January, Mrs Marguerite Oswald appeared at the State Department in Washington, DC, where she spoke with a Mr Boster and a Mr Hickey. She has testified that she told these men that she was under the impression that her son, Lee, was a US agent, and that she was destitute and just getting over a sickness.

On 1 February 1961, the Department of State in Washington forwarded to the Moscow Embassy a request informing the Embassy that Oswald's mother was worried about him, and asking that he get in touch with her, if possible (which is not exactly what her pitch was).

Then on 13 February 1961, the American Embassy in Moscow received a letter from Oswald postmarked Minsk on 5 February, asking that he be readmitted to the United States.

Considering the timing of the State Department message and Oswald's letter, the Warren Commission opined that 'the simultaneity of the two events was apparently coincidental'. The basis for this conclusion is stated to be that, 'The request from Marguerite Oswald went from Washington to Moscow by sealed diplomatic pouch and there was no evidence that the seal had been tampered with. The officer of the Department of State who carried the responsibility for such matters has testified that the message was not forwarded to the Russians after it arrived in Moscow.'

Obviously, if a message from Mrs Oswald was removed in Moscow from a sealed diplomatic pouch but never forwarded to the Russians, it could bear no cause and effect relationship to Lee's letter. In theory, Mrs Oswald's message would still be lying around the Embassy someplace when Lee's letter arrived. However, if we move from the text of the Warren Report and go instead to Appendix XV, we find that what went to the Moscow Embassy was not a message from private citizen, Marguerite Oswald, to private citizen, Lee Oswald. Quite the contrary, the message was from the State Department to the Moscow Embassy and it read: 'The Embassy is requested to inform the [Soviet] Ministry of Foreign Affairs that Mr Oswald's mother is worried as to his present safety, and is anxious to hear from him.' In this Appendix, it is asserted that this request had not been acted upon by the 13th because the diplomatic pouch which left Washington for Moscow on the 1st did not reach Moscow until the 10th or 11th.

Within Oswald's letter is a statement which, if true, would preclude any possibility of a link between his letter and the State Department missive. That statement is in the form of a complaint by Oswald in this letter that he had written an earlier letter which had not been answered. However, the Warren Commission found that there is evidence that such a letter was never sent – specifically, Oswald's diary refers to this February letter as his 'first request'.

Oswald's letter noted that he did not appear personally because he could not leave Minsk without permission. The Second Secretary, Richard Snyder, answered on 28 February that Oswald would have to appear at the Embassy personally to discuss his return to the United States. A second letter from Oswald, posted on 5 March, reached the Embassy on 20 March; it reiterated that he was unable to leave Minsk without permission, and asked that preliminary inquiries be put in the form of a questionnaire and sent to him.

The Warren Commission noted that, 'The Soviet authorities had undoubtedly intercepted and read the correspondence between Oswald and the Embassy and knew of his plans. Soon after the correspondence began, his monthly payments from the "Red Cross" were cut off.'

Sometime in the second week of March, Miss Katherine Mallory, who was on tour in Minsk with the University of Michigan Symphonic Band, found herself surrounded by curious Russian citizens. A young man who identified himself as a Texan and former Marine stepped out of the crowd and asked if she needed an interpreter; he interpreted for her for the next 15 or 20 minutes. Later he told her that he despised the United States and hoped to stay in Minsk for the rest of his life. Miss Mallory was unable to swear that her interpreter was Oswald, but was personally convinced that it was he.

A few days later, probably on 17 March, Oswald attended a dance at the Palace of Culture for Professional Workers in Minsk, where he met 19-year-old Marina Nikolayevna Prusakova. They met again at another dance a week later, danced together most of the evening, and when he walked her home they arranged to meet again the following week.

However, on Thursday, 30 March, Oswald was admitted to the Clinical Hospital, where Marina worked as a pharmacist. By the time he left the hospital on 11 April, he had asked her to be his fiancée, and she had agreed to consider it.

After his discharge from the hospital he visited Marina regularly at her aunt and uncle's apartment, where she had lived since the previous fall (she never knew her father; her mother died in 1957, and she subsequently left her stepfather with whom she did not get along).

By 20 April, they had filed notice with the registrar of their intent to marry, and had obtained the special consent necessary for an alien to marry a citizen. After waiting the usual ten days, they were married on 30 April.

Marina testified that when she agreed to marry Oswald, she believed – based upon his statements to her – that he did not intend to, and indeed could not, return to the United States. Oddly enough, this would also have to mean that nothing was said to Marina when she applied for permission to marry this alien who the authorities knew was intending to leave the country.

But of greater curiosity is the fact that this would have to mean that her intended's plans to leave the country were kept from her by the beloved uncle with whom she lived, for that uncle was not some ordinary, uninformed soviet citizen – on the contrary, her uncle, Colonel Ilya Vasilyevich Prusakov, was a high-ranking official in the Minsk MVD.

Oswald's diary says that he told Marina 'in the last days of June' that he was anxious to return to the United States. Yet, on 25 May, the Moscow Embassy received a letter mailed in Minsk about ten days earlier, in which Oswald asked for assurances that he would not be prosecuted if he returned, and informing the

Embassy that he had married a Russian woman who would seek to accompany him to the United States. At about this time, the Oswalds began to make inquiries in Soviet offices about exit visas.

It is interesting to note Oswald's social activities at this time. Among his stated reasons for wanting to leave the Soviet Union were complaints about the sameness of the food, and the complaint that there were no places of recreation. Yet, the Warren Commission relates that, 'While these preparations were being made, the Oswalds apparently enjoyed their new life. They ate most of their meals in cafes or at restaurants where they worked. For amusement they went boating, attended the opera, concerts, the circus, and films; occasionally, they gathered with a group of friends for a cooperative meal at someone's apartment.'

Weeks went by, but Lee received no response to his letter informing the Embassy of his desire to bring his new bride with him to the United States. Then, on 8 July, he appeared at the Embassy in Moscow. It being Saturday, the offices were closed.

He used the house telephone to reach Snyder, who came to the office, talked with him briefly, and suggested that he return on the following Monday. Oswald called Marina and asked her to join him in Moscow, which she did, arriving on Sunday.

At the Embassy on Monday, Marina waited outside during Oswald's interview with Snyder, who asked to see his Soviet papers and questioned him closely about his life in Russia and possible expatriating acts. Oswald stated that he was not a citizen of the Soviet Union and had never formally applied for citizenship, that he had never taken an oath of allegiance to the Soviet Union, and that he was not a member of the factory trade union organization. He said that he had never given Soviet officials any confidential information that he had learned in the Marines, had never been asked to give such information, and 'doubted' that he would have done so had he been asked.

The Warren Commission concluded that 'Some of Oswald's statements during this interview were undoubtedly false. He had almost certainly applied for citizenship in the Soviet Union and, at least for a time, been disappointed when it was denied. He possessed a membership card in the union organization. In addition, his assertion to Snyder that he had never been questioned by Soviet authorities concerning his life in the United States is simply unbelievable.'

Snyder concluded that Oswald had not expatriated himself and returned to him his passport, stamped valid only for direct travel to the United States. Accompanied by his wife, Lee came to the Embassy again on the following day to initiate procedures for her admission to the United States as an immigrant.

Marina has testified that when the news of her visit to the American Embassy reached Minsk, she was dropped from membership in 'Komsomol', the Communist Youth Organization, and that 'meetings were arranged' at which 'members of the various organizations' attempted to dissuade her from leaving the Soviet Union. She also says that her aunt and uncle did not speak to her for 'a long time'. Indeed, Lee wrote to the Embassy on 4 October to request that the US Government officially intervene to facilitate his and his wife's applications for exit visas. He stated that there had been systematic and concerted attempts to intimidate Marina into withdrawing her application for a visa, which had resulted in her being hospitalized for a five-day period on 22 September for nervous exhaustion.

There is no record of such hospitalization and Marina agrees there was no such hospitalization. As to the rest of the harrassment and outrage, if it was sincere and not for show, it makes even more incomprehensible the apparently blasé approach of the authorities and her uncle to her courtship by and marriage to Oswald after he had applied for readmission to the United States.

The Embassy replied to Oswald's letter on 12 October, saying that it had no way of influencing Soviet conduct on such matters and that its experience had been that action on applications for exit visas was 'seldom taken rapidly'.

On 25 December 1961, Marina was called to the local passport office in Minsk, where she was told that authority had been received to issue exit visas to her and her husband. The Oswalds did not pick up their exit visas immediately, one reason probably being the fact that Marina was pregnant with their first child, June, who was born on 15 February.

In the meantime, the American Embassy in a letter dated 5 January suggested that since there might be difficulties in obtaining an American visa for Marina, Oswald should consider returning alone and bringing her over later. He replied on the 16th that he would not leave Russia without her. There was apparently less urgency about the departure for the United States after June was born, as Oswald wrote to his mother and brother that he would probably not arrive for several months.

On 1 June, Oswald signed a promissory note at the Embassy for a repatriation loan of $435.71. He and his family boarded a train for Holland, passing through Minsk that night. They crossed the Soviet frontier at Brest on 2 June. Two days later they departed from Holland on the SS *Maasdam*, which landed at Hoboken, New Jersey, on 13 June, where they were met by Spas T. Raikin, a representative of the Travelers Aid Society, which had been contacted by the Department of State. The society referred the Oswalds to the New York City Department of Welfare, which helped them find a room at the Times Square Hotel. On the afternoon of 14 June, the Oswalds left New York by plane for Fort Worth.

BOOK 2

CHAPTER

8

The Diary That Wasn't

It has been pointed out that there are significant problems with each of the sources utilized to reconstruct Oswald's thoughts and activities while in the Soviet Union.

For many years Oswald's 'Historic Diary' was the virtually unchallenged primary source of information on this period of his life, purporting, as it does, to be his contemporaneous documentation of events.

However, some skeptics pointed to certain entries in the diary which they said reflected information which could only have become known after the supposed time of the entries.

The House Select Committee on Assassinations had a number of documents about which there were various questions; inevitably, Oswald's diary came to be amongst them.

In order to resolve these questions, the Committee first asked the President of the American Society of Questioned Document Examiners for his recommendations on the leading experts in the field of questioned document examination, specifically handwritten documents. The Committee then asked each of the people he recommended for their suggestions as to whom the Committee might retain for these purposes.

Three names appeared consistently. After ascertaining that none had had a connection with the FBI or the Kennedy case, the Committee requested that this impartial panel undertake an examination of various documents.

The panel members, all of whom belonged to the American Society of Questioned Document Examiners, were Joseph P. McNally, David J. Purtell and Charles C. Scott. The Committee stated their qualifications thus:

'McNally received a BS and an MPA in police science from the John Jay College of Criminal Justice, University of New York City in 1967 and 1975 respectively. He started in the field of questioned document identification in 1942 with the New York Police laboratory. He has been supervisor of the document identification section of the police laboratory, training officer in the police academy, commanding officer of the police laboratory, and handwriting expert in the district attorney's office of New York County. He retired from the police department with the rank of captain in 1972 and entered private practice. He serves as a consultant to New York's Human Resources Administration. McNally is a fellow of the American Academy of Forensic Sciences, and a member of the International Association for Identification, and the American Society for Testing and Materials. He has lectured at the University of New York City, Rockland College, and the New York Police Academy. [. . .]

'Purtell received a Ph.B, with a major in mathematics and chemistry, from Northwestern University in 1949. He began his career in questioned document identification in 1942 with the Chicago Police Department, where he served as document examiner in the scientific crime detection laboratory. He retired in 1974 as chief document examiner and captain of police, and entered private practice in 1973. He is a fellow of the

American Academy of Forensic Sciences and served as chairman of the questioned document section and chairman of the program committee. He is past vice president and president of the American Society of Questioned Document Examiners. Purtell has lectured at Northwestern University, the University of Illinois, the University of Indiana and St Joseph's College, among other schools. He has presented and published numerous scientific papers. [. . .]

'Scott received an AA degree from Kansas City Junior College in 1930 and a JD from the University of Missouri School of Law in 1935, whereupon he became a member of the Missouri bar. While attending law school, he founded the *University of Missouri at Kansas City Law Review* and was its first editor-in-chief. He began his career as a questioned document examiner with the Federal Reserve Bank in 1935 and has been in private practice since 1946. The first edition of his three-volume book, *Photographic Evidence*, was published in 1942. Now in its second edition, it has become the standard textbook on the subject. He served on the first board of directors of the American Board of Forensic Document Examiners. He has conducted seminars on scientific document examination for more than 20 State bar associations, written numerous professional articles, and, since 1954, has been an adjunct professor of law at the University of Missouri School of Law.'

The panel followed standard procedures and techniques in its examinations. The writings and signatures were looked at individually and in juxtaposition with each other, taking into consideration the gross characteristics of the writing process, writing skill, slant, speed, proportions of the letters, ratio of small to capital letters, height ratio, lateral spacing, and overall writing pattern. Significant differences were looked for. A stereoscope microscope was used for minute examination and comparison of individual letters and characteristics.

One of the issues addressed to these experts queried 'Was the "historic diary" written in one sitting?' As to this, the panel concluded that, 'Because of the poor condition of the historical diary, they are unable to conclude firmly whether it was written at one or more than one sitting. On balance, it appears to have been written at one or a few sittings.'

The problem referred to regarding the condition of the diary can best be understood from the comments of David J. Purtell: 'With respect to the timespan of the historical diary, an answer cannot be provided because of the present condition of the paper. The documents had been processed by the silver nitrate method in an attempt to develop latent fingerprints. While a recognized method, the drawback is that it soils the paper; the silver nitrate which remains on the paper causes it to turn black in time. Today, the pages are in very poor condition, and though the message can be read in part, it is a very difficult task. One observation that can be reported is that one sheet of paper is of a different weight (thickness) than the other sheets.'

However, although scientifically dating the age of the writing might have proven helpful, inability to do so did not prevent addressing the truly crucial issue, which might be stated in the question: 'Was this document an accumulation of random entries each entry having been made on the date indicated contemporaneous with the events being recorded?'

As to that very important question, the answer is most unsettling, for it appears to be rather clear that this document, upon which so much reliance has been placed in reconstructing the defection, is a phony. In other words, Lee Harvey Oswald's 'diary' was not a diary at all.

As Joseph P. McNally reported, 'A check was made of the historical diary. The 12 pages were written with the same type of writing instrument. The paper used for 11 of the 12 pages is similar; only the last page differs – it is appreciably thinner. The writing has a continuity from page to page and line to line that is indicative of being written about, or at, the same time. It does not give the impression of being "random", as would be expected of a diary extended over a period of time. It appears that this diary has been written within a short period of time and not over any extensive period.'

This determination not only calls into question the entire reconstruction of Oswald's life in Russia, but also gives rise to a most disturbing new question: 'Why?'

BOOK 2

CHAPTER

9

Yuri Nosenko, KGB Defector

Some CIA agents, including a Chief of Counter-
Intelligence in the Agency's Soviet Branch, told the
House Select Committee on Assassinations in 1978 that
they believed it was possible that Lee Harvey Oswald
had been recruited by the Soviet KGB during his
military tour at Atsugi Air Base in Japan, as the CIA
had identified a KGB program aimed at recruiting US
military personnel during the period Oswald was
stationed there.

This was not a new concern. From the time of his
arrest for the killing of President Kennedy, a primary
concern was the question: 'Had Oswald been enlisted
by the Soviet secret police, the dreaded KGB?'

Then, in February 1964, only three months after the
assassination, a most fortuitous event occurred: a Russian named Yuri Nosenko sought political asylum in the
United States.

According to CIA records, Nosenko declared that he
had been a KGB agent; that in 1959 and again in 1963
he had been assigned to the KGB's American Tourist
Section; that in that assignment he had reviewed
Oswald's KGB file; and that he could categorically

deny that Oswald had in any way been connected with the KGB.

Nosenko's assertions did not end the inquiry into whether Oswald had a KGB connection. In fact, they only tended to complicate it.

This complication arose because some officials of the Central Intelligence Agency expressed doubt that Nosenko was a bona fide defector, which might mean that Nosenko's 'defection' was instead an effort to mislead – a disinformation mission.

According to CIA records, back in 1962, whilst a security escort to a Soviet disarmament delegation in Geneva, Switzerland, Nosenko had offered to sell information to the CIA for 900 Swiss francs, claiming he needed the money to replace KGB funds he had spent on a drinking spree. After his defection he admitted that he had not really needed the money but had felt that an offer to merely give the information away for nothing would be rejected, as had been the case with similar offers by other Soviet agents. (This admission has not received all the study it deserves. For example, how would Nosenko have known of those prior offers, and why was Nosenko supposedly so anxious to pass information to the US as to make up such a story in order to be able to do so?)

Nonetheless, the CIA had made that 1962 deal with Nosenko. According to the records, at that time he asserted that he would never defect because he could never leave his family, and he told the CIA never to contact him in the Soviet Union. However, he assured them that he would make contact the next time he came abroad.

On 23 January 1964, eight weeks after the Kennedy assassination, Nosenko was once again in Geneva as escort to a disarmament delegation. Claiming that he was now disillusioned with his Government, and insisting that he would soon not be able to leave the Soviet Union again, Nosenko declared that he wished to immediately defect.

The CIA stalled, but Nosenko was adamant. Then, 'On 4 February, Nosenko revealed he had received a telegram ordering him to return to Moscow directly. He said he feared the KGB was aware he was working with the West, and his life depended on his being permitted to defect immediately.' Persuaded by his plea, the CIA accepted Nosenko as a defector. Nosenko would later admit that the recall telegram was a fake, and that he had made up the story in order to get the CIA to agree to his defection without further delay.

The FBI, having been informed by the CIA that Nosenko had information about Oswald, interviewed him upon his arrival in the United States. He reiterated what he had told the CIA regarding his knowledge of Oswald, including the reassuring fact that the KGB had never had any contact with President Kennedy's assassin.

The conclusion of the report of this FBI interview reads: 'On 4 March 1964, Nosenko stated that he did not want any publicity in connection with this information but stated he would be willing to testify to this information before the Presidential Commission provided such testimony is given in secret and absolutely no publicity is given either to his appearance before the Commission or to the information itself.' The report also notes that two days later Nosenko inquired if his offer had been given to the appropriate authorities, and he was assured that this had been done.

By April 1964, officials of both the Soviet Russia and the Counter-Intelligence sections of the CIA were raising serious doubts as to whether Nosenko was a bona fide defector. The bases for their misgivings were stated to be that:

(1) Many leads provided by Nosenko had been of the 'giveaway' variety, that is, information that is no longer of significant value to the KGB, or information which in the probable judgement of the KGB is already being probed by Western intelligence, so that there is

more to be gained from having a dispatched agent 'give it away' and thereby gain credibility.

(2) A background check of Nosenko – of his schooling, military career and his activities as an intelligence officer – had led US officials to suspect Nosenko was telling them a 'legend', that is, supplying them with a fabricated identity. Certain aspects of Nosenko's background did not check out, and certain events he described seemed highly unlikely.

(3) Two defectors who had preceded Nosenko were skeptical of him. One was convinced Nosenko was on a KGB mission, the purpose of which was to neutralize information one of the defectors had provided.

(4) Information Nosenko had given about Oswald aroused their suspicions. The chief of the Soviet Russia section had difficulty accepting the statements about Oswald, characterizing them as seeming 'almost to have been tacked on or to have been added, as though it didn't seem to be part of the real body of the other things he had to say, many of which were true'.

On 4 April 1964, the CIA placed Nosenko in isolation and commenced 'hostile interrogations'. The atmosphere was set by conducting a polygraph test wherein the CIA polygrapher was to accuse Nosenko of lying no matter what the test really showed.

Presumably that did not require any great acting ability in this case, for in his report – in which he was to state his true conclusions – the polygrapher declared that Nosenko had indeed lied.

During 1964, Nosenko was interviewed on five occasions wherein at least some questions dealt with Lee Harvey Oswald. His story as it relates to Oswald has been summarized as follows:

'Nosenko related that he was assigned to the Seventh Department of the Second Chief Directorate when Oswald arrived in the Soviet Union in 1959, at which time Nosenko's section had responsibility for counter-intelligence operations against American tourists.

'At the time Oswald asked to remain in Russia, Nosenko reviewed information the KGB had on the American. Soon after Oswald went to Minsk, Nosenko was transferred and lost contact with him. However, he became re-involved in the case right after the assassination.

'Nosenko said that as soon as President Kennedy's assassin was identified as a man who had lived in the Soviet Union, the KGB ordered that Oswald's file be flown to Moscow and reviewed to determine whether there had been any contact between him and Soviet intelligence. Nosenko said further he was assigned to the review of Oswald's file. Based on that review, as well as his earlier contact with the case, he was able to report positively that Oswald had neither been recruited nor contacted by the KGB.'

In October 1966, Nosenko was given his second polygraph test, during which he was again asked about Oswald. The CIA examiner was the same one who had administered the first test and he once again concluded that Nosenko was lying.

The Soviet Russia Section of the CIA wrote a 900-page report based on its interrogations of Nosenko, which was trimmed to 447 pages by the time it was submitted in February 1968. It came to the conclusion that Nosenko:

(1) Did not serve in the naval reserve as he had claimed.

(2) Did not join the KGB at the time or in the manner he described.

(3) Did not serve in the American Embassy section of the KGB at the time he claimed, and was not a senior case officer or deputy chief of the seventh department, as he stated he had been.

(4) Was not chief of the American Embassy section.

(5) Was not a deputy chief of the seventh department in 1962, as he had claimed.

From the time this report was first being drafted, the

thrust of its conclusions was known by, and seemed to create quite a dilemma for, the leadership of the CIA. As a result, in mid-1967 a career security officer was assigned to write a critique of the handling of Nosenko. His conclusion – that Nosenko was who he claimed to be and that he was supplying valid information – led to the official CIA position that Nosenko was a bona fide defector.

On 8 August 1968, Nosenko was given a third polygraph test. Only two of the questions on this test related to information he had supplied about Oswald. This time Nosenko was deemed to have passed the test.

The official position of the CIA relative to the various polygraphs thereupon was stated to be that the third test – the one Nosenko passed – was considered to be a valid test.

As to the first two tests – both of which Nosenko had failed – the official CIA position became that both of those tests were invalid or inconclusive.

In October 1968, the security officer who had been selected by the CIA brass issued a report which disputed each and every conclusion of the report of the Soviet Russia Section written eight months earlier.

However, neither of these reports paid very much attention to the Oswald aspect of the Nosenko case, and neither even attempted to analyze Nosenko's statements about Oswald. The combined total for both reports amounts to 730 pages, only fifteen of which deal in any respect with Oswald.

The security officer's report did, nonetheless, reach the conclusion that Nosenko was not dispatched by the Soviet Government to give false information to the US officials about Oswald. He listed the reasons for this conclusion thus:

(1) Nosenko's first contact with the CIA was in June 1962, 17 months prior to the assassination.

(2) Information provided by Nosenko was not sufficient in 'nature, scope and content' to convince US authorities of no Soviet involvement in the assassination.

(3) Even if the KGB were involved in the assassination, the Soviets would assume that US authorities would, in turn, believe only a few senior officers would be aware of it, and Nosenko would not be one of them.

Amongst the documents obtained by the House Committee is information on finances, in which we learn that:

'Prior to Nosenko's defection on 4 February 1964, he was promised $50,000 for previous cooperation, $10,000 for his identification in 1962 of a particular espionage agent, and $25,000 a year compensation for future services.'

These were not exactly pauper's wages. The average annual earnings of fulltime employees in the US in the year 1964 were $5,503.*

* Historical Statistics of the United States, US Department of Commerce, Bureau of the Census, 1975, page 164, Series D 722–727.

BOOK 2

CHAPTER

10

Pick your Polygraph

The House Select Committee undertook its own investigation of the Nosenko case, which involved both the review of existing documentation and the eliciting of new evidence.

As part of its investigation, the Committee retained Richard O. Arther to conduct an independent analysis of Yuri Nosenko's three polygraph tests.

'Arther received a BS with honors in police science from Michigan State University in 1951, and an MA in psychology from Columbia University in 1960. Arther has been in private practice in New York City since 1963. He founded Scientific Lie Detection, Inc. and co-founded the National Training Center of Polygraph Science. He has taught at Brooklyn College, Seton Hall University, the John Jay College of Criminal Justice and the Graduate School of Public Administration of New York University. Arther has authored over 200 professional articles and two books. He is a member of the Academy of Certified Polygraphists and the Amercian Polygraph Association. [. . .]

'A polygraph examination records physiological responses to questions asked. The polygraphist attempts to design the examination in such a way that the truthful person will react to the control questions and the lying person to the relevant questions. The test structure must be constructed so that it poses a threat to both the truthful and untruthful person.

'The polygraphist attempts to determine the "psychological set" of the examinee. He tries to determine, by reading the physiological activity of the examinee in the polygraph charts, what questions or question areas pose the greatest threat to the examinee's well-being. A "psychological set" is a person's fears, anxieties, and apprehension, [which] are channeled toward that situation causing the greatest threat to the individual's well-being. He will tune in on that which is of a greater threat, and tune out that of a lesser threat.

'Responses to questions are recorded on a polygraph chart, which consists of tracings produced by three different types of psychological reactions associated with the circulatory, nervous, and respiratory systems:

(1) The breathing pattern is recorded by means of a rubber tube placed around the person's chest.

(2) The Galvanic skin response is measured by placing the attachments on either the fingers or the palms.

(3) Changes in blood pressure, heart beat, and pulse rate are obtained by a standard blood pressure cuff placed around the upper arm.

'Questions are broken down into three categories:

(1) Relevant – those pertinent to the investigation.

(2) Irrelevant – hopefully, meaningless, non-emotion-producting ones to get the person used to being questioned and giving answers.

(3) Control – non-relevant, to which it can be assumed the person will lie during the test. These provide a standard for comparing the responses to relevant questions.

'If a person reacts more to a proper control question than to the relevant questions, then he is considered to be truthful to the relevants. On the other hand, if he reacts more to the relevants than to the proper control question, he is considered to be lying to the relevants.

'Relevant, irrelevant and control questions are interspersed throughout the polygraph chart. The examination may consist of various series covering various relevant issues. Each relevant issue must be asked a minimum of two times in a series, but as many times as necessary to conclude that relevant issue successfully. Each series should have a minimum of two charts, but, as many charts as necessary to conclude the relevant issues in that series successfully.

'The procedure for a polygraph examination is as follows: The polygraphist first conducts a pre-test interview, during which the test questions are read to the person exactly as they are going to be asked. It is vital that all questions be properly worded and discussed with the person. Then the actual test is conducted.'

Having conducted his independent analysis, Richard O. Arther concluded that the second test – in which the examiner determined Nosenko was lying – was the most valid and reliable of the three examinations administered to Yuri Nosenko.

As for the third test – where the examiner found Nosenko to be telling the truth – Mr Arther, in addressing the only two questions on that exam which related to the information Nosenko had supplied about Oswald, characterized the first such question as 'atrocious' and the second such question as 'very poor' for use in assessing the validity of Nosenko's responses.

The fact is that this third examiner had even found Nosenko to be truthful when he answered 'No' to the question, 'Is there any possibility that the KGB would dispatch an officer to defect to the Americans?'.

BOOK 2

CHAPTER

11

Not Worthy of Belief

The House Select Committee, in considering whether
Nosenko was a bona fide defector, was interested to
know why the CIA had apparently failed (or refused)
to ascertain that there were inconsistencies within
Nosenko's various statements, as well as between some
of Nosenko's statements and knowledge from other
sources.

As part of its investigation on these points, the
Committee took the deposition of the CIA employee
who interviewed Nosenko on 3 and 27 July 1964. It
turned out that this person who the CIA had detailed to
question Nosenko, was in no position to challenge
Nosenko either on general knowledge or specifically on
Oswald. In his deposition this CIA employee told the
Committee he was not an expert on the KGB, nor had
he any previous experience with KGB defectors. When
asked about his knowledge of Oswald, since it was in
his interviews that the most detailed questions about
Oswald were asked, he replied, 'I cannot specifically
recall having read any files pertaining to Lee Harvey
Oswald. Certainly I had read and heard a lot about him
in the newspapers, television, and radio. I may have

had the opportunity to read some previous debriefings of Nosenko concerning Oswald, but I am not sure of that.'

As to the security officer who wrote the 1968 report, when he was asked if he ever spoke to Nosenko about Oswald, he said, 'No. Well, all I have you have there (Nosenko's three page statement). I did a write-up on it. I didn't see that it seriously conflicted with what we had.'

He was then asked, 'And did you ever question him about what he wrote?' To this he responded, 'No, because I had no reason to disbelieve him.'

Questioned further as to why he did not compare all of Nosenko's statements on Oswald, he replied, 'I did not have all the information on the Oswald investigation. That was an FBI investigation.'

The follow-up inquiry was, 'Well, was it available to you if you had asked the FBI for their reports of what Oswald had said to them?' The answer was, 'It might, under certain circumstances, but in this case here, as far as our office was concerned, the Oswald matter was an FBI matter.'

Given the apparent failure of the CIA to critically evaluate the credibility of Nosenko's statements about Oswald, the Committee undertook to do this job, and, in review of all the evidence, the Committee noted that there had been significant inconsistencies over the years in Nosenko's story. A few of these will now be discussed.

In his interviews in 1964, among the points Nosenko stressed was that there had been no physical or technical surveillance on Oswald (in fact, he had even claimed that the KGB did not know that Marina was a friend of Oswald until they applied for marriage because there was no surveillance on Oswald to show that he knew her).

He claimed that he could unequivocally state this because he had thoroughly reviewed Oswald's KGB file. Yet, when being pressed on a slightly different tack in 1978, Nosenko claimed that he had been unable to read the entire Oswald file because it consisted of seven or eight thick volumes of documents due to all the surveillance reports.

Nosenko insisted that the KGB never had any contact whatsoever with Oswald, not even an interview. They not only did not question Oswald when he asked to defect, but they also did not interview him later when it was decided he would be permitted to remain in Russia. At no time did the KGB talk to Oswald.

Yet, when the Committee asked Nosenko, 'Would the KGB have any interest in an American student?', he replied 'As I told you yesterday, the KGB is interested in students, but particularly those students who are studying the Russian language, Russian history, Russian economy.'

A subsequent question began 'Is it your testimony that Lee Harvey Oswald, who was a student, who was a professed Marxist, who had . . .' At this point Nosenko interrupted. 'Students. I never heard that he was a student.'

This is a fascinating statement by a man who claimed to know all there was to know about Oswald in the Soviet Union. Russian documents supplied to the United States presumably from the files Nosenko claimed to have reviewed show that upon his arrival in Moscow Oswald registered at the Hotel Berlin as a 'student'; and in his application for an identity card at the Visa and Registration Office at the Moscow City Council, Oswald had filled out item 13 (occupation) with the word 'student'.

When asked, 'And exactly why did no KGB officer ever speak to Oswald before they made the decision about whether to let him defect?', Nosenko answered, 'We didn't consider him an interesting target.' But, when asked if he knew of any other defector who was turned away because he was uninteresting, Nosenko answered 'No'.

The head of the CIA Soviet Russia Section from 1963

to 1968 was asked by the Committee if he knew of comparable situations in which someone was not questioned, was just left alone, as Nosenko said Oswald was. He replied that he did not know of any former Soviet intelligence officer or other knowledgeable source to whom he had spoken who felt that this would have been possible. 'If someone did,' he said, 'I never heard of it.'

Nosenko was forced to admit that the KGB would have been 'very interested' in the fact that Oswald worked as a radar operator at an air base from which the super secret U-2 spy planes took off and landed. But, Nosenko maintained, the KGB never spoke with Oswald and so it didn't know that he had any connection with the U-2 flights.

As the Committee summarized this tale, 'In short, Nosenko's Oswald story is as follows: The KGB, although very interested in the U-2, never learned anything about it from Oswald because it didn't know he had any knowledge of the aircraft. Why? Because Oswald was never questioned by the KGB because the decision was made that Oswald was of no interest to Soviet intelligence.'

Even John Hart, who appeared before the Committee to support the CIA's assessment that Nosenko was a bona fide defector, had to concede as follows: 'I find it very hard to believe that the KGB had so little interest in this individual. Therefore, if I were in the position of deciding whether to use the testimony of Mr Nosenko on this case or not, I would not use it.'

Mr Hart was asked, '. . .[Y]ou have someone in the Soviet Union who announces he wants to stay, that he wants to live there, that he wants to become a Soviet citizen, and the KGB according to Mr Nosenko decides that on the basis of his application to come to the country he is uninteresting. Now, does that strike you as plausible, based on your information and your knowledge of intelligence and counter-intelligence activities, that the KGB would dismiss that kind of request merely by looking at the entrance applications, and not make an effort to talk to the person, to see what information they might be able to impart?'

The answer to that question by this Nosenko apologist was: 'Congressman, I find it implausible. I might say that if this had ever been the case within the expertise of any of us who had anything to do with Soviet operations, it would have greatly facilitated our tasks in connection with putting people into the Soviet Union . . .'.

Hart's enthusiastic support for Nosenko's bona fides as a defector was rebutted at length by the Deputy Chief, SB Division (a man referred to only as Mr D. C.) who, at the time of Nosenko's first contact with the CIA in Geneva, had served as head of the CIA's section responsible for counter-intelligence against the Soviet intelligence services, and later, as the deputy chief of the Soviet Bloc Division of the CIA, had assisted in further interrogations of Nosenko. As relates to Oswald, the testimony of this witness is dramatic and informative:

'Here was this young American, Lee Harvey Oswald, just out of the Marine Corps, already inside the USSR and going to great lengths to stay there and become a citizen. The KGB never bothered to talk to him, not even once, not even to get an idea whether he might be a CIA plant (and although even Nosenko once said, I think, that the KGB feared he might be). Can this be true?

'Could we all be wrong in what we've heard about rigid Soviet security precautions and about their strict procedures and disciplines, and about how dangerous it is in the USSR for someone to take a risky decison (like failing to screen an applicant for permanent residence in the USSR)? Of course not.'

BOOK 2

CHAPTER

12

A Disinformation Mission?

Having evaluated all of the evidence, the Committee declared, not surprisingly, that they were 'certain Nosenko lied about Oswald'.

However, that still left a question which the Committee could not answer: *Why* did Nosenko lie about Oswald?

As for that issue, all they could do was to observe: 'The reasons he would lie about Oswald range from the possibility that he merely wanted to exaggerate his own importance to the disinformation hypothesis with its sinister implications.'

To this they appended a footnote: 'Beyond those reasons for falsification that can be attributed to Nosenko himself, there has been speculation that the Soviet Government, while not involved in the assassination, sent Nosenko on a mission to allay American fears. Hence, while his story about no connection between Oswald and the KGB might be false, his claim of no Soviet involvement would be truthful.'

The Committee's comments on the question 'Why did Nosenko lie about Oswald?' appear to imply that there is absolutely nothing in the evidence which might prove helpful in trying to answer that question. Perhaps so.

The Committee also appears to be indicating that they have at least set the outer bounds – the range – of the possible answers to that perplexing question. Again, perhaps so.

Yet, careful analysis of the available evidence seems to hint that there may be a very different and perhaps more logical explanation to the Nosenko enigma.

Let us re-examine the known facts and consider if there are reasonable inferences which such facts may warrant.

We are told that Nosenko sold information to the CIA in 1962.

We are later told that Nosenko 'said he feared the KGB was aware he was working with the West, and his life depended on his being permitted to defect immediately'.

Suppose we reword these facts into language more meaningful to our inquiry.

As of 1962, the CIA had compromised Nosenko, and thereby, as of 1962 the CIA 'owned' Nosenko – could at any time force him to do their bidding – because they held over his head the ever present threat of leaking to the Soviets the facts about Nosenko's sale of information to the CIA.

The language ascribed to Nosenko is also informative: 'He said he feared the KGB was aware he *was working* with the West. . .' The tense used hints at something quite to the contrary of the implication in the summary that there had been merely a single contact prior to the time of the defection.

But we need not depend on semantics to show that there had been an ongoing relationship between Nosenko and the CIA. The information in another part of this body of work relative to finances would seem to rather clearly demonstrate that there in fact had been such a relationship:

'Prior to Nosenko's defection on 4 February 1964,

he was promised $50,000 for previous cooperation, $10,000 for his identification, in 1962, of a particular espionage agent, and $25,000 a year for future services.'

In the narrative we are told of only one contact, that being in 1962, and the nature of that contact is said to be the sale of information for the sum of 900 Swiss francs. So, as for the one stated contact, the CIA already had its information and Nosenko already had his money.

For what, then, was the sum of $60,000 being promised, if not for services provided during an ongoing relationship prior to the defection? Indeed, the very language tells us that is just what this $60,000 was for: '$50,000 for previous cooperation', and '$10,000 for his identification, in 1962, of a particular espionage agent'.

So, the evidence would seem to be conclusive that for some period of time preceding his defection, Yuri Nosenko had been a CIA asset – an undercover agent in place – who had been providing valuable services and information to the CIA.

Can there be any question but that under normal circumstances Nosenko's most valuable role to the CIA would be to remain as an agent in place?

Logically, should the CIA want to encourage him to defect, thereby losing a well-placed spy?

Yet, if they were not encouraging him to defect, how else does one explain the statement: '*Prior to Nosenko's defection* on 4 February 1964, *he was promised* $50,000 for previous cooperation, $10,000 for his identification, in 1962, of a particular espionage agent, and $25,000 a year compensation for future services'?

Here was a KGB officer the CIA had 'turned', and over whom they had permanent blackmail privileges. Are we to believe that the soft-hearted CIA let him off the hook just because he wanted out?

No, we are told that he was permitted to defect because he reported that he had received a telegram recalling him immediately to Moscow, and that he feared the Soviets knew he was working with the West, so that his life was in danger if not allowed to defect.

But let's look a bit more closely at this rationalization.

Is there any believable explanation as to why – before allowing this asset, this compromised KGB officer, to defect – no one demanded that he produce the alleged telegram supposedly ordering him back to his death in Moscow?

Here, supposedly, was the proof Nosenko needed to persuade the CIA to permit him to defect. Would anyone have believed it had he said he had destroyed this crucial life-saving evidence? What would he have said: That he destroyed it to keep it a secret? If so, from whom?

We can conclude they never asked for the telegram, since:

(1) We know that no such telegram was sent and so could not have been produced.

(2) Had the telegram been called for, there is no credible excuse Nosenko could have offered for failing to produce it.

It would appear, therefore, that in order to accept the alleged story of Nosenko's defection, we must first accept the premise that in utter dereliction of their duties, the responsible CIA officials permitted a valuable spy, a turned KGB officer, to hornswoggle them into accepting the story of a phantom recall telegram which they never even asked to see, and, in addition, that before permitting him the pleasure of bamboozling them, they first promised him amounts of money which were by 1964 standards most substantial indeed.

The alternative would seem to be that we have not been told a complete and accurate story about Nosenko's defection, which would certainly raise the question as to why we were misled.

All of this leads inexorably to the following questions:

(1) Did the CIA (or elements thereof) order the

defection of the CIA's longtime agent, Yuri Nosenko?

(2) Was it merely a coincidence that Nosenko's defection happened to come at a time when intense scrutiny was being addressed to the background of Lee Harvey Oswald?

(3) By insisting that his testimony about Oswald be given in secret and with absolutely no publicity given, either to his appearance before the Commission or to the information itself, was Nosenko participating in an effort to keep the Russians from knowing that false information was being provided under the cover that it came from them?

Let's follow that last thought for a moment.

Who controlled the input of information if Nosenko's testimony about Oswald had been kept secret from all except those for whose ears it was intended?

What might the investigators be anticipated to suspect when elements of the CIA advise them that Nosenko might be a false defector?

Was Nosenko's Oswald story intentionally designed so that absolutely no one could possibly believe it?

When this possibly false defector relates his blatantly untrue Oswald story, are the listeners expected to conclude that the untrue Oswald story provides the final proof that he was, indeed, a false defector?

When the listeners conclude that this false defector has told an untrue Oswald story, are they to suspect that someone might have sent the false defector?

Are the listeners to suspect that whoever sent the false defector with the untrue Oswald story might have had a reason to want to deflect attention away from some connection they had with Oswald?

Does this mean that it was intended that the investigators should be led to believe that the KGB was trying to deflect attention away from its Oswald connection?

And, finally, if Nosenko was indeed on a disinformation mission, a mission to deflect attention away from an Oswald connection, and if it was not the KGB which sent him, then who sent him and why?

BOOK 2

CHAPTER

13

Who Sent Nosenko?

As if there were not already enough twists and turns to the Nosenko story, there is *possibly* yet another explanation to this increasingly bizarre puzzle. The word 'possibly' is emphasized here because the evidence upon which this chapter is based was not authenticated by any of the official investigations we have been relying upon – at least not directly.

A writer named Edward Jay Epstein, utilizing the Freedom Of Information Act, obtained documents detailing the differing CIA perceptions of Yuri Nosenko, which might best be described as: the 'official' CIA position that he was a bona fide defector; and the 'contrarian' unofficial view that he was a false defector.

Mr Epstein's book, *Legend*, was published in 1978, and it provided to the general public its first real knowledge of Nosenko. *Legend*, based in good part on adopting the contrarian view of Nosenko, made out a strong case that the Russians were seeking to deflect attention away from some relationship they had with Lee Harvey Oswald.

As it turns out, during his preparation for the book,

Mr Epstein spoke with the CIA official previously identified as Mr D. C. In his testimony to the House Select Committee, Mr D. C. acknowledged talking with Epstein in that regard, indicating that the primary help he provided to Mr Epstein was to insure that there were no errors in the Nosenko story now being disseminated to the public.

Specifically, Mr D. C. stated in his sworn testimony that while he may not agree with some of the emphasis, '[T]he facts that Mr Epstein has in the book are generally accurate.'

This leads us into yet another labyrinth, for in *Legend* Mr Epstein relates certain facts relating to Yuri Nosenko for which we have no official verification except for this blanket 'Amen' by Mr D. C.

However, these are facts about which Mr D. C. would have firsthand knowledge, and so his endorsement under oath of the accuracy of the facts in Mr Epstein's book is uniquely meaningful. It will be remembered that Mr D. C. has previously been identified as having been in 1962 the head of the CIA's section responsible for counter-intelligence against the Soviet intelligence services. As such, he would have had more than a mere passing interest in a KGB officer who first contacted the Agency in 1962 offering information. More to the point, he testified that he was directly responsible for the case of Yuri Nosenko from 1962 to 1967.

Mr Epstein in his book discloses that at the time of his first meeting with the CIA in 1962, Nosenko had related a story as to how the KGB had come to uncover and execute a CIA 'mole', Pytor Semyonovich Popov.

Popov, a lieutenant colonel in Soviet military intelligence, had for some time been perhaps the highest placed and most valuable CIA spy in Russia. The Agency had an understandable interest in how Popov had come to be discovered, since one obvious possibility which existed was that he had been betrayed by someone on the US side. Nosenko said that Popov had been detected through a new Soviet surveillance technique, which would indicate – comfortingly – that there had been no breach of security within the CIA.

Mr Epstein also discloses that in what would have been late 1958 or early 1959, Richard Bissell, the father of the U-2 spy plane program, told the CIA deputy director of plans, Richard Helms, that Popov had been sending out information that the Russians now had ascertained some specific information about the super secret U-2. This was shocking news, since if they had discovered many of the flight characteristics of the U-2, this could accelerate their ability to design a control system which would permit their high-altitude rockets to knock the planes from the sky. Helms and Bissell wondered how the Soviets could be gaining such knowledge.

Sometime later in 1959, at a meeting in Moscow with his CIA case officer, Popov revealed that the KGB had caught on to him, indicating with hand gestures that he had been wired for sound and passing a note scribbled out on six pages of toilet paper. In September 1959, Popov was arrested and subsequently executed by Soviet counter-intelligence.

Obviously, Nosenko's information that Popov had been caught through a new Soviet surveillance technology would be comforting only if Nosenko were believed. If there were reason to doubt him, it would follow that he might have been sent to deflect attention away from the truth; to wit, that Popov had been identified by a Soviet mole within the American intelligence community.

It is a tribute to their usual tight-mouthed discipline that we laymen tend to view the CIA as a monolithic organization of single-minded people. Spy novels aside, the testimony of and about Yuri Nosenko provides us with a rare glimpse into the real and very human world of the intelligence agent.

We learn, for example, that at the time Nosenko presented himself in 1962, there was an internal struggle within the CIA as to the bona fides of a Russian defector identified as 'X'. Six months earlier, X had defected bringing information that there was a Russian mole highly placed in the American intelligence community. The question arose: Was X sent to sow dissent and distrust in the Agency, or did the intelligence community have the very serious problem of a mole?

The problem becomes more complex. Mr D. C. told the House Select Committee that at the time of Nosenko's initial contact in 1962, he was suspicious of Nosenko because he believed Nosenko was deflecting information which had been given in the previous months by X. In other words, Mr D. C. says that from the word go he believed Nosenko was providing false information in order to deflect American attention away from the information which X had given.

Yet John Hart testified that, 'The first important communication which went back from Geneva after the two American emissaries had met with Mr Yosenko was sent by a man who . . . I am going to call . . . the deputy chief of the SB Division, Soviet Bloc Division, throughout my testimony [elsewhere Hart makes clear that he is referring to the man as the deputy chief of the Soviet Bloc Division although he did not as yet hold that rank]. The deputy chief, who is the chief interrogator over there, sent back a telegram to Washington on 11 June 1962, in which he said "Subject", meaning Nosenko, "has conclusively proved his bona fides. He has provided info of importance and sensitivity. Subject now completely cooperative. Willing to meet when abroad and will meet as often and as long as possible in his departure in Geneva from 15 June."

'On 15 June both Nosenko and the Deputy Chief SB departed from Geneva, Mr Nosenko to return to Moscow and his KGB duties, the Deputy Chief SB to return to Washington.

'In the course of my investigation, I asked the gentleman, who was for many years chief of the CIA

counter-intelligence staff, to describe to me what
ensued after the arrival in Washington of DCSB, and I
shall give you a brief quote which was recorded and
transcribed and which is held in our files. This is the
chief of the counter-intelligence staff of the CIA
speaking:

'"We got the first message from Deputy Chief SB –
that is the one I have just previously quoted to you – on
Nosenko from Geneva, and Deputy Chief SB was
ordered back to Washington, and we had a big meeting
here on Saturday morning, and Deputy Chief SB
thought he had the biggest fish of his life. I mean he
really did. And everything I heard from him, however,
was in direct contrast from what we had heard from Mr
X".'

In 1978 Mr D.C. told the House Committee, 'In 1962
he made it absolutely clear to us that he would never
defect, under no circumstances . . . He not only said he
wouldn't defect but he wouldn't accept contact with us
inside the Soviet Union. However, he would see us
whenever he came out on official duty on Soviet
delegations abroad. In January of 1964 he came out and
stupefied us with this statement that he now wants to
defect.'

We know from previous chapters that this rendition
would appear to be incomplete, since the records
indicate that there was an ongoing relationship after
Nosenko's return to Russia during which he acted as an
American agent in place.

In a 1976 internal CIA memorandum, the Chief of
the Soviet Russia Division (SR Division) is quoted as
stating in a memo dated 10 February 1964, 'First I
assured Subject [Mr Nosenko] that I was satisfied that
he was genuine. Based on this, and assuming his
continued "cooperation" I said we would proceed to
make arrangements to bring him to the States. Second,
I confirmed our agreement to pay him $25,000 for each
year in place ($50,000) plus $10,000 for [a sensitive
case] and our readiness to contract for his services at

$25,000 per year. Third, I explained the polygraph he would be expected to take as final proof of his bona fides.'

In a memo dated 17 February 1964, the Chief of the SR Division writes, 'None of the events of the past few days including the way the Soviets played the pre-confrontation publicity or the confrontation itself changes the substance of the conclusions contained in my 10 February memorandum. However, there is greater evidence now I believe for the view that this operation is designed for long-range goals of utmost importance to the Soviets. One of these is probably a massive propaganda assault on CIA in which Subject, most probably as a "re-defected CIA agent", will play a major but not necessarily the sole role.'

We know from previous chapters that from the time of Nosenko's defection, a long and bitter internal battle ensued as to Nosenko's bona fides. And from the material discussed immediately above we can understand that the perceptions of the various CIA factions as to Nosenko were shaped to a great extent by their perception of X.

But what has all this to do with Oswald?

An interesting fact is glossed over in the Nosenko/Oswald summaries of the House Committee. Mr D.C., who was the man on the scene, testified that, 'Nosenko *before* his defection, . . . was meeting us under clandestine circumstances in Geneva. He was telling us about Lee Harvey Oswald. We, of course, took that and got it as straight and as thoroughly as we could under the circumstances. After he defected and came to the United States, it was made clear . . . that the FBI, as the primary investigative agency on the President's assassination, would manage the further and detailed questioning of Mr Nosenko in the United States on his knowledge of Lee Harvey Oswald.'

There is nothing in that rendition to indicate that the FBI was warned at this time that Nosenko's bona fides were in question. Indeed, the conclusion of the FBI report of their interview with Nosenko makes no such reference. Instead, it relates the famous offer by Nosenko to testify before the Warren Commission and the statement that the offer had been passed on to the appropriate authorities. [The records show that at a later date J. Edgar Hoover expressed himself as believing that Nosenko was a valid defector but that Mr X was a provocateur].

It would appear from the official summaries that – only after the Warren Commission had been briefed on Nosenko's story that Oswald had never been contacted by the KGB – the CIA met informally with Commission member Allen Dulles to inform him that Nosenko's bona fides were in doubt.

The official summaries imply that the doubts began after the Commission had been told Nosenko's Oswald story. However, the testimony of Mr D.C. contradicts that, and indeed, indicates that the doubts went back to the time of the 1962 contact.

Whatever the truth on these matters, the result is the same:The Warren Commission received information which could only lead them to suspect an Oswald/KGB connection, thereby deflecting them from considering any other possible connection.

For a period of time after his defection, the monies promised to Nosenko before his defection were not paid. Obviously, whether the challenges to his bona fides were sincere or a sham, it wouldn't do to be paying him monies at that time. By the late 60s, the money had been worked out, and by the time of the House hearings in 1978, Nosenko was receiving in excess of $35,000 per year as a 'consultant'.

In a memorandum to the Director of Central Intelligence dated 5 October 1972, Harold J. Osborn, Director of Security, states: 'An analysis of this case clearly indicates that Mr Nosenko has been an extremely valuable source, one who has identified many hundreds of Soviet Intelligence Officers, and he has otherwise provided a considerable quantity of useful information on the organization of the KGB, its operational doctrine, and methods. [Sensitive info has] been forwarded to the Federal Bureau of Investigation based on data from Mr Nosenko. He has conducted numerous special security reviews on Soviet subjects of specific intelligence interest, and he has proven himself to be invaluable in exploring counter-intelligence leads. He recently authored a book which is of interest to the Agency. In effect, Mr Nosenko has shown himself to be a productive and hardworking defector, who is "rehabilitated" and favorably disposed towards the Agency.'

Then, in 1978, the House Committee received testimony by and about Nosenko which could only cause them to suspect an Oswald/KGB connection, thus deflecting them also from even considering some other possible connection. The question arises: How or why is it that this 'extremely valuable' CIA employee delivers testimony about Oswald which the CIA then disowns as implausible and incredible?

After Nosenko again asserted he could state positively that Soviet intelligence had had no interest in ex-Marine Oswald because they didn't think he was interesting, a CIA official named David Murphy made sure everyone understood that was nonsense: 'They will talk to a marine about close order drill. You follow me? It doesn't require that he be known to have been a radar operator or a . . . they would talk to him about his military affiliations just as we would . . . We in Germany will talk to a private in the East German Border Guards, period. The GRU would be interested in talking to a private. He was a corporal in the Marine Corps, who had stated to a consul in a consular office, which is manned by the Soviets, Soviet locals and what have you, fully accessible to the Soviets, unlike the higher floors of the Embassy, that he wanted to talk about his experiences, that he wanted to tell all. I guess I found it difficult to believe; this is one of the things that made (or one of the things that created) an atmosphere of disbelief: that there must be something to this case that is important, vitally important to the Soviet Union, and we can't understand it.'

CIA Director Richard Helms, while on the one hand supporting Nosenko's bona fides as a defector, left no room for doubt in his testimony that the Committee should disbelieve Nosenko on Oswald.

In response to the question, 'Given your work in the whole field of intelligence, is it reasonable for this Committee to assume that with Oswald's background and his attempt to defect, that he would be an "uninteresting target" to the KGB?', Richard Helms testified, 'I simply do not understand that assertion. I would have thought, to begin with, that any American who went to the Russian Government and said "I want to defect to the Soviet Union" would have immediately been taken over by the KGB to find out what his game was because, after all, the KGB's charter is to protect the Soviet state against infiltration.

'How would they know that he was serious about this? How would they know that the CIA had not sent him to make a fake defection and to try to get into Soviet society through this device? So for that reason, if not for many others, I find it quite incredible, the assertion by Nosenko that Oswald was never interrogated or was never in touch with the KGB while he was in the Soviet Union. This really stretches one's credulity. It goes back to the testimony this morning that this is the hardest thing about the whole Nosenko case to swallow, and I have not been able to swallow it in all these years.'

The morning testimony to which Helms was referring began with a question by Chairman Stokes: 'If it were clearly proven that Nosenko's statements concerning Oswald were untrue, what significance would you attach to such a finding insofar as the broader question of his overall bona fides are concerned?'

To which Helms replied, 'I think, Mr Stokes, that is just the point. This is the issue which remains, as I understand it, to this very day, that no person familiar with the facts, of whom I am aware, finds Mr Nosenko's comments about Lee Harvey Oswald and the KGB to be credible. That still hangs in the air like an incubus. I think, therefore, this tends to sour a great deal of one's opinion of all the other things he may have contributed to the knowledge of the intelligence community about Soviet affairs and Soviet agents and so forth.

'I do not know how one resolves this bone in the throat. And therefore, if I sit here before you and say, Mr Stokes, I believe that Mr Nosenko is a bona fide defector and you can rely on everything he says, I am in effect saying now, Mr Stokes, you can rely on what he says about Lee Harvey Oswald. And I would not like to make that recommendation to you. That is where this thing lies and it is a most difficult question even at this late date.'

The true culmination of all this came a little further on, when Chairman Stokes asked: 'So it leaves you with the conclusion, then, that if Nosenko was lying about Oswald, that Oswald would in fact be left as being an agent of the KGB?', to which Helms responded 'By implication'.

It would seem more accurate to say: If Nosenko was lying about Oswald, then, by implication, Oswald would be left as being the agent of whoever sent Nosenko.

BOOK 2

CHAPTER 14

The Agency

In 1964, the CIA advised the Warren Commission that the Agency had never had a relationship of any kind with Lee Harvey Oswald. CIA Director John A. McCone testified not only that Oswald was not an agent, employee, informant of the CIA, and was never associated or connected directly or indirectly in any way whatsoever with the Agency, but, further, he swore that:

'The Agency never contacted him, interviewed him, talked with him, or solicited any reports or information from him, or communicated with him directly or in any other manner.'

Does this sound strikingly like what Nosenko said as regards the KGB and Oswald? Is it any more believable?

Is it believable that the CIA, which routinely attempts to solicit information from Americans traveling to Russia, would not even contact and attempt to debrief a returning defector who had lived in Russia for some two and a half years?

Let us accept that, for whatever reason, it is believable.

Is it believable if we consider the interest the CIA would clearly have – if not in this particular defector, as such – in adding to their information as to how the Russians handle defectors, should they want to 'plant' a defector?

Is it still believable if we now add the following additional facts?

(1) The returning defector had been a Marine radar operator carrying a security clearance of 'Confidential'

(2) He had worked at an air base where the super secret U-2 spy plane took off and landed

(3) Since his defection, Francis Gary Powers had been shot down over Russia in the first ever successful downing of a U-2.

Let us now add another little-known, but vital fact to the inquiry we have just begun.

It has been reported in passing that during his years in the Soviet Union, Oswald worked in the Belorussian Radio and Television Factory in Minsk.

It so happens that the CIA had a very great interest in this particular radio factory. They actively collected and carefully accumulated reams of information on the plant, and there were volumes of documents on the facility maintained in the Office of Research and Reports.

Given the CIA's interest in this particular radio factory, is it believable that the CIA would not even attempt to debrief Oswald when he re-defected?

What are we to make of this categorical denial by the CIA that they ever had even the slightest contact with Oswald?

Let us look more carefully at this new piece of information, and see if it might tie in with any knowledge we learned earlier.

To do that, let's explore two seemingly unrelated questions and see if there may be some point of convergence between them.

(1) Why was the CIA so interested in the Minsk radio factory?

(2) How did the Russians come to assign Oswald to this facility?

Since neither the CIA nor the Russians have been forthcoming with answers to these questions, we must approach the issue from a somewhat different tack.

Are we to assume that the CIA's interest in this plant was because they were concerned that the Russians were about to swamp American markets with Russian radios or TVs?

Or, is it more logical to ask if there might have been some military implications to some of the activities at the Minsk radio plant?

What type of activities might take place at a radio plant that might have military implications?

Let's return to a topic we discussed much earlier.

Radio waves are used in a very important system which has significant military implications. By definition, radar is 'a method of detecting distant objects and determining their position, velocity, or other characteristics by analysis of very high frequency radio waves reflected from their surfaces'.

Surely, if the Russians were doing some radar work at this plant, that fact would seem to provide an answer to both of the questions we are currently exploring. It would explain the CIA's interest in the plant, and it would explain why the Russians sent Oswald there.

But where does that lead us?

We know from the testimony of John Hart that the CIA had, as part of its operations, the task of 'putting people into the Soviet Union'. Why would they want to infiltrate people into the Soviet Union?

Is it reasonable to assume that the CIA did not on mere whim expose people to the great physical risk of 'putting them into the Soviet Union'? Is it reasonable to assume that such risks were undertaken only in order to procure specific information which second-hand reports could not adequately provide?

Let us take as a given the great interest the CIA had in this plant, together with the presumption that they must have had a good reason for that interest – for example, radar. Let us then assume hypothetically that the CIA desired to put their own man into that plant.

How might they go about infiltrating this spy into the plant?

Well, if the reason for the CIA interest was Russian radar work at that plant, it may seem a good bet that if the Russians had an American defector who was a radar operator, they might wish to utilize his knowledge at the Minsk plant.

Of course, for that to happen, the CIA's man must be a radar operator – regardless of whether he really has the aptitude for that specialty or not.

If, for example, the man selected had on his aptitude tests scored significantly below the average in arithmetic and pattern code analysis, that would not deter from his being assigned to radar, since the radar assignment would be not because of his aptitude, but because of his future mission.

And if he finished his first six-week radar course forty-sixth in a class of fifty-four, that was no reason to drop him from the specialty.

All that was needed was to help him place seventh in the class of thirty who went on to the second six-week radar course.

So, in our hypothesis, we now have ourselves Lee Harvey Oswald, radar operator. But we need more. We need a radar operator who will be accepted as a bona fide defector.

There happens to be an interesting thing about this Oswald. Within the recent past, preceding his entry to the Marines, he has been demonstrating an interest in socialism and communism.

And, since entering the service, this Oswald has

become more and more blatant in overtly showcasing his interest in things Russian, to the point where his fellow Marines call him 'Oswaldskovich', apparently to his pleasure. He has his name written in Russian on one of his jackets; he plays records of Russian songs 'so loud that one could hear them outside the barracks'; he frequently makes remarks in Russian, and uses expressions like 'da' and 'nyet' and addresses others and is addressed as 'Comrade'; he has been known to have come over and said jokingly, 'You called?' when one of his fellow Marines plays a particular record of Russian music; he makes a point of expressing a preference for the red pieces in chess, forming the 'Red Army'; he regularly and openly reads a Russian language newspaper; and he is openly studying the Russian language.

Certainly, the last place one would wish to station such a Marine with this great vulnerability to things Russian, would be at Atsugi Air Base in Japan, near which there is known to be operating a KGB program aimed at recruiting US military personnel.

Not that one need worry that the Russians would encourage Oswald to defect. They, as assuredly as the CIA, would want a new asset to remain in place as an undercover agent – a spy.

However, contact with this KGB program, together with a history of being a malcontent as evidenced by two court martials, might be persuasive items on his résumé at a later point.

Despite the claim by CIA officials that it was possible Oswald had been recruited by the KGB during his military tour of duty overseas, it is more logical to presume that had he truly been recruited there, the Russians would not have wanted him to defect for the reasons stated above. However, if they did want him to defect, they surely would not have needed to send him halfway around the world to Gregory Golub in Helsinki, Finland – only a narrow body of water separates Japan from Russia. Nor would Oswald or the Russians have been much concerned with the niceties of his finishing his enlistment if he were a true defector.

Is there any more logical explanation for Oswald's trek from New Orleans to Le Havre to London to Helsinki than that someone directed him to Gregory Golub, who could get him an entry visa without prior approval of Moscow?

Who was that? It surely wasn't the Russians. If they wanted Oswald in Russia, they did not need to send him to someone who could get him in without prior approval. Moreover, we know that Oswald was neither expected nor welcomed in Moscow, as evidenced by his reception – or lack thereof – when he arrived.

On the other hand, if the CIA had their radar operator whom they wished to clandestinely infiltrate into the Soviet Union, how better could they attempt to 'put him into the Soviet Union' than by directing him to Gregory Golub, who was not only known to have authority to issue entry visas without prior Moscow approval, but also was known to have exercised that right without prior investigation?

A former CIA finance officer named James Wilcott provided the House Select Committee on Assassinations with information that Lee Harvey Oswald had been a CIA agent who had received financial disbursements under an assigned cryptonym (a code designation for an agency project) and that he himself had disbursed payments for Oswald's project. In the face of categorical denials by every other CIA witness and the absence of any documentation to the contrary, the Committee concluded that Wilcott's allegation was not worthy of belief.

The Committee also had testimony from CIA personnel that a review of Agency files would not always indicate whether an individual was affiliated with the Agency in any capacity. And they recognized that there was not always an independent means of verifying that all materials requested from the Agency had, in fact, been provided. The Committee acknowledged that the very institutional characteristics that are designed to prevent penetration by foreign powers (such as the Agency's strict compartmentalization and the complexity of its enormous filing system) have the simultaneous effect of making congressional inquiry difficult.

Accordingly, the Committee specifically pointed out that, 'Any finding that is essentially negative in nature – such as that Lee Harvey Oswald was neither associated with the CIA in any way, nor ever in contact with that institution – should explicitly acknowledge the possibility of oversight.'

There are certain things that must be analyzed which are relevant to the question of whether Oswald was a true defector or an American agent.

As of October 1959, the State Department had information which should have caused it to prepare a 'lookout card' for Lee Harvey Oswald. A lookout card was filed in the lookout file in the Passport Office, and whenever anyone applied for a passport from any city in the world, his application was immediately forwarded to this office and his name and date of birth checked against the lookout file and if a lookout card was filed, appropriate action, including the possible refusal of a passport, was taken. No such lookout card pertaining to Lee Harvey Oswald was ever located and the Warren Commission reported that 'certain file entries indicate that such card was never prepared'.

In itself, the absence of a lookout card may prove little. However, as part of a mosaic of oddities, it may take on some meaning.

Since long before the time we are discussing, the CIA has maintained what are known as 201 files. '201 files are opened when a person is considered to be of potential intelligence or counter-intelligence significance. The opening of such a file is designed to serve the purpose of placing certain CIA information pertaining to that individual in one centralized records system. The 201 file is maintained in a folder belonging to the Directorate for Operations, the Agency component responsible for clandestine activities.'

A confidential State Department telegram dated 31 October 1959, sent from Moscow to Washington and forwarded to the CIA, reported that Oswald, a recently discharged Marine, had appeared at the US Embassy in Moscow to renounce his American citizenship and 'has offered Soviets any information he has acquired as [an] enlisted radar operator'. At least three other communications of a confidential nature that gave more detail on the Oswald case were sent to the CIA in about the same time period. Agency officials questioned by the Committee testified that the substance of the 31 October 1959 cable was sufficiently important to warrant the opening of a 201 file. Oswald's file, however, was not opened until 9 December 1960.

An Agency memorandum dated 18 September 1975 indicates that Oswald's file was opened on 9 December 1960 in response to the receipt of five documents: two from the FBI, two from the State Department and one from the Navy. This explanation, however, is inconsistent with the presence in Oswald's file of four State Department documents dated in 1959 and a fifth dated 25 May 1960.

The 18 September 1975 memo also states that Oswald's file was opened on 9 December 1960 as a result of his 'defection' to the USSR on 31 October 1959 and renewed interest in Oswald brought about by his queries concerning possible re-entry into the United States. There is no official indication, however, that Oswald expressed to any US Government official an intention to return to the United States until mid-February 1961 (although there is the statement in Oswald's letter – inconsistent with his diary – stating it was a 'second request'). The Committee interviewed a number of Agency people who attempted to explain away the above situation. The Committee, even after accepting their analysis of what had happened, declared, 'Even so, this analysis only explained why a file on Oswald was finally opened; it did not explain the seemingly long delay in the opening of the file.'

The form used to initiate the opening of a 201 file contains a box entitled 'Other Identification'. Lee Harvey Oswald's form had in that box the designation 'AG'. The Agency's explanation of this designation was that AG was a code meaning 'actual or potential defectors to the East or the Sino/Soviet block including Cuba'. Unfortunately, no one on the Committee asked why the CIA would need a secret code on their internal records to denote that the subject had defected or might defect: why not just enter 'defector' or 'potential defector'? Confusingly, another CIA witness said the 'A' represented Communism while the 'G' would represent some category within the Communist structure. All the Agency witnesses were most adamant that the one thing that AG did not stand for was AGency.

The form used to initiate the opening of Oswald's 201 file contains a notation that this file was to be 'restricted'. The CIA admittedly had a practice of restricting access to agents' files to persons on a 'need-to-know' basis. This restriction meant that any person seeking access to the file would first have to notify the restricting officer. The explanation offered by the CIA on this restriction was that the restricting officer had done so simply to allow her to remain aware of any developments that might have occurred with regard to the file. However, no explanation was offered as to why this was necessary. Obviously, if the usual practice was for the person opening the file to be kept abreast of developments, there would be no need to mark a file 'restricted' in order to kick the file back to her.

At the time Oswald was in the Soviet Union, the CIA had a program known as 'HT-Lingual', the purpose of which was to obtain intelligence and counter-intelligence information from letters sent between the United States and Russia. Intercepted letters and envelopes would be photographed and then returned to the mails.

Despite the fact that Oswald was known to have sent or received more than fifty communications during his stay in the Soviet Union, the CIA represented that they had only one letter in their possession directly related to Oswald, a letter dated 6 July 1961 sent by Marguerite Oswald. The Committee, having questioned why the Agency ostensibly had just this one Oswald letter, stated, 'In essence, the Agency's response suggested that HT-Lingual only operated 4 days a week, and, even then, proceeded on a sampling basis.'

The Committee's review of HT-Lingual files pertaining to the Oswald case resulted in the discovery amongst other things of a reproduction of an index card regarding Lee Harvey Oswald dated 9 November 1959, which stated that Oswald was a recent defector to the USSR and a former Marine. It also bears the notation 'CI/Project/RE' and some handwritten notes.

The Committee questioned former employees of the CIA who may have had some knowledge pertaining to the HT-Lingual project in general and this card in particular. Some of these employees recognized the card as relating to the HT-Lingual project, but were unable to identify the meaning of the notation 'CI/Project/RE'. However, one employee testified that the 'CI/Project' was 'simply a name of convenience that was used to describe the HT-Lingual project'. Another testified that 'CI/Project' was the name of the component that ran the HT-Lingual project, and that 'RE' represented the initials of a person who had been a translator of foreign language documents.

The Agency's explanation for the term 'CI/Project/RE' was that there existed an office within the counter-intelligence staff that was known as 'CI/Project', a cover title that had been used to hide the true nature of the office's function of exploiting the material produced by the HT-Lingual project, and that RE represented the initials of a former employee. Thus, the Agency said, the full meaning of the notation was that on 9 November 1959, an employee whose initials were RE placed Oswald's name on the 'watch list' for the HT-Lingual project for the reason stated on the card: that Oswald was a recent defector to the USSR and a former Marine.

The Agency's response also offered explanations for the handwritten material on the card, which was the number '7–305', and the notation 'N/R–RI,20 Nov.59'.

The number 7–305, they said, was a reference to the communication from the CI staff to the Office of Security expressing the CI staff's interest in seeing any mail to or from Oswald in the Soviet Union.

The notation 'N/R–RI,20 Nov.59', according to the Agency, signified that a name trace run through the central records register indicated that there was no record for Lee Oswald as of that date.

How do these explanations of the Agency stand up to examination? Let's start at the end.

They claim that 'N/R–RI,20 Nov.59' signifies that a name trace run through the central records register indicated that there was no record for Lee Oswald as of that date. Yet, that is in direct conflict with other Agency records which indicate the receipt of a telegram concerning Oswald on 31 October 1959, and of two telegrams from the Navy concerning him on 3 and 4 November 1959.

They claim that the handwritten number 7–305 is a reference to the communication from the CI staff to the Office of Security expressing the CI staff's interest in seeing *any* mail to or from Oswald in the Soviet Union. Is this supposed to mean that the picking up of Oswald's letters is not to be left to chance (sampling)? But how does this square with the Agency's position that they have only one of the more than fifty communications to or from Oswald? Does it mean that the Office of Security is being advised that any Oswald communications which do happen to be picked up should be forwarded to the CI staff?

Wouldn't that then make it rather superfluous for RE to also note that Oswald's name be placed on a watch list for the HT-Lingual Project, which is the Agency's explanation for the entry CI/Project/RE?

One aspect of that explanation which deserves more thought is the Agency's interpretation of 'CI/Project'. They say there was an office within the counter-intelligence staff that was known as CI/Project, a cover title that had been used to hide the true nature of the office's functions; and further they say that in fact this office was responsible for the exploitation of the material produced by the HT-Lingual project.

That sounds good if you say it fast. But when you say it slow and consider what you are saying, certain questions emerge. For example, what would be the purpose of having the HT-Lingual project at all unless you were going to exploit the material it produced? If we take as a given that all the material is being gathered in the expectation of being exploited, doesn't it follow that all the material being produced would be of interest to the office responsible for exploiting the material? So, why would this particular card have on it a notation 'CI/Project', supposedly identifying the exploitation unit?

Two Agency employees gave slightly different explanations for CI/Project, one stating that this was a name of convenience to describe the HT-Lingual project, and the other that it was the name of the component that ran the HT-Lingual project. To these explanations, the comments in the preceding paragraph might with equal force be made, and, in addition, it may well be asked why the code name HT-Lingual had been invented if it was going to need yet another code name, CI/Project, to refer to it?

Richard E. Snyder, it will be remembered, was the consular official in the US Embassy in Moscow who had handled the Oswald case both in 1959 at the time of the defection, and in 1961 at the time the re-defection was initiated. It so happens that during 1949–50, while awaiting his foreign service appointment with the State Department, Snyder had worked for the CIA. However, Snyder swore to the Committee, he had had no contact with the CIA since resigning from the Agency in March 1950, other than a letter written in 1970 or 1971 inquiring about employment on a contractual basis.

The Committee found that Snyder's CIA file revealed that at one time prior to 1974 it had been red flagged and maintained on a segregated basis. The file contained a routing indicator that stated that the file had been red flagged because of a 'DCI (Director of Central Intelligence) statement and a matter of cover' concerning Snyder. In response to a Committee inquiry, the CIA indicated that the DCI statement presumably refered to comments which former Director Richard Helms had made in 1964 concerning the Oswald case (which was then under intense study) when Helms was Deputy Director for Plans. The CIA also stated that Snyder's file had been flagged at the request of DDO/CI (Directorate of Operations/Central Intelligence) to insure that all inquiries concerning Snyder would be referred to that office. The Agency was unable to explain the reference to 'cover' because according to its records Snyder had never been assigned any cover while employed. Further, the Agency stated that 'There is no record in Snyder's official personnel file that he ever worked, directly or indirectly, in any capacity for the CIA after his resignation on 26 September 1950' (he had said March).

The Committee did not regard this explanation as satisfactory, especially since Snyder's 201 file indicated that for approximately one year during 1956–7 he had been used by an Agency case officer as a spotter at a university campus because of his access to others who might be going to the Soviet Union, nor was the Agency able to explain specifically why someone considered it necessary to red flag the Snyder file.

Knowing that Snyder may have had a CIA role while in Moscow, when combined with the fact that it was common knowledge that the Russians had hundreds of bugs in the Embassy, gives rise to the intriguing possibility that Snyder and Oswald were engaging in a charade for the benefit of eavesdropping Russian ears, when Oswald went to the Embassy to announce that he had important information he was going to give to the Russians. There can be no question that that act (together with the newspaper interest in Oswald, which was also initiated by Snyder) got some action from the Russians, who had been cautious about Oswald to that point.

Shortly after Lee Oswald had married Marina at the end of April 1961, a Dr Alexis H. Davidson began a tour of duty as the US Embassy physician in Moscow. Davidson stated to the Committee that in connection with this assignment, he had received some 'superficial' intelligence training. This training, he said, mainly involved lectures on Soviet life and instructions on remembering and reporting Soviet names and military activities.

For reasons which will be immediately made clear, Davidson could not have attempted to claim total naiveté with respect to intelligence matters. And perhaps his training was not quite so 'superficial' as he claimed.

The fact is that for at least a year during his Moscow tour of duty, Davidson served as part of the signal system for a CIA agent who was a highly placed GRU officer, Colonel Oleg Penkovsky. When the Soviets finally broke the Penkovsky case in 1963, Davidson was publicly declared *persona non grata*.

Meanwhile, back in 1961 and 1962, while Davidson was still on duty in Moscow, Lee Harvey Oswald was in the process of beginning his re-defection. What, if any, relationship this physician/agent had with Lee Harvey Oswald has never been ascertained.

However, after the assassination of President Kennedy, it was discovered that the name of Dr Davidson's mother and her address in Atlanta, Georgia were in Oswald's address book under the heading 'Mother of US Embassy Doctor'. In addition, it was determined that the flight that the returning Oswalds took from New York to Dallas on 14 June 1962 had stopped in Atlanta.

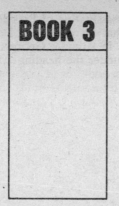

BOOK 3

THE INTELLIGENCE
CONNECTION

BOOK 3

CHAPTER

15

The Aristocratic Spy

Upon his return from Russia in June 1962, Oswald and his family lived for several months in Fort Worth, Texas. In October, Lee went alone to Dallas, got a job, and at the beginning of November moved his wife and daughter to Dallas.

They remained in the Dallas area until April 1963, when Lee moved to New Orleans, leaving his wife and daughter in Irving, a suburb of Dallas, at the home of Ruth Paine, whom they had first met in February.

His little family rejoined Lee in mid-May and they resided together in New Orleans until 22 September when Marina (who was eight months pregnant) and June returned to live at Ruth Paine's. They remained at Ruth Paine's even after Lee moved back to Dallas on 3 October; and, though Lee visited from time to time, it was at Ruth Paine's that Marina was living on 20 October, when she gave birth to their second daughter, Rachel; and it was at Ruth Paine's that she was residing with their children on 22 November 1963.

From the time of their arrival from Russia, Lee and Marina had become acquainted with the growing number of people of the Russian-speaking community in the Dallas–Fort Worth area, who were attracted to each other by a common background, language and culture. With just one exception, Lee himself appears to have had only short-lived contacts with these people.

The exception, George de Mohrenschildt, was more than just a close friend; he was also a man for whom Oswald had appreciable respect.

De Mohrenschildt had an impressive pedigree. Amongst his ancestors was Baron Hilienfelt, a Baltic Swede who fought in the American Army of Independence; and an uncle, Ferdinand de Mohrenschildt, had been First Secretary of the last Russian Embassy in Washington under the Czarist Government.

His father, Sergius Alexander von Mohrenschildt, a 'marshall of nobility' in Minsk Province, had served as director of the Nobel interests in Czarist Russia. Following the Revolution, Sergius was jailed several times by the Communist regime and then was banished for life to Siberia, from where he escaped with his family to Poland.

George's brother, Dimitri, had served in the Czarist Russian Imperial Navy. After the Revolution he joined anti-Communist groups for which he was jailed by the Communists and sentenced to death. Released in a prisoner exchange, Dimitri had emigrated to the United States in 1920 where he remained a 'ferocious anti-Communist'.

George had been about ten years of age when he fled with his parents from Russia to Poland. After attending a Polish cavalry military academy, he studied in Antwerp and attended the University of Liège from which he received a doctor's degree in international commerce in 1928.

In 1938, he emigrated to the United States, where he went to to work as a salesman for the Shumaker Co. in New York. The chief of export for the Shumaker Co., Pierre Fraiss, soon became one of de Mohrenschildt's best friends. Fraiss was connected with French intelligence, and before long de Mohrenschildt was working for Fraiss collecting facts on people involved in pro-German activities. This intelligence work for Fraiss took him around the United States.

It also involved contacting oil companies in the United States about selling oil to the French in competition against German oil supplies during the war. In 1944 de Mohrenschildt entered the University of Texas, from where he received a master's degree in petroleum geology and petroleum engineering in 1945. From that time on he became active as a petroleum engineer throughout the world.

It appears, though, that petroleum engineering may not have been all he was doing throughout the world.

For example, following his trip in 1957 to Yugoslavia for the International Cooperation Administration, de Mohrenschildt was debriefed on that country on several occasions by the CIA in the person of their agent J. Walton Moore.

There were a number of further contacts between Moore and de Mohrenschildt for debriefing purposes during the ensuing years, at which some of the subjects discussed included China and Latin America. Interestingly enough, de Mohrenschildt told the Warren Commission that he 'asked Moore and Ft. Worth attorney Max Clark about Oswald to reassure himself that it was "safe" for the de Mohrenschildts to assist Oswald. According to his testimony, de Mohrenschildt was told by one of the persons he talked to about Oswald, although he said he could not remember who it was, that "the guy seems to be OK".' Since there is no indication who Clark was or whether he had any contact at all with Oswald, the question arises as to what basis CIA agent Moore might have had for giving the 'OK' to this returned defector.

By 'happenstance', at the time of the Bay of Pigs invasion de Mohrenschildt was in Guatemala City, the control center of the CIA's multi-million dollar invasion preparation operation.

One of de Mohrenschildt's world-wide contacts was

with Clemard Joseph Charles, President of the Banque Commerciale d'Haiti. In early May 1963, Charles began a visit to the United States. Colonel Sam Kail, an Army Intelligence officer who was working in Miami, contacted Dorothe Matlack of the office of the Army Chief of Staff for Intelligence. The work of Mrs Matlack, who served as Assistant Director of the Office of Intelligence of the Army, included 'human source collection of intelligence' and involved serving in a liaison capacity with the Central Intelligence Agency. Colonel Kail suggested that Mrs Matlack talk to Charles when he visited Washington, DC, because of Charles' relationship to President Duvalier of Haiti and Haiti's strategic position relative to Cuba.

On 7 May 1963, Mrs Matlack met in the Capitol with Charles and de Mohrenschildt, apparently after having first made hotel reservations for them. Because of the potential political information Charles could give about the current situation in Haiti, she decided that the CIA should become the primary contact with Charles, and so she also arranged for Charles to meet with Tony Czaikowski of the CIA, whom she introduced as a professor from Georgetown University.

The House Select Committee related that, 'A *Washington Post* article by Norman Gale, dated 29 September 1964, reported that Haitian President François Duvalier had received two T-28 fighter planes from Dallas, Texas. The article stated the planes were flown to Haiti illegally. According to the article, Duvalier made down payment on the planes with a letter of credit drawn on the Banque Commerciale of Port-au-Prince, Haiti. The article identified Clemard Joseph Charles as president and principal stockholder of the bank and a close ally of Duvalier. The article stated that Charles visited the United States earlier in 1964 to buy boats and other weapons, and that he visited Dallas during that trip.'[. . .]

'In an airgram dated 2 May 1967 from the Department of State to the American Embassy at Port-au-

Prince, Haiti, it was reported that a man named Edward Browder had leased a plane for one year starting on 24 November 1964 in the name of a phony company and had flown the plane to Port-au-Prince and left it there. The airgram reported also that Browder later cashed a check for $24,000 signed by Clemard Joseph Charles. Another airgram from the State Department to the Embassy dated 25 May 1967 verified that the check to Browder was drawn from the personal account of Clemard Joseph Charles at Manufacturers Hanover Trust Bank.

'Edward Browder was interviewed by the Committee at the Federal Penitentiary at MacNeill Island, Washington, where he was serving a 25-year sentence for securities violations. During his interview, Browder discussed a series of gun-running and smuggling operations he was involved in during the 1960s that were intended to result in the eventual overthrow or assassination of Fidel Castro. Browder stated that this work included assistance by the CIA in the form of money and operations. Browder said that during that period he did purchase at least two B-25 planes to be used in "smuggling operations" which would be used to assist the gun-running and raids against Cuba.'

The House Committee interviewed Joseph Dryer, a Palm Beach, Florida, stockbroker who, they had learned, had known George de Mohrenschildt in Haiti. According to Dryer, during the 1950s and 60s, he, Clemard Joseph Charles, and George de Mohrenschildt were associated with a woman named Jacqueline Lancelot, who owned a well-known restaurant in Petionville, Haiti. Dryer said the restaurant was frequented by many American intelligence personnel from the American Embassy, and other foreigners. Lancelot, he said, had contact with the American intelligence operatives and passed them information about the Duvalier government. Dryer said that his relationship with Lancelot included passing messages for her to people in the United States whom Dryer assumed were connected in some way to the CIA.

Dryer also told the Committee the following bit of hearsay information. He said that Lancelot had told him shortly after the Kennedy assassination that a 'substantial' sum of money, $200,000 or $250,000, had been deposited in de Mohrenschildt's account in a Port-au-Prince bank (not Charles' bank). According to Dryer, Lancelot said her source of information was the person who handed out the funds at the bank; that the money was subsequently paid out, although she did not know to whom; and de Mohrenschildt left Haiti soon after.

Given this hint at George de Mohrenschildt's fascinating and exciting exploits over the years, his 1962–3 friendship with Lee Harvey Oswald surely made for a rather strange pairing, to say the least. De Mohrenschildt, sophisticated and well educated, was a man who moved easily in the social and professional circles of wealthy Texas oilmen and the so-called 'White Russian' community in Dallas, many of whom were avowed right-wingers. Oswald, because of his 'lowly' background which did not include much education or influence, and because of his Marxist ideological positions, was shunned by most of the people de Mohrenschildt counted among his friends.

When Oswald first moved to Dallas on 9 October 1962, before he even established a residence, he opened a post office box (#2915) at the Dallas General Post Office. His application for the box listed his address as that of George de Mohrenschildt's daughter, Alexandra de Mohrenschildt Taylor.

Finally, there is this intriguing 'teaser' of the George de Mohrenschildt story. It appears that de Mohrenschildt had some type of association with a man named William Avery Hyde. This is, an intriguing teaser because Hyde just happened to be the father of Ruth Paine, the woman with whom Marina and the children were permanently residing after September 1963.

And on 14 October 1963 (18 days after the front page of the *Dallas Morning News* announced that JFK would be visiting Dallas in November), this same Ruth Paine placed a most fateful telephone call to Roy S. Truly, the superintendent of the Texas School Book Depository in downtown Dallas. As a direct result of that phone call, Lee Harvey Oswald began his employment at the Depository, which overlooked Dealey Plaza, where, some five weeks later, John Fitzgerald Kennedy was assassinated.

BOOK 3

CHAPTER

16

Covert Operations

As can be discerned from even our very brief glimpse of George de Mohrenschildt and his associates, American intelligence in the 50s and 60s might be described as being both 'passive' (receiving information) and 'active' (gun-running, etc.). But we have, to this point, seen just a tip of the iceberg of the 'active' side of the picture.

'Following the end of World War II, many nations in Eastern Europe and elsewhere fell under Communist influence or control. The defeat of the Axis powers was accompanied by rapid disintegration of the Western colonial empires. World War II had no sooner ended than a new struggle began. The Communist threat, emanating from what came to be called the "Sino-Soviet bloc", led to a policy of containment intended to prevent further encroachment into the "Free World".

'United States strategy for conducting the Cold War called for the establishment of interlocking treaty arrangements and military bases throughout the world. Concern over the expansion of an aggressive Communist monolith led the United States to fight two major wars in Asia. In addition, it was considered necessary to wage a relentless cold war against Communist expansion wherever it appeared in the "back alleys of the world". This called for a full range of covert activities in response to the operations of Communist clandestine services.

'The fear of Communist expansion was particularly acute in the United States when Fidel Castro emerged as Cuba's leader in the late 1950s. His takeover was seen as the first significant penetration by the Communists into the Western Hemisphere. United States leaders, including most Members of Congress, called for vigorous action to stem the Communist infection in this hemisphere. These policies rested on widespread support and encouragement.

'Throughout this period, the United States felt impelled to respond to threats which were, or seemed to be, skirmishes in a global Cold War against Communism. Castro's Cuba raised the specter of a Soviet outpost at America's doorstep. Events in the Dominican Republic appeared to offer an additional opportunity for the Russians and their allies. The Congo, freed from Belgian rule, occupied the strategic center of the African continent, and the prospect of Communist penetration there was viewed as a threat to American interests in emerging African nations. There was great concern that a Communist takeover in Indochina would have a "domino effect" throughout Asia. Even the election in 1970 of a Marxist president in Chile was seen by some as a threat similar to that of Castro's takeover in Cuba.[. . .]

'Covert action is activity which is meant to further the sponsoring nation's foreign policy objectives, and to be concealed in order to permit that nation to plausibly deny responsibility.[. . .]

'From 1955 to 1970, the basic authority for covert operations was a directive of the National Security Council, NSC5412/2. This directive instructed the CIA to counter, reduce and discredit "International Communism" throughout the world in a manner consistent with United States foreign and military policies. It also directed the CIA to undertake covert operations to achieve this end and defined covert operations as any covert activities related to propaganda, economic warfare, political action (including sabotage, demolition and assistance to resistance movements) and all activities compatible with the directive.[. . .]

'Beginning in 1955, the responsibility for authorizing CIA covert action operations lay with the Special Group, a subcommittee of the National Security Council composed of the President's Assistant for National Security Affairs, the Director of Central Intelligence, the Deputy Secretary of Defense and the Under Secretary of State for Political Affairs.'

A look at covert actions conducted in the Congo and the Dominican Republic should prove instructive for the material in following chapters.

'In the summer of 1960, there was great concern at the highest levels in the United States government about the role of Patrice Lumumba in the Congo. Lumumba, who served briefly as Premier of the newly independent nation, was viewed with alarm by United States policymakers because of what they perceived as his magnetic public appeal and his leanings toward the Soviet Union.

'Under the leadership of Lumumba and the new President, Joseph Kasavubu, the Congo declared its independence from Belgium on 30 June 1960. In the turbulent month that followed, Lumumba threatened to invite Soviet troops to hasten the withdrawal of Belgian armed forces. The United Nations Security Council requested Belgium's withdrawal and dispatched a neutral force to the Congo to preserve order. In late July, Lumumba visited Washington and received pledges of economic aid from Secretary of State Christian Herter. By the beginning of September, Soviet airplanes, trucks, and technicians were arriving in the province where Lumumba's support was strongest.[. . .]

'The evidence indicates that it is likely that President Eisenhower's expression of strong concern about Lumumba at a meeting of the National Security Council on 18 August 1960, was taken by Allen Dulles [Director of the CIA] as authority to assassinate Lumumba.[. . .]

'The week after the 18 August NSC meeting, a presidential advisor reminded the Special Group of the "necessity for very straightforward action" against Lumumba and prompted a decision not to rule out consideration of "any particular kind of activity which might contribute to getting rid of Lumumba". The following day, Dulles cabled a CIA Station Officer in Leopoldville, Republic of the Congo, that "in high quarters" the "removal" of Lumumba was "an urgent and prime objective". Shortly thereafter the CIA's clandestine service formulated a plot to assassinate Lumumba.[. . .]

'In the summer of 1960, DDP [Deputy Director for Plans] Richard Bissell asked the Chief of the Africa Division, Bronson Tweedy, to explore the feasibility of assassinating Patrice Lumumba. Bissell also asked a CIA scientist, Joseph Scheider, to make preparations to assassinate or incapacitate an unspecified "African leader". Scheider procured toxic biological materials in response to Bissell's request, and was then ordered by Tweedy to take these materials to the Station Officer in Leopoldville.[. . .]

'In mid-September, after losing a struggle for the leadership of the government to Kasavubu and Joseph Mobutu, Chief of Staff of the Congolese armed forces, Lumumba sought protection from the United Nations forces in Leopoldville.[. . .]

'The evidence indicates that the ouster of Lumumba did not alleviate the concern about him in the United States government. Rather, CIA and high Administration officials continued to view him as a threat. During this period, CIA officers in the Congo advised and aided Congolese contacts known to have an intent to assassinate Lumumba. The officers also urged the "permanent disposal" of Lumumba by some of these Congolese contacts. Moreover, the CIA opposed re-opening Parliament after the coup because of the likelihood that Parliament would return Lumumba to power.[. . .]

'In late September, Scheider delivered the lethal substances to the Station Officer in Leopoldville [Hedgman] and instructed him to assassinate Patrice Lumumba. The Station Officer testified that after requesting and receiving confirmation from CIA Head-quarters that he was to carry out Scheider's instructions, he proceeded to take "exploratory steps" in furtherance of the assassination plot. . . .

'Scheider explained that the toxic material was to be injected into some substance that Lumumba would ingest: "it had to do with anything he could get to his mouth, whether it was food or a toothbrush, so that some of the material could get to his mouth".

'Hedgman said that the means of assassination was not restricted to use of toxic material provided by Scheider. He testified that he may have "suggested" shooting Lumumba to Scheider as an alternative to poisoning. Scheider said it was his "impression" that Tweedy and his Deputy empowered him to tell the Station Officer that he could pursue other means of assassination. Station Officer Hedgman testified that, although the selection of a mode of assassination was left to his judgement, there was a firm requirement that "if I implemented these instructions it had to be a way which could not be traced back either to an American or the United States government".[. . .]

'Scheider's mission to the Congo was preceded and followed by cables from Headquarters urging the "elimination" of Lumumba transmitted through an extraordinarily restricted "Eyes Only" channel – including two messages bearing the personal signature of Allen Dulles.'

The 'extraordinarily restricted' channel, known as

the PROP channel, 'indicated extraordinary sensitivity and restricted circulation at CIA Headquarters to Dulles, Bissell, Tweedy, and Tweedy's Deputy. The PROP designator restricted circulation in the Congo to the Station Officer. Tweedy testified that the PROP channel was established and used exclusively for the assassination operation.[. . .]

'Throughout the fall of 1960, while Lumumba remained in UN protective custody, the CIA continued to view him as a serious political threat. One concern was that if Parliament were re-opened and the moderates failed to obtain a majority vote, the "pressures for Lumumba's return will be almost irresistible." Another concern at CIA Headquarters was that foreign powers would intervene in the Congo and bring Lumumba to power. Lumumba was also viewed by the CIA and the Administration as a stalking horse for "what appeared to be a Soviet effort to take over the Congo".'

On 15 October 1960, Bronson Tweedy dispatched a cable 'via the PROP channel for Hedgman's "Eyes Only", which prevented the message from being dispatched to anyone else, including the Ambassador'.

Amongst other things in this cable which dealt with the subject of the assassination of Lumumba, Tweedy requested 'the Station Officer's reaction to the prospect of sending a senior CIA case officer to the Congo on a "direct assignment to concentrate entirely this aspect".'

In his response two days later, Station Officer Hedgman concluded his cable 'with the following cryptic recommendation, reminiscent of his testimony that he may have "suggested" shooting Lumumba to Scheider as an alternative to poisoning: "If Case Officer sent, recommend HQS pouch soonest high powered foreign make rifle with telescopic scope and silencer. Hunting good here when lights right. However as hunting rifles now forbidden, would keep rifle in office pending opening of hunting season." Tweedy testified that the Station Officer's recommendation clearly referred to sending to the Congo via diplomatic pouch a weapon suited for assassinating Lumumba. The oblique suggestion of shooting Lumumba at the "opening of hunting season" could be interpreted as a plan to assassinate Lumumba as soon as he was seen outside the residence where he remained in UN protective custody. Tweedy interpreted the cable to mean that "an operational plan involving a rifle" had not yet been formulated by the Station Officer and that the "opening of hunting season" would depend upon approval of such a plan by CIA headquarters.[. . .]

'Michael Mulroney, a senior CIA officer in the Directorate for Plans, testified that in October 1960 he had been asked by Richard Bissell to go to the Congo to carry out the assassination of Lumumba.[. . .] At the time, Mulroney was the Deputy Chief of an extra-ordinarily secret unit within the Directorate of Plans.[. . .] Mulroney said that he refused to partici-pate in an assassination operation, but proceeded to the Congo to attempt to draw Lumumba away from the protective custody of the UN guard and place him in the hands of Congolese authorities.[. . .]

'According to Mulroney there was a "very, very high probability" that Lumumba would receive capital pun-ishment at the hands of the Congolese authorities. But he "had no compunction about bringing him out and then having him tried by a jury of his peers". Despite Mulroney's expressed aversion to assassination and his agreement to undertake a more general mission to "neutralize" Lumumba's influence, Bissell continued pressing him to consider an assassination opera-tion.[. . .]

'Shortly after Mulroney's arrival in the Congo, he was joined by QJ/WIN, a CIA agent with a criminal background. Late in 1960, WI/ROGUE, one of Hedgman's operatives, approached QJ/WIN with a proposition to join an "execution squad".[. . .]

'WI/ROGUE was an "essentially stateless" soldier of fortune, "a forger and former bank robber". The CIA sent him to the Congo after providing him with plastic surgery and a toupee so that Europeans traveling in the Congo would not recognize him.[. . .] CIA's Africa Division recommended WI/ROGUE as an agent in the following terms: "He is indeed aware of the precepts of right and wrong, but if he is given an assignment which may be morally wrong in the eyes of the world, but necessary because his case officer ordered him to carry it out, then it is right, and he will dutifully undertake appropriate action for its execution without pangs of conscience. In a word, he can rationalize all actions."'

A 14 November 1960 PROP cable from the Station Officer to Tweedy states that a CIA agent had learned that Lumumba's 'political followers in Stanleyville desire that he break out of his confinement and proceed to that city by car to engage in political activity . . . Decision on breakout will probably be made shortly. Station expects to be advised by [agent] of [what] decision was made . . . Station has several possible assets to use in event of breakout and studying several plans of action'.

Lumumba left UN custody on 27 November 1960. A cable the next day advised '[Station] working with [Congolese Government] to get roads blocked and troops alerted [block] possible escape route'. (CIA Cable, Leopoldville to Director, 28 November 1960.)

A CIA Cable on 29 November 1960 read, 'View change in location target, OJ/WIN anxious go Stanleyville and expressed desire execute plan by himself without using any apparat.'

The reply the following day from the Chief of the Africa Division to the Station Officer said 'Concur QJ/WIN go Stanleyville . . . We are prepared consider direct action by QJ/WIN but would like your reading on security factors. How close would this place [the United States] to the action?[. . .]

'Early in December, Mobutu's troops captured Lumumba while he was traveling toward his stronghold at Stanleyville and imprisoned him.[. . .]

'There is no doubt that the CIA and the Congolese government shared a concern in January 1961 that Lumumba might return to power, particularly since the Congolese army and police were threatening to mutiny if they were not given substantial pay raises.'

On 12 January 1961, 'Station Officer Hedgman reported that a mutiny "almost certainly would bring about [Lumumba] return power" and said he had advised the Congolese government of his opinion that the army garrison at Leopoldville "will mutiny within two or three days unless drastic action taken satisfy complaints".[. . .]

'The next day, Hedgman cabled Headquarters: "Station and Embassy believe present government may fall within few days. Result would almost certainly be chaos and return [Lumumba] to power." Hedgman advised that reopening the Congolese Parliament under United Nations supervision was unacceptable because: "The combination of [Lumumba's] powers as demagogue, his able use of goon squads and propaganda and spirit of defeat within [government] coalition which would increase rapidly under such conditions would almost certainly insure [Lumumba] victory in Parliament . . . Refusal take drastic steps at this time will lead to defeat of [United States] policy in Congo."[. . .]

'On 17 January, authorities in Leopoldville placed Lumumba and two of his leading supporters, Maurice Mpolo and Joseph Okito, aboard an airplane bound for Bakwanga. Apparently the aircraft was redirected in midflight to Elisabethville in Katanga Province "when it was learned that United Nations troops were at Bakwanga airport". On 13 February, the government of Katanga reported that Lumumba and his two companions escaped the previous day and died at the hands of hostile villagers.

'The United Nations Commission on Investigation was "not convinced by the version of the facts given by the provincial government of Katgana". The Commission concluded instead that Lumumba was killed on 17

January, almost immediately after his arrival in Katanga, probably with the knowledge of the central government and at the behest of the Katanga authorities: "The Commission wishes to put on record its view that President Kasavubu and his aides . . . should not escape responsibility for the death of Mr Lumumba, Mr Okito and Mr Mpolo. For Mr Kasavubu and his aides had handed over Mr Lumumba and his colleagues to the Katanga authorities knowing full well, in doing so, that they were throwing them into the hands of their bitterest political enemies."[. . .]

'[T]he Station Officer clearly had prior knowledge of the plan to transfer Lumumba to a state where it was probable that he would be killed. Other supporters of Lumumba who had been sent to Bakwanga earlier by Leopoldville authorities "were killed there in horrible circumstances, and the place was known as the 'slaughterhouse'."[. . .]

'Hedgman acknowledged that the CIA was in close contact with some Congolese officials who "quite clearly knew" that Lumumba was to be shipped to Katanga "because they were involved". But Hedgman said that these Congolese contacts "were not acting under CIA instructions if and when they did this".

'Rafael Trujillo came to power in the Dominican Republic in 1930. For most of his tenure, the United States Government supported him and he was regarded throughout much of the Caribbean and Latin America as a protégé of the United States. Trujillo's rule, always harsh and dictatorial, became more arbitrary during the 1950s. As a result, the United States' image was increasingly tarnished in the eyes of many Latin Americans.

'Increasing American awareness of Trujillo's brutality and fear that it would lead to a Castro-type revolution caused United States officials to consider various plans to hasten his abdication or downfall.

'As early as February 1960, the Eisenhower Administration gave high level consideration to a program of covert aid to Dominican dissidents.[. . .] During the spring of 1960, the US Ambassador to the Dominican Republic, Joseph Farland, made initial contact with . . . a group of dissidents regarded as moderate, pro-United States and desirous of establishing a democratic form of government.[. . .] 'During the course of a cocktail party in the Dominican Republic, a leading dissident made a specific request to Ambassador Farland for a limited number of rifles with telescopic sights. The Ambassador promised to pass on the request. He apparently did so after returning to Washington.[. . .]

'Prior to his final departure from the Dominican Republic in May 1960, the Ambassador introduced his Deputy-Chief-of-Mission, Henry Dearborn, to the dissident leaders, indicating that Dearborn could be trusted.

'Then on 16 June 1960, CIA Headquarters cabled a request that Dearborn become the "communications link" between the dissidents and CIA. The cable stated that Dearborn's role had the unofficial approval of Assistant Secretary of State for Inter-American Affairs, Roy R. Rubottom. Dearborn agreed. He requested, however, that the CIA confirm the arrangement with the dissidents as being that the United States would "clandestinely" assist the opposition to "develop effective force to accomplish Trujillo overthrow", but would not "undertake any overt action itself against Trujillo government while it is in full control of Dominican Republic". CIA Headquarters confirmed Dearborn's understanding of the arrangement.[. . .]

'Events occurring during the summer of 1960 further intensified hemispheric opposition to the Trujillo regime. In June, agents of Trujillo tried to assassinate Venezuelan President Betancourt. As a result, the OAS (Organization of American States) censured the Trujillo government. At the same time, in August 1960 the United States interrupted diplomatic relations with the Dominican Republic and imposed economic sanctions. With the interruption of diplomatic relations, the United States closed its Embassy. Most American personnel, including the CIA Chief of Station, left the Dominican Republic. With the departure of the CIA Chief of Station, Dearborn became *de facto* CIA Chief of Station and was recognized as such by both CIA and the State Department. Although in January 1961 a new CIA Chief of Station came to the Dominican Republic, Dearborn continued to serve as a link to the dissidents.

'Dearborn came to believe that no effort to overthrow the Trujillo government could be successful unless it involved Trujillo's assassination. He communicated this opinion to both the State Department and the CIA.[. . .]

'On 19 January 1961, the last day of the Eisenhower Administration, Consul General Dearborn was advised that approval had been given for supplying arms and other material to the Dominican dissidents.[. . .]

'In a 15 March 1961 cable, a Station officer reported that Dearborn had asked for three .38 caliber pistols for issue to several dissidents.[. . .] [A] 7 June 1961 CIA memorandum, unsigned and with no attribution as to source, states that two of the three pistols were passed by a Station officer to a United States citizen who was in direct contact with the action element of the dissident group.[. . .]

'In a 26 March 1961 cable to CIA Headquarters, the Station asked for permission to pass to the dissidents three 30 caliber M1 carbines. The guns had been left behind in the Consulate by Navy personnel after the United States interrupted formal diplomatic relations in August 1960 . . . On 31 March 1961, CIA Headquarters cabled approval of the request to pass the carbines. The carbines were passed to the action group contact on 7 April 1961. Eventually, they found their way into the hands of one of the assassins, Antonio de la Maza.[. . .]

'On 7 April 1961, a Pouch Restriction Waiver

Request and Certification was submitted seeking permission to pouch "four M3 machine guns and 240 rounds of ammunition on a priority basis for issuance to a small action group to be used for self protection" . . . The Waiver Request was approved by Richard Bissell, as DDP, on 10 April 1961 . . . The machine guns were pouched to the Dominican Republic and were received by the Station on 19 April 1961.[. . .]

'By 17 April 1961, the Bay of Pigs invasion had failed. As a result, there developed a general realization that precipitous action should be avoided in the Dominican Republic until Washington was able to give further consideration to the consequences of a Trujillo overthrow and the power vacuum which would be created. A cable from Headquarters to the Station, on 17 April 1961, advised that it was most important that the machine guns not be passed without additional Headquarters approval.[. . .]

'Dearborn recalls receiving instructions that an effort be made to turn off the assassination attempt and testified that efforts to carry out the instructions were unsuccessful. In effect, the dissidents informed him that this was their affair and it could not be turned off to suit the convenience of the United States government.

'On 30 April, 1961, Dearborn advised Headquarters that the dissidents had reported to him the assassination attempt was going to take place during the first week of May. The action group was reported to have in its possession three carbines, four to six 12-gauge shotguns and other small arms. Although they reportedly still wanted the machine guns, Dearborn advised Headquarters that the group was going to go ahead with what they had, whether the United States wanted them to or not.'

State Department memoranda dated 15 May stressed that it was 'highly desirable for the United States to be identified with and to support the elements seeking to overthrow Trujillo [and] recommended that Consul General inform the dissidents that if they succeed "at their own initiative and on their own responsibility in forming an acceptable provisional government they can be assured that any reasonable request for assistance from the US will be promptly and favorably answered".'[. . .]

'Late in the evening of 30 May 1961, Trujillo was ambushed and assassinated near San Cristobal, Dominican Republic. The assassination closely paralleled the plan disclosed by the action group to American representatives in the Dominican Republic and passed on to officials in Washington at both the CIA and the State Department. The assassination was conducted by members of the action group, to whom the American carbines had been passed, and such sketchy information as is available indicates that one or more of the carbines was in the possession of the assassination group when Trujillo was killed. The evidence indicates, however, that the actual assassination was accomplished by handguns and shotguns.'

BOOK 3

CHAPTER

17

Strange Bedfellows

As noted previously, '[T]he fear of Communist expansion was particularly acute in the United States when Fidel Castro emerged as Cuba's leader in the late 1950s. His takeover was seen as the first significant penetration by the Communists into the Western Hemisphere. United States leaders, including most Members of Congress, called for vigorous action to stem the Communist infection in this hemisphere. These policies rested on widespread popular support and encouragement. Throughout this period, the United States felt impelled to respond to threats which were, or seemed to be, skirmishes in a global Cold War against Communism. Castro's Cuba raised the specter of a Soviet outpost at America's doorstep . . .'

After discussing other countries, the Senate Select Committee went on to a lengthy study of the Cuban situation.

'Efforts against Castro did not begin with assassination attempts. From March through August 1960, during the last year of the Eisenhower Administration, the CIA considered plans to undermine Castro's charismatic appeal by sabotaging his speeches.

'According to the 1967 Report of the CIA's Inspector General, an official in the Technical Services Division (TSD) recalled discussing a scheme to spray Castro's broadcasting studio with a chemical which produced effects similar to LSD, but the scheme was rejected because the chemical was unreliable. During this period, TSD impregnated a box of cigars with a chemical which produced temporary disorientation, hoping to induce Castro to smoke one of the cigars before delivering a speech.

'The Inspector General also reported a plan to destroy Castro's image as "The Beard" by dusting his shoes with thallium salts, a strong depilatory that would cause his beard to fall out. The depilatory was to be administered during a trip outside Cuba, when it was anticipated Castro would leave his shoes outside the door of his hotel room to be shined. TSD procured the chemical and tested it on animals, but apparently abandoned the scheme because Castro cancelled his trip.[. . .]

'A notation in the records of the Operations Division, CIA's Office of Medical Services, indicates that on 16 August 1960 an official was given a box of Castro's favorite cigars with instructions to treat them with lethal poison. The cigars were contaminated with a botulinum toxin so potent that a person would die after putting one in his mouth. The official reported that the cigars were ready on 7 October 1960; TSD notes indicate that they were delivered to an unidentified person on 13 February 1961. The record does not disclose whether an attempt was made to pass the cigars to Castro.[. . .]

'In August 1960, the CIA took steps to enlist members of the criminal underworld with gambling syndicate contacts to aid in assassinating Castro.[. . .]

'The earliest concrete evidence of the operation is a conversation between DDP Bissell and Colonel Sheffield Edwards, Director of the Office of Security. Edwards recalled that Bissell asked him to locate someone to assassinate Castro. Bissell confirmed that he requested Edwards to find someone to assassinate Castro and believed that Edwards raised the idea of contacting members of a gambling syndicate operating in Cuba. Edwards assigned the mission to the Chief of the Operational Support Division of the Office of Security.[. . .]

'Edwards and the Support Chief decided to rely on Robert A. Maheu to recruit someone "tough enough" to handle the job. Maheu was an ex-FBI agent who had entered into a career as a private investigator in 1954. A former FBI associate of Maheu's was employed in the CIA's Office of Security and had arranged for the CIA to use Maheu in several sensitive covert operations in which "he didn't want to have an Agency person or a government person get caught". Maheu was initially paid a monthly retainer by the CIA of $500, but it was terminated after his detective agency became more lucrative. The Operational Support Chief had served as Maheu's case officer since the Agency first began using Maheu's services, and by 1960 they had become close personal friends.

'Sometime in late August or early September 1960, the Support Chief approached Maheu about the proposed operation.' It was decided that Maheu 'would contact John Rosselli, an underworld figure with possible gambling contacts in Las Vegas, to determine if he would participate in a plan to "dispose" of Castro . . . Maheu had known Rosselli since the late 1950s. [. . .]

'At first Maheu was reluctant to become involved in the operation because it might interfere with his relationship with his new client, Howard Hughes. He finally agreed to participate because he felt that he owed the Agency a commitment. . . . The Support Chief testified that Maheu was told to offer money, probably $150,000, for Castro's assassination.

'According to Rosselli, he and Maheu met at the Brown Derby Restaurant in Beverly Hills in early September 1960. Rosselli testified that Maheu told him that "high government officials" needed his cooperation in getting rid of Castro, and that he asked him to help recruit Cubans to do the job.[. . .]

'Maheu and Rosselli both testified that Rosselli insisted on meeting with a representative of the Government. A meeting was arranged for Maheu and Rosselli with the Support Chief at the Plaza Hotel in New York.[. . .]

'It was arranged that Rosselli would go to Florida and recruit Cubans for the operation.[. . .] During the week of 24 September 1960 the Support Chief, Maheu, and Rosselli met in Miami to work out the details of the operation.[. . .] After Rosselli and Maheu had been in Miami for a short time, and certainly prior to 18 October, Rosselli introduced Maheu to individuals on whom Rosselli intended to rely: "Sam Gold", who would serve as a "back-up man", or "key" man, and "Joe", whom "Gold" said would serve as a courier to Cuba and make arrangements there.[. . .]

'The Support Chief testified that he learned the true identities of his associates one morning when Maheu called and asked him to examine the "Parade" supplement to the *Miami Times*. An article on the Attorney General's ten most-wanted criminals list revealed that "Sam Gold" was Momo Salvatore Giancana, a Chicago-based gangster, and "Joe" was Santos Trafficante, the Cosa Nostra chieftain in Cuba.'

Momo Salvatore ('Sam') Giancana was not exactly a candidate for monkhood. In addition to his more obvious disqualifications, Sam would have had serious problems with the vow of silence. In an 18 October 1960 memo to Richard Bissell, J. Edgar Hoover reported that Giancana had recently told several friends that Fidel Castro was to be done away with shortly by a girl dropping a pill into his drink. The Committee related that 'The identity of this "girl" referred to by Giancana has not been conclusively ascertained, but it is reasonable to assume that Trafficante was in a position to recruit a mistress of Castro because of his numerous contacts in the Cuban gambling and prostitution circles.'

Nor was silence the only monk's vow with which Giancana would have had difficulty. He had a great fondness for the women. One of his girl friends in Las Vegas became the center of a bizarre event – bizarre if only because it was such an eerie precursor of the Watergate foul-up.

'In late October 1960, Maheu arranged for a Florida investigator, Edward DuBois, to place an electronic "bug" in a room in Las Vegas. Dubois' employee, Arthur J. Balletti, flew to Las Vegas and installed a tap on the phone. The Support Chief characterized the ensuing events as a "Keystone Comedy act". On 31 October 1960, Balletti, believing that the apartment would be vacant for the afternoon, left the wiretap equipment unattended. A maid discovered the equipment and notified the local sheriff, who arrested Balletti and brought him to the jail. Balletti called Maheu in Miami, tying "Maheu into this thing up to his ear". Balletti's bail was paid by Rosselli.[. . .]

'The Support Chief testified that during the early stages of negotiations with the gambling syndicate, Maheu informed him that a girl-friend of Giancana was having an affair with the target of the tap. Giancana wanted Maheu to bug that person's room; otherwise, Giancana threatened to fly to Las Vegas himself. Maheu was concerned that Giancana's departure would disrupt the negotiations, and secured the Support Chief's permission for a bug to insure Giancana's presence and cooperation.[. . .]

'Rosselli testified that Maheu had given him two explanations for the tap on different occasions: first, that Giancana was concerned that his girl-friend was having an affair; and, second, that he had arranged the tap to determine whether Giancana had told his girl friend about the assassination plot, and whether she was spreading the story.'

During the investigation of this affair, Colonel Edwards mislead the FBI, informing the Bureau that 'the CIA would object to Maheu's prosecution because it might reveal sensitive information relating to the abortive Bay of Pigs invasion'. Subsequently, 'Herbert J. Miller, Assistant Attorney General, Criminal Division, advised the Attorney General that the "national interest" would preclude any prosecutions based upon the tap. Following a briefing of the Attorney General by the CIA, a decision was made not to prosecute.'

Another of Giancana's girl-friends, Judith Campbell Exner, reportedly was introduced to John F. Kennedy by Frank Sinatra, and a long-term 'relationship' between her and JFK bloomed until it was brought to a sudden and unceremonious end when J. Edgar Hoover intervened.

The Committee circumspectly reported this affair as follows: 'Evidence before the Committee indicates that a close friend of President Kennedy had frequent contacts with the President from the end of 1960 through mid-1962; FBI reports and testimony indicate that the President's friend was also a close friend of John Rosselli and Sam Giancana and saw them often during this same period . . . White House telephone logs show 70 instances of phone contact between the White House and the President's friend, whose testimony confirms frequent phone contact with the President himself . . . On 27 February 1962, Hoover sent identical copies of a memorandum to the Attorney General and Kenneth O'Donnell, Special Assistant to the President. The memorandum stated that information developed in connection with a concentrated FBI investigation of John Rosselli revealed that Rosselli had been in contact with the President's friend. The memorandum also reported that the individual was maintaining an association with Sam Giancana, described as "a prominent Chicago underworld figure". Hoover's memorandum also stated that a review of the telephone toll calls from the President's friend's residence revealed calls to the White House.[. . .]

'The association of the President's friend with the "hoodlums" and that person's connection with the President was again brought to Hoover's attention in a memorandum preparing him for a meeting with the President planned for 22 March 1962 . . . On 22 March, Hoover had a private luncheon with President Kennedy. There is no record of what transpired at that luncheon. According to the White House logs, the last telephone contact between the White House and the President's friend occurred a few hours after the luncheon.'

The Senate Select Committee was curious about the claim made by the Support Chief that he first learned the identities of Sam Gold and Joe because of an article in the "Parade" supplement of the *Miami Times*. We learn from the 1978 House Committee Report that in 1975 the Senate Committee had 'conducted a search of supplements to all Miami newspapers for the requisite time period and could not locate any such article. The Committee consequently searched "Parade" magazine for the fall of 1960, all of 1961, and all of 1962, the years that spanned the entire operation. The Committee found that on 21 January 1962, "Parade" published an article entitled "The Untold Story: Our Government's Crackdown on Organized Crime", written by Jack Anderson, which contained a listing of the top 10 hoodlums in the country as well as several photographs of mobsters, including Santos Trafficante. The article focused on the efforts of Attorney General Robert F. Kennedy's campaign against organized crime and mentioned both Giancana and Trafficante. Although this "Parade" article appears to correspond with the Support Chief's and Maheu's descriptions, it is over 1 year past the beginning months of the operation. Indeed, it occurred 9 months after the completion of Phase I of the plots'.

The House Committee goes on to comment: 'It

appears the Support Chief and Maheu are not telling the truth in an attempt to look for an ex-*post facto* reason for continuing the operation after the introduction of two of the top organized crime figures in the United States. Implicit in their contention is that while the CIA wished to solicit criminal sources to assassinate Castro, it would not knowingly have recruited any figures from the top echelon of organized crime.[. . .]

'[T]his CIA plot to assassinate Castro was necessarily a highly volatile and secret operation. Once Roselli introduced additional contacts into the scene, it is not logical that the CIA would have neglected to verify the identities of such principals. On the contrary, it is more believable that the CIA ascertained the true identities of "Sam Gold" and "Joe" at an early stage and progressed consciously forward in the operation, confident that these two persons, in the words attributed to Colonel Sheffield Edwards, were individuals "tough enough" to handle the job.'

'After meeting several times in Miami and deciding upon poison pills as the method of assassination, the IG report [Inspector General] states that Trafficante made the arrangements for the assassination of Castro with one of his contacts inside Cuba on one of the trips he allegedly made to Havana, Cuba. This contact was a Cuban official who held a position close to Castro.

'The IG report then stated that Rosselli passed the pills to Trafficante. Rosselli subsequently told the Support Chief that the pills were delivered to the Cuban official in Cuba. The Cuban official apparently retained the pills for a few weeks and then returned them since he was no longer in a position to fulfill any plan. The Cuban official was no longer in a position to kill Castro because he had lost his Cuban post.

'With the Cuban official unable to perform, the syndicate looked elsewhere. Rosselli next told the Support Chief, sometime during early 1961, that Trafficante knew a man prominent in the Cuban exile movement who could accomplish the job. After receiving approval, Trafficante approached this person about assassinating Castro and reported that he was receptive. The IG report stated that the Support Chief again distributed pills that eventually reached the Cuban exile leader.'

The Senate Report states: 'The Cuban claimed to have a contact inside a restaurant frequented by Castro.[. . .] The attempt met with failure. According to the Inspector General's Report, Edwards believed the scheme failed because Castro stopped visiting the restaurant where the "asset" was employed.[. . .]'

'The Inspector General's Report divides the gambling syndicate operation into Phase I, terminating with the Bay of Pigs, and Phase II, continuing with the transfer of the operation to William Harvey in late 1961. The distinction between a clearly demarcated Phase I and Phase II may be an artificial one, as there is considerable evidence that the operation was continuous, perhaps lying dormant for the period immediately following the Bay of Pigs.

'In early 1961, Harvey was assigned the responsibility for establishing a general capability within the CIA for disabling foreign leaders, including assassination as a "last resort". The capability was called Executive Action and was later included under the cryptonym ZR/RIFLE.[. . .]'

'Harvey's notes reflect that Bissell asked him to take over the gambling syndicate operation from Edwards and that they discussed the "application of ZR/RIFLE program to Cuba" on 16 November 1961.'

The House Report informs us that, 'The Support Chief then introduced Harvey to Rosselli. During this phase, the CIA decided against using Giancana or Trafficante; instead, a person referred to as "Maceo" entered the plot as the person who would help provide Castro contacts. In addition, the plots still utilized the services of the Cuban exile leader.[. . .]

'In June 1962 Rosselli reported to Harvey that the

Cuban exile leader dispatched a three-man team to Cuba with the general assignment of recruiting others to kill Castro and, if the opportunity arose, to kill him themselves, maybe through the use of pills. In September 1962, Rosselli reported to Harvey in Miami that the "medicine" was reported in place, that the three-man team was safe, and that the Cuban exile leader was prepared to dispatch another three-man team to infiltrate Castro's bodyguard. In December 1962, Rosselli and Harvey agreed that not much seemed to be occurring and by February 1963, Harvey terminated the plots.'

The Senate Report states that 'Two plans to assassinate Castro were explored by Task Force W, the CIA section then concerned with covert Cuban operations, in early 1963. Desmond Fitzgerald, Chief of the Task Force, asked his assistant to determine whether an exotic seashell, rigged to explode, could be deposited in an area where Castro commonly went skin diving. The idea was explored by the Technical Services Division and discarded as impractical.

'A second plan involved having James Donovan (who was negotiating with Castro for the release of prisoners taken during the Bay of Pigs operation) present Castro with a contaminated diving suit.[. . .] The Technical Services Division bought a diving suit, dusted the inside with a fungus that would produce a chronic skin disease (Madura foot), and contaminated the breathing apparatus with a tubercule bacillus. The Inspector General's Report states that the plan was abandoned because Donovan gave Castro a different diving suit on his own initiative. Helms testified that the diving suit never left the laboratory [and characterized the plan as "cockeyed"].'

In the fall of 1963, another operation against Castro began. Since early 1961, the CIA had had an important asset inside Cuba in the person of a highly-placed Cuban official who was referred to by the cryptonym AM/LASH.

'As a high-ranking leader who enjoyed the confidence of Fidel Castro, AM/LASH could keep the CIA informed of the internal workings of the regime. It was also believed that he might play a part in fomenting a coup within Cuba.

'From the first contact with AM/LASH until the latter part of 1963, it was uncertain whether he would defect or remain in Cuba. His initial requests to the CIA and FBI for aid in defecting were rebuffed.[. . .]

'At a meeting in the fall of 1963, AM/LASH stated that he would remain in Cuba if he "could do something really significant for the creation of a new Cuba" and expressed a desire to plan the "execution" of Fidel Castro.' Desmond Fitzgerald, Chief of the Special Affairs Staff (formerly called Task Force W) 'met AM/LASH in late fall 1963 and promised him that the United States would support a coup against Castro. When later interviewed for the Inspector General's Report, Fitzgerald recalled that AM/LASH repeatedly requested an assassination weapon, particularly a "high-powered rifle with telescopic sights that could be used to kill Castro from a distance". Fitzgerald [originator of the exploding seashell brainstorm] stated that he told AM/LASH that the United States would have "no part of an attempt on Castro's life".' However, a contemporaneous memorandum by the case officer involved states 'C/SAS [Fitzgerald] approved telling AM/LASH he would be given a cache inside Cuba. Cache could, if he requested it, include . . . high-powered rifles with scopes.[. . .] AM/LASH was told on 22 November 1963 that the cache would be dropped in Cuba.

'Another device offered to AM/LASH was a ballpoint pen rigged with a hypodermic needle. The needle was designed to be so fine that the victim would not notice its insertion.[. . .] Helms confirmed that the pen was manufactured "to take care of a request from him that he have some device for getting rid of Castro, for killing him, murdering him, whatever the case may be".

[. . .] On 22 November, 1963, Fitzgerald and the case officer met with AM/LASH and offered him the poison pen, recommending that he use Blackleaf-40, a deadly poison which is commercially available. The Inspector General's Report noted that "it is likely that at the very moment President Kennedy was shot, a CIA officer was meeting with a Cuban agent . . . and giving him an assassination device for use against Castro." [. . .]

'CIA cables indicate that one cache of arms for AM/LASH was delivered in Cuba in March 1964 and another in June.[. . .] Documents in the AM/LASH file establish that in early 1965, the CIA put AM/LASH in contact with B-1, the leader of an anti-Castro group.[. . .] In June 1965, CIA terminated all contact with AM/LASH and his associates for reasons related to security.'

BOOK 3

CHAPTER

18

Castro Retaliation?

In March 1967, President Lyndon Johnson learned of allegations which had recently been asserted by a Washington lawyer named Edward Morgan, and that the FBI had refused to investigate the charges.

Morgan was saying that one of his clients had told him that the United States had attempted to assassinate Fidel Castro in the early 1960s, and Castro had decided to retaliate.

President Johnson instructed 'that the FBI interview [the lawyer] concerning any knowledge he might have regarding the assassination of President Kennedy'. On 21 March 1967, two agents of the Washington Field Office sent FBI Headquarters a memorandum of their interview with Morgan.

The Senate Select Committee summarized the memo as follows:

'(1) The lawyer had information pertaining to the assassination, but that it was necessary for him in his capacity as an attorney to invoke the attorney-client privilege since the information in his possession was derived as a result of that relationship.

'(2) His clients, who were on the fringe of the

underworld, were neither directly nor indirectly involved in the death of President Kennedy, but they faced possible prosecution in a crime not related to the assassination and through participation in such crime they learned of information pertaining to the President's assassination.

'(3) His clients were called upon by a governmental agency to assist in a project which was said to have the highest governmental approval. The project had as its purpose the assassination of Fidel Castro. Elaborate plans were made; including the infiltration of the Cuban government and the placing of informants within key posts in Cuba.

'(4) The project almost reached fruition when Castro became aware of it; by pressuring captured subjects he was able to learn the full details of the plot against him and decided "if that was the way President Kennedy wanted it, he too could engage in the same tactics".

'(5) Castro thereafter employed teams of individuals who were dispatched to the United States for the purpose of assassinating President Kennedy. The lawyer stated that his clients obtained this information "from 'feedback' furnished by sources close to Castro", who had been initially placed there to carry out the original project.

'(6) His clients were aware of the identity of some of the individuals who came to the United States for this purpose and he understood that two such individuals were now in the State of New Jersey.

'(7) One client, upon hearing the statement that Lee Harvey Oswald was the sole assassin of President Kennedy "laughs with tears in his eyes and shakes his head in apparent disagreement".

'(8) The lawyer stated if he were free of the attorney-client privilege, the information that he would be able to supply would not directly identify the alleged conspirators to kill President Kennedy. However, because of the project to kill Fidel Castro, those participating in the project, whom he represents, developed through feedback information that would identify Fidel Castro's counter-assassins in this country who could very well be considered suspects in such a conspiracy.

'The transmittal slip accompanying this memorandum noted, "No further investigation is being conducted by the Washington Field Office unless it is advised to the contrary by the Bureau."[. . .]

'Both agents testified that they were "surprised" during the interview when the lawyer recounted United States assassination efforts targeted at Fidel Castro. These agents stated that they could not evaluate the lawyer's allegations or question him in detail on them, since they had not been briefed on the CIA assassination efforts.'

The House Select Committee observed, 'Had the interviewing agents known of the CIA-underworld plots against Castro, they would have been aware that the lawyer had clients who had been active in the assassination plots . . . Neither the Field agents who interviewed the lawyer nor the Headquarters supervisory agents assigned to the assassination case could provide any explanation for the Bureau's failure to conduct any follow-up investigation. When they were informed of the details of CIA assassination efforts against Castro, each of these agents stated that the allegations and specific leads provided should have been investigated to their logical conclusions.'

The concept of a Castro retaliation theory has been discounted on the following rationalizations:

(1) That Castro has denied it.

(2) That it would not make sense for Castro to do it.

(3) That Morgan's client was manipulating the facts.

(4) That Castro didn't know about the US plots against him.

The first two items are easily dealt with by asking the

questions: Why would anyone believe Castro's denial, and what grounds are there for assuming that Castro would have been so logical?

The third item refers to the fact that one of Morgan's clients was John Rosselli, who was at the time trying to avoid deportation. There is no doubt that given such a source, one must take any information with a large grain of salt. However, the fact that the source is a Rosselli does not necessarily mean the information is untrue. Indeed, if the government really believed that such a source necessarily made information untrue, they would have to drop a very large percentage of their criminal prosecutions since they are based on 'turning' someone. The fact is that much of law enforcement is premised on the reality that only when a Rosselli is being threatened by some penalty to be imposed upon himself, will he divulge information as to others. Moreover, the first part of the information Morgan was supplying is now known to be true.

Consideration of the balance of Morgan's information leads us to item four, the proposition that Castro could not have known about US plots against him and so would have had no reason to retaliate.

It will be recalled that an intricate part of the CIA-Mafia plot against Castro involved Salvatore Trafficante's role as a courier. The IG Report states that, 'At that time the gambling casinos were still operating in Cuba, and Trafficante was making regular trips between Miami and Havana on syndicate business.'

The House Select Committee observed, 'If Trafficante was actually traveling between Miami and Havana, the implications are interesting. He was either willing to risk being detained again or had acquired assurance from the Cuban Government regarding his safety. In any event, the presence of Trafficante during the fall of 1960 in Cuba raises the possibility of a more cooperative relationship between himself and the Cuban Government than believed previously. Such a relationship during the period when Trafficante was scheming to assassinate Castro invites the theory that Trafficante was possibly informing the Cuban Government of activities in the Miami area in general and of the plots in particular. In return for such information, Trafficante could have been promised lost gambling operations as well as support and a Cuban sanctuary for the smuggling of contraband into the United States.'

Trafficante was not the only potential source for Castro to learn of the US plots against his life. Joseph Langosch, the Chief of Counter-Intelligence for the CIA's Special Affairs Staff in 1963 (the component responsible for CIA operations against the Government of Cuba and the Cuban Intelligence Services) told the House Select Committee that 'The AM/LASH operation prior to the assassination of President Kennedy was characterized by the special affairs staff, Desmond FitzGerald and other senior CIA officers as an assassination operation initiated and sponsored by the CIA . . . [A]s of 1962 it was highly possible that the Cuban Intelligence Services were aware of AM/LASH and his association with the CIA.'

Any question that Castro knew of the US plots against his life would seem to be resolved by this quote from the Report of the House Select Committee regarding 'an interview that Premier Castro held on 7 September 1963 with Associated Press Reporter Daniel Harker. In that interview, Castro warned against the United States "aiding terrorist plans to eliminate Cuban leaders". He stated, according to Harker, that US leaders would be in danger if they promoted any attempt to eliminate the leaders of Cuba.'

None of this proves that President Kennedy was assassinated by Castro in retaliation for US assassination plots against him. However, possible Castro retaliation plots are not the only Cuban aspect to our story.

In fact, in one fashion or another, Cuba lies at the very center of this web.

BOOK 3

CHAPTER

19

Anti-Castro Cubans

The House Select Committee, after an exhaustive analysis of the whole Cuban situation, stated that, '[T]he Committee ascertained that as a consequence of the efforts, the failure and the eventual unwillingness of the Kennedy administration to liberate Cuba from Castro, [anti-Castro activists and organizations] acquired the means, motive and opportunity to assassinate the President.'

In addition to its Report, the House published a special study on this subject in which it observed: 'If it can be said to have a beginning, the anti-Castro Cuban exile movement was seeded in the early-morning hours of New Year's Day 1959 when a DC-4 lifted from the fog-shrouded Camp Columbia airfield in Havana. Aboard the plane was Fulgencio Batista, the military dictator of Cuba for the previous 6 years. Batista was fleeing the country, his regime long beset by forces from within and without, now crumbling under pressure from rebel forces sweeping down from the mountains. When dawn came, the bells tolled in Havana and, 600 miles away, Fidel Castro Ruz began his triumphal march to the capital. For seven days

Castro and his 26th of July Movement rebels moved down Cuba's Central Highway while thousands cheered and threw flowers in their path. Castro finally arrived in Havana on 8 January and characteristically gave a speech. Clad in his green fatigue uniform while three white doves, which someone had dramatically released, circled above him, Castro boldly proclaimed: "There is no longer an enemy!"

'That was not true, of course, and he knew it. A hard core of Batistianos had fled the country early, many long before their leader, and were already concocting counter-revolutionary plots from their refuges in the United States, the Dominican Republic and elsewhere.

'And it was not very long after Castro took power that a sense of betrayal began to grow among those who had once been his strongest supporters. As each day went by it became more apparent that Castro's revolution was, as one chronicler noted, "leading inexorably toward an institutionalized dictatorship in which individuals were contemptuously shorn of their rights and dissenters were met with charges of treasonable conduct, counter-revolutionary activity or worse". Then, too, there was a large number of public executions. Within 2 weeks of his reign, Castro shot 150 ex-Batista officials. Within 3 months, there were at least 506 executions.

'The disillusionment for many Cubans deepened when it became obvious that the form of Castro's rule was turning toward Communism and that Castro's attitude toward the United States was engendering a hostile relationship. The publishing of Castro's Agrarian Reform Law in May 1959, was a significant sign. It was far more radical than had been expected and was obviously designed to strip both Cuban and American-owned sugar firms of their immensely valuable cane lands. A few weeks later the chief of Castro's air force, Major Pedro Diaz-Lanz, resigned, charging "there was Communist influence in the armed forces and Government". Then, when Castro's own hand-picked president, Manuel Urrutia, announced at a press conference that he rejected the support of the Communists and said, "I believe that any real Cuban revolutionary should reject it openly", Castro immediately forced him to resign and accused him of actions "bordering on treason".

'And so, after the broken pledges of free elections and a free press, the mass trials and executions, the assumption of unlimited power and the bellicose threats against the United States, it slowly became apparent to many Cubans that Fidel Castro was not the political savior they had expected.

'Then, on 19 October 1959, there occurred an incident which precipitated the formation of the first organized anti-Castro opposition within Cuba. Major Huber Matos, one of Castro's highest ranking officers and considered by most Cubans to be one of the key heroes of the revolution, resigned from the Army in protest against the increasing favoritism shown to known Communists. The next day Matos was arrested, charged with treason, subsequently tried and sentenced to 20 years in prison. Shortly afterward, Castro himself called a secret meeting of the National Agrarian Reform Institute managers at which he outlined a plan to communize Cuba within three years. There the suspicions of Dr Manuel Artime, the manager in Oriente Province, were confirmed. "I realized," Artime later said, "that I was a democratic infiltrator in a Communist government".

'Artime returned to Oriente and began organizing students and peasants to fight against Castro and Communism. By early November each province in Cuba had an element of Artime's new underground movement. It was called the Movimiento de Recuperación Revolucionaria (MRR). It was the first anti-Castro action group originating from within Castro's own ranks.

'By the summer of 1960, it had become obvious both within and without Cuba that the foundation for an eventual confrontation between Castro and anti-Castro forces had been laid. The Eisenhower administration had canceled the Cuban sugar quota. Soviet first deputy chairman Anastas Mikoyan had visited Havana and Raul Castro had gone to Moscow. Ernesto "Che" Guevara had proclaimed publicly that the revolution was on the road set by Marx, and Allen Dulles of the Central Intelligence Agency had said in a speech that Communism had perverted Castro's revolution. By then, Castro had seized more than $700 million in US property within Cuba.

'On 17 March 1960, President Eisenhower authorized the CIA to organize, train and equip Cuban refugees as a guerilla force to overthrow Castro. Soon it became common knowledge within Cuba that a liberation army was being formed and that a political structure in exile had been created. As the flight from Cuba increased in size and fervor, the exile community in the United States grew in spirit and confidence.[. . .]

'By April 1961, the more than 100,000 Cubans who had fled Castro's revolution lived in anticipation of its overthrow. They had been buoyed in that hope by public pronouncements of support from the US Government. In his State of the Union Address, President Kennedy had spoken of "the Communist base established 90 miles from the United States", and said that "Communist domination in this hemisphere can never be negotiated". In addition, the Cuban exiles had been organized, directed and almost totally funded by agencies of the US Government, principally the CIA.

'From an historical perspective, in light of its later radical change, the attitude of the Cuban exiles toward the US Government prior to the Bay of Pigs is especially significant. Author Haynes Johnson who in writing a history of the invasion collaborated with the top Cuban leaders, including brigade civilian chief Manuel Artime, described that attitude in detail: "From the beginning, the Cuban counter-revolutionists viewed their new American friends with blind trust. Artime was no exception. He, and later virtually all of the Cubans involved, believed so much in the Americans – or wanted so desperately to believe – that they never questioned what was happening or expressed doubts about the plans. Looking back on it, they agree now that their naiveté was partly genuine and partly reluctance to turn down any offer of help in liberating their country. In fact, they had little choice; there was no other place to turn. Some, of course, were driven by other motives: political power and personal ambition were involved. Even more important was the traditional Cuban attitude toward America and Americans. To Cubans the United States was more than the colossus of the north, for the two countries were bound closely by attitudes, by history, by geography and by economics. The United States was great and powerful, the master not only of the hemisphere but perhaps of the world, and it was Cuba's friend. One really didn't question such a belief. It was a fact; everyone knew it. And the mysterious, anonymous, ubiquitous American agents who dealt with the Cubans managed to strengthen that belief."

'This "blind trust" by the Cuban exiles in the US Government prior to the Bay of Pigs was specifically noted by the military commander of the 2506 Brigade, Jose (Pepe) Perez San Roman: "Most of the Cubans were there", he said, "because they knew the whole operation was going to be conducted by the Americans, not by me or anyone else. They did not trust me or anyone else. They just trusted the Americans. So they were going to fight because the United States was backing them."

'The débâcle at the Bay of Pigs was not only military tragedy for the anti-Castro Cuban exiles but also a painful shattering of their confidence in the US Government. The exile leaders claimed the failure of the invasion was a result of the lack of promised air support, and for that they directly blamed President Kennedy. Particularly galling to them was Kennedy's public declaration to Soviet Premier Khrushchev at the height of the invasion, when the Brigade was being slaughtered in the swamps of Bahia de Cochinos: "I repeat now that the United States intends no armed intervention in Cuba."

'Even those exile leaders who were willing to rationalize the extent of Kennedy's responsibility were dissuaded when Kennedy himself admitted the blame. Cuban Revolutionary Council leader Manuel Antonio de Varona, in his executive session testimony before the Committee, told of the President gathering the Council members together at the White House when it became clear that the invasion was a disaster. Varona recalled: "We were not charging Mr Kennedy with anything; we just wanted to clarify. We knew that he didn't have any direct knowledge of the problem, and we knew he was not in charge of the military effects directly. Nevertheless, President Kennedy, to finish the talks, told us he was the one – the only one responsible."

'A few days after that meeting, the White House issued a public statement declaring that President Kennedy assumed "sole responsibility" for the US role in the action against Cuba.

'The acceptance of responsibility did not cut the bitter disappointment the Cuban exiles felt toward the US Government and President Kennedy. Much later, captured and imprisoned by Castro, Brigade Commander San Roman revealed the depth of his reaction at the failure of the invasion: "I hated the United States," he said, "and I felt that I had been betrayed. Every day it became worse and then I was getting madder and madder and I wanted to get a rifle and come and fight against the US."

'Prominent Cuban attorney Mario Lazo wrote a book caustically titled *Dagger in the Heart*. Lazo wrote: "The Bay of Pigs defeat was wholly self-inflicted in Washington. Kennedy told the truth when he publicly accepted responsibility . . . The heroism of the beleaguered Cuban Brigade had been rewarded by betrayal, defeat, death for many of them, long and cruel imprisonment for the rest. The Cuban people and the Latin American nations, bound to Cuba by thousands of subtle ties of race and culture, were left with feelings of astonishment and disillusionment, and in many cases despair. They had always admired the United States as strong, rich, generous – but where was its sense of honor and the capacity of its leaders? The mistake of the Cuban fighters for liberation was that they thought too highly of the United States. They believed to the end that it would not let them down. But it did."

'President Kennedy was well aware of the bitter legacy left him by the Bay of Pigs débâcle. It is not now possible to document the changes in Kennedy's personal attitude brought about by the military defeat, but the firming of US policy toward Cuba and the massive infusion of US aid to clandestine anti-Castro operations in the wake of the Bay of Pigs was editorially characterized by Taylor Branch and George Crile in *Harper's Magazine* as "the Kennedy vendetta".

'What can be documented is the pattern of US policy between the period of the Bay of Pigs failure in April 1961 and the Cuban missile crisis in October 1962. That pattern, replete with both overt and covert maneuvers, had a significant effect on the reshaping of Cuban exile attitudes and, when it was abruptly reversed, could have provided the motivation for involvement in the assassination of President Kennedy.

'In retrospect, the period between the Bay of Pigs and the Cuban missile crisis can be considered the high-water mark of anti-Castro activity, almost every manifestation of the US policy providing a reassurance of support of the Cuban cause. As a matter of fact, only a few days after the Bay of Pigs invasion, President Kennedy delivered a particularly hard-line address before the American Society of Newspaper Editors on the implications of Communism in Cuba. "Cuba must not be abandoned to the Communists", he declared. In appealing for support from Latin America, he indicated that the United States would expect more from the nations of the hemisphere with regard to Cuba and asserted that the United States would not allow the doctrine of non-intervention to hinder its policy. Said Kennedy, "Our restraint is not inexhaustible", and spoke of Cuba in the context of the "new and deeper struggle".

'When Castro, in a May Day speech, declared Cuba to be a socialist nation, the State Department retorted that Cuba was a full-fledged member of the Communist bloc.

'Another US response was the establishment of the Alliance for Progress, after years of relatively little attention to Latin America's economic and social needs. President Kennedy gave the Alliance concept a memorable launching in a speech in March 1961 when he called for vigorous promotion of social and economic development in Latin America through democratic means and, at the same time, pledged substantial financial and political support.

'While the campaign to broaden its Cuban policy base was being pursued, the United States was proceeding on another course. In one of the first unilateral efforts to isolate Cuba from its allies, the United States in September 1961 announced it would stop assistance to any country that assisted Cuba. In December, Kennedy extended the denial of Cuba's sugar quota through the first half of 1962.

'Meanwhile, the secret policy aimed at removing Castro through assassination continued as FBI chief J. Edgar Hoover informed Attorney General Robert Kennedy in May that the CIA had used the Mafia in "clandestine efforts" against Castro. In that month, poison pills to be used in a plot to kill Castro were passed to a Cuban exile in Miami by a Mafia figure. In November 1961, Operation Mongoose, designed to enlist 2,000 Cuban exiles and dissidents inside Cuba to overthrow Castro, was initiated.

'Although the bitter after-taste of the Bay of Pigs invasion lingered in the Cuban exile community, those who remained active in the fight against Castro came to realize that these subsequent actions of the Kennedy administration were manifestations of its determination to reverse the defeat. What Kennedy had euphemistically termed "a new and deeper struggle" became, in actuality, a secret war.

'The nerve center of the United States' "new and deeper struggle" against Castro was established in the heartland of exile activity, Miami. There, on a secluded, heavily wooded 1,571-acre tract that was part of the University of Miami's south campus, the CIA set up a front operation, an electromics firm called Zenith Technological Services. Its code name was JM/WAVE and it soon became the largest CIA installation anywhere in the world outside of its headquarters in Langley, Virginia.

'The JM/WAVE station had, at the height of its activities in 1962, a staff of more than 300 Americans, mostly case officers. Each case officer employed from 4 to 10 Cuban "principal agents" who, in turn, would each be responsible for between 10 and 30 regular agents.

'In addition, the CIA set up 54 front corporations – boat shops, real estate firms, detective agencies, travel companies, gun shops – to provide ostensible employment for the case officers and agents operating outside of JM/WAVE headquarters. It also maintained hundreds of pieces of real estate, from small apartments to palatial homes, as "safe houses" in which to hold secret meetings. As a result of its JM/WAVE operation, the CIA became one of Florida's largest employers.

'It was the JM/WAVE station that monitored, more or less controlled, and in most cases funded the anti-Castro groups. It was responsible for the great upsurge in anti-Castro activity and the lifted spirits of the Cuban exiles as American arms and weapons flowed freely through the training camps and guerilla bases spotted around south Florida. Anti-Castro raiding parties that left from small secret islands in the Florida Keys were given the "green light" by agents of the JM/WAVE station. The result of it all was that there grew in the Cuban exile community a renewed confidence in the US Government's sincerity and loyalty to its cause.

'Then came the Cuban missile crisis. The more fervent Cuban exiles were initially elated by the possibility that the crisis might provoke a final showdown with Castro.

'For several months there had been increasing pressure on President Kennedy to take strong measures against the build-up of the Soviet presence in Cuba, which was becoming daily more blatant. In a report issued at the end of March 1962, the State Department said that Cuba had received from the Soviet Union $100 million in military aid for the training of Cuban pilots in Czechoslovakia and that the Soviet Union also had provided from 50 to 75 Mig fighters as well as tons of modern weapons for Cuba's ground forces. Fortifying the Cuban exiles' hope for action was the fact that the increasing amounts of Soviet weapons moving into Cuba became the dominant issue in the news in the succeeding months, leading to congressional calls for action and a series of hard-line responses from President Kennedy. In September, Kennedy declared that the United States would use "whatever means may be necessary" to prevent Cuba from exporting "its aggressive purposes by force or threat of force" against "any part of the Western Hemisphere".

'The fervent hope of the Cuban exiles – that the Cuban missile crisis would ultimately result in the United States smashing the Castro regime – was shattered by the manner in which President Kennedy resolved the crisis. Cuba itself was relegated to a minor role as tough negotiations took place between the United States and Soviet Union, specifically through communication between President Kennedy and Premier Khrushchev.

'The crisis ended when President Kennedy announced that all IL-28 bombers were being withdrawn by the Soviets and progress was being made on the withdrawal of offensive missiles and other weapons from Cuba.

'In return, Kennedy gave the Soviets and the Cubans a "no invasion" pledge.

'If Kennedy's actions at the Bay of Pigs first raised doubts in the minds of the Cuban exiles about the President's sincerity and determination to bring about the fall of Castro, his handling of the missile crisis confirmed those doubts. Kennedy's agreement with Khrushchev was termed "a violation" of the pledge he had made 3 days after the Bay of Pigs invasion that the United States would never abandon Cuba to Communism. Wrote one prominent exile: "For the friendly Cuban people, allies of the United States, and for hundreds of thousands of exiles eager to stake their lives to liberate their native land, it was a soulshattering blow."

'The bitterness of the anti-Castro exiles was exacerbated by the actions the US Government took to implement the President's "no invasion" pledge Suddenly there was a crackdown on the very training camps and guerilla bases which had been originally established and funded by the United States, and the exile raids which once had the Government's "green light" were now promptly disavowed and condemned.

'On 31 March 1963, a group of anti-Castro raiders were arrested by British police at a training site in the Bahamas. The US State Department admitted it had given the British the information about the existence of the camp. That same night another exile raiding boat was seized in Miami Harbor. On 3 April, the Soviet Union charged that the United States "encourages and bears full responsibility" for two recent attacks on Soviet ships in Cuban ports by anti-Castro exile commandos. The United States responded that it was "taking every step necessary to insure that such attacks are not launched, manned or equipped from US territory". On 5 April, the Coast Guard announced it was throwing more planes, ships, and men into its efforts to police the straits of Florida against anti-Castro raiders. As a result of the crackdown, Cuban exile sources declared that their movement to rid their homeland of Communism had been dealt "a crippling blow" and that they had lost a vital supply link with anti-Castro fighters inside Cuba.

'There were numerous other indications of the US crackdown on anti-Castro activity following the missile crisis. The Customs Service raided what had long been a secret training camp in the Florida Keys and arrested the anti-Castro force training there. The FBI seized a major cache of explosives at an anti-Castro camp in Louisiana. Just weeks later, the US Coast Guard in cooperation with the British Navy captured another group of Cuban exiles in the Bahamas. In September, the Federal Aviation Administration issued "strong warnings" to six American civilian pilots who had been flying raids over Cuba. Shortly afterward, the Secret Service arrested a prominent exile leader for conspiring to counterfeit Cuban currency destined for rebel forces inside Cuba. In October, the Coast Guard seized 4 exile ships and arrested 22 exile raiders who claimed they were moving their operations out of the United States.

'The feeling of betrayal by the Cuban exiles was given reinforcement by prominent sympathizers outside their community, as well as by Kennedy's political opponents. Captain Eddie Rickenbacker, chairman of the Committee for the Monroe Doctrine, asserted: "The Kennedy administration has committed the final betrayal of Cuban hopes for freedom by its order to block the activities of exiled Cuban freedom fighters to liberate their nation from Communism." Senator Barry Goldwater accused Kennedy of "doing everything in his power" to keep the flag of Cuban exiles "from ever flying over Cuba again". Richard Nixon urged the end of what he called the "quarantine" of Cuban exiles.

'Of course, the most strident reactions came from within the anti-Castro community itself. Following the US Government's notification that it would discontinue its subsidy to the Cuban Revolutionary Council, its president, Jose Miro Cardona, announced his resignation from the council in protest against US policy. The Cuban exile leader accused President Kennedy of "breaking promises and agreements" to support another invasion of Cuba. Miro Cardona said the change in American policy reflected the fact that Kennedy had become "the victim of a master play by the Russians". [. . .]

'Against the pattern of US crackdown on Cuban exile activity during this period, however, emerges a countergrain of incidents that may have some bearing on an examination of the Kennedy assassination. These incidents involve some extremely significant Cuban exile raids and anti-Castro operations which took place, despite the crackdown, between the time of the missile crisis and the assassination of the President. [. . .]

'In retrospect, this much is clear. With or without US Government support and whether or not in blatant defiance of Kennedy administration policy, there were a number of anti-Castro action groups which were determined to continue – and, in fact, did continue – their operations. The resignation of Miro Cardona actually split the Cuban Revolutionary Council down the middle and precipitated a bitter dispute among the exile factions. The more moderate contended that without US support there was little hope of ousting Castro and that the exiles should concentrate their efforts in mounting political pressure to reverse Washington's shift in policy. Other exile groups announced their determination to continue the war against Castro and, if necessary, to violently resist the curtailment of their para-military activities in the Kennedy administration. In New Orleans, for instance, Carlos Bringuier, the local leader of the Cuban Student Directorate (DRE) who, coincidentally, would later have a contact with Lee Harvey Oswald, proclaimed, in the wake of the Miro Cardona resignation, that his group "would continue efforts to liberate Cuba despite action by the United States to stop raids originating from US soil".

'The seeds of defiance of the Kennedy administration may have been planted with the exiles even prior to the Bay of Pigs invasion. In his history of the invasion, Haynes Johnson revealed that shortly before the invasion, "Frank Bender", the CIA director of the invasion preparations, assembled the exile leaders together at the CIA's Guatemala training camp: "It was now early in April and Artime was in the camp as the civilian representative of the Revolutionary Council. Frank called Pepe (San Roman) and (Erneido) Oliva again. This time he had startling information. There were forces in the administration trying to block the invasion, and Frank might be ordered to stop it. If he received such an order, he said, he would secretly inform Pepe and Oliva. Pepe remembers Frank's next words this way: 'If this happens you come here and make some kind of show, as if you were putting us, the advisers, in prison, and you go ahead with the program as we have talked about it, and we will give you the whole plan, even if we are your prisoners.' . . . Frank then laughed and said: 'In the end we will win.'"

'That, then, is the context in which the Committee approached the question of whether or not the John F. Kennedy assassination was a conspiracy involving anti-Castro Cuban exiles. It also considered the testimony of the CIA's chief of its Miami JM/WAVE station in 1963, who noted, "'assassination' was part of the ambience of that time".'

As the quote attributed to 'Frank Bender' makes clear, there was rather less than total respect and admiration for President Kennedy by at least some CIA personnel. This was, it should be noted, not a one-way street.

Although Kennedy accepted 'sole responsibility' for

the Bay of Pigs débâcle, privately he blamed the CIA. Use here of the word 'privately' should not be misunderstood to mean 'secretly'; it really is used to distinguish Kennedy's true feelings from his 'official' statements. He didn't make much of a secret about his disdain for the CIA, which was such that, as the House Report relates, he vowed to 'splinter the agency into a thousand pieces'.

The net result of all of this was that John Kennedy wound up with two sets of enemies who shared mutual interests and the capacity for violence.

BOOK 3

CHAPTER

20

Kennedy Had Enemies

Elements of the CIA, and anti-Castro Cubans, were not John Kennedy's only bitter enemies.

'In an era when the United States was confronted with intractable, often dangerous, international and domestic issues, the Kennedy administration was inevitably surrounded by controversy as it made policies to deal with the problems it faced. Although a popular President, John F. Kennedy was reviled by some, an enmity inextricably related to his policies. [. . .]

'Kennedy appointed Blacks to high administration posts and to Federal judgeships. He gave Attorney General Robert F. Kennedy his sanction for vigorous enforcement of civil rights laws to extend voting rights, end segregation and fight racial discrimination. [. . .]

'Violence erupted soon after Kennedy took office. In May 1961, the Congress of Racial Equality staged a series of freedom rides in Alabama in an effort to integrate buses and terminals. One bus was burned by a mob in Anniston, Alabama. An angry segregationist crowd attacked demonstrators in Montgomery, Alabama, and several persons were injured. Attorney

General Kennedy ordered several hundred US marshals to Montgomery to protect the demonstrators. National Guardsmen with fixed bayonets scattered a mob that tried to overwhelm the marshals, who were protecting a mass meeting at a Black church where civil rights leader Martin Luther King, jun., was speaking. [. . .]

'Trouble exploded again in 1962 when James Meredith, a 29-year-old Black Air Force veteran, gained admission to the all-white University of Mississippi. Meredith had been refused admission, despite Federal court orders requiring that he be enrolled. The Kennedy administration supported an effort to force compliance by the State, but Governor Ross Barnett was equally determined to defy the orders. In his fourth attempt to enroll at the university, Meredith arrived in Oxford on 30 September, escorted by 300 US marshals. He was met by a mob of 2,500 students and segregationist extremists who howled, "Two four one three, we hate Kennedy . . ." A bloody night-long riot that left two dead and scores injured was quelled only after Federal troops had been dispatched by President Kennedy. [. . .]

'Blacks continued demonstrations for equal rights in the spring of 1963. In April and May, Dr King led an attack on what he called "the most segregated city in the United States", Birmingham, Alabama. Demonstrators were met by police dogs, electric cattle prods and fire hoses. [. . .]

'In June 1963, Alabama Governor George Wallace, in defiance of a Federal court order, stood on the steps of the University of Alabama to prevent the admission of two Black students. Wallace bowed, however, to National Guard troops that had been federalized by the President . . . In the same month, Medgar Evers, the NAACP field secretary for Mississippi, was shot to death in front of his home in Jackson, Mississippi. [. . .]

'On 28 August 1963, an inter-racial group of more than 200,000 persons joined "The March for Jobs and

Freedom" in Washington, DC, to urge the Congress to pass the comprehensive civil rights legislation the Kennedy administration envisioned. Violence shattered the hopeful mood in the wake of the Washington march when a bomb exploded on 17 September at the Sixteenth Street Baptist Church in Birmingham, Alabama during a Sunday School session. Four young Black girls were killed and 23 other persons were injured. [. . .]

'In October, *Newsweek* magazine reported that the civil rights issue alone had cost Kennedy 3.5 million votes, adding that no Democrat in the White House had ever been so disliked in the South. In Georgia, the marquee of a movie theatre showing *PT109* read "See how the Japs almost got Kennedy". [. . .]

'As the policies of the Kennedy administration broke new ground, political extremists in the United States seemed increasingly willing to resort to violence to achieve their goals. In an address at the University of Washington in Seattle on 16 November 1961, President Kennedy discussed the age of extremism: two groups of frustrated citizens, one urging surrender and the other urging war. He said: "It is a curious fact that each of these extreme opposites resembles the other. Each believes that we have only two choices: appeasement or war, suicide or surrender, humiliation or holocaust, to be either Red or dead."

'The radical right condemned Kennedy for his "big Government" policies, as well as his concern with social welfare and civil rights progress. The ultra-conservative John Birch Society, Christian Anti-Communist Crusade led by Fred C. Schwarz, and the Christian Crusade led by Revd Billy James Hargis attracted an anti-Kennedy following. The right wing was incensed by Kennedy's transfer of General Edwin A. Walker from his command in West Germany to Hawaii for distributing right-wing literature to his troops. The paramilitary Minutemen condemned the administration as "soft on Communism" and adopted guerilla warfare tactics to prepare for the fight against the Communist foe. At the other extreme, the left labeled Kennedy a reactionary disappointment, a tool of the "power elite".'

There was, however, another domestic issue which presented President Kennedy with, perhaps, his foremost enemy – an enemy all the more dangerous to him since it had contacts with, and could mobilize and utilize segments of, his other enemies.

BOOK 3

CHAPTER

21

Enemy No. 1, The Mob

The House Committee, in its special volume on organized crime, relates that, 'Up to the 1960s the . . . groups of organized crime were in an enviable position. They had an organization that few believed existed and about which little was known. Its leaders – and hence the organization itself – were protected by low-level members who actually performed the criminal acts, many of which Federal and other agencies considered to be beyond their purview or legislative mandate. At best, organized crime was assigned a low priority at State and local levels of law enforcement, and even this was easily nullified by corruption and politics. At the Federal level, even where there was concern, effective action was hampered by inadequate enabling legislation. [. . .]

'The only major national investigation to be conducted during the period from prohibition until the late 1950s was that of the Senate Select Committee to Investigate Organized Crime in Interstate Commerce, chaired by Senator Estes Kefauver. The Committee held hearings in major cities across the country. It built up a substantial body of knowledge that indicated that there was a national and highly successful syndicate known as the Mafia, involved in a wide range of criminal activities throughout the United States and abroad. Violence was key to its success, as was corruption, and it was completely ruthless. As a result of the Committee's findings, Congress passed some gambling legislation, similar investigations were precipitated at the State and local levels, and in 1954, the Federal Government took further action by setting up the Organized Crime and Racketeering Section in the Department of Justice. Its main function was to coordinate the effort against organized crime, but it found little cooperation from other agencies.

'It was in 1957 that organized crime once again came into national attention. On 14 November, a significant meeting took place outside the village of Appalachian, New York. The aftermath was perhaps not what the participants had anticipated, for not only was the cloak of secrecy partially pulled aside, but the event ultimately led to the greatest campaign to date against organized crime.

'On that day, Sergeant Edgar Crosswell of the New York State Police noted that a large number of people were converging on the estate of Joseph Barbera, sen., many from far away. Crosswell had long been interested in Barbera, at the time the distributor for a major soda bottling company. Barbera had come from northern Pennsylvania, where he had a long police record that included two arrests for homicide (he was not convicted of either).

'Because the meeting was on private property, no direct police action could be taken. Crosswell himself watched the entrance from nearby. A tradesman from the village, while making a delivery, noticed Crosswell and alerted those at the meeting.

'Many of Barbera's guests elected to depart. Some did so by car and were detained, once on public roads, for the purpose of identification. Others who fled onto adjoining posted acreage were picked up for possible trespass. Most of those who remained on Barbera's estate could not be identified.

'In all, 63 people were detained and identified. Local hotel records, auto rental contracts and one report of a motor vehicle accident provided investigators with the names of still others. The evidence showed that they had come from New England, New York, New Jersey, Pennsylvania, Florida, Missouri, Texas, Colorado, Ohio, Illinois, and northern and southern California. They included many of the leading organized crime figures, such as Santos Trafficante, Vito Genovese, Carmine Galante, John Ormento and Sam Giancana . . . The evidence supported a conclusion that the gathering was to have been a national meeting of . . . criminals and their associates. [. . .]

'Because a number of attendees at the Appalachian meeting were directly or indirectly involved in union affairs, some were called before the Senate Select Committee on Improper Activities in the Labor or Management Fields, chaired by Senator John L. McClellan. These hearings became known as the McClellan Committee hearings. Senator John F. Kennedy was a member of this Committee; his brother, Robert F. Kennedy, was its chief counsel. [. . .]

'By 1960, the FBI had accumulated substantial knowledge about . . . organized criminal groups . . . Nevertheless, the FBI did not make organized crime a top priority until the Kennedy administration arrived in Washington . . . With the advent of [the Kennedy] administration, organized crime investigations were assigned a high priority . . . As a first step, Robert Kennedy dramatically expanded the number of attorneys in the Organized Crime and Racketeering Section of the Criminal Division of the Justice Department and made clear to the FBI that organized crime was to be a high priority. The category within which these investigations were carried at Justice was shown in FBI files to be AR, or anti-racketeering. He also put together a list of 40 organized crime figures who were to be targeted for investigation. This was soon followed by a second list of 40. The Attorney General quickly requested new legislation to improve the Department's ability to attack organized crime. [. . .]

'The scope and success of this campaign by the Kennedy administration can be easily seen in the following . . . Between 1960 (prior to the Kennedy administration) and 1963, there was:

(1) A 250 percent increase in the number of attorneys – from 17 to 60.

(2) More than a 900 percent increase in days in the field – from 660 to 6,172

(3) A 1,250 percent increase in days in grand jury – from 100 to 1,353.

(4) A 1,700 percent increase in days in court – from 61 to 1,081.

From 1961 to 1963, there was:

(1) A 500 percent increase in defendants indicted – from 121 to 615.

(2) A 400 percent increase in defendants convicted – from 73 to 288. [. . .]

'As the year 1963 progressed, there were many signs that the constant pressure was taking its toll.'

As the House Committee stated in its final report: 'The zeal of the Kennedy brothers signified the roughest period for organized crime in Department of Justice history. Historian Arthur Schlesinger, jun., wrote in *Robert Kennedy and His Times* that, as a result of the Attorney General's pressure, the national Government took on organized crime as it had never done before". Schlesinger observed: "In New York, Robert Morgenthau, the Federal Attorney, successfully prosecuted one syndicate leader after another. The Patriarca gang in Rhode Island and the De Cavalcante gang in New Jersey were smashed. Convictions of racketeers by the Organized Crime Section [together with] the Tax Division steadily increased – 96 in 1961, 101 in 1962, 373 in 1963. So long as John Kennedy sat in the White House, giving his Attorney General absolute backing, the underworld knew that the heat was on."

'The Attorney General focused on targets he had become acquainted with as counsel for the Rackets Committee. He was particularly concerned about the alliance of the top labor leaders and racketeers as personified by Teamster President James R. Hoffa. Schlesinger wrote that "the pursuit of Hoffa was an aspect of the war against organized crime". He added: "The relations between the Teamsters and the syndicate continued to grow. The FBI electronic microphone, planted from 1961 to 1964 in the office of Anthony Giacalone, a Detroit hood, revealed Hoffa's deep if wary involvement with the local mob. For national purposes a meeting place was the Rancho La Costa Country Club near San Clemente, California, built with $27 million in loans from the Teamsters' pension fund; its proprietor, Morris B. Dalitz, had emerged from the Detroit [sic. Cleveland] underworld to become a Las Vegas and Havana gambling figure. Here the Teamsters and the mob golfed and drank together. Here they no doubt reflected that, as long as John Kennedy was President, Robert Kennedy would be unassailable."'

Schlesinger may well be right that Jimmy Hoffa came to realize that the key was John, not Robert, since John could always replace Robert; but if John were gone, Robert was out of office. However, the House Select Committee found that 'Hoffa and at least one of his Teamster lieutenants, Edward Partin, apparently did, in fact, discuss the planning of an assassination conspiracy against President Kennedy's brother, Attorney General Robert F. Kennedy, in July or August of 1962 . . . In an interview with the Committee, Partin reaffirmed the account of Hoffa's discussion of a possible assassination plan, and he stated that Hoffa had believed that having the Attorney General murdered would be the most effective way of ending the Federal Government's intense investigation of the Teamsters and organized crime. Partin further told the Committee that he suspected that Hoffa may have approached him about the assassination proposal because Hoffa believed him to be close to various figures in Carlos Marcello's syndicate organization. Partin, a Baton Rouge Teamsters official with a criminal record, was then a leading Teamsters Union official in Louisiana . . . While the Committee was aware of the apparent absence of any finalized method or plan during the course of Hoffa's discussion about assassinating Attorney General Kennedy, he did discuss the possible use of a lone gunman equipped with a rifle with a telescopic sight, the advisability of having the assassination committed somewhere in the South, as well as the potential desirability of having Robert Kennedy shot while riding in a convertible . . . Edward Partin told the Committee that Hoffa believed that by having Kennedy shot as he rode in a convertible, the origin of the fatal shot would be obscured . . . The context of Hoffa's discussion with Partin about an assassination conspiracy further seemed to have been predicated upon the recruitment of an assassin without any identifiable connection to the Teamster organization or Hoffa himself.'

The special organized crime volume of the House Committee Report informs us that by 1963, 'Santos Trafficante's gambling operations in Florida were in trouble. [. . .] Sam Giancana in Chicago was also feeling the pressure. Giancana's concern could be readily understood. For some time he had been the subject of intense coverage by the FBI. By the spring of 1963, it had become "bumper-to-bumper", almost 24 hours per day – while driving, on the golf course, in restaurants, wherever he was . . . As a consequence, Giancana was staying away from his home base in Chicago to a significant degree, and it was creating problems. [. . .]

'Later in July 1963, on two weekends, Sam Giancana and Phyllis McGuire, the singer, were together at the Cal-Neva Lodge on Lake Tahoe, Nevada. One of these weekends Frank Sinatra, who owned 50 percent of the Lodge (as well as having an interest in the Sands in Las Vegas) was with them. On 2 August 1963 Giancana and McGuire were also guests at Frank Sinatra's Palm Springs, California, home, having flown there on Sinatra's plane. These and other similar facts appeared in the Chicago newspapers and other media and resulted in action by the Nevada Gaming Commission, which had listed Giancana as a person not to be allowed in any premises licenced for gambling. Sinatra refused to deny his close relationship with Giancana and decided to sell his interests rather than run the risk of a suspended licence. Later that month, the FBI learned of rumbling in the higher echelons of organized crime in Chicago over Giancana's absenteeism and bad publicity.'

Other La Cosa Nostra leaders were also experiencing difficulties, but few more than Carlos Marcello. 'The FBI determined in the 1960s that because of Marcello's position as head of the New Orleans Mafia family (the oldest in the United States, having first entered the country in the 1880s), the Louisiana organized crime leader had been endowed with special powers and privileges not accorded to any other La Cosa Nostra leaders. As the leader of "the first family" of the Mafia in America, according to FBI information, Marcello has been the recipient of the extraordinary privilege of conducting syndicate operations without having to seek the approval of the national commission.'

In a special section dealing exclusively with Carlos Marcello, the House Committe relates, 'The exact place of Marcello's birth on 6 February 1910 has long been in doubt, and at one point was a central question in a lengthy deportation proceeding. Nevertheless, it is generally believed that Marcello was born in Tunis, North Africa, with the name Calogero Minacore.

'Marcello's first contact with the law came on 29 November 1929, when he was arrested at the age of 19 by New Orleans police as an accessory before and after the robbery of a local bank. The charges were subsequently dismissed. Less than 6 months later, on 13 May 1930, he was convicted of assault and robbery and was sentenced to the State penitentiary for 9 to 14 years. He served less than 5 . . . In 1935, after receiving a pardon by the Governor of Louisiana, Marcello's early underworld career continued, with charges being filed against him for a second assault and robbery, violation of Federal Internal Revenue laws, assault with intent to kill a New Orleans police officer, and yet another assault and robbery. Marcello was not prosecuted on the various charges. In 1938, as part of what Federal agents described as "the biggest marihuana ring in New Orleans history", Marcello was arrested and charged with the sale of more than 23 pounds of illegal substance. Despite receiving another lengthy prison sentence and a $76,830 fine, Marcello served less than 10 months and arranged to settle his fine for $400. Other charges were brought against Marcello over the next several years, stemming from such alleged offenses as narcotics sale, a high speed automobile chase, and assaulting an investigative reporter; these were never prosecuted, and the records have since disappeared.

'During the 1940s, Marcello became associated with New York Mafia leader Frank Costello in the operation of a slot machine network. Costello was then regarded by some authorities as one of the most influential leaders of organized crime in the United States and was commonly referred to in the newspapers as the Mafia's "boss of all bosses" or "prime minister of the underworld". Marcello's association with Costello in various Louisiana gambling activities had come about following a reported agreement between Costello and Senator Huey Long that allowed for the introduction of slot machines into New Orleans.

'Marcello was also involved in Louisiana gambling through his family-owned Jefferson Music Company, which came to dominate the slot machine, pinball and juke box trade in the New Orleans area. By the late

1940s, in an alliance with Joseph Poretta, Marcello had taken control of the largest racing wire service in New Orleans, the Southern News Service and Publishing Co., which served Louisiana's prosperous gambling network. Marcello and other associates also gained control of the two best-known gambling casinos in the New Orleans area, the Beverly Club and New Southport Club; the Beverly Club brought Marcello into partnership with the syndicate financier, Meyer Lansky.

'By the late 1950s, the Nola Printing Co. of New Orleans, a gambling wire service controlled by the Marcello interests, was serving bookmakers and relay centers throughout the State of Louisiana, as well as areas as diverse as Chicago, Houston, Miami, Hot Springs, Indianapolis and Detroit and cities in Alabama and Mississippi.

'In a statement prepared for the House Judiciary Committee in 1970, [Aaron M. Kohn, the managing director of the Metropolitan Crime Commission of New Orleans and a former FBI agent] outlined the continuing expansion of Marcello's holdings during the 1940s and 1950s: "Marcello and his growing association developed their capital or bankroll through extensive gambling, including casinos, slot machines, pinball, handbooks, layoff, football pools, dice card games, roulette and bingo; also narcotics, prostitution, extortion, clipjoint operations, B-drinking, marketing stolen goods, robberies, burglaries, and thefts. Their criminal enterprise required, and had, corrupt collusion of public officials at every critical level including police, sheriffs, justices of the peace, prosecutors, mayors, governors, judges, councilmen, licencing authorities, State legislators, and at least one Member of Congress."

'When Marcello appeared as a witness before the Kefauver Committee on 25 January 1951, he invoked the fifth amendment and refused to respond to questioning on his organized crime activities. Subsequently convicted of contempt of Congress for refusing to respond to the directions of the chair, Marcello was later successful in having his conviction overturned. In its final report, the Kefauver Committee concluded that Marcello's domination of organized crime in Louisiana had come about in large part due to the "personal enrichment of sheriffs, marshals, and other law enforcement officials" who received payoffs for "their failure to enforce gambling laws and other statutes relating to vice". The Kefauver report further noted that, "In every line of inquiry, the Committee found . . . the trail of Carlos Marcello."

'The Kefauver report also raised the question of why Marcello, who "has never become a citizen", "had not been deported".

'In early 1953, partly as a result of the national attention he received from the Kefauver Committee investigation, Marcello finally became the subject of deportation proceedings. [. . .]

'Carlos Marcello was called to testify before the McClellan Committee on 24 March 1959, during the Committee's extended investigation of labor racketeering and organized crime. Serving as chief counsel to the Committee was Robert F. Kennedy; his brother, Senator John F. Kennedy, was a member of the Committee. In response to Committee questioning, Marcello again invoked the fifth amendment in refusing to answer any questions relating to his background, activities, and associates.

'At the conclusion of Marcello's appearance before the Committee, Senator Sam Ervin of North Carolina requested of the Chair permission to ask the New Orleans underworld leader one final question: "I would like to know how you managed to stay in the United States for 5 years, 9 months and 24 days after you were found ordered deported as an undesirable person." Marcello's response to the question – "I wouldn't know" – provoked Ervin to state that "the American people's patience ought to run out on this" and that "those who have no claim to any right to remain in America, who come here and prey like leeches upon law-abiding people ought to be removed from this country". Senator Karl Mundt joined in Ervin's denunciation, urging prompt action by the Attorney General, and Senator Carl Curtis further remarked to Marcello that, "I think you ought to pack up your bags and voluntarily depart." [. . .]

'Carlos Marcello and his syndicate became a primary target of investigation by the Department of Justice during the Kennedy administration. Attorney General Robert F. Kennedy viewed him as one of the most powerful and threatening Mafia leaders in the Nation and ordered that the Justice Department focus on him, along with other figures such as Teamster President Hoffa and Chicago Mafia leader Sam Giancana.

'In Marcello's case, the intent of the Kennedy administration was made known even before Inauguration Day, 20 January 1961. On 28 December 1960, the *New Orleans States-Item* reported that Attorney General-designate Kennedy was planning specific actions against Marcello. An FBI report from that period noted: "On 12 January 1961, a [source] advised that Carlos Marcello is extremely apprehensive and upset and has [been] since the *New Orleans States-Item* newspaper on 28 December 1960 published a news story reporting that . . . Robert F. Kennedy stated he would expedite the deportation proceedings pending against Marcello after Kennedy takes office in January 1961."

'The Bureau's La Cosa Nostra file for 1961 noted that Marcello flew to Washington, DC shortly after the inauguration of President Kennedy and was in touch with a number of political and business associates. While there he placed a telephone call to the office of at least one Congressman.

'Bureau records further indicate that Marcello initiated various efforts to forestall or prevent the anticipated prompt deportation action. An FBI report noted that Marcello may have tried a circuitous approach. Through a source, the Bureau learned of another Mafia leader's account of how Marcello had reportedly proceeded. Philadelphia underworld leader Angelo Bruno discussed a specific attempt by Marcello to forestall an action by the immigration authorities. According to the Philadelphia underworld leader Marcello had enlisted his close Mafia associate, Santos Trafficante of Florida, in the reported plan. Trafficante in turn contacted Frank Sinatra to have the singer use his friendship with the Kennedy family on Marcello's behalf. This effort met with failure and may even have resulted in intensified Federal efforts against Marcello. [. . .]

'On 3 March 1961, General Joseph Swing of the Immigration and Naturalization Service advised the FBI that: "The Attorney General had been emphasizing the importance of taking prompt action to deport notorious hoodlums. In this connection, the Marcello case is of particular interest. A final order of deportation has been entered against Marcello but this fact is being held in strictest confidence."

'On the afternoon of 4 April 1961, 8 years after he was ordered deported, Carlos Marcello was finally ejected from the United States.

'As he walked into the INS office in New Orleans for his regular appointment to report as an alien, he was arrested and handcuffed by INS officials. He was then [unceremoniously] rushed to the New Orleans airport and flown to Guatemala. Marcello's attorneys denounced the deportation later that day, terming it "cruel and uncivilized", and noted that their client had not been allowed to telephone his attorney or see his wife. [. . .]

'On 10 April 1961, 6 days after he was deported, the Internal Revenue Service filed a $835,396 tax lien against Marcello and his wife. On 23 April, news reports disclosed that Marcello was being held in custody by Guatemalan authorities in connection with what were reported to be false citizenship papers he had presented on arrival there 6 April. On 4 May, Guatemalan President Miguel Fuentes ordered that Marcello be expelled; he was driven to and released at the El Salvador border late that night.

'On 19 May 1961, a Federal court in Washington ruled that Marcello's deportation was fully valid and denied a motion by his attorneys that it be declared illegal. With that ruling, Marcello's re-entry to the country was prohibited.

'Less than 2 weeks later, Marcello secretly gained entry into the United States. On 2 June 1961, confirming widespread rumors that their client had somehow slipped back in, Marcello's attorneys announced he had returned and was in hiding. Federal investigators have never been able to establish in detail his means of entry.

'On 5 June 1961, after Attorney General Kennedy dispatched 20 Federal agents to Shreveport, Louisiana, to conduct a search for Marcello, the Louisiana crime leader voluntarily surrendered in New Orleans and was ordered held in an alien detention center at McAllen, Texas. On 8 June, a Federal grand jury indicted him for illegal re-entry; on 11 July, the INS ruled he was an undesirable alien and once again ordered him deported.

'On 16 June 1961, the FBI received a report that a US Senator from Louisiana might have sought to intervene on Marcello's behalf. This Senator had reportedly received "financial aid from Marcello" in the past and was sponsoring a Louisiana official for a key INS position from which assistance might be rendered. [. . .]

'On 30 October 1961, Attorney General Kennedy announced the indictment of Marcello by a Federal grand jury in New Orleans on charges of conspiracy in falsifying a Guatemalan birth certificate and committing perjury. [. . .]

'On 20 December 1961, with Marcello free on a $10,000 bond, the five-member Board of Immigration

Appeals upheld the deportation order against Marcello, denying another appeal by Marcello attorneys that it be declared invalid.

'In October 1962, a Bureau of Narcotics report described Marcello as "one of the Nation's leading racketeers" and noted that he was "currently under intense investigation by the Internal Revenue Service Intelligence Division for tax fraud". The report also noted that Marcello was then instituting a further legal step to forestall deportation. Marcello's attorneys had filed a legal writ in an effort to set aside his Federal conviction on narcotics charges from 24 years earlier. This conviction was one of the key factors in the ongoing deportation proceedings against him.

'On 31 October 1962, a Federal court ruled against Marcello's attempt to have the 1938 drug conviction nullified. The court said that his claim that he had not counsel present when he pled guilty to the narcotics charge on 29 October 1938, was false, as was his claim that he had not known of his rights and could not afford an attorney.

'On 15 February 1963, in apparent response to Attorney General Kennedy's request for continuing action against Marcello, FBI Director J. Edgar Hoover directed the New Orleans FBI office to intensify its coverage of Marcello and his organization. He ordered that a "special effort" be made to upgrade the level of the investigation of Marcello, and suggested increased use of informants as well as the possible initiation of electronic surveillance . . . Two unsuccessful attempts were made to effect such surveillance, failures attributable in all likelihood to the security system employed by Marcello at the various locations from which he operated. [. . .]

'On 4 November 1963, Marcello went on trial in New Orleans on Federal charges of conspiracy in connection with his alleged falsification of a Guatemalan birth certificate. Eighteen days later, on 22 November 1963, he was acquitted. The news of President Kennedy's murder in Dallas reached the courtroom shortly before the verdict was announced.'

The above review makes clear that by 1963, top Mafia leaders and their labor cronies had been the subjects of an unprecedented, unremitting, relentless campaign against them; a campaign which could not be terminated by merely getting rid of Robert Kennedy, who could be replaced with a like-minded person by President Kennedy, whose program this was.

The Kefauver Committee had stated among its conclusions: 'The domination of the Mafia is based fundamentally on "muscle" and "murder". The Mafia is a secret conspiracy against law and order which will ruthlessly eliminate anyone who stands in the way of its success in any criminal enterprise in which it is interested. It will destroy anyone who betrays its secrets. It will use any means available – political influence, bribery, intimidation, et cetera, to defeat any attempt on the part of law enforcement to touch its top figures.'

Information of perhaps more than passing interest to our story was provided in the testimony of Aaron Kohn to the House Select Committee. According to Kohn, the 1930 crime which resulted in his first conviction – a grocery store robbery – had been personally planned by the then 20-year-old Carlos Marcello, using an interesting method of operation: 'Marcello had shielded his own complicity in the crime by inducing two juveniles to carry out the robbery . . . Marcello and a confederate had supplied the juveniles with a gun and instructions on their "getaway". The plan had gone awry when the two were later apprehended and pressured by authorities to identify the "higher-ups".' Kohn also noted that Marcello 'was referred to as a Fagin' in press accounts at the time, in an apparent reference to the Dickens character who recruited juveniles to carry out his crimes.

Organized crime had become somewhat more sophisticated by mid-century, as the House Committee noted in its final report:

'In its investigation, the Committee noted three cases, for the purposes of illustration, in which the methodology employed by syndicate figures was designed to insulate and disguise the involvement of organized crime. These did not fit the typical pattern of mob killing, as the assassination of a President would not. While the atypical cases did not involve political leaders, two of the three were attacks on figures in the public eye.

'In the first case, the acid blinding of investigative reporter Victor Riesel in April 1956, organized crime figures in New York used a complex series of go-betweens to hire a petty thief and burglar to commit the act. Thus, the assailant did not know who had actually authorized the crime for which he had been recruited. The use of such an individual was regarded as unprecedented, as he had not been associated with the syndicate, was a known drug user, and outwardly appeared to be unreliable. Weeks later, Riesel's assailant was slain by individuals who had recruited him in the plot. [. . .]

'The second case, the fatal shooting of a well-known businessman, Sol Landie, in Kansas City, Missouri, on 22 November 1970, involved the recruitment, through several intermediaries, of four young Black men by members of the local La Cosa Nostra family. Landie had served as a witness in a Federal investigation of gambling activities directed by Kansas City organized crime leader Nicholas Civella. The men recruited for the murder did not know who had ultimately ordered the killing, were not part of the Kansas City syndicate, and had received instructions through intermediaries to make it appear that robbery was the motive for the murder. All of the assailants and two of the intermediaries were ultimately convicted.

'The third case, the shooting of New York underworld leader Joseph Columbo before a crowd of 65,000 people in June 1971, was carried out by a young Black man with a petty criminal record, a nondescript loner who appeared to be alien to the organized crime group that had recruited him through various go-betweens. The gunman was shot to death immediately after the shooting of Columbo, a murder still designated as unsolved. [. . .]

'The Committee found that these three cases, each of which is an exception to the general rule of organized crime executions, had identifiable similarities. Each case was solved, in that the identity of the perpetrator of the immediate act became known. In two of the cases, the assailant was himself murdered soon after the crime. In each case, the person who wanted the crime accomplished recruited the person or persons who made the attack through more than one intermediary. In each case, the person suspected of inspiring the violence was a member of, or connected to, La Cosa Nostra. In each case, the person or persons hired were not professional killers, and they were not part of organized criminal groups. In each case, the persons recruited to carry out the acts could be characterized as dupes or tools who were being used in a conspiracy they were not fully aware of. In each case, the intent was to insulate the organized crime connection, with a particular requirement for disguising the true identity of the conspirators, and to place the blame on generally nondescript individuals.'

BOOK 3

CHAPTER

22

Jack Ruby, Mobster

Way back in late 1946, a well-known episode in organized crime history took place. In one of the more brazen efforts made during that post-war period of criminal expansion, representatives of the Chicago Mafia who were attempting to move into Dallas, Texas, sought to facilitate the maneuver by bribing Sheriff-elect Steve Guthrie. The proposed bribe was no less than a partnership in a gambling operation to be set up and financed by the mob, and kept free of trouble and competition by the Guthrie. The episode became known because Guthrie reported it and the contact man, Paul Roland Jones, was prosecuted and convicted of attempted bribery.

The scheme was to open a nightclub or restaurant downstairs, which would serve as a front for the gambling operation upstairs. As Sheriff Guthrie recalled the event years later, the person he was constantly told would manage the 'front' was Jack Ruby.

Whether or not Ruby (born Jacob Rubinstein in Chicago, 1911) was actually involved in this scheme is no longer capable of definitive proof. It is clear, however, that Ruby and members of his family were acquainted with individuals who were involved, including Chicago gangsters who had moved to Dallas in 1946–7.

In 1947 Jack Ruby moved to Dallas and established himself as a nightclub operator. After the Silver Spur, a country and western club, he opened the Sovereign, which eventually became the Carousel Club, a striptease joint.

During his years in Chicago, Ruby had also been acquainted with David Yaras and Lenny Patrick. The House Select Committee, it said, 'established that Yaras and Patrick were, in fact, notorious gunmen, having been identified by law enforcement authorities as executioners for the Chicago mob and closely associated with Sam Giancana, the organized crime leader in Chicago . . . Yaras and Patrick are believed to have been responsible for numerous syndicate executions, including the murder of James Ragan, a gambling wire service owner. The evidence implicating Yaras and Patrick in syndicate activities is unusually reliable. Yaras, for example, was overheard in a 1962 electronic surveillance discussing various underworld murder contracts he had carried out and one he had only recently been assigned.' Ruby's relationship with Patrick himself can be traced to at least the summer of 1963, and with a Patrick associate to at least the fall of 1963. Yaras, who relocated to Miami in the late 50s, had been more of a friend to Ruby, and his brother Sam, who lived in Dallas, was acquainted with Ruby.

Among Ruby's closest friends in Dallas was Lewis McWillie, who Ruby 'idolized'. McWillie had been engaged in gambling activities all his adult life, which brought him into relationships with various organized crime and gambling figures, including R. D. Matthews, a Dallas and Las Vegas gambler; Joseph Civillo, the Dallas organized crime figure; and Sam Yaras, the brother of Dave Yaras.

In September 1958, McWillie moved to Cuba and

managed the Tropicana Casino until May 1960. He worked as a pitboss at the Capri Hotel-Casino in Cuba from May 1960 to 2 January 1961, when he left Cuba for Nevada where he worked at the Cal-Neva Lodge, and then at various Las Vegas clubs.

Shortly after Fidel Castro took over in Cuba at the beginning of 1959, Elaine Mynier, a girl-friend of Lewis McWillie and an acquaintance of Jack Ruby, took a vacation in Cuba. She carried with her a coded message from Ruby to McWillie, containing various sets of numerals and letters.

At some point thereafter, Ruby purchased in Dallas and sent to McWillie in Cuba, one or more Colt Cobra guns which McWillie had requested.

On at least three occasions in the late summer and early fall of 1959, Ruby made quick trips from Miami into Cuba, apparently as some type of courier; on one of these round trips he traveled on to New Orleans upon his return.

It appears that Ruby did not spend all his time in Cuba visiting with McWillie. On at least one occasion during his time in Cuba, he went to Trescornia, a minimum security detention camp where the Castro Government was holding those who controlled extensive gambling interests in Cuba under a policy that would subsequently lead to confiscation of all underworld holdings in Cuba.

Jack Ruby's purpose in going to Trescornia was to visit with Santos Trafficante, the Florida crime boss who had controlled mob gambling in Cuba, and who would soon be a prime figure in the upcoming CIA-Mafia plots to assassinate Castro.

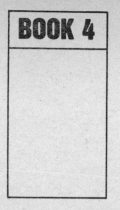

BOOK 4

THE WEB TIGHTENS

Curious Activities

For someone who, out of disillusionment with Soviet life, had picked up his family and left Russia, Lee Harvey Oswald continued to manifest most remarkable interests.

He wrote to the Soviet Embassy in Washington asking how to subscribe to Russian periodicals and for information on 'any periodicals or bulletins which you may put out for the benefit of your citizens living, for a time, in the USA.' He subsequently subscribed to several Russian journals. In December 1962, the Soviet Embassy received a card in Russian, signed 'Marina and Lee Oswald,' which conveyed New Year's greetings and wishes for 'health, success and all the best' to the employees at the Embassy (an interesting personal touch, considering that there is no evidence that either Lee or Marina had ever been to or had any contact with anyone at that Embassy, other than Lee's letter asking about literature).

Soon after his return to the US in June 1962, Lee had begun again manifesting an interest in Communism. In August he subscribed to the *Worker*. He also started to correspond with the Communist Party, USA, and the

Socialist Workers Party, and he also wrote for additional literature from these organizations. In October of 1962, he attempted to join the Socialist Workers Party, but his application was not accepted since there was no chapter in the Dallas area. Undaunted, he also wrote to them offering his assistance in preparing posters; and he entered a subscription to their affiliated publication, the *Militant*. In November 1962 he also wrote to the Socialist Labor Party in New York requesting literature. He wrote also to the Communist Party and asked whether, in view of his prior defection, he should 'continue to fight, handicapped as it were by past record compete with anti-progressive forces, aboveground or should always remain in the background, i.e., underground.' The Party replied that 'often it is advisable for some people to remain in the background not underground.'

At about 9 p.m. on 10 April 1963, Major General Edwin A. Walker, the controversial hero of the right wing, was sitting at his desk on the first floor of his home in Dallas when a bullet fired from outside his home entered the room and missed him. The official reconstruction was that the gunman had rested his rifle on the fence of Walker's yard. The evidence strongly points to the probability that Oswald fired the shot.

There were no eyewitnesses to the actual shooting, but the police spoke to a teenage boy in a neighboring house who said that after hearing the shot, he saw some men speeding down the alley at the rear of Walker's home in a light green or light blue Ford, either a 1959 or 1960 model. He said he also saw another car, a 1958 Chevrolet, black with white down the side, in a church parking lot adjacent to Walker's home; the car door was open and a man was bending over the back seat as though he was placing something on the floor of the car.

On the night of the incident, police interviewed Robert Surrey, an aide to Walker. Surrey said that on

Saturday 6 April, at about 9 p.m., he had seen two men sitting in a dark purple or brown 1963 Ford at the rear of Walker's house. Surrey also said the two men got out of the car and walked around the house. Surrey said he was suspicious and followed the car, noting that it had no licence plate.

If we are to assume that this was a true assassination attempt by Oswald, we must be willing to believe that this same man who at least twice hit a moving target from a rakishly high angle across Dealey Plaza, couldn't hit a stationary target only across the yard from him. If it wasn't a true assassination attempt, then it had to be a phony designed to give some credentials to Walker or Oswald or both. Whether it was real or phony may never be known, but that is relatively unimportant.

There is a much more meaningful angle to this Walker incident – an angle which must be pondered and remembered: every bit of the credible evidence makes it absolutely clear that Lee Harvey Oswald was not acting alone!

The evidence demonstrates that there were at least three others involved with Oswald in this Walker conspiracy: there were 'some' in the car in the alley, and at least two in the car in the church parking lot where a man was putting something on the back floor (it is uncontroverted that Oswald did not drive).

During the period Oswald was in New Orleans, from the end of April to late September 1963, he was engaged in activity purportedly on behalf of the now defunct Fair Play for Cuba Committee (FPCC), an organization centered in New York which was highly critical of US policy toward the Cuban Government under Fidel Castro. In May 1963, after having obtained literature from the FPCC, Oswald applied for and was granted membership in the organization.

When applying for membership, Oswald wrote to

national headquarters that he had 'been thinking about renting a small office at my own expense for the purpose of forming a FPCC branch here in New Orleans. Could you give me a charter?' (This offer to rent an office at his own expense was being made by a man who at the most – accepting the generous financial reconstruction of the Warren Committee – ended up the month of May with a grand total of $129.58 to his name.)

The FPCC responded to the effect that even if Oswald were able to organize the few members FPCC had in the New Orleans area, he would still need an equal number of new members just to be able to conduct a legal executive board for the chapter. They also strongly recommended against opening an office for a number of reasons, not the least of which was that having an identifiable location made it too easy for the 'lunatic fringe' on the other side to make trouble. Their suggestion was to use a Post Office box instead of an address.

On 3 June 1962, Oswald opened box No. 30061 at the Lafayette Square Substation in New Orleans. However, it seems clear that this was not in response to the suggestion of FPCC. For one thing, he had already been using a PO box, having maintained one at the General Post Office while in Dallas. Moreover, on this box he now opened in New Orleans, he did not list FPCC as one of the additional names entitled to receive mail at that box; he listed only Marina Oswald and A. J. Hidell (one of Oswald's aliases).

Oswald thereafter informed national headquarters that against their advice he had decided 'to take an office from the very beginning', and that he was going to have membership cards printed, which he did. He wrote three further letters to the New York office, in one of which he discussed his activity in passing out circulars on the street.

On at least three occasions, Oswald did, in fact, distribute commercially printed literature consisting of handbills demanding 'Hands off Cuba' in large letters and application forms for his FPCC chapter. Once while doing so, he was arrested and fined for being involved in a disturbance with anti-Castro Cuban refugees. His activities received some attention in the New Orleans press, and he twice appeared on a local radio program representing himself as a spokesman for the Fair Play for Cuba Committee.

Despite these activities, the FPCC chapter which Oswald purportedly formed in New Orleans was entirely fictitious.

Nor is there any evidence that Oswald ever opened an office as he claimed to have done. Although literature he was passing out contained the rubber stamp imprint 'FPCC, 544 Camp St., New Orleans, La.', investigation has established that neither the Fair Play for Cuba Committee nor Lee Harvey Oswald ever maintained an office at that address.

This address puzzle is particularly mystifying, since Oswald was passing out literature presumably designed to win over converts to his pro-Castro group; should he win people over, presumably he would like them to contact him. Why, then, would he list on the literature an address with which he had no connection – an address where he could not be contacted – when he had a post office box he could have listed where they could have contacted him (just as headquarters had suggested). The way he did it, how would someone reading the literature bearing the 544 Camp Street address have contacted Oswald in order to join him?

The disturbance with anti-Castro Cubans referred to above was described by the Warren Commission as follows.

'On 5 August, he visited a store managed by Carlos Bringuier, a Cuban refugee and avid opponent of Castro and the New Orleans delegate of the Cuban student directorate. Oswald indicated an interest in joining the struggle against Castro. He told Bringuier that he had been a Marine and was trained in guerilla warfare, and that he was willing not only to train Cubans to fight Castro but also to join the fight himself. The next day Oswald returned to the store and left his "Guidebook for Marines" for Bringuier.

'On August 9, Bringuier saw Oswald passing out Fair Play for Cuba leaflets. Bringuier and his companions became angry and a dispute resulted. Oswald and the three Cuban exiles were arrested for disturbing the peace. Oswald spent the night in jail and was interviewed by a lieutenant of the New Orleans Police Department . . . On 16 August, Oswald, assisted by at least one other person who was a hired helper, again passed out Fair Play for Cuba literature, this time in front of the International Trade Mart. That night, television newscasts ran pictures of Oswald's activities . . . William Stuckey, a radio broadcaster with a program called *Latin Listening Post*, had long been looking for a member of the Fair Play for Cuba Commmittee to appear on his program. He learned of Oswald from Bringuier . . . Stuckey arranged for a debate between Oswald and Bringuier on a 25-minute daily public affairs program called *Conversation Carte Blanche* which took place on 21 August.'

BOOK 4

CHAPTER

24

The FBI and Oswald

The Warren Commission reasoned that Oswald had met Bringuier 'by presenting himself as hostile to Premier Castro in an apparent attempt to gain information about anti-Castro organizations operating in New Orleans'.

Perhaps so. However, infiltration is not a one-way street.

Consider, for example, the FBI's counter-intelligence program against the Communist Party (COINTELPRO). Begun in 1956, COINTELPRO was expanded by a March 1960 directive to make a greater effort to prevent Communist infiltration (COMINT). This program against the Communist Party, USA (CPUSA COINTELPRO) was supplemented by SWP COINTELPRO, initiated on 12 October 1961 and directed against the Socialist Workers Party, which was targeted because of its '"open" espousal of its lines "through running candidates for public office" and its direction and/or support of "such causes as Castro's Cuba and integration problems arising in the South".' White Hate groups including the Ku Klux Klan also merited their own COINTELPROs.

Among the favorite COINTELPRO methods was the use of fictitious organizations. The Senate Select Committee described this routine as follows.

'There are basically three kinds of "notional" or fictitious organizations. All three were used in COINTELPRO attempts to factionalize.

'The first kind of "notional" was the organization whose members were all Bureau informants. Because of the Committee's agreement with the Bureau not to reveal the identity of informants, the only example which can be discussed publicly is a proposal which, although approved, was never implemented. That proposal involved setting up a chapter of the WEB DuBois Club in a Southern city which would be composed entirely of Bureau informants and fictitious persons. The initial purpose of the chapter was to cause the CPUSA expense by sending organizers into the area, cause the Party to fund Bureau coverage of out-of-town CP meetings by paying the informants' expenses, and receiving literature and instructions. Later, the chapter was to begin to engage in deviation from the Party line so that it would be expelled from the main organization "and then they could claim to be the victim of a Stalinist-type purge". It was anticipated that the entire operation would take no more than 18 months.

'The second type of "notional" was the fictitious organization with some unsuspecting (non-informant) members. For example, Bureau informants set up a Klan organization intended to attract membership away from the United Klans of America. The Bureau paid the informant's personal expenses in setting up the new organization, which had, at its height, 250 members.

'The third type of "notional" was the wholly fictitious organization, with no actual members, which was used as a pseudonym for mailing letters or pamphlets. For instance, the Bureau sent out newsletters from something called "The Committee for Expansion of Socialist Thought in America" which attacked the CPUSA from the "Marxist right" for at least two years.'

To the discussion of this last type of 'notional', we can add that obviously the setting up of such a fictitious organization can manufacture some very nice credentials for someone looking to pass himself off as something he is not.

Passing out pro-Castro literature on the street, getting into an altercation with anti-Castro Cubans, getting arrested for same, and supporting Castro in a debate on radio will all do wonders for showcasing someone as pro-Castro.

An FBI intelligence program aimed at Castro sympathizers had originally begun in 1960. After the Bay of Pigs invasion in 1961, the FBI intensified its coverage of pro-Castro Cuban activities. Particular attention came to be paid to the Fair Play for Cuba Committee.

'FBI field offices were advised [on 27 April 1961] that "increasing anti-United States attitudes and demonstrations stemming from the Cuban situation and 'cold war' tensions are cause for concern" and that pro-Castro groups might "react militantly to an emergency situation". In particular, the activities of the Fair Play for Cuba Committee revealed "the capacity of a nationality group organization to mobilize its efforts in such a situation so as to arrange demonstrations and influence public opinion". Hence, all field offices were to "be most alert to the possibility of demonstrations by nationality groups which could lead to incidents involving violence".'

On 25 July 1961, Director Hoover submitted a report to President Kennedy's Special Assistant for National Security, McGeorge Bundy, on the status of the internal security programs of the Interdepartmental Intelligence Conference. The report (in part) stated, 'The Fair Play for Cuba Committee is the principal outlet for pro-Castro propaganda and agitation on the part of US nationals sympathetic to the Castro regime. There are indications that this organization is receiving funds from the Cuban Government. In addition, investigation has shown that this group has been heavily infiltrated by the Communist Party, USA (CPUSA), and the Socialist Workers Party (SWP) . . . In fact, some chapters of the group have been directly organized by and under the complete control of the CPUSA or the SWP.'

The FBI has consistently denied that Oswald was an undercover agent, which may well be the case. However, there are certain things which seem to have to be disregarded before wholeheartedly accepting such assurances.

Oswald's actions in 1959 (defection to the Soviet Union in 1959; informing the American Embassy in Moscow that he was going to renounce his American citizenship and apply for Soviet citizenship; and his statement that he intended to reveal radar secrets to the Soviet Union) required, per FBI procedures, that a 'security case' be opened with Oswald as the subject. That was indeed done, and the security case was, as it should have been, still open when Oswald re-defected in 1962.

The Bureau indicates that it wasn't until almost three weeks after his return from Russia that they first interviewed Oswald. This was done by Special Agents John W. Fain and B. Tom Carter at the Fort Worth FBI office on 26 June 1962, at which time they say that Oswald denied he had told State Department officials at the American Embassy in Moscow that he was going to renounce his American citizenship, apply for Soviet citizenship, and reveal radar secrets to the Soviets.

Moreover, Fain told the House Select Committee, when he asked Oswald to take a polygraph test, Oswald refused to even be polygraphed on whether he had dealings with Soviet intelligence. Fain did not report Oswald's refusal to be polygraphed when he testified before the Warren Commission on 6 May 1964, 'despite', as the Senate Committee observed, 'detailed questioning by Commission members Ford and Dulles as to the discrepancies in Oswald's statements and Fain's reaction to them'.

A second interview on 16 August 1962 (this time by Fain and Special Agent Arnold J. Brown, in the back seat of Fain's automobile) yielded similar denials.

These agents all described Oswald as giving incomplete answers and demonstrating a bad attitude towards the Bureau: he was said to be cold, arrogant, uncooperative and evasive. Despite Oswald's reported attitude and demonstrable lies, the Bureau closed the Oswald security case on 26 August 1962.

The Senate Committee commented that, 'Although wide-ranging interviews were a basic investigative technique commonly used by the Bureau to develop background information on subjects of security investigations, no neighborhood or employment sources were checked in Oswald's case, nor was his wife interviewed.

'The FBI did not interview Marina Oswald prior to the assassination' despite the existence of a Bureau program 'which monitored the activities of Soviet immigrants and repatriates to detect possible foreign intelligence ties'.

Oswald's subscribing in September 1962 to the *Worker*, which the Bureau characterized as 'an east coast Communist Newspaper', came to the attention of the New York Field Office on 28 September 1962 (presumably through surveillance at that newspaper). This act, the Bureau concedes, contradicted statements attributed to Oswald in his FBI interviews that he was 'disenchanted with the Soviet Union'. Yet despite this, Oswald's security case was not re-opened. After the assassination, FBI Assistant Director Gale agreed that had standard Bureau procedures been followed, 'In light of Oswald's defection, the case should have been re-opened at the first indication of Communist sympathy or activity (i.e., September 1962).'

Then, on 26 March 1963, the Oswald security case was suddenly re-opened, the stated basis purportedly being his subscription to the *Worker* the previous September. It is curious, however, that shortly after

Oswald received this official certification that he was a security problem, he wrote a letter to the Fair Play for Cuba Committee claiming that he had passed out FPCC literature in Dallas with a placard around his neck reading 'Hands Off Cuba – Viva Fidel'.

Despite the fact that the Oswald security case was now ostensibly re-opened as of the end of March 1963, Marina Oswald was still not interviewed by the Bureau, the alleged reason for this being that there was information that Oswald had been drinking to excess and beating his wife, and that the relevant FBI manual provision required a 'cooling off' period. After the assassination, FBI Director Hoover agreed that this could only be characterized as 'an asinine excuse', and Assistant Director Gale conceded that, in fact, 'the best time to get information from her would be after she was beaten up by her husband'.

After his arrest following the Kennedy assassination, it was found that Oswald's address book contained the name, address, telephone number and automobile licence plate number of FBI agent James P. Hosty. Approximately two to three weeks earlier, Oswald had delivered a note addressed to Hosty at the FBI office in Dallas. Hosty said the note was threatening or complaining in nature, ordering him to stop bothering Oswald's wife. And well it might have, for in this period of time Oswald made a great show of writing to the Soviet Embassy to advise them that the FBI was trying to inhibit his activities on behalf of the Fair Play for Cuba Committee.

However, we will never know what was really in Oswald's note, because following the assassination – under the order, he said, of J. Gordon Shanklin, head of the Dallas FBI office – Agent Hosty destroyed it.

BOOK 4

CHAPTER

25

Oswald and the FBI

Clearly, the FBI accounts of the various contacts make it very clear that Oswald was un-cooperative and, indeed, antagonistic toward the Bureau. He wanted nothing to do with them.

Consider, however, the testimony of a man named Adrian Alba, who told the House Select Committee that as an employee and part owner of the Crescent City Garage in New Orleans, he had, in the summer of 1963, become acquainted with Lee Harvey Oswald, who at that time worked next door at the Reily Coffee Co. Oswald had spent many of his working hours at the garage, where he read gun magazines and discussed guns with Alba.

Alba related that one day an FBI agent entered his garage and requested to use one of the Secret Service cars garaged there. The FBI agent showed Alba his credentials, and Alba allowed him to take a Secret Service car, a dark green Studebaker. Later that day or the next day, Alba says he saw the FBI agent in the car handing a white envelope to Oswald in front of the Reily Coffee Co. There was no exchange of words, Alba says, and Oswald, in a bent position, turned away trom the car window and held the envelope close to his chest as he walked to the Reily Coffee Co. Alba says he believes he observed a similar transaction a day or so later as he was returning from lunch, but on this occasion he was farther away and failed to see what was handed to Oswald.

A factor which must be considered in evaluating the credibility of Alba is the fact that he did not relate his account of the transactions between Oswald and the FBI agent when he testified before the Warren Commission in 1964. He explained to the Committee in 1978 that he first remembered these incidents in 1970, when his memory was triggered by a television commercial showing a merchant running to and from a taxi to assist a customer. Alba's failure to relate this information to the Warren Commission unarguably may be a reason in and of itself to disbelieve him. On the other hand, it doesn't necessarily mean his story is untrue, any more than the fact that agent Fain failed to tell the Warren Commission that Oswald refused a polygraph means that is not true.

However, in evaluating the FBI's story as to Oswald's dealings with them, there is an undisputed fact which must be evaluated, because it is so seemingly inconsistent with the Bureau's position that Oswald was un-cooperative, antagonistic, and wanted nothing to do with them. Given that posture, how does one rationalize the fact – which the Bureau concedes to be true – that while he was in the New Orleans jail on 10 August 1963, in relation to the altercation with the anti-Castro Cubans, Lee Harvey Oswald – by his own request – was paid an official visit by FBI agent Quigley?

Incidentally, even if it is concluded that Oswald's reported overtures to Carlos Bringuier and the anti-Castro Cubans were contrived (phony), that would not necessarily prove that Oswald was not working for the FBI.

On 23 May 1961, shortly after the Bay of Pigs, FBI field offices were instructed that 'The failure of the recent invasion attempt by Cuban rebel forces has accentuated the problem of investigating anti-Castro and pro-Castro groups and individuals in the United States. In addition to discharging our security and criminal responsibilities we are faced with the necessity of acquiring and providing other agencies informative and valid intelligence data relative to the objectives and activities of both factions as well as data regarding key personalities . . . In order to discharge these investigative and intelligence responsibilities with maximum effectiveness it is essential that particular attention be afforded the development on a broadly expanded basis of sources and informants in a position to provide knowledgeable data regarding pro-Castro and anti-Castro activities.'

The Senate Committee said: 'After the missile crisis, CIA operations against Cuba apparently decreased, while operations by Cuban exile groups on their own continued. On 18 March 1963, there was a reported attack on a Soviet vessel off the northern coast of Cuba by members of two exile groups, Alpha 66, and the Second National Front of Escambray. There was another reported attack on a Soviet vessel off the northern coast of Cuba on the evening of 26–27 March 1963, by members of another anti-Castro group, Commandos L-66.

'This apparently caused considerable concern within the US Government that such activity by Cuban exile groups could produce confrontation with the Soviets. One witness stated, "the whole apparatus of government, Coast Guard, Customs, Immigration and Naturalization, FBI, CIA, were working together to try to keep these operations from going to Cuba".

'These moves to restrict exile activities had an impact on New Orleans at the time Lee Harvey Oswald was living there. As reported on page one of the *New Orleans Times-Picayune* on 1 August 1963, the FBI seized more than a ton of dynamite, 20 bomb casings, napalm material and other devices at a home in the New Orleans area on 31 July. Newspaper interest in the seizure continued with prominent articles in the *Times-Picayune* on 2 August and 4 August. [. . .]

'Additional FBI reports provided to the Warren Commission detailed other facts connected to this anti-Castro activity in New Orleans at the time of Oswald's contact with Bringuier. On 24 July, according to FBI reports, ten Cuban exiles arrived in New Orleans from Miami. These ten joined an existing group of exiles at a "training camp" north of New Orleans, which was directed by the same individuals who were involved in procuring the dynamite the FBI seized. By late July, some 28 Cuban exiles were at the training camp, allegedly awaiting transportation to Guatemala where they would work for a lumber company.

'Some of those who owned the land on which the Cuban exiles were staying became concerned about the FBI interest in the anti-Castro activities and ordered them to leave. Carlos Bringuier was called upon to assist in getting this group back to Miami.'

The Senate Committee went on to observe, 'Although this was the extent of the Warren Commission investigation of this incident, at least one FBI report, on the seizure of materials, which was not provided the Warren Commission, raises additional questions about the purpose of Oswald's contact with Bringuier . . . A report of the Miami Office of the FBI [dated 3 October 1963] revealed some of the information the FBI had on this incident:

(1) On 14 June 1963, information was received that a group of Cuban exiles had a plan to bomb the Shell refinery in Cuba.

(2) On 15 June, United States Customs Agents seized a twin Beechcraft airplane on the outskirts of Miami, Florida, along with a quantity of explosives. [. . ., . . ., . . ., "A" and . . ., along with American . . .] were involved and detained, but not arrested, by

the United States Customs Agents. It was ascertained that [. . .] supplied the money and explosives for this operation. [He] is well known as a former gambling concession operator in Havana.

(3) On 19 July 1963, [. . .] advised that there was another plan to bomb Cuba, using bomb casings and dynamite located on the outskirts of New Orleans, Louisiana.

(4) On 31 July 1963, the Federal Bureau of Investigation (FBI) at New Orleans, Louisiana, obtained a search warrant and seized 2,400 pounds of dynamite and 20 bomb casings near Lacombe, Louisiana. This material was located on the property of [. . .], brother of [. . .], [of] Miami Beach and former operator of a casino in the Nacional Hotel, Havana, Cuba.

(5) Investigation determined that this dynamite was purchased at Collinsville, Illinois, by ["B"] for "A", who was involved in the 14 June 1963 seizures at Miami. "A" transported the dynamite to New Orleans in a rented trailer. Also involved in this bomb plot were . . .

(6) [. . .] advised on 14 June 1963, "B" of Collinsville, Illinois, recently arrived in Miami, Florida, in a Ford station wagon with a load of arms for sale. American adventurers and mercenaries, [. . .] and [. . .], took "B" around to meet the different Cuban exile leaders in Miami.

'On another occasion, an intelligence agency conducted a sensitive operation which developed information on the location of arms caches and training camps in another country. That information was given to the other country, which then raided the camps and seized the materials. Raids and seizures such as these apparently were commonplace throughout the summer and fall of 1963. Those individuals apparently sponsoring this activity were angered by these raids and seizures.'

BOOK 4

CHAPTER

26

The Return of Svengali

As discussed previously, despite what Oswald had told the Fair Play for Cuba Committee headquarters about renting an office, and despite his stamp on literature he was distributing stating that FPCC was located at 544 Camp Street, investigation following the assassination revealed that neither the FPCC nor Lee Harvey Oswald had ever rented an office at that address.

Troubled by questions such as why Oswald would list an address with which he had absolutely no relationship, the House Select Committee conducted its own investigation of the possibility of a connection between Oswald and 544 Camp Street.

It turns out that the building located at 544 Camp Street, the Newman Building, occupied a corner lot where Camp Street meets Lafayette Street. Its other entrance was addressed 531 Lafayette Street. The Camp Street address was the main entrance for two tenants who have no relation to our story.

The Lafayette Street address, however, was the main entrance of Guy Banister Associates, a private investigative firm.

Guy Banister, after a 20-year career, had retired

from the FBI in 1954 to become assistant superintendent for the New Orleans Police Department. After a falling out with the mayor of New Orleans, Banister had left public service and formed his own private detective agency.

According to FBI files, Banister had become excessively involved in anti-Communist activities after his separation from the Bureau, and testified before various investigating bodies about the dangers of Communism. Early in 1961, Banister helped draw up a charter for the Friends of Democratic Cuba, an organization set up as the fund-raising arm of Sergio Arcacha Smith's branch of the Cuban Revolutionary Council.

The FBI files also indicate that Banister was running background investigations on those Cuban students at Louisiana State University who sought to join Smith's anti-Castro group, ferreting out any pro-Castro sympathizers among them.

Also extremely active in Sergio Arcacha Smith's anti-Castro group was a man we have met previously – the man who had been Lee Harvey Oswald's commander in the Civil Air Patrol – David Ferrie.

Ferrie shared Banister's anti-Communism and anti-Castro fervor. In fact, Ferrie had actually had to be asked 'to discontinue his remarks at a speaking engagement in July 1961 before the New Orleans chapter of the Military Order of World Wars. His topic was the Presidential administration and the Bay of Pigs fiasco. The organization put a stop to Ferrie's remarks when he became too critical of President Kennedy.'

Ferrie had not bothered to renew his CAP commander charter when it ran out in 1954, although he continued to wear the insignia of the CAP on his fatigues. He did renew his commander charter in 1959, when he augmented his cadet's standard CAP rifle training by instituting an association with the New Orleans Cadet Rifle Club.

'Ferrie also started a group called the "Falcon Squadron", composed of Ferrie's closest CAP associates.

A group within this group, the "Omnipotents", was allegedly starting to train cadets in what to do in the event of a major attack on the United States.

'Ferrie's job and ownership of an airplane enabled him to travel around the country with relative ease. He told officials he frequently traveled to Texas and other parts of the South, including Miami. He also visited New York on occasion. The amount of time Ferrie spent in these cities could not be determined. In August 1959, while in Miami, Ferrie was put under a 24-hour surveillance by customs agents who believed he was involved in gun smuggling. Following a brief investigation, including a tapping of his telephone conversations, it was determined that Ferrie was not involved in any illegal activity, but merely planning an outing for his "scouts". The investigation was dropped.

'Ferrie also became involved in other activities. In 1959, he had found an outlet for his political fanaticism in the anti-Castro movement. By early 1961, Ferrie and a young man whom Ferrie had first met in the CAP, Layton Martens, were working with Sergio Arcacha Smith, head of the Cuban Revolutionary Front delegation in New Orleans.

'Ferrie soon became Smith's eager partner in counter-revolutionary activities. He reportedly built two miniature submarines, which he planned to use for an attack on Havana Harbor, obtained several rifles and mortars for the proposed invasion, and was reportedly teaching Cubans how to fly. Further, several of Ferrie's cadets claimed to have taken trips to Cuba in Ferrie's airplane.

'Ferrie was also involved with Arcacha Smith, adventurer Gordon Novel and Layton Martens in a raid on a munitions dump in Houma, Louisiana.' Others who were said to have participated in the raid, in which various weapons, grenades and ammunition were stolen, were Andrew Blackmon, a Ferrie associate and former CAP cadet, and Guy Banister, whose involvement may have been limited to storing the stolen material.

'In September 1961, the US Border Patrol received information that Ferrie was attempting to purchase a C-47 airplane for $30,000 and reportedly had a cache of arms in the New Orleans area. The report was never verified. [. . .]

'Arcacha Smith wrote to Eastern Airlines' then-president Eddie Rickenbacker on Ferrie's behalf requesting a 60- or 90-day leave with pay for full-time work for the CRC. The request was denied. Nevertheless, Ferrie's vacation in April 1961 coincided with the Bay of Pigs invasion. Ferrie's role, if any, is not known.'

Guy Banister did investigative work both directly for Ferrie and for Ferrie's lawyer, G. Wray Gill, in connection with the charges brought against Ferrie by Eastern Airlines, his employer, and by the New Orleans police alleging crimes against nature, and extortion. In return, Ferrie provided Banister research services, such as analysis of autopsy reports.

Ferrie and Banister also worked together over some period of time with attorney Gill for the defense of another of Gill's clients who was involved in a deportation case – Carlos Marcello.

'Ferrie's involvement with Marcello may have begun as early as the spring of 1961. An unconfirmed Border Patrol report of February 1962 alleges that Ferrie was the pilot who flew Marcello back into the United States from Guatemala after he had been deported in April 1961 as part of the US Attorney General Robert Kennedy's crackdown on organized crime. This may have helped Ferrie establish an enduring relationship with the Marcello organized crime family.'

The return of Marcello to the United States coincided chronologically with Ferrie's activities with the Cuban Revolutionary Council. According to Carlos Quiroga, a Cuban who had been involved with the CRC, Ferrie often provided Arcacha Smith with funds, stating 'Ferrie lent him [Arcacha Smith] money when he needed it for his family . . . He [Ferrie] had $100 bills around all the time', even after he lost his job with the airlines.

As a result of his work with Guy Banister, David Ferrie spent a good deal of time at Banister's office at the Newman Building, and he and Banister were frequent customers at Mancuso's coffee shop on the first floor. Less than a block away were the Reily Coffee Co., where Oswald worked, and the Crescent City Garage, whose owner, Adrian Alba, testified that he had often seen Oswald in Mancuso's.

Following his much-publicized altercation and subsequent debate with the anti-Castro leader, Carlos Bringuier, near the end of August 1963, Oswald largely passed out of sight in New Orleans until mid-September.

During this period, Oswald reportedly appeared in Clinton, Louisiana, where a voting rights demonstration organized by the Congress of Racial Equality was in progress. Clinton, the county seat of East Feliciana Parish, was about 130 miles from New Orleans.

'There were six witnesses in Clinton who saw Oswald there, among them a State representative, a deputy sheriff and a registrar of voters . . . In addition to the physical descriptions they gave that matched that of Oswald, other observations of the witnesses tended to substantiate their belief that he was, in fact, the man they saw. For example, he referred to himself as "Oswald", and he produced his Marine Corps discharge papers as identification.'

The reason Oswald had to produce identification was because he was applying to be registered as a voter in East Feliciana Parish. But, as far as we know, he produced legitimate identification, so that none of the papers he produced contained an address which would qualify him to be registered as a resident of East Feliciana Parish. Apparently, the pretext he offered was that he had been seeking employment at East

Louisiana State Hospital, in nearby Jackson, Louisiana, and had been told that his job would depend on his becoming a registered voter, and so he had come to Clinton for that purpose. He was, it would appear, unsuccessful in attempting to be registered as a voter in East Feliciana Parish.

'Some of the witnesses said that Oswald was accompanied by two older men whom they identified as [David] Ferrie and [a man named Clay] Shaw.'

The House Select Committee found that 'the Clinton witnesses were credible and significant . . . If the witnesses were not only truthful but accurate as well in their accounts, they established an association of an undetermined nature between Ferrie, Shaw and Oswald less than 3 months before the assassination.'

There the matter has stood since then: 'an association of an undetermined nature' involving Oswald, David Ferrie and a third man. In other words, a mystery. But perhaps there are a few potential clues that have been overlooked.

The central question would seem to be: 'Was it only a mere coincidence that a "big-city boy" like Oswald happened to be applying to be registered as a voter out in East Feliciana Parish, just at the very time that an organized Black voting registration drive was taking place in that parish?'

Perhaps so. But let's look at a little background.

The Senate Committee, in a special volume on the Federal Bureau of Investigation, relates that in the late 50s and early 60s, in addition to its own mandate, the FBI had 'the role of an investigative agency, acting for the Justice Department, required by law to serve the Civil Rights Division, which was in turn charged with the responsibility of enforcing Federal laws with respect to civil rights . . . [T]he Civil Rights Division was to enforce the Civil Rights Acts of 1957 and 1960 – a twin responsibility to go after (A) public officials who practiced racial discrimination in registration or voting, and (B) anyone, public official or private citizen, who interfered with registration or voting by threats, intimidation, or coercion by any means. [. . .]

'In 1960 the Department of Justice believed that there was massive wide-spread racial discrimination in voting in five Deep South States (Alabama, Georgia, Louisiana, Mississippi and South Carolina) and in some counties in Florida, North Carolina and Tennessee. [. . .]

'Shortly after the Civil Rights Act of 1960 went into effect, record demands were made for 15 counties in [five] states – McCormick, Hampton and Claredon Counties, South Carolina; Webster, Fayette and Early Counties, Georgia; Wilcox, Sumpter and Montgomery Counties, Alabama; East Feliciana, Quachita and East Carroll Parishes, Louisiana; and Boliva, Leflore, and Forrest Counties, Mississippi.'

By 1964, 'The result of four years of work was a tremendous accumulation of proof of racial discrimination of voting throughout the States of Alabama, Mississippi and Louisiana.'

An example of one aspect of the Bureau's activity in this field is the 27 June 1963 memorandum on the subject 'Racial Matters' which FBI Headquarters sent to the Special Agents in charge of all field offices; in part, the memorandum reads:

'In order that the Bureau's information will be complete and absolutely current, it is essential that all offices promptly [send] information concerning racial demonstrations . . . arrests arising out of racial problems, results of court action, and any other pertinent information. Steps shall be taken to furnish pertinent information so that it will be received prior to midnight on the day of occurrence . . . When activities continue throughout the night, the Bureau is to be telephonically advised of the current status of the activities before 7 a.m., Eastern Daylight Savings Time.

'Each office must also assume responsibility for following up scheduled racial activity and promptly advising the Bureau of subsequent developments.

Whenever the Bureau has been advised that a meeting, demonstration or other pertinent activity will take place, coverage must be continued and the Bureau promptly informed as to whether the anticipated activity actually occurred, and pertinent details of what transpired. If a planned racial activity is cancelled or postponed, the Bureau should also be promptly advised.'

Given the above background, together with the other information we now know about Lee Harvey Oswald, it would seem appropriate to at least entertain the following questions:

(1) Might Oswald's business in Clinton have been part of the coverage of this Black voting registration drive organized by the Congress of Racial Equality, such as is mandated in the 'Racial Matters' memo sent from FBI headquarters to all field offices only two months earlier?

(2) Might the purpose of having Oswald apply to be registered as a voter in East Feliciana Parish, be to test whether an outside white would be treated better than local Blacks?

The so-called 'Clinton Sightings' of Oswald have significance beyond the possibility that they tie the FBI to Oswald, for they rather firmly tie the supposed pro-Castro Communist, Oswald, together with the staunch anti-Communist, anti-Castro partisan, David Ferrie.

Nor is this the only evidence tying Oswald and Ferrie together in this fateful period of time. There is a fascinating link which has been largely overlooked despite the fact that there are credible witnesses to its existence.

A Ferrie associate named Layton Martens told the police that after the assassination, W. Wray Gill (Carlos Marcello's lawyer, for whom Ferrie had been doing some work) had 'come by to relay a message to Ferrie that his library card was found among Oswald's effects'. The House Select Committee dismissed this with the comment that 'Marten's story was unsubstantiated'.

However, they subsequently relate that 'Oswald's former landlady in New Orleans, Mrs Jesse Garner, told the Committee she recalled that Ferrie visited her home on the night of the assassination and asked about Oswald's library card'. And, 'A neighbor of Oswald's, Mrs Doris Eames, told New Orleans district attorney investigators in 1968 that Ferrie had come by her house after the assassination, inquiring if Mr Eames had any information regarding Oswald's library card. Eames told Ferrie he had seen Oswald in the public library but apparently had no information about the library card Oswald used.'

Ferrie's interest in this card clearly points to an active association between Oswald and Ferrie in this period of time.

BOOK 4

CHAPTER

27

Closet Anti-Communist?

The Clinton sightings are not Oswald's only possible contact with virulent anti-Castro Cuban zealots.

Antonio Veciana Blanch was the founder of Alpha 66 which, 'throughout 1962 and most of 1963, was one of the most militant of the exile groups. Its repeated hit-and-run attacks had drawn public criticism from President Kennedy in the spring of 1963, to which Veciana replied, "We are going to attack again and again"'

Veciana told the House Select Committee that originally he had been recruited to work against the Castro Government in the middle of 1960, by a man who called himself Maurice Bishop, who purported to be with a construction firm headquartered in Belgium. Veciana related that prior to the time the American Embassy in Cuba was closed in January 1961, Bishop had suggested that he go there and contact certain officials for help in his anti-Castro activity. Veciana recalled that one of the names Bishop had given him was Sam Kail.

The Committee ascertained that Colonel Sam Kail 'served as the US Army attaché at the US Embassy in

Havana from 3 June 1958 until the day the Embassy closed, 4 January 1961. His primary mission as military attaché was that of intelligence. Later, in February 1962, he was transferred to Miami where he was in charge of the unit that debriefed newly-arrived Cuban refugees. Although he reported directly to the Chief of Army Intelligence in Washington, Kail said he assumed his unit was actually functioning for the CIA.' (The Committee doesn't mention that Kail, as we know, was also involved with Clemard Charles, the friend of George de Mohrenschildt.)

Veciana says that in mid-1961 he fled Cuba because Bishop told him Castro's agents were becoming suspicious of his activities.

'Shortly after he settled in Miami, Veciana testifies, Bishop contacted him again. [. . .]

'Early in their relationship in Miami, Bishop asked Veciana to monitor the activities of an anti-Castro operation called "Cellula Fantasma". Veciana said he attended a few meetings of the group and described the operation as a leaflet-dropping mission over Cuba which involved known soldier of fortune, Frank Fiorini Sturgis [later of Watergate fame]. [. . .]'

The result of Veciana and Bishop re-establishing contact eventually led to Veciana's founding of Alpha 66 which, according to Veciana, was the brainchild of Bishop (whose main thesis was that Cuba had to be liberated by Cubans). 'Alpha 66 became one of the most active of the anti-Castro exile groups, buying guns and boats, recruiting and training commandos, and conducting numerous raids on Cuba. [. . .]'

'According to Veciana, the man behind all of Alpha 66's strategy was Maurice Bishop. Over the 12-year period of their association, Veciana estimated he met with Bishop more than 100 times . . . Besides contacts with Bishop in Havana and Miami, Veciana also had meetings with him in Dallas, Washington, Las Vegas and Puerto Rico and in Caracas, Lima, and La Paz in South America.' Veciana testified that over the years

that he knew Bishop, he had 'at least five meetings with
him in Dallas'.

One of these Dallas meetings, which Veciana
believed 'was in late August 1963', took place 'in the
lobby of a large office building in the downtown section
of the city. [. . .] When Veciana arrived for the meeting, Bishop was there talking with [a young man] . . .
[The young man] remained with Bishop and Veciana
only for a brief time as they walked toward a nearby
coffee shop . . . [The young man] then departed, and
Bishop and Veciana continued their meeting alone.

'Veciana testified that he recognized the young man
with Bishop as Lee Harvey Oswald after seeing photographs of him following the Kennedy assassination.
There was absolutely no doubt in his mind that the man
was Oswald, not just someone who resembled him.
Veciana pointed out that he had been trained to
remember the physical characteristics of people and
that if it was not Oswald it was his "exact" double.'

In late September 1963, three men appeared at the
Dallas home of Silvia Odio, a member of the Cuban
Revolutionary Junta, or JURE, to ask for help in
preparing a fundraising letter for JURE. The House
Committee tells us Mrs Odio stated that 'two of the
men appeared to be Cubans, although they also had
characteristics that she associated with Mexicans. The
two individuals, she remembered, indicated that their
"war" names were "Leopoldo" and "Angelo". The
third man, an American, was introduced to her as
"Leon Oswald", and she was told that he was very
much interested in the anti-Castro Cuban cause.

'Mrs Odio stated that the men told her that they had
just come from New Orleans and that they were about
to leave on a trip. The next day, one of the Cubans
called her on the telephone and told her that it had
been his idea to introduce the American into the
underground "because he is great, he is kind of nuts".
The Cuban also said that the American had been in the

Marine Corps and was an excellent shot, and that the American had said that Cubans "don't have any guts because President Kennedy should have been assassinated after the Bay of Pigs, and some Cubans should have done that, because he was the one that was holding the freedom of Cuba actually". Mrs Odio claimed the American was Lee Harvey Oswald.

'Mrs Odio's sister, who was in the apartment at the time of the visit by the three men and who stated that she saw them briefly in the hallway when answering the door, also believed that the American was Lee Harvey Oswald.'

The Warren Commission concluded that Mrs Odio was mistaken. They did so, not on the basis that she and her sister were not believable, but because they concluded that other evidence made it impossible for Oswald to have been in Dallas when she said this occurred. Essentially, they concluded that the event had to have happened on either the 26th or 27th of September: if on the 26th, they asserted they had firm evidence that Oswald was on a bus from Houston to Mexico City; and if on the 27th, Oswald could not have traveled from Dallas and reached Mexico City when they knew he did, unless he had private transportation. The fact is, as the House Select Committee quoted J. Wesley Liebeler, the Warren Commission assistant counsel, 'There really is no evidence at all that Oswald left Houston on that bus.'

As to having private transportation, we now know that Oswald had at least one associate, David Ferrie, who had his own airplane.

The House Select Committee stated it 'was inclined to believe Silvia Odio. From the evidence provided in the sworn testimony of the witnesses, it appeared that three men did visit her apartment in Dallas prior to the Kennedy assassination and identified themselves as members of an anti-Castro organization. Based on a judgement of the credibility of Silvia and Annie Odio, one of these men at least looked like Lee Harvey

Oswald and was introduced to Mrs Odio as Leon Oswald.'

That last sentence is really the important finding, because from at least one aspect of our inquiry, it doesn't matter if Oswald was there or not.

Once a determination is made that the Odios are truthful when they say that the man looked like and was introduced as Oswald, the implications become, if anything, more staggering if he was not there: that would mean that less than eight weeks before the assassination, these two men showcased an imposter who looked like and was passed off as Oswald – and the next day one of them called to tell Mrs Odio that this 'Oswald' was an ex-Marine who was an excellent shot and who had talked about killing Kennedy.

In mid September 1963, Lee Harvey Oswald applied for and received a Mexican tourist card. The tourist card immediately preceding his in numerical sequence was issued to William G. Gaudet, a newspaper editor. Two days later, Gaudet departed on a 3- or 4-week trip to Mexico and other Latin American countries. This happened to coincide with Oswald's visit to Mexico City between 27 September and 3 October 1963.

Gaudet, who had once been employed by the CIA, had continued thereafter to serve 'as a source of information obtained during his trips abroad' and, in addition, 'he occasionally performed errands for the Agency'. The Agency's records purport that their contacts with Gaudet ended in 1961, but he testified that they continued through at least 1969, and were never formally terminated.

'Gaudet said he could not recall whether his trip to Mexico and other Latin American countries in 1963 involved any intelligence-related activity. He was able to testify, however, that during that trip he did not encounter Oswald, whom he had previously observed on occasion at the New Orleans Trade Mart. . . Gaudet testified that he had never met Oswald, although he had known of him prior to the assassination because Oswald had distributed literature near his office. Gaudet also stated that on one occasion he observed Oswald speaking to Guy Banister on a street corner.'

While in Mexico City, Oswald visited both the Cuban and Soviet Embassies, representing that he intended to travel to the Soviet Union, and requesting an 'in-transit' Cuban visa to permit him to enter Cuba on 30 September on the way to the Soviet Union.

The evidence is, however, that what he was attempting – or wanted to appear to be attempting – was to use the in-transit visa to get into Cuba legitimately.

When Oswald left Mexico City, he went to Dallas, where he arrived on 3 October. On 9 November he sent a letter to the Soviet Embassy in Washington to 'inform [them] of recent events since my meetings with Comrade Kostin in the Embassy of the Soviet Union, Mexico City, Mexico'.

The 'recent events' amounted to a declaration that the FBI was trying to inhibit his activities: 'The Federal Bureau of Investigation is not now interested in my activities in the progressive organization "Fair Play for Cuba Committee" of which I was secretary in New Orleans (state Louisiana) since I no longer reside in that state. However, the FBI has visited us here in Dallas, Texas, on November 1st. Agent James P. Hasty [sic] warned me that if I engaged in FPCC activities in Texas the FBI will again take an "interest" in me.'

The fact is that if Oswald's Mexico trip was on the level, the FBI most certainly should have been aggressively checking up on him. 'Under the relevant FBI manual provisions then in effect, any contact such as Oswald's with the Soviet Embassy in Mexico City required that immediate investigative action at the appropriate field office be undertaken.'

Yet, 'despite the fact that both the Dallas and New Orleans field offices were aware that Oswald had been in contact with the Soviet Embassy in Mexico City, there is no evidence that either of these field offices intensified their "efforts" to locate and interview Oswald. Most surprising, however, is that the "Soviet experts" at FBI headquarters did not intensify their efforts in the Oswald case after being informed that Oswald had met with Vice Consul Kostikov at the Soviet Embassy in Mexico City. Not only were these experts familiar with Soviet activities in general, but they knew that Kostikov was a member of the KGB. Further, the Bureau's Soviet experts had reason to believe he was an agent within the KGB's Department which carries out assassination and sabotage. They were also aware that American citizen contacts with the Soviet Embassy in Mexico City were extremely rare.'

BOOK 4

CHAPTER 28

'He Is Going To Get Hit'

On September 11 1962 at Churchill Farms, his 3,000-acre swampland plantation outside New Orleans, Carlos Marcello and three associates were discussing 'the pressure law enforcement agencies were bringing to bear on the Mafia brotherhood as a result of the Kennedy administration'. One of those present was Edward Becker, a man with ties to Joseph Sica, the Mafia leader of Los Angeles, and a close friend of Carl Roppolo, reputedly Carlos Marcello's favorite nephew.

In 1969 Ed Reid, a writer on organized crime and a former editor of the *Las Vegas Sun*, published *The Grim Reapers*, which contained what Becker had told him regarding something which had occurred at that Churchill Farms meeting. Becker authenticated so much of Reid's rendition as appears below when he testified before the House Select Committee, from whose work the following excerpts are taken:

'It was then that Carlos' voice lost its softness, and his words were bitten off and spit out when mention was made of US Attorney General Robert Kennedy, who was still on the trail of Marcello:

'"Livarsi na petra di la scarpa!" Carlos shrilled the Mafia cry of revenge: "Take the stone out of my shoe!"

'"Don't worry about that little Bobby son of a bitch," he shouted. "He's going to be taken care of!"

'Ever since Robert Kennedy had arranged for his deportation to Guatemala, Carlos had wanted revenge. But as the subsequent conversation . . . showed, he knew that to rid himself of Robert Kennedy he would first have to remove the President. Any killer of the Attorney General would be hunted down by his brother; the death of the President would seal the fate of his Attorney General.

'No one at the meeting had any doubt about Marcello's intentions when he abruptly arose from the table. Marcello did not joke about such things. In any case, the matter had gone beyond mere "business"; it had become an affair of honor, a Sicilian vendetta. Moreover, the conversation at Churchill Farms also made clear that Marcello had begun to plan a move. He had, for example, already thought of using a "nut" to do the job.

'Roughly 1 year later President Kennedy was shot in Dallas – 2 months after Attorney General Robert Kennedy had announced to the McClellan Committee that he was going to expand his war on organized crime. And it is perhaps significant that privately Robert Kennedy had singled out James Hoffa, Sam Giancana, and Carlos Marcello as being among his chief targets.'

Becker told the House Committee that '"Marcello was very angry" and had "clearly stated that he was going to arrange to have President Kennedy murdered in some way"; and that Marcello's statement had been made in a serious tone and sounded as if he had discussed it previously to some extent. Becker commented that Marcello had made some kind of a reference to President Kennedy's being a dog and Attorney General Robert Kennedy the dog's tail, and had said "the dog will keep biting you if you only cut off its tail", but that if the dog's head were cut off, the dog would die.

'Becker stated that Marcello also made some kind of reference to the way in which he allegedly wanted to arrange the President's murder. Marcello "clearly indicated" that his own lieutenants must not be identified as the assassins, and that there would thus be a necessity to have them use or manipulate someone else to carry out the actual crime.'

The House Committee specifically noted that 'as a consequence of his underworld involvement', Edward Becker 'had a questionable reputation for honesty and may not be a credible source of information'.

On the other hand, the House Committee commented that Jose Aleman, who testified to a similar event involving Santos Trafficante, 'appeared to be a reputable person, who did not seek to publicize his allegations, and he was well aware of the potential danger of making such allegations against a leader of La Costa Nostra'.

Trafficante, it will be remembered, had such good business ties to the anti-Castro Cuban exile community that the CIA had used him as their contact man for their Castro assassination plots. Jose Aleman was described by the Committee as 'a prominent Cuban exile'.

Aleman told the House Committee's investigators that in September 1962, Santos Trafficante met with him relative to financial difficulties Aleman was then experiencing. A relative of Aleman's had helped someone get out of a Cuban jail, and Trafficante in return was offering to arrange a loan from the Teamsters for Aleman. In the course of this meeting, Trafficante was 'talking of the many problems in the country and of Kennedy's role in causing problems generally and in particular causing problems for certain individuals'. Speaking to a Cuban exile in late 1962, Trafficante may have had good reason to believe that it was sympathetic ears which heard him assert that 'a lot of people weren't going to forget the problems Kennedy had caused them, including Hoffa. [. . .] Trafficante brought up Jimmy Hoffa's name and said Hoffa would never forgive the Kennedys for what they did to him.'

When Trafficante began to talk in specifics, Aleman at first thought Trafficante was talking about knocking Kennedy off in the next election. So Trafficante, 'trying to make Aleman realize that he was not saying Kennedy would be defeated in the 1964 election, rather that he would not make it to the election, said: ". . . You don't understand me. Kennedy's not going to make it to the election. He is going to get hit". [. . .]

'Aleman stated that during the course of the discussion, Trafficante had made clear to him that he was not guessing that the President was going to be killed. Rather he did in fact know that such a crime was being planned . . . [and] . . . Trafficante had given him the distinct impression that Hoffa was to be principally involved in the elimination of Kennedy.'

The House Committee relates that, 'On 9 November 1963 an informant for the Miami police, William Somersett, secretly recorded a conversation with a right-wing extremist named Joseph A. Milteer, who suggested there was a plot in existence to assassinate the President with a high-powered rifle from a tall building. Miami Police intelligence officers met with Secret Service agents on 12 November and provided a transcript of the Somersett recording. It read in part:

Somersett: I think Kennedy is coming here 18 November to make some kind of speech. I don't know what it is, but I imagine it will be on TV.

Milteer: You can bet your bottom dollar he is going to have a lot to say about the Cubans; there are so many of them here.

Somersett: Well, he'll have a thousand bodyguards, don't worry about that.

Milteer: The more bodyguards he has, the easier it is to get him.

Somersett: Well, how in the hell do you figure would be the best way to get him?
Milteer: From an office building with a high-powered rifle.

Somersett: They are really going to try to kill him?
Milteer: Oh, yeah; it is in the working.

Somersett: Hitting this Kennedy is going to be a hard proposition. I believe you may have figured out a way to get him, the office building and all that. I don't know how them Secret Service agents cover all them office buildings everywhere he is going. Do you know whether they do that or not?
Milteer: Well, if they have any suspicion, they do that, of course. But without suspicion, chances are they wouldn't.'

'During the meeting at which the Miami Police Department provided this transcript to the Secret Service, it also advised the Secret Service that Milteer had been involved with persons who professed a dislike for President Kennedy and were suspected of having committed violent acts, including the bombing of a Birmingham, Alabama, church in which four young girls had been killed. They also reported that Milteer was connected with several radical right-wing organizations and traveled extensively throughout the United States in support of their views. [. . .]

'[T]he information gathered "was furnished [to] the agents making the advance arrangements before the visit of the President" [to Miami on 18 November 1963]. PRS [Protective Research Section] then closed the case, and copies of its report were sent to the Chief of Secret Service and to field offices in Atlanta, Philadelphia, Indianapolis, Nashville, Washington, and Miami.

'The Milteer threat was ignored by Secret Service personnel in planning the trip to Dallas. PRS Special Agent-in-Charge Bouck, who was notified on 8

November that the President would visit Miami on 18 November, told the Committee that relevant PRS information would have been supplied to the agents conducting advance preparations for the scheduled trip to Miami, but no effort was made to relay it to Special Agent Winston G. Lawson, who was responsible for the trip to Dallas, or to Forrest Sorrels, Special Agent-in-Charge of the Dallas office. Nor were Sorrels or any Secret Service agent responsible for intelligence with respect to the Dallas trip informed of the Milteer threat before 22 November 1963.'

As part of its examination of the evidence, the House Committee discussed the following fascinating episode. On 20 November 1963, 'a woman known as Rose Cheramie, a heroin addict and prostitute with a long history of arrests, was found . . . lying on the road near Eunice, Louisiana, bruised and disoriented'. Cheramie was taken to a private hospital in Eunice, treated for minor abrasions, and the police were called.

Francis Fruge, a lieutenant with the Louisiana State Police, responded. Though the woman needed no further medical care, she appeared to be under the influence of drugs, so Fruge took her to the jail and put her in a cell to sober up. However, as the woman began to display severe symptoms of withdrawal, Fruge called a doctor, who sedated the woman, and Fruge proceeded to transport her to the State hospital in Jackson, Louisiana.

During the trip to Jackson, Fruge asked Cheramie some 'routine' questions. Fruge told the Committee, '"She related to me that she was coming from Florida to Dallas with two men who were Italians or resembled Italians. They had stopped at this lounge . . . and they'd had a few drinks and had gotten into an argument or something. The manager of the lounge threw her out and she got on the road and hitchhiked to catch a ride, and this is when she got hit by a vehicle." Fruge said the lounge was a house of prostitution called the Silver Slipper.

'Fruge asked Cheramie what she was going to do in Dallas: "She said she was going to, number one, pick up some money, pick up her baby, and to kill Kennedy."

'Fruge claimed during these intervals that Cheramie related the story she appeared to be quite lucid.' He had her admitted to the hospital late on 20 November.

While in the hospital, Cheramie reportedly told a Dr Bowers before the assassination 'that President Kennedy was going to be killed'; and after the assassination she reportedly told a Dr Weiss that 'she had worked for Jack Ruby', and that while 'she did not have any specific details of a particular assassination plot against Kennedy . . . the "word in the underworld" was that Kennedy would be assassinated. [. . .]

'On 22 November, when he heard the President had been assassinated, Fruge said he immediately called the hospital and told them not to release Cheramie until he had spoken to her. The hospital administrators assented but said Fruge would have to wait until the following Monday before Cheramie would be well enough to speak to anyone. Fruge waited.

'Under questioning, Cheramie told Fruge that the two men traveling with her from Miami were going to Dallas to kill the President. For her part, Cheramie was to obtain $8,000 from an unidentified source in Dallas and proceed to Houston with the two men to complete a drug deal. Cheramie was also supposed to pick up her little boy from friends who had been looking after him.

'Cheramie further supplied detailed accounts of the arrangement for the drug transaction in Houston. She said reservations had been made at the Rice Hotel in Houston. The trio was to meet a seaman who was bringing in 8 kilos of heroin to Galveston by boat. Cheramie had the name of the seaman and the boat he was arriving on. Once the deal was completed, the trio would proceed to Mexico.

'Fruge . . . contacted the chief customs agent in Galveston who reportedly verified the scheduled docking of the boat and the name of the seaman. Fruge believed the customs agent was also able to verify the name of the man in Dallas who was holding Cheramie's son. Fruge recalled that the customs agent had tailed the seaman as he disembarked from the boat, but then lost the man's trail. Customs closed the case. [. . .]

'During a flight from Houston, according to Fruge, Cheramie noticed a newspaper with headlines indicating investigators had not been able to establish a relationship between Jack Ruby and Lee Harvey Oswald. Cheramie laughed at the headline, Fruge said. Cheramie told him she had worked for Ruby, or "Pinky", as she knew him, at his nightclub in Dallas and claimed Ruby and Oswald "had been shacking up for years". Fruge said he called Captain Will Fritz of the Dallas Police Department with this information. Fritz answered, he wasn't interested. Fritz and the Louisiana State Police dropped the investigation into the matter.

'Four years later, however . . . during the course of the New Orleans DA's investigation . . . Fruge attempted to corroborate the version she had given him [as to how she had ended up by the side of the road, and the number and identity of her companions]. Fruge spoke with the owner of the Silver Slipper Lounge. The bar owner, a Mr Mac Manual . . . told Fruge that Cheramie had come in with two men who the owner knew as pimps engaged in the business of hauling prostitutes in from Florida. When Cheramie became intoxicated and rowdy, one of the men "slapped her around" and threw her outside.

'Fruge claims he showed the owner of the bar a "stack" of photographs and mug shots to identify. According to Fruge, the bar-owner chose the photos of a Cuban exile, Sergio Arcacha Smith, and another Cuban Fruge believed to be named Osanto.'

In 1961, Arcacha Smith had befriended David Ferrie and both were believed to have ties with Carlos Marcello. Arcacha Smith moved from the New Orleans area in 1962 to go to Miami and later to settle in

Houston. The weekend following the assassination, Ferrie took a trip to Houston and *Galveston* for a little 'rest and relaxation'.

The House Committee informs us that in Chicago, on 21 November 1963, Thomas Mosley, an FBI informant, had a conversation with 'a Cuban exile, an outspoken critic of President Kennedy named Homer S. Echevarria'. Mosley 'for some time . . . had been involved in negotiating the sale of illegal arms' with Echevarria. On 21 November, 'Echevarria had said his group now had "plenty of money" and that they were prepared to proceed with the purchases "as soon as we [or they] take care of Kennedy". [. . .]

'. . .Echevarria was a member of the 30th of November (Cuban exile) Movement . . . an associate of his who had also spoken directly with Mosley about the arms sales was Juan Francisco Blanco-Fernandez, military director for the Cuban Student Revolutionary Directorate (DRE), and that the arms purchases were being financed through Paulino Sierra Martinez, a Cuban exile who had become a Chicago lawyer. Mosley inferred from his conversation with Echevarria and Blanco that Sierra's financial backers consisted in part of "hoodlum elements" who were "not restricted to Chicago". [. . .]

'The Committee found that the 30th of November Movement was receiving financial backing through the Junta del Gobierno de Cuba en el Exilio (JGCE), a Chicago-based organization led by Sierra. JGCE was essentially a coalition of predominantly right-wing anti-Castro groups. It had been formed in April 1963 and abolished abruptly in January 1964. During its short life, JGCE apparently acquired enormous financial backing, secured at least in part from organized gambling interests in Las Vegas and Cleveland. JGCE actively used its funds to purchase large quantities of weapons and to support its member groups in conducting military raids on Cuba. The affiliates of JGCE, in addition to the 30th of November Movement, included Alpha 66, led by Antonio Veciana Blanch, and the MIRR, whose leader was the militant anti-Castro terrorist, Orlando Bosch Avila. [. . .]

'Bosch was interviewed by the Committee in Cuartel San Carlos prison in Venezuala. He is charged with complicity in the 6 October 1975 bombing of a Cuban Airlines plane which resulted in the deaths of 73 people . . . Whether or not Bosch was the principal conspirator in the bombing of the Cuban airliner, it is known that his Cuban Power movement, which merged with other Cuban activists in 1976 to form a Cuban Secret Government, engaged in acts of terrorism. This latter group was linked with numerous recent bombing incidents, an assassination attempt against Henry Kissinger, the assassination of Orlando Letelier in Washington, DC, and the bombing of the Cuban Airlines plane.'

BOOK 4

CHAPTER

29

The Assassin's Assassin

At 12.30 p.m., 22 November 1963, as the President's open limousine proceeded at approximately 11 m.p.h along Elm Street through Dealey Plaza toward the Triple Underpass, shots fired from a rifle mortally wounded President Kennedy. At 1.22 p.m. a rifle was found in the Texas School Book Depository which subsequently was identified as being owned by Lee Harvey Oswald, but by that time Oswald was already in custody. In the meantime, Oswald was involved in what has been described as his escape.

The Warren Report stated: 'The possibility that accomplices aided Oswald in connection with his escape was suggested by the testimony of Earlene Roberts, the housekeeper at the 1026 North Beckley roominghouse. She testified that at about 1 p.m. on 22 November, after Oswald had returned to the roominghouse, a Dallas police car drove slowly by the front of the 1026 North Beckley premises and stopped momentarily; she said she heard its horn several times.' Oswald hurriedly left the house, and a few seconds later, shortly after 1 p.m., she saw him standing at a bus stop in front of the house. However, the bus did not go to where the scene of action now shifted.

About a mile away, at approximately 1.15 p.m., patrolman J. D. Tippit was driving east on 10th Street. About 100 feet past Patton Avenue he stopped his vehicle and spoke to Lee Harvey Oswald, who then approached the car and engaged in some conversation with Tippit. Tippit got out and started to walk around the front of the car. As Tippit reached the left front wheel, Oswald pulled out a revolver and shot Tippit dead. About a half-hour later, Oswald was arrested while sitting in the Texas Theater.

Two days later, as Oswald was being brought through the basement of the Dallas Police Station to be transferred to the county jail, Jack Ruby shot and killed Lee Harvey Oswald. Ruby would later explain that he had killed Oswald to spare Jackie Kennedy from having to return for Oswald's trial.

Perhaps Ruby's concern for Jackie was the reason he killed Oswald. However, there is evidence which points to the more troubling possibility that Ruby's role was to shut Oswald's mouth (as we saw in the Joe Columbo assassination and the Victor Reisel blinding, discussed in Chapter 21).

If this second scenario is correct, two of the questions which immediately follow are:

For whom was Ruby acting? and, Was Ruby the only one who had been given the task of getting rid of Oswald?

The House Select Committee investigated and reported on a number of intriguing relationships of Jack Ruby.

Since 14 October, the very same day on which Ruth Payne called Roy Truly at the Texas School Book Depository, Lee Harvey Oswald had been living at Earlene Roberts' home in the Oak Cliff section of Dallas, and maintaining a Post Office box at the terminal annex. Coincidentally enough, Jack Ruby also lived in the Oak Cliff section of Dallas and had a Post Office box at the terminal annex. A fellow boarder at Oswald's roominghouse, John Carter, was friendly with a close friend and employee of Ruby, Wanda Killam. Bertha Cheek, the sister of Oswald's landlady, visited Jack Ruby at his nightclub on 18 November 1963.

Jack Ruby's closest friend, to whom he spoke every day, was Ralph Paul. Ruby was constantly indebted to Paul for loans to operate his nightclubs, and Paul actually held a half interest in the Carousel until early 1964. Ruby became friendly with a good friend of Paul's, Austin Cook, a member of the ultra-conservative John Birch Society, and the owner of Austin's Barbeque. For about three years prior to the assassination, Cook had been employing a moonlighting Dallas policeman as a security guard at Austin's Barbeque. The policeman's name was J. D. Tippett.

Tippit's tie-in to friends of Jack Ruby would seem to permit at least the speculative query: Was Tippit's contact with Oswald shortly after the assassination merely a chance encounter, or did Tippit have a mission which Oswald sensed and reacted to?

As noted earlier, there is evidence that in the summer of 1963, Jack Ruby had placed a call to Chicago to Lenny Patrick, who was said to be 'one of the Chicago Mafia's leading assassins, responsible, according to Federal and State law enforcement files, for the murders of over a dozen mob victims'. Patrick was not the only unsavory character to whom Ruby spoke.

The House Committee undertook an extensive study of Ruby's telephone activity, from which the following excerpts are taken.

'A chronological consolidation of the telephone calls made by [Jack] Ruby from the five separate business and home telephones he used uncovered a significant increase in the number of calls made in October and November 1963. The average number leapt from around 25 to 35 in the months of May through September to approximately 75 in October and approximately 96 during the first 3½ weeks of November. [. . .]

'An extensive computer analysis of his telephone toll

records for the month prior to the President's assassination revealed that he either placed calls to or received calls from a number of individuals who may be fairly characterized as having been affiliated, directly or indirectly, with organized crime. These included Irwin Weiner, a Chicago bondsman well-known as a frontman for organized crime and the Teamsters Union; Robert "Barney" Baker, a lieutenant of James R. Hoffa and associate of several convicted organized crime executioners; Nofio J. Pecora, a lieutenant of Carlos Marcello, the Mafia boss in Louisiana; Harold Tannenbaum, a New Orleans French Quarter nightclub manager who lived in a trailer park owned by Pecora; McWillie, the Havana gambler; and Murray "Dusty" Miller, a Teamster deputy of Hoffa and associate of various underworld figures. [. . .]

'Between June and August of 1963, Jack Ruby placed seven long distance calls to Lewis J. McWillie . . . In 1959, Ruby had visited Lewis McWillie in Havana, where McWillie was working in an organized crime-controlled casino. Jack Ruby's phone calls to McWillie occurred on 27 June, 2 September (two calls), 4 September, 19 September, 20 September and 22 September. The first two calls were placed to McWillie's home number, the remaining five calls were to McWillie's place of business, the Thunderbird Casino in Las Vegas. [. . .]

'On the afternoon of 26 October 1963, Jack Ruby placed a long distance phone call to Irwin S. Weiner in Chicago, with whom he spoke for 12 minutes. Weiner was and is a prominent bondsman in Chicago, who has been closely linked with such figures as James Hoffa, Santos Trafficante, Sam Giancana, Paul and Allen Dorfman. Weiner, according to Federal and State law enforcement files, is alleged to have served as a key functionary in the longtime relationship between the Chicago Mafia and various corrupt union officials, particularly during Hoffa's reign as President of the Teamsters Union. Additionally, Weiner has been involved in a business relationship with two men long identified as executioners for the Chicago Mafia – Felix "Phil" Alderisio and Albert "Obie" Frabotta. [. . .]

'At 9.13 p.m., 30 October 1963, 4 days after his call to Irwin Weiner, Jack Ruby placed a call to the Tropical Court Tourist Park, a trailer park in New Orleans. The number Ruby called, 242–5431, was listed as the business office of the Tropical Court, and the duration of the call was one minute. In a partial compilation of numbers called by long distance by Ruby, transmitted to the Warren Commission by the FBI in early 1964, a notation was made indicating that this Ruby call to the Tropical Court went to N. J. Pecora. The Warren Commission did not, however, interview or investigate Pecora and made no mention of him in its Report.

'Nofio J. Pecora, alias Joseph O. Pecoraro, was the owner of the Tropical Court Tourist Park. He ran the park from a one-man office located on the premises, the office Ruby had called on 30 October. Pecora, a former heroin smuggler, was alleged to be a close associate of Carlos Marcello. The FBI, Justice Department, and Metropolitan Crime Commission of New Orleans have identified Pecora as one of Marcello's three most trusted aides. Law enforcement surveillance reports have indicated a particularly close Marcello-Pecora relationship during the early 1960s, with Pecora always close at hand at Marcello's Town and Country Motel headquarters on the outskirts of New Orleans.

'On 7 November 1963 Ruby received a collect call from Robert G. (Barney) Baker of Chicago. The call lasted 17 minutes. Baker is said to have been a top lieutenant and reputed "enforcer" for Teamster President James Hoffa. A former boxer and ex-convict, Baker was perhaps Hoffa's best known assistant during the McClellan Committee investigation of labor racketeering in the late 1950s. The Senate investigation, coordinated by then chief counsel Robert F. Kennedy, had detailed Baker's role as Hoffa's personal liaison to various leading Mafia figures. In his McClellan testimony, Baker recited a long list of Mafia hit men with whom he had been associated. In 1960, Robert F. Kennedy wrote of Baker, "Sometimes the mere threat of his presence in a room was enough to silence the men who would otherwise have opposed Hoffa's reign." [. . .]

'On 8 November 1963, the day after he received the call from Barney Baker, Ruby placed a call to Murray W. (Dusty) Miller at the Eden Roc Hotel in Miami. The call lasted four minutes. Dusty Miller was another key lieutenant of Teamster President James Hoffa, and as head of the powerful southern conference of the union, he was regarded as a possible successor to Hoffa. Miller, who had been a Teamster leader in Dallas, was associated with numerous underworld figures. [. . .]

'At 5.22 p.m., 8 November 1963, 31 minutes after he called Dusty Miller, Jack Ruby placed a call to Barney Baker in Chicago. This call lasted 14 minutes. [. . .]

'The Committee found that the evidence surrounding the calls was generally consistent – at least as to the times of their occurrence – with the explanation that they were for the purpose of seeking assistance in a labor dispute. Ruby, as the operator of two nightclubs, the Carousel and the Vegas, had to deal with the American Guild of Variety Artists (AGVA), an entertainers' union. Ruby did in fact have a history of labor problems involving his striptease performers, and there was an ongoing dispute in the early 1960s regarding amateur performers in Dallas area nightclubs. Testimony to the Committee supported the conclusion that Ruby's phone calls were, by and large, related to his labor troubles. In light of the identity of some of the individuals, however, the possibility of other matters being discussed could not be dismissed.

'In particular, the Committee was not satisfied with the explanations of three individuals closely associated with organized crime who received telephone calls from Ruby in October or November 1963.

'Weiner, the Chicago bondsman, refused to discuss his call from Ruby on 26 October 1963 with the FBI in 1964, and he told a reporter in 1976 that the call had nothing to do with labor problems. In his executive session testimony before the Committee, however, Weiner stated that he had lied to the reporter, and he claimed that he and Ruby had, in fact, discussed a labor dispute. The Committee was not satisfied with Weiner's explanation of his relationship with Ruby. Weiner suggested Ruby was seeking a bond necessary to obtain an injunction in his labor troubles, yet the Committee could find no other creditable indication that Ruby contemplated seeking court relief, nor any other explanation for his having to go to Chicago for such a bond.

'Barney Baker told the FBI in 1964 that he had received only one telephone call from Ruby (on 7 November 1963) during which he had curtly dismissed Ruby's plea for assistance in a nightclub labor dispute. The Committee established, however, that Baker received a second lengthy call from Ruby on 8 November. The Committee found it hard to believe that Baker, who denied the conversation ever took place, could have forgotten it.

'The Committee was also dissatisfied with the explanation of a call Ruby made on 30 October 1963, to the New Orleans trailer park office of Nofio J. Pecora, the long-time Marcello lieutenant. Pecora told the Committee that only he would have answered his phone and that he never spoke with Ruby or took a message from him. The Committee considered the possibility that the call was actually for Harold Tannenbaum, a mutual friend of Ruby and Pecora who lived in the trailer park, although Pecora denied he would have relayed such a message.

'Additionally, the Committee found it difficult to dismiss certain Ruby associations with the explanation that they were solely related to his labor problems. For example, James Henry Dolan, a Dallas AGVA representative, was reportedly an acquaintance of both

Carlos Marcello and Santos Trafficante. While Dolan worked with Ruby on labor matters, they were also allegedly associated in other dealings, including a strong-arm attempt to appropriate the proceeds of a one-night performance of a stage review at the Adolphus Hotel in Dallas called *Bottoms Up*. The FBI, moreover, has identified Dolan as an associate of Nofio Pecora. The Committee noted further that reported links between AGVA and organized crime figures have been the subject of Federal and State investigations that have been underway for years. The Committee's difficulties in separating Ruby's AGVA contacts from his organized crime connections was, in large degree, based on the dual roles that many of his associates played. [. . .]

'According to FBI records, AGVA has been used frequently by members of organized crime as a front for criminal activities.

'In assessing the significance of these Ruby contacts, the Committee noted, first of all, that they should have been more thoroughly explored in 1964 when memories were clearer and related records (including, but not limited to, additional telephone toll records) were available. Further, while there may be persuasive arguments against the likelihood that the attack on Oswald would have been planned in advance on the telephone with an individual like Ruby, the pattern of contacts did show that individuals who had the motive to kill the President also had knowledge of a man who could be used to get access to Oswald in the custody of the Dallas police. In Ruby, they also had knowledge of a man who had exhibited a violent nature and who was in serious financial trouble. The calls, in short, established knowledge and possible availability, if not actual planning.'

The House Committee reported that it had 'also investigated the relationship between Ruby and the Dallas Police Department to determine whether members of the department might have helped Ruby get access to Oswald for the purpose of shooting him. Ruby had a friendly and somewhat unusual relationship with the Dallas Police Department, both collectively and with individual officers, but the Committee found little evidence of any significant influence by Ruby within the force that permitted him to engage in illicit activities. Nevertheless, Ruby's close relationship with one or more members of the police force may have been a factor in his entry to the police basement on 24 November 1963.

'Both the Warren Commission and a Dallas Police Department investigative unit concluded that Ruby entered the police basement on 24 November 1963, between 11.17 a.m., when he apparently sent a telegram, and 11.21, when he shot Oswald, via the building's Main Street ramp as a police vehicle was exiting, thereby fortuitously creating a momentary distraction. The Committee, however, found that Ruby probably did not come down the ramp, and that his most likely route was an alleyway located next to the Dallas Municipal Building and a stairway leading to the basement garage of police headquarters.

'The conclusion reached by the Warren Commission that Ruby entered the police basement via the ramp was refuted by the eyewitness testimony of every witness in the relevant area, only Ruby himself excepted. It was also difficult for the Committee to reconcile the ramp route with the 55-second interval (derived from viewings of the video tapes of the Oswald murder) from the moment the police vehicle started up the ramp and the moment Ruby shot Oswald. Ruby would have had to come down the ramp after the vehicle went up, leaving him less than 55 seconds to get down the ramp and kill Oswald. Even though the Warren Commission and the Dallas police investigative unit were aware of substantial testimony contradicting the ramp theory, they arrived at their respective conclusions by relying heavily on Ruby's own assertions and what they perceived to be the absence of a plausible alternative route.

'The Committee's conclusion that Ruby entered from the alley was supported by the fact that it was much less conspicuous than the alternatives, by the lack of security in the garage area and along the entire route, and by the testimony concerning the security of the doors along the alley and stairway route. This route would also have accommodated the 4-minute interval from Ruby's departure from a Western Union office near police headquarters at 11.17 a.m. to the moment of the shooting at 11.21.'

The House Committee declared that, 'Based on a review of the evidence, albeit circumstantial, the Committee believed that Ruby's shooting of Oswald was not a spontaneous act, in that it involved at least some premeditation. Similarly, the Committee believed that it was less likely that Ruby entered the police basement without assistance, even though the assistance may have been provided with no knowledge of Ruby's intentions. The assistance may have been in the form of information about plans for Oswald's transfer or aid in entering the building or both.

'The Committee found several circumstances significant in its evaluation of Ruby's conduct. It considered in particular the selectively recalled and self-serving statements in Ruby's narration of the events of the entire 22–24 November weekend in arriving at its conclusions. It also considered certain conditions and events.

'The Committee was troubled by the apparently unlocked doors along the stairway route and the removal of security guards from the area of the garage nearest the stairway shortly before the shooting; by a Saturday night telephone call from Ruby to his closest friend, Ralph Paul, in which Paul responded to something Ruby said by asking him if he was crazy; and by the actions and statements of several Dallas police officers, particularly those present when Ruby was initially interrogated about the shooting of Oswald.

'There is also evidence that the Dallas Police Department withheld relevant information from the Warren Commission concerning Ruby's entry to the scene of the Oswald transfer. For example, the fact that a polygraph test had been given to Sergeant Patrick Dean in 1964 was never revealed to the Commission, even though Dean was responsible for basement security and was the first person to whom Ruby explained how he had entered the basement. Dean indicated to the Committee that he had "failed" the test, but the Committee was unable to locate a copy of the actual questions, responses and results.

'The Committee noted that other Ruby activities and movements during the period immediately following the assassination – on 22 and 23 November – raised disturbing questions. For example, Ruby's first encounter with Oswald occurred over 36 hours before he shot him. Ruby was standing within a few feet of Oswald as he was being moved from one part of police headquarters to another just before midnight on 22 November. Ruby testified that he had no trouble entering the building, and the Committee found no evidence contradicting his story. The Committee was disturbed, however, by Ruby's easy access to headquarters and by his inconsistent accounts of his carrying a pistol. In an FBI interview on 25 December 1963, he said he had the pistol during the encounter with Oswald late in the evening of 22 November. But when questioned about it by the Warren Commission, Ruby replied, "I will be honest with you. I lied about it. It isn't so, I didn't have a gun."

'Finally, the Committee was troubled by reported sightings of Ruby on Saturday, 23 November, at Dallas police headquarters and at the county jail at a time when Oswald's transfer to the county facility had originally been scheduled. These sightings, along with one on Friday night, could indicate that Ruby was pursuing Oswald's movements throughout the weekend.'

'The Committee also questioned Ruby's self-professed motive for killing Oswald, his story to the Warren Commission and other authorities that he did it out of sorrow over the assassination and sympathy for the President's widow and children. Ruby consistently claimed that there had been no other motive and that no one had influenced his act. A handwritten note by Ruby, disclosed in 1967, however, exposed Ruby's explanation for the Oswald slaying as a fabricated legal ploy. Addressed to his attorney, Joseph Tonahill, it told of advice Ruby had received from his first lawyer, Tom Howard, in 1963: "Joe, you should know this. Tom Howard told me to say that I shot Oswald so Caroline and Mrs Kennedy wouldn't have to come to Dallas to testify. OK?"'

'The Committee examined a report that Ruby was at Parkland Hospital shortly after the fatally wounded President had been brought there on 22 November 1963. Seth Kantor, a newsman then employed by Scripps-Howard who had known Ruby, later testified to the Warren Commission that he had run into him at Parkland and spoken with him shortly before the President's death was announced. While the Warren Commission concluded that Kantor was mistaken, the Committee was impressed by the opinion of Burt W. Griffin, the Warren Commission counsel who directed the Ruby investigation and wrote the Ruby section of the Warren report. Griffin told the Committee he had come to believe, in light of evidence subsequently brought out, that the Commission's conclusion about Kantor's testimony was wrong.'

Subsequent to Ruby's apprehension, he was given a polygraph examination. There is general agreement by everyone who has reviewed the test (Warren Commission,

FBI, House Committee) that it was unsatisfactorily administered. However, while unable to interpret the test as an overall piece, the panel retained by the House Committee did observe – contrary to what had been concluded in 1964 – that, because it produced the largest valid GSR reaction together with a constant suppression, Ruby was possibly lying when he answered 'No' to the question 'Did you assist Oswald in the assassination?'

The Committee noted several other areas of telephone contact or relationship of probative interest. Of note is the fact that they are not likely to be explainable on the basis of Ruby's labor problems.

'The Committee found that Barney Baker had placed a telephone call to another onetime associate of Jack Ruby on the evening of 21 November 1963. The person Baker called was David Yaras of Miami. Yaras was a close friend and partner of Lenny Patrick. He had also been acquainted with Ruby during their early years in Chicago. Like Lenny Patrick, Dave Yaras has served, it is alleged, as a key lieutenant of Chicago Mafia leader Sam Giancana, reputedly as an executioner.'

The Committee also found that shortly before midnight on 21 November 1963, Jack Ruby had drinks at the Cabana Motel with Jean Aase West, and a mutual friend, Lawrence Meyers. The Committee further found that, while in Chicago on 24 September 1963, Miss West had received a 15-minute telephone call from an 'investigator' working for New Orleans Mafia boss, Carlos Marcello.

The man who placed that call to Chicago, to this person who was in Dallas with Ruby on the eve of the assassination, was the staunch anti-Communist, anti-Castro activist who had once been Oswald's CAP squadron leader, the man who only weeks before this call had been with Oswald in Clinton, Louisiana – David Ferrie.

BOOK 4

CHAPTER

30

The Rosetta Stone

The overwhelming and conclusive evidence is that President John F. Kennedy had at least two sets of bitter enemies within the US, each of which had the means, motive and opportunity to assassinate him; and each of which had an unbroken history demonstrating absolutely no reluctance to the use of force. The evidence is inescapable that these two groups – organized crime and anti-Castro Cuban exiles – owed their very existence to their continued use of violence.

That is not to say that all members of organized crime or all anti-Castro Cuban exiles were involved in the Kennedy assassination. No such finding is warranted – or necessary.

However, the proof is that important elements from each group were involved in very specific planning to murder the President.

Importantly, those very same elements had a common bond, having been united (to provide their unique services) by the CIA, some of whose agents secretly continued to encourage their projects long after being ordered to stop them.

The evidence is, to say the least, abundant that the

CIA, and indeed all of the American intelligence community including the FBI, routinely utilized what can only be described as a motley group of people to perform various services for them. Here in our own little story we find that Congressional investigations have identified the following people to have been involved with American intelligence: Yuri Nosenko, a KGB officer; Richard E. Snyder, consular officer in the US Embassy in Moscow; Dr Alexis H. Davidson, US Embassy physician in Moscow; George de Mohrenschildt, friend of Oswald; John Rosselli, Mafia; Sam Giancana. Mafia; Santos Trafficante, Mafia; Guy Banister, anti-Castro activist; Sergio Arcacha Smith, anti-Castro activist; Antonio Veciana Blanch, anti-Castro activist; Homer S. Echevarria, anti-Castro activist; and Orlando Bosch Avila, anti-Castro activist, amongst others.

Even if one rejects the implication pointed to in this book that Oswald was himself an American intelligence agent, it seems unarguable that he was not the loner he has been made out to be, and that he was associated with people who were, at the least, involved on the periphery of American intelligence.

As the Kennedy years proceeded, the Mafia and the anti-Castro activists – who might be forgiven for believing that their CIA activities had earned them the right to be ignored – instead found themselves more and more the primary targets of relentless and unmerciful campaigns instigated and prosecuted by the Kennedy administration.

Given the fact that these were people who truly existed both by and for violence, it should not be surprising that certain elements of these deadly enemies of the President might see his assassination as the answer to their problems.

Those who challenge the official findings by questioning whether Oswald pulled the trigger are probably missing the central issue, for even if he did (as the proof suggests), the more important point is that the evidence also rather strongly indicates that he was the designated 'nut', specifically chosen to be identified and then eliminated.

If we eliminate Jack Ruby's alleged reason for killing Oswald (the lawyer-inspired 'protect Jackie'), we are left in our search for his motive with the evidence of Ruby's mob background and associates – that, and our common sense.

Indeed, the question of Ruby's motive may well be the 'Rosetta Stone' of the Kennedy assassination, for if Ruby was acting for others, those others had to have a reason to want Oswald eliminated.

Those who are satisfied with a 'non-conspiratorial' explanation for Ruby's rub-out of Oswald will probably have wasted their time reading this book. Those who remain unsatisfied with such a seemingly illogical rationalization might, it is hoped, have had their interest piqued by the material discussed in this book and might, it is further hoped, contribute their own thoughts towards a general rethinking of this web.

SOURCES

Warren Report *Report of the President's Commission on the Assassination of President John F. Kennedy*, published by the US Government Printing Office (1964).

Assassinations *Alleged Assassination Plots Involving Foreign Leaders*, conducted by the Select Committee to Study Governmental Operations with respect to Intelligence Activities, United States Senate, published by the US Government Printing Office (1975).

Senate Select *Investigation of the Assassination of President John F. Kennedy*, conducted by the Senate Select Committee to Study Governmental Operations with Respect to Intelligence Activities, United States Senate, published by the US Government Printing Office (1976).

House Select *Investigation of the Assassination of President John F. Kennedy*, conducted by the Select Committee on Assassinations of the US House of Representatives, published by the US Government Printing Office (1979).

DOCUMENTS

INVESTIGATION OF THE ASSASSINATION OF PRESIDENT JOHN F. KENNEDY

HEARINGS

BEFORE THE

SELECT COMMITTEE ON ASSASSINATIONS

OF THE

U.S. HOUSE OF REPRESENTATIVES

NINETY-FIFTH CONGRESS

SECOND SESSION

SEPTEMBER 27, 28, AND DECEMBER 29, 1978

VOLUME V

Printed for the use of the Select Committee on Assassinations

U.S. GOVERNMENT PRINTING OFFICE

35-379 O   WASHINGTON : 1979

For sale by the Superintendent of Documents, U.S. Government Printing Office
Washington, D.C. 20402
Stock Number 052-070-04907-3

plete than that of the FBI or the Warren Commission in 1963 and 1964. It is also fair to comment that had this sort of investigation taken place at that time when the evidence was fresh, it is possible, though hardly a sure thing, that a lot more information might have been forthcoming. But the committee must face this fact. The question of organized crime involvement is still and open one. Nothing that has been uncovered excludes it and much that is new points toward it. Yet frustration may be the result of this committee's efforts too.

To address the issues raised by this frank recognition of the possibility of ultimate frustration and comment on the investigation of the Warren Commission and this committee, as well as the future, the committee has invited the Hon. Burt W. Griffin to appear here today. Judge Griffin was an assistant counsel for the Warren Commission. As such, he shared responsibility for the investigation of Jack Ruby and the shooting of Lee Harvey Oswald. Judge Griffin received a B.A. cum laude from Amherst College in 1954 and an LL.B. degree from Yale in 1959. Judge Griffin has served as the Director of the Cleveland Office of Economic Opportunity, Legal Service Program, as well as the Director of the Legal Aid Society.

In January 3, 1975, he was appointed judge of the Court of Common Pleas of Cuyahoga County, Ohio. It would be appropriate at this time, Mr. Chairman, to call Judge Griffin.

Chairman STOKES. Judge, I ask you to stand, please, and be sworn. Do you solemnly swear the testimony you will give before this committee is the truth, the whole truth and nothing but the truth, so help you God?

Judge GRIFFIN. I do.

Chairman STOKES. Thank you, you may be seated.

Judge Griffin, it is a real pleasure to welcome you here. Mr. Blakey, Judge Griffin happens to be not only a long-time close friend, but one of Cleveland's most distinguished jurists. We welcome you here this afternoon, Judge.

TESTIMONY OF JUDGE BURT W. GRIFFIN, FORMER ASSISTANT COUNSEL FOR THE WARREN COMMISSION AND JUDGE OF THE COURT OF COMMON PLEAS, CUYAHOGA COUNTY, OHIO

Judge GRIFFIN. Mr. Chairman, and my good friend, Louis Stokes. Let me say it is a pleasure for me to be here before your committee. I say it with only one reservation, and I think, Mr. McKinney, this may bring back some memories to you because the last time that I had an opportunity to appear before this committee in executive session, I was about an hour late because I found deficiencies in the Metro transportation system. Last night, your committee was very kind and offered to spare me that indignity and sent Mr. Mathews with Mr. Blakey's car to the airport to pick me up.

I regret to say that when we got out to Mr. Blakey's car, it didn't work. And I found myself behind the car trying to push Mr. Mathews to get it started. So I would suggest that if there are any other areas of investigation for this committee to undertake that there might be some in the field of transportation.

Mr. EDGAR. Would the gentleman yield at that point?

Chairman STOKES. The gentleman is recognized.

Mr. EDGAR. As a very strong advocate of public transit, I think the Metro system is getting better, and I would suggest if you are ever in that predicament again, you might try using it. I have been to the gentleman's city of Cleveland and you have a very fine public transit system. I hope we can have those fine systems throughout the Nation.

Judge GRIFFIN. I thank you, Mr. Edgar, for the advice, and I am sure that I will consider it seriously.

Let me say in seriousness, that the purpose of my remarks is to discuss with the committee the question of what is the proper process for investigating political murders that have national implications. That is what I would like to reflect upon in these minutes with the committee.

I propose to begin that inquiry with a brief discussion of what I perceive to have been the goals of the Warren Commission and the Warren Commission's successes and failures. And I would like to end with some suggestions for dealing with future political murders.

It is a sad thing to think about, but I think we cannot escape the honest judgment that we will have in this country, political murders in the future and we will, I am sorry to say, in all probability, have Presidents who are assassinated in the future. So that I think more important than attempting to reach a conclusion as to how President Kennedy happened to be killed and why and who all may have participated in that, as important as that inquiry is, the real questions are not for the past, but the real questions for this committee are for the future.

The Warren Commission was designed primarily to achieve four goals. First, to establish the true facts surrounding the assassination of President Kennedy and the murder of Lee Harvey Oswald. Second, to accomplish that mission in a manner that would satisfy the broadest segment of influential people and the American public in general. Third, to do it in a manner that would not unnecessarily disrupt the stability of the national government and its conduct of international affairs or jeopardize the national security. And, fourth, to conduct this inquiry in a manner that would avoid damaging the reputations or employment of individuals against whom there did not exist convincing evidence of criminal conduct.

Those goals were not in every respect stated by the Commission, but I believe that they indeed were the goals of the Commission, and I think that the first two goals, that is, of finding the truth and, second, of accomplishing that investigation in a manner that would be persuasive, were actually articulated in the official Commission documents.

The third goal, that is the one that related to the stability of the National Government and the problems of national security, was communicated by the President of the United States to Chief Justice Warren.

The fourth goal, that being a civil libertarian goal, although it may not have been articulated in any official documents, was, in fact, the philosophy of Chief Justice Warren, as I had the opportunity to witness his conduct of the Warren Commission.

In a rather brief manner, I would like to summarize the reasons for these goals, and I will be brief because I think that the reasons are obvious, but it is perhaps worth mentioning them.

President Kennedy's death was surrounded with suspicions of conspiratorial intrigue that could easily have fed efforts at domestic and international turmoil. If the suspicions were true, there would be a need for serious corrective action, but if the suspicions were unfounded and were not abated, the mere suspicions could provide strong weapons in the hands of individuals who desired to manipulate public opinion and power for unjustified ends.

The Warren Commission began its inquiry on the very heels of one of the most unfortunate eras in American political history. It was what we all look back upon now as the McCarthy era. And the conduct of investigations into matters of internal security during that period cast not only a blot upon the conduct of senatorial committees, but of congressional committees as well, and I think that we—many of us, if not a vast majority of us—look back upon that period with a great deal of embarrassment and sorrow.

There was another period which none of us is old enough to remember where the same kind of political ambitions based upon unfounded suspicions and fears brought the United States into war, and that is the period of the Spanish-American War, which has been well documented and the role that irresponsible newspaper people had to play in the creation of that war is well known to any student of history. So that the fears about the inability to find the truth and to document it in a persuasive manner were not inconsiderable or insubstantial ones, as far as the members of the Warren Commission were concerned.

And it was important that a reliable body be established to investigate and report honestly the facts that surrounded the murder of Lee Harvey Oswald and of President Kennedy in order to minimize the possibility of such disastrous consequences.

At the outset of the Warren Commission's activities, speed seemed to be an important element in the Commission's operations. Initially, the White House informed the Commission that it should complete its work and make its report prior to the national political conventions that were scheduled for the summer of 1964. The emphasis on speed stemmed from the early perceptions of this problem that I have been alluding to—preventing the unnecessary disruption of public policy and political power.

At the outset, the timetable seemed reasonable, but as the scope of the investigation became apparent, such a deadline became obviously unrealistic. The goal of speed came into conflict with the goal of completeness, for many of the suspicions, which the obvious facts generated, could not be explored fully in the 5 months that were originally projected for the Warren Commission's investigation.

In retrospect, it seems to me that speed was not the political necessity that the White House originally envisioned. The Warren report was itself not issued until late September 1964, and I reflected as I came here today that I believe that today or tomorrow is the 14th anniversary of the issuance of that report. This was, of course, after both the Republican and Democratic national conventions had nominated their candidates for President. And the issue of the assassination of President Kennedy never became an issue in that Presidential election campaign.

At no time prior to the report's issuance did any Member of Congress attempt to use the uncertainties of the assassination to oppose Johnson administration policies. So long as the Commission was operating, the White House, in fact, achieved its goal of preventing the uncertainties that surrounded the assassination from interfering with its own conduct of public policy. I believe that the initial emphasis on speed reflected the recollections which I have made of McCarthyism which were still vivid to President Johnson and members of the Commission when we began our work in early 1964.

I would like to turn at this point then to discuss the question of how the Commission came to terminate its investigation. Pressure for a quick report was not, in my experience, what induced the Commission to curtail its investigation of areas that are now a public concern and under investigation by this committee. The reasons for stopping the investigation by the Warren Commission were that to anyone with substantial criminal investigatory experience, and you must remember that Chief Justice Warren had been the prosecutor of Alameda County for 20 years before he became Governor of the State of California, to anyone with such investigative experience, the evidence seemed overwhelming that Oswald was the assassin and the conspiracy questions that remained were entirely speculative. They were based upon political or underworld acquaintanceships but devoid of any concrete evidence on any participation in a murder or in the planning of a murder.

As a practical matter, the Commission leadership decided not to pursue further the various speculative theories on conspiracy unless two things could be found. First, unless they could find substantial evidence that a specific suspected conspirator had had personal contact with Lee Oswald or Jack Ruby during the period when that person could have counseled or assisted Oswald or Ruby in the events of November 21–23, 1963.

And second, and the two would have to go together, unless there was some evidence that such suspected conspirator desired to kill President Kennedy or was involved in a common political activity with Lee Harvey Oswald.

Although the criteria that I have mentioned were not applied at the beginning of any line of inquiry so as to stop an exploration of at least a minimal sort at the beginning, they were applied after months of investigation in deciding to close out a particular line of inquiry. It was believed by the Commission's leadership that any further investigation not so founded would require an in-depth probing of the life of any possible conspirator. The mere act of continuing to investigate such individuals, would be a form of accusation that could severly injure innocent people. It seemed unwarranted to conduct such an in-depth investigation merely upon speculation that a conspiratorial link might exist. The cost and length of such investigation seemed immense.

The likelihood of success seemed remote and the possible infringement of civil liberties seemed serious.

Those two criteria, I might point out, also became the standards that the Commission ultimately used for concluding that "no evidence," the famous and much maligned language of the Commission report, that no evidence of any conspiracy had been found. The committee, in my opinion, Mr. Stokes, must seriously consider in reaching its own conclusions whether or not it is proper to depart from the standard of proof that I suggest was followed by the Warren Commission and whether it is proper to apply those standards in making its own judgments as to how far to continue any investigation.

I would like then, with that background, to turn to what I believe to be the successes and failures of the Warren Commission.

The overriding short-term political objective of President Johnson in establishing the Warren Commission was achieved. That is, the determination of public policy was not substantially affected by the uncertainties of the assassination and no member of Congress or political opponent of President Johnson was able to mobilize public sentiment through manipulation of fears that grew out of these uncertainties.

Second, the factfinding goal of the Warren Commission was partially, if not substantially, achieved. The Commission developed an extensive body of information about the assassination and related events. That information not only formed the basis of the Commission's conclusion but has provided, up to this committee's commencement of its investigation, the most solid evidence upon which the Commission's critics have relied. Almost no probative evidence bearing upon the identity of participants in the murders has been uncovered by the legions of Warren Commission critics. No witness, unknown at the time of the original investigation, has come forward with information showing that any specific person assisted or encouraged either Oswald or Ruby in their murders. The most significant newly discovered information has been that evidence in the possession of governmental agencies was deliberately withheld from the Warren Commission. If that evidence had been provided to the Commission, I personally have no doubt that our investigation, that is the investigation of the Warren Commission, would have been extended substantially.

And I would like to point out a major success which Warren Commission critics tend largely to ignore. That is, that the civil liberties of Americans were conscientiously protected by the Commission and the Commission did not become an official witch hunt that destroyed the reputations and lives innocent citizens. That success resulted both from the manner in which the Commission conducted its inquiry and from the standards that it applied in deciding to terminate the inquiry. This is a success, Mr. Chairman, which I believe the select committee should recognize and would do well to applaud, lest that accomplishment be forgot.

However, it must be recognized that a decision to terminate governmental investigation also unleashed a private witch hunt, and the committee must evaluate that byproduct.

Let me turn next to what I believe were the failures of the Warren Commission. It is clear that the Warren Commission failed to prevent the assassination from becoming a long-term political issue.

I distinguish here between an issue that remains of public curiosity, such as one might say would be an issue concerning the assassination of President Lincoln at this stage, and between that kind of issue and an issue that actually affects in a substantial way the time, money, and decisions of public policy and public officials.

A second failure, and a glaring failure, was its inability, the Commission's inability, to gain full cooperation from the investigative agencies.

The committee, I know, has carefully examined the areas in which the CIA, the FBI, and the Dallas Police Department failed to provide candid and, I might say, loyal assistance to the Warren Commission, and I will not attempt to go into those.

The third failure of the Commission relates to this problem of cooperation with investigative agencies. It is the use by the Commission of liaison personnel from other agencies.

In retrospect, Mr. Chairman, I believe that the Commission needed its own staff presence on the premises of the FBI, CIA, and the Dallas Police Department, with unrestricted access to their files, and with freedom to speak privately and without approval to any employee of each agency.

Instead, the FBI and the CIA established their own liaison personnel at the Commission offices. All contacts with the FBI and CIA personnel were cleared, first through agency channels of those agencies, and the agent's reports were reviewed by their supervisors before being forwarded to the Commission.

There was, I think, at least a middle ground that the Commission might have adopted in hindsight. The investigative staffs of those agencies might have been assigned to the Commission and controlled by the Commission and the Commission then might have made the decision as to how it would keep the agencies advised of the Commission's progress, as it, the Commission deemed appropriate.

I think there was also a failure by the Warren Commission of investigative tactics. The style of the Commission's own staff was in retrospect not fully one of criminal investigators. The rules that governed the staff discouraged off the record conversations with witnesses and emphasized almost exclusively transcribed depositions. Transcribed depositions did not lend themselves to candor, if the deponent feared that this candor could injure him.

The Commission itself failed to utilize the instruments of immunity from prosecution or prosecution for perjury with respect to witnesses whose veracity it doubted.

In each case, the failure to have any of its own staff stationed within the agencies, the system of agency-Commission communications, the failure to employ its own staff investigators, and the restraints on Commission interviewing techniques, and the reluctance to use immunity grants and perjury prosecutions, the Commission chose an investigatory course that would cause the least damage to individual citizens and to existing public agencies. I believe that is the reason that the Commission chose that approach.

There was a belief among the Commission leadership that the investigatory approaches which were rejected were likely to produce more resistance than truth from public agencies and that the possibility of success by those rejected methods was outweighted by the possible unjustified injury to individual citizens and existing governmental operations.

You must remember, Mr. Chairman, that in those days we trusted the various agencies of Government with whom we dealt, much more than we trust them now.

At no time, however, despite these investigatory techniques did those limitations ever prevent a Commission staff member from making an inquiry that he believed was relevant. The consequence, nonetheless, was the Commission was powerless to combat deliberate deceit by an investigative agency.

A fifth difficulty or failure, as I look back upon the Warren Commission, evolved from the difficulties of conducting a conspiracy investigation through a special commission. The investigatory techniques that the Commission utilized were in fact the standard investigatory techniques of the Federal Bureau of Investigation at that time and were reasonably suited to an investigation which depended on testimony from independent witnesses who generally desired to tell the truth.

The primary investigatory approach utilized by the FBI in connection with the murders of President Kennedy and Lee Harvey Oswald was directly and immediately to confront a witness or a suspect with questions. This approach, of course, was important to preserving the memory of an honest witness, but for a possible coconspirator it largely served to keep any possible conspirators fully appraised of the ongoing investigations.

To my knowledge, in that period, the FBI never established a list of possible conspirators with either Jack Ruby or Lee Oswald, and if it had such a list, it never placed them under surreptitious investigation, or if it did so, the existence and nature of such investigations was certainly never revealed to me, and I had responsibility for investigating Jack Ruby.

Nor was there any indication that the FBI in that period used its own agents in an undercover capacity under any circumstances, or pursued the practice in that period of our history of infiltrating suspect groups, except through paid informants.

Indeed, it was my experience as an Assistant U.S. attorney in the years of 1960, 1961, and 1962, that J. Edgar Hoover strongly opposed using his own employees in an undercover capacity. By contrast, during that same period of time, the U.S. Secret Service did have its own employees trained to investigate counterfeiting by undercover means. I think a comparison of the two agencies during that period of time would reveal that the Secret Service had been much more successful in investigating counterfeiting conspiracies than the FBI had been against organized crime.

The FBI fully used its standard investigatory techniques for approximately 2 months before any member of the Warren Commission was able to initiate his own investigation. That 2-months delay substantially undermined the ability of the Commission to investigate a conspiracy.

First, obviously all tracks were cold and any conspirator had 2 months to flee or hide.

Second, all possible suspects and conspirators had ample time to learn what direction the Government's investigation was taking.

All in all, I want to thank all persons who had anything to do with the way in which we were able to present these hearings. It is particularly important to me, and I think all members of this committee, to have the American people understand the nature of the undertaking this committee has undertaken, has; in our opinion, from the very beginning been a very serious undertaking. We were all determined these hearings would not be conducted in any kind of a circus atmosphere, they would have all of the professionalism of the House of Representatives behind them, they would be done professionally and competently. The Chair feels that has been accomplished and I appreciate the cooperation that we have received from everyone in being able to perform our work in that manner.

Thank you, and at this time, I will ask Judge Preyer if he will assume the Chair.

Mr. PREYER [now presiding]. Well, I hope the rest of the afternoon won't be anticlimactic after the Chairman's statement.

Have a good trip, Mr. Chairman, you have earned it.

Chairman STOKES. Thank you.

Mr. PREYER. Judge Griffin, we appreciate your statement, your deeply thoughtful statement. I think you went well beyond just talking about the facts of the Warren Commission study and the facts of this Commission's study and you have got into the question of the meaning of it, and you have talked to us about the meaning of criminal law and political murders and uses of history. It is certainly a stimulating paper.

We have one historian, at least, who is a member of this panel, and the Chair at this time would recognize Mr. Fithian.

Mr. FITHIAN. Thank you, Mr. Chairman and, judge, we welcome you to the committee hearings today, and you have given us some very thoughtful food for thought, recommendations, some of which I suspect we won't be able to carry out but some we will.

I have two or three categories of things I would like to explore with you, and I think rather than just ask for continuance of time repeatedly, I would like to take one of those areas first and then after others have had their chance to ask questions, perhaps I could get additional time.

I want now to go directly to the policy questions and policy recommendations that you make, which are large, I would like to return to those, but in 5 minutes before the second set of bells ring, I would like to explore some specific questions that come out of your testimony.

First, on your preliminary draft, which I went over last night, and repeated today, you indicated that certain things might have been done differently had you known certain kinds of information. Now, for your information, it seems to me as one member of this committee that upon occasion and sometimes even frequently the two agencies that we questioned most carefully, the CIA and the FBI, frequently excused themselves for not giving information to the Warren Commission by saying something like this—"we gave them whatever they asked for." But if the Warren Commission didn't know of its existence, the question logically arises, how could they ask for it.

And when we talked to the Warren Commission members, including the President, the former President, and J. Lee Rankin, we seemed to get that refrain, we couldn't ask for something we didn't know existed. It reminds me ever so much of the chicken and egg dilemma that we get into sometimes in life.

But assuming that at some future date some other commission, some other group, some other time, might be faced with the same kind of problem for a political assassination, could you make any specific recommendations as to how we could break that at the outset institutionally or structurally?

Judge GRIFFIN. Well, you are talking specifically, I presume, about the failure of the CIA to reveal that they had supported, as I understand the evidence, actually initiated attempts to assassinate Premier Castro?

Mr. FITHIAN. That is one example. There are other lesser lights in the discussion.

Judge GRIFFIN. Certainly I think that is the most troublesome one.

I don't know what your evidence is as to what the President knew. I think that decision has to be made at the highest level, and I think that unless the President himself was kept ignorant, and I believe that the Attorney General has to be considered in this case, since he was the brother of the President, it strikes me that when you have a situation that seems to indicate, and I think it is a question that you must develop the facts on, that the decision may have been made at that level to keep information from the Commission. I don't think there is anything we can do about it.

Mr. FITHIAN. You don't think there is anything that the Commission could do about it?

Judge GRIFFIN. No; as far as what we do about that situation in the future, I think you are going to stumble onto that information.

Incidentally, I think, as I understand the evidence before this Commission, Allen Dulles, I believe, was privy to that information and did not convey it to the rest of the Commission members.

I would rather answer the question this way: I think it might be legitimate to keep that information from a commission provided within the governmental process there was an assurance that the President knew that there was a complementary investigation going on and that ultimately all of that information would be preserved and come to light. I am troubled even by that kind of suggestion.

Mr. FITHIAN. Yes.

Judge GRIFFIN. But I recognize that if it had been known in 1964 that the CIA was attempting to assassinate Fidel Castro, I think the possibilities were very great in that period that pressures would have been brought in this country to begin a war against Cuba which might have had implications that would have brought this country into a thermonuclear war with the Soviet Union.

Those are frightening consequences and I have frankly myself wondered whether the reason Chief Justice Warren said to us that our investigation had those implications, was that something that had been communicated to him by the President in that regard.

But I think in the long run if that decision is made and if made by a responsible official, that that is what is crucial, if it were

Do you have any indication that your findings would have been different——

Judge GRIFFIN. I think that our findings——

Mr. FITHIAN. After 15 years?

Judge GRIFFIN. I would make this observation. I think our findings on Oswald's motive would have been different, and this is a question that I don't hear discussed very often, but I happen to believe it is a very important question, because I think if an analysis of the evidence indicates that the greatest possibility is that Oswald was motivated to do this because he was aware through his so-called underground, or whatever you want to call these sources, grassroots sources, that the CIA was involved in an assassination to murder, in plot to murder President Kennedy, then it becomes clear that the motive for the assassination was supplied by this activity of the CIA, and that raises a very vital question of public policy, and if that were to be the conclusion of this committee, it would have implications that would go beyond these particular events that you are studying.

So I think we would have had to pursue that. We frankly ducked, I think, everybody who has read the report knows, we ducked the question of motive. I do not think we could have ducked the question of motive under those circumstances.

Mr. FITHIAN. Are you satisfied with regard to the question of motive or the testimony that, the information that has come about and been reiterated time and again, that Lee Harvey Oswald's most likely motive for pulling the trigger was because he was mentally or psychologically bent in the direction of trying to become somebody important?

Judge GRIFFIN. Yes; I think that is a factor, but that does not explain why he selected President Kennedy or why he did it when he did. I mean, we know, I think many of us accepted this point, that Oswald attempted to assassinate General Walker. What motivated Oswald at that particular time to select Walker?

If Oswald in November of 1963, with all his personality problems, with the sense of total inadequacy that was being given him by his wife, was then in such a psychological state that he was prepared to pull another General Walker, it might not have been President Kennedy he might have gone after someone else and, therefore, it becomes very important that something, that perhaps that the U.S. Government did is what supplied the impetus to select President Kennedy rather than some other person.

Mr. FITHIAN. I have one more minor matter, then I would like to ask a policy recommendation question.

You use the word, very powerful words on page 12, of the consequences, nonetheless, that the Commission was powerless to combat, and you used the word "deliberate deceit by an investigative agency."

Judge GRIFFIN. Yes, sir.

Mr. FITHIAN. Can you give me any indication, is that your conclusion, it was deliberate deceit?

Judge GRIFFIN. I think the CIA deliberately deceived the Warren Commission, based on evidence that I have seen. I think the answer that they have given that they didn't provide the information because nobody asked them is the kind of statement I get from criminal defendants time in and time out, presiding over ordinary trials, and I think it is patent to me.

The FBI conducted, I think the Hosty incident, I am satisfied it was deliberate and not accidental, although that we did find out about. I am not familiar with what you have found out as far as withholding of information by the FBI so I wouldn't really comment upon anything beyond what happened in the Hosty episode.

Mr. FITHIAN. Finally, you make a very fervent plea for open hearings, open investigations, procedures in public, et cetera.

Judge GRIFFIN. At some point.

Mr. FITHIAN. Given the emotions of the 1963 and 1964 period, when you were working with the Warren Commission, is it not probable that the Warren Commission really couldn't have conducted a public hearing at that time?

Judge GRIFFIN. I think that merits very serious consideration. I think, as I reflect upon my state of trauma and what I think was the state of trauma of this country, even when the Commission came out, the Commission's report came out, it may be that with an event of that magnitude at that time, so close to the events, that a proper judgment is under those circumstances that there cannot be any public hearings.

I would think, however, that if one focused on the question in an intense way there would still be a way to structure public hearings that could avoid the trauma and could preserve the ultimate visual record for presentation at another time.

Mr. FITHIAN. Thank you, Judge.

I recognize the gentleman from Connecticut, Mr. McKinney.

Mr. McKINNEY. Judge, let me assure you our subway is running better and better everyday.

Judge GRIFFIN. Thank you, Mr. McKinney.

Mr. McKINNEY. Good to see you.

We have discussed these points before and they will be in the record. So, very briefly, I gather you are suggesting that this committee come forth with almost a body of Federal law that would set up a certain line to follow in the case of any public assassination?

Judge GRIFFIN. Mr. McKinney, I don't know whether legislation is needed in this area. I am inclined to believe that a recommendation from this committee that would be implemented administratively by the executive branch might deal with a lot of the problems and might in fact be a preferred way to do it, because I do think there has to be flexibility, and when you write a statute you are frozen for a long time.

But I think, for example, the recommendation I made about continuing this investigation in some way through the Justice Department, even after this committee ceases to operate, is one that could be implemented, and I think the further suggestion that a responsibility of the Justice Department should be to create a game plan which could be immediately implemented in the event of a future assassination. I think that could be implemented and those things could be done without legislation.

Mr. McKINNEY. I think one of the problems that we have had, in retrospect, relates to the trauma of the times. It would seem to me that we need to set up some sort of a pattern as to what must happen in a sequence.

INVESTIGATION OF THE ASSASSINATION
OF PRESIDENT JOHN F. KENNEDY

HEARINGS

BEFORE THE

SELECT COMMITTEE ON ASSASSINATIONS

OF THE

U.S. HOUSE OF REPRESENTATIVES

NINETY-FIFTH CONGRESS

SECOND SESSION

SEPTEMBER 22, 25, AND 26, 1978

VOLUME IV

Printed for the use of the Select Committee on Assassinations

U.S. GOVERNMENT PRINTING OFFICE
WASHINGTON : 1979

41-373 O

For sale by the Superintendent of Documents, U.S. Government Printing Office
Washington, D.C. 20402

Stock Number 052-070-04906-5

-JFK Exhibit F-534-

15

Department of State

35

Action
PPT
Info
L
INR
EUR
P
CU
SCMC
TSIA
SCS
SY
DCL
IRC
CIA
OSD
NAVY
(J)

Control: 20261
Rec'd: OCTOBER 31, 1959
7:59 A.M.

FROM: MOSCOW

TO; Secretary of State

NO: 1304, OCTOBER 31, 1 P.M.

FOR PG

LEE HARVEY OSWALD, UNMARRIED AGE 20 PP 1733242 ISSUED SEPT 10, 1959 APPEARED AT EMB TODAY TO RENOUNCE AMERICAN CITIZENSHIP, STATED APPLIED IN MOSCOW FOR SOVIET CITIZENSHIP FOLLOWING ENTRY USSR FROM HELSINKI OCT 15. MOTHER'S ADDRESS AND HIS LAST ADDRESS US 4936 COLLINWOOD ST., FORT WORTH TEXAS. SAYS ACTION CONTEMPLATED LAST TWO YEARS. MAIN REASON "I AM MARXIST". ATTITUDE ARROGANT AGGRESSIVE. RECENTLY DISCHARGED MARINE CORPS. SAYS HAS OFFERED SOVIETS ANY INFORMATION HE HAS ACQUIRED AS ENLISTED RADAR OPERATOR.

IN VIEW PETRULLI CASE WE PROPOSE DELAY EXECUTING RENUNCIATION UNTIL SOVIET ACTION KNOWN OR DEPT ADVISES. DESPATCH FOLLOWS. PRESS INFORMED.

FREERS

JR

CONFIDENTIAL

JFK Exhibit F-534

REPORT

OF THE

SELECT COMMITTEE ON ASSASSINATIONS
U.S. HOUSE OF REPRESENTATIVES

NINETY-FIFTH CONGRESS

SECOND SESSION

———

FINDINGS AND RECOMMENDATIONS

———

MARCH 29, 1979.—Committed to the Committee of the Whole House
on the State of the Union and ordered to be printed

———

U.S. GOVERNMENT PRINTING OFFICE

43–112 O   WASHINGTON : 1979

four-man assassination team, although he claimed to remember Vallee's name in connection with a 1963 Chicago case. (67) He did not recognize Vallee's photograph when shown it by the committee. (68)

The questionable authenticity of the Bolden account notwithstanding, the committee believed the Secret Service failed to make appropriate use of the information supplied it by the Chicago threat in early November 1963.

Similarly, the Secret Service failed to follow up fully on a threat in Miami, also in November 1963. On November 9, 1963, an informant for the Miami police, William Somersett, had secretly recorded a conversation with a rightwing extremist named Joseph A. Milteer, who suggested there was a plot in existence to assassinate the President with a high-powered rifle from a tall building. (69) Miami Police intelligence officers met with Secret Service agents on November 12 and provided a transcript of the Somersett recording. (70) It read in part:

> SOMERSETT. I think Kennedy is coming here November 18 to make some kind of speech. I don't know what it is, but I imagine it will be on TV.
>
> MILTEER. You can bet your bottom dollar he is going to have a lot to say about the Cubans; there are so many of them here.
>
> SOMERSETT. Well, he'll have a thousand bodyguards, don't worry about that.
>
> MILTEER. The more bodyguards he has, the easier it is to get him.
>
> SOMERSETT. What?
>
> MILTEER. The more bodyguards he has, the easier it is to get him.
>
> SOMERSETT. Well, how in the hell do you figure would be the best way to get him?
>
> MILTEER. From an office building with a high-powered rifle.

*   *   *   *   *   *   *

> SOMERSETT. They are really going to try to kill him?
> MILTEER. Oh, yeah; it is in the working.

*   *   *   *   *   *   *

> SOMERSETT. * * * Hitting this Kennedy is going to be a hard proposition. I believe you may have figured out a way to get him, the office building and all that. I don't know how them Secret Service agents cover all them office buildings everywhere he is going. Do you know whether they do that or not?
>
> MILTEER. Well, if they have any suspicion, they do that, of course. But without suspicion, chances are that they wouldn't.

During the meeting at which the Miami Police Department provided this transcript to the Secret Service, it also advised the Secret Service that Milteer had been involved with persons who professed a dislike for President Kennedy and were suspected of having committed violent acts, including the bombing of a Birmingham, Ala., church in which four young girls had been killed. They also reported that Milteer was connected with several radical rightwing organizations and traveled extensively throughout the United States in support of their views. (71)

Although it would have been possible to read Milteer's threats as hollow speculation, the Secret Service did not dismiss them lightly. The case agent in the Miami office forwarded a report and a recording of the Somersett-Milteer conversation to the Protective Research Section.(72) Robert I. Bouck, special agent in charge of PRS, then requested that the Miami office make discreet inquiries about Milteer.(73)

On November 18, 1963, Special Agent Robert Jamison of the Miami Secret Service office, in an interview with Somersett, had him place a telephone call to Milteer at his home in Valdosta, Ga., to verify he was in that city.(74) In addition, Jamison learned that Somersett did not know the identity of any violence-prone associates of Milteer in the Miami area.(75) The November 26 Miami field office report indicated that the information gathered "was furnished the agents making the advance arrangements before the visit of the President * * *."(76) PRS then closed the case, and copies of its report were sent to the Chief of Secret Service and to field offices in Atlanta, Philadelphia, Indianapolis, Nashville, Washington, and Miami.(77)

The Milteer threat was ignored by Secret Service personnel in planning the trip to Dallas. PRS Special Agent-in-Charge Bouck, who was notified on November 8 that the President would visit Miami on November 18, told the committee that relevant PRS information would have been supplied to the agents conducting advance preparations for the scheduled trip to Miami,(78) but no effort was made to relay it to Special Agent Winston G. Lawson, who was responsible for preparations for the trip to Dallas,² or to Forrest Sorrels, special agent-in-charge of the Dallas office. Nor were Sorrels or any Secret Service agent responsible for intelligence with respect to the Dallas trip informed of the Milteer threat before November 22, 1963.(80)

Following the assassination, Somersett again met with Milteer. Milteer commented that things had gone as he had predicted. Somersett asked if Milteer actually had known in advance of the assassination or had just been guessing. Milteer asserted that he had been certain beforehand about the inevitability of the assassination.(81)

Bouck and Inspector Thomas Kelley, who was assigned to represent the Secret Service in the investigation of the Kennedy assassination, testified to the committee that threat information was transmitted from one region of the country to another if there was specific evidence it was relevant to the receiving region.(82) The fact was, however, that two threats to assassinate President Kennedy with high-powered rifles, both of which occurred in early November 1963, were not relayed to the Dallas region.

(3) *Inspection of the motorcade route.*—During the Secret Service check of the Dallas motorcade route, Special Agent-in-Charge Sorrels commented that if someone wanted to assassinate the President, it could be done with a rifle from a high building.(83) President

² Lawson, on November 8, visited the PRS office in Washington to check geographical indexes. They revealed no listing of any individual or group that posed a potential danger to the President in the territory of the Secret Service regional office that included Dallas and Fort Worth.(79)

Kennedy himself had remarked he could be shot from a high building and little could be done to stop it. (84) But such comments were just speculation. Unless the Secret Service had a specific reason to suspect the occupants or activities in a certain building, it would not inspect it. (85) The committee found that at the time of the Dallas trip, there was not sufficient concern about the possibility of an attack from a high building to cause the agents responsible for trip planning to develop security precautions to minimize the risk.

The Warren Commission commented that a building survey conducted under a "level of risk" criterion might well have included the Texas School Book Depository. (86) Although the agent in the lead vehicle had some responsibility to scan the route for danger, (87) this would have been woefully inadequate to protect against a concealed sniper. Television films taken in Dallas on November 22, 1963 show foot patrolmen facing the motorcade but not the crowd or the buildings. (88) The police captain in charge of security on the route was not instructed to have his men watch the buildings, although they were ordered to watch the crowds. (89) The committee found that if the threats that the PRS was aware of had been communicated to agents responsible for the Dallas trip, additional precautions might have been taken.[3]

(4) *Performance at the time of the assassination.*—The committee concluded that Secret Service agents in the motorcade were inadequately prepared for an attack by a concealed sniper. Using films and photographs taken of the motorcade at the time of the firing of the shots and immediately thereafter, the committee studied the reactions of Secret Service agents. (96) In addition, the committee questioned agents who had been in the motorcade with respect to their preparedness to react to gunfire.

The committee found that, consistent with the protective procedures and instructions they had been given, (97) the Secret Service agents performed professionally and reacted quickly to the danger. But the committee also found that a greater degree of awareness of the possibility of sniper fire could have decreased reaction time on the part of the agents and increased the degree of protection afforded the President.[4]

No actions were taken by the agent in the right front seat of the Presidential limousine to cover the President with his body, although it would have been consistent with Secret Service procedure for him

[3] The committee's investigation of the Vallee and Milteer threats dealt primarily with the Secret Service response to them. It also, however, investigated any actual connection they might have had with the assassination. In the Vallee case, the committee contacted relatives and his union (90) and visited his most recent known address (91) but was unable to develop additional information. Although Milteer as well as Somersett had since died, the committee did obtain the names and addresses of rightwing associates of Milteer. It found no connection to Oswald or Ruby or their associates. (92) The committee also investigated information that Milteer had called a friend from Dallas on the morning of November 22, 1963, (93) as well as an allegation that Milteer appeared in a photograph of the Presidential motorcade in Dallas. (94) The committee's investigation—which included an analysis of the photograph in question by forensic anthropologists—could find no evidence that Milteer was in Dallas on the day of the assassination. (95) In its investigation, therefore, the committee was unable to find a connection between the threat in Chicago or the threat in Miami with the assassination in Dallas.

[4] The committee, of course, noted that if sniper fire had been expected, the motorcade should have been canceled. The committee learned that instruction received by Secret Service agents in 1978 in responding to a variety of emergency threats and attacks was far more intensive than it was in 1963. (98)

to have done so. (*99*) The primary function of the agent was to remain at all times in close proximity to the President in the event of such emergencies. (*100*) The committee found that the instructions to the driver of the limousine were inadequate to maximize his recognition of, and response to, such emergencies. (*101*) He should have been given the responsibility to react instantaneously on his own initiative and to take evasive action. Instead, his instructions were to act only at the judgment of the agent in the right passenger seat, who had general supervisory responsibilities. (*102*)

The committee found from its acoustical analysis that approximately 8.3 seconds elapsed from the first shot to the fatal head shot. (*103*) Under the circumstances, each second was crucial, and the delay in taking evasive action while awaiting instructions should have been avoided. Had the agents assigned to the motorcade been alert to the possibility of sniper fire, they possibly could have convinced the President to allow them to maintain protective positions on the rear bumper óf the Presidential limousine, and both shielded the President and reacted more quickly to cover him when the attack began. The committee recognized, however, that President Kennedy consistently rejected the Secret Service's suggestions that he permit agents to ride on the rear bumper of the Presidential limousine or permit motorcycles to ride parallel to the limousine and in close proximity to it. (*104*)

Although the conduct of the agents was without firm direction and evidenced a lack of preparedness, (*105*) the committee found that many of the agents reacted in a positive, protective manner. Agent Clint Hill, assigned to protect the First Lady, reacted almost instantaneously. (*106*) Agent Thomas "Lem" Johns left Vice President Johnson's follow-up car in an effort to reach the Vice President's limousine, but he was left behind momentarily in Dealey Plaza as the procession sped away to Parkland Hospital. (*107*) Photographic analysis revealed that other agents were beginning to react approximately 1.6 seconds after the first shot. (*108*)

In reviewing the reactions of the agents, the committee also reexamined the allegation that several had been out drinking the evening before and the morning of the assassination. (*109*) Four of the nine agents alleged to have been involved were assigned to the motorcade and had key responsibilities as members of the President's follow-up car. (*110*) The supervisor of the agents involved advised that each agent reported for duty on time, with full possession of his mental and physical capabilities and was entirely ready to perform his assigned duties. (*111*) Inspector Thomas Kelley, who was in charge of an evaluation of Secret Service performance in the assassination, testified before the committee that an investigation of the drinking incident led to a conclusion that no agent violated any Secret Service rule. (*112*)

In an effort to reach its own conclusion about the drinking incident, the committee reviewed film coverage of the agents' movements at the time of the shooting. The committee found nothing in the reactions of the agents that would contradict the testimony of the Secret Service officials. (*113*)

236

(b) The responsibility of the Secret Service to investigate the assassination was terminated when the Federal Bureau of Investigation assumed primary investigative responsibility.

The committee found that the investigation by the Secret Service after the assassination was terminated prematurely when President Johnson ordered that the FBI assume primary investigative responsibility.*(114)* Although the initial investigative efforts of the Secret Service lacked coordination, individual field offices with information that might have been related to the assassination had started their own investigations and pursued them aggressively.

How the Secret Service responded after the assassination is illustrated by the investigation conducted by the Chicago Secret Service office. After the assassination, the acting special agent-in-charge of the Chicago field office wrote an urgent report indicating he had received reliable information about "a group in the Chicago area who (sic) may have a connection with the JFK assassination."*(115)* This report was based on information received after the assassination from a reliable informant who reported a conversation he had had on November 21, 1963.*(116)* The informant, Thomas Mosley, reported that for some time he had been involved in negotiating the sale of illegal arms with a Cuban exile, an outspoken critic of President Kennedy named Homer S. Echevarria.*(117)* On November 21, Echevarria had said his group now had "plenty of money" and that they were prepared to proceed with the purchases "as soon as we [or they] take care of Kennedy."*(118)*

After receiving the initial report, the Secret Service surveilled subsequent meetings between Mosley and Echevarria,*(119)* received reports from Mosley about the conversations,*(120)* and discussed the progress of the investigation with the local FBI office.*(121)* By December 3, 1963, a fuller picture of Echevarria was obtained *(122)* and reported to the Protective Research Section.*(123)* By that date, it appeared that Echevarria was a member of the 30th of November (Cuban exile) Movement,*(124)* that an associate of his who had also spoken directly with Mosley about the arms sales was Juan Francisco Blanco-Fernandez, military director for the Cuban Student Revolutionary Directorate (DRE),*(125)* [5] and that the arms purchases were being financed through Paulino Sierra Martinez, a Cuban exile who had become a Chicago lawyer.*(126)* Mosley inferred from his conversation with Echevarria and Blanco that Sierra's financial backers consisted in part of "hoodlum elements" who were "not restricted to Chicago." *(127)*

The committee's investigation provided substantial corroboration for the Secret Service's concern about the Mosley allegations. The committee found that the 30th of November Movement was receiving financial backing through the Junta del Gobierno de Cuba en el Exilio (JGCE), a Chicago-based organization led by Sierra. JGCE was essentially a coalition of predominantly right-wing anti-Castro groups.*(128)* It had been formed in April 1963 and abolished abruptly in January 1964.*(129)* During its short life, JGCE apparently acquired enormous financial backing, secured at least in part from

---

[5] As previously noted, the FBI had learned that the Miami-based DRE had a representative in New Orleans, Carlos Bringuier, who had contact with Oswald in the summer of 1963 (see section I C 3 on anti-Castro Cuban exiles).

organized gambling interests in Las Vegas and Cleveland. (*130*) JGCE actively used its funds to purchase large quantities of weapons and to support its member groups in conducting military raids on Cuba. (*131*) The affiliates of JGCE, in addition to the 30th of November Movement, included Alpha 66, led by Antonio Veciana Blanch,⁶ and the MIRR, whose leader was the militant anti-Castro terrorist, Orlando Bosch Avila. (*132*)

The Secret Service recognized the need to investigate the alleged plots by Cuban exile groups more fully, especially that of Echevarria's 30th of November group. (*133*) But when the progress of the investigation was discussed with the FBI, the FBI responded that the 30th of November group was not likely to have been involved in any illegal acts. (*134*) ⁷ The Secret Service initially was reluctant to accept this representation in light of the evidence it had developed that indicated the group was in fact involved in illegal activities, (*137*) and therefore began preparations to place an undercover agent in Echevarria's groups to investigate his activities more closely. (*138*) On November 29, 1963, however, President Johnson created the Warren Commission and gave the FBI primary investigative responsibility. (*139*) Although the Secret Service understood the President's order to mean primary, not exclusive, investigative responsibility, (*140*) the FBI, according to testimony of former Secret Service Chief James J. Rowley and Inspector Thomas J. Kelley, soon made it clear that it did not consider the Secret Service to be an equal collaborator in the post-assassination investigation. Rowley testified that "in the ultimate," there was "no particular jurisdiction" on the part of the Secret Service to cooperate in the post-assassination investigation. (*141*) Inspector Kelley testified that an order came down not only to the Secret Service but to the Dallas Police Department that the FBI would take "full responsibility," (*142*) not joint responsibility, for the postassassination investigation of conspiracies.

In summary, the committee concluded that the Secret Service did in fact possess information that was not properly analyzed and put to use with respect to a protective investigation in advance of President Kennedy's trip to Dallas. Further, it was the committee's opinion that Secret Service agents in the Presidential motorcade in Dallas were not adequately prepared for an attack by a concealed sniper. Finally, the committee found that the investigation by the Secret Service of a possible assassination conspiracy was terminated prematurely when President Johnson ordered that the FBI assume primary investigative responsibility.

2. THE DEPARTMENT OF JUSTICE FAILED TO EXERCISE INITIATIVE IN SUPERVISING AND DIRECTING THE INVESTIGATION BY THE FEDERAL BUREAU OF INVESTIGATION OF THE ASSASSINATION

The position of Attorney General was created by law in 1789, but not until after the Civil War did the role of the chief legal officer of the

---

⁶ See section I C 3 on anti-Castro Cuban exiles.
⁷ As discussed in the section on the FBI investigation, the Bureau's Nationalities Intelligence Section, the most knowledgeable about anti-Castro Cuban exile activities, did not actively participate in the investigation, nor did the Bureau ever fully investigate the question of Cuban involvement. (*135*) After the Secret Service provided the results of its Echevarria investigation to the FBI, the FBI conducted only a limited investigation and closed the case on him. (*136*)

INVESTIGATION OF THE ASSASSINATION OF PRESIDENT JOHN F. KENNEDY

APPENDIX TO HEARINGS

BEFORE THE

SELECT COMMITTEE ON ASSASSINATIONS

OF THE

U.S. HOUSE OF REPRESENTATIVES

NINETY-FIFTH CONGRESS

SECOND SESSION

VOLUME XII

CONSPIRACY WITNESSES IN DEALEY PLAZA
OSWALD-TIPPIT ASSOCIATES
GEORGE de MOHRENSCHILDT
DEPOSITIONS OF MARINA OSWALD PORTER
THE DEFECTOR STUDY
OSWALD IN THE SOVIET UNION: AN INVESTIGATION OF
YURI NOSENKO

MARCH 1979

Printed for the use of the Select Committee on Assassinations

U.S. GOVERNMENT PRINTING OFFICE
43-792   WASHINGTON : 1979

For sale by the Superintendent of Documents, U.S. Government Printing Office
Washington, D.C. 20402

Stock No. 052-070-04983-9

years old.(94) Benavides said the man pulled over in his car "when he heard the scare" but did not get out of the car.(95) He was located about six cars from the police car.(96)

(37)   The committee did not locate any public documents or Warren Commission reports which identified the driver of the red car. However, through investigation in Dallas, the committee did locate and interview a man who said he was at the scene of the Tippit shooting but never came forward with information.

(38)   Committee investigators interviewed Jack Ray Tatum at his office at the Baylor University Medical Center in Dallas on February 1, 1978. Tatum stated that on the afternoon of November 22, 1963, he was driving north on Denver Street and stopped at Tenth Street.(97) At that point he saw a police squad car, and a young white male walking on the sidewalk near the squad car.(98) Both the police car and the young man were heading east on Tenth Street.(99) As Tatum approached the squad car, he saw the young male leaning over the passenger side of the police car with both hands in his zippered jacket.(100) Tatum said that as he drove through the intersection of Tenth and Patton Streets he heard three shots in rapid succession; Tatum said he went through the intersection, stopped his car and turned to look back.(101) At that point he saw the police officer lying on the ground near the front of the police car, with the young male standing near him.(102) Tatum said the man ran toward the back of the police car with a gun in his hand.(103) The man then stepped back into the street and shot the police officer as he was lying on the ground.(104) The man then started to run in Tatum's direction.(105) Tatum said he then sped off in his car and last saw the man running south on Patton toward Jefferson.(106)

XI. Austin's Barbeque

(39)   The FBI interviewed Austin Cook on May 15, 1964. Cook said that he had employed J. D. Tippit at his drive-in, Austin's Barbeque, at 2321 West Illinois in Dallas, for about 3 years at the time of the assassination.(107) Tippit worked on Friday and Saturday nights from 10 p.m. to 2 a.m. at the barbeque as a "deterrent" to any teenage trouble from youths who frequented the establishment.(108) Cook told the FBI that he was a member of the John Birch Society, but that he had never discussed politics with Tippit and did not believe Tippit was interested in politics.(109)

(40)   Cook told the FBI that he never heard Tippit mention Lee Harvey Oswald or Jack Ruby or any of Jack Ruby's clubs.(110) The FBI report of the interview with Cook did not mention whether Cook had any knowledge of or acquaintance with Ruby or Oswald.

(41)   The committee interviewed Cook on March 9, 1978. Cook was asked if he had known Jack Ruby. Cook replied that he may have met Ruby, but he could not recall.(111) He stated further that if he had met Ruby, that would have been the extent of their association. (112)

(42)   In discussing his business, Cook told the committee that he originally went into business in 1946 in a grocery store at Ninth and Jefferson Streets in Dallas.(113) Cook bought the store from a woman

named Bowman. (*114*) Her son, Bert, stayed on at the store for about 6 months after Cook bought it, and Cook and Bert Bowman remained friends for many years. (*115*)

(43) Cook said that he and Bowman became partners in 1950 at a place they named the Bull Pen at 2321 West Illinois. (*116*) That business ended about 1958 when Bowman bought out his share of the establishment and took the name Bull Pen with him. (*117*) Cook then renamed the business Austin's Barbeque. (*118*)

(44) Cook stated that about 8 or 10 years ago, Ralph Paul bought the Bull Pen from Bowman, and Bowman in turn opened Pudnuh's in Arlington, Tex. (*119*)

(45) Bert Bowman's wife was interviewed by FBI Special Agents Robert Lish and David Barry on November 24, 1963. She stated that she had known Ralph Paul since he first moved to Dallas from New York about 1951. (*120*) Mrs. Bowman said that at the time of the assassination, Ralph Paul was living in the lower level of the Bowman home on Copeland Road in Dallas. (*121*) Mrs. Bowman said Ralph Paul was a close friend of Jack Ruby and had been of financial assistance to both Jack Ruby and Bert Bowman over the years. (*122*)

(46) According to Mrs. Bowman, Ralph Paul expressed great concern for his friend Jack Ruby after the shooting of Oswald. (*123*) On November 24, 1963, Paul told Mrs. Bowman that he had spent the whole day at a lawyer's office. (*124*)

(47) Mrs. Bowman said she was not acquainted with any friends of Paul. (*125*) However, on one occasion he brought a woman to the house whom he introduced as Tammy. (*126*) About 4½ years before, Paul had brought Jack Ruby by the house. (*127*) Mrs. Bowman said that Ruby remained for only a short time. (*128*)

(48) On March 9, 1978, committee investigators interviewed Maebert Leolla Cook, the former wife of Austin Cook. Mrs. Cook related that she knew J. D. Tippit when she still worked with her husband at Austin's Barbeque, where Tippit worked as a security guard. (*129*) Mrs. Cook stated further that she did not know either Lee Harvey Oswald or Jack Ruby, but that Ralph Paul was a mutual friend of the Cooks and Jack Ruby. (*130*)

Submitted by:

Ms. SURELL BRADY,
Staff Counsel.

REFERENCES

(*1*) The Warren Commission did, however, request that the FBI conduct a "limited" background investigation on Tippit. That check included interviews of the Tippit family, associates and business acquaintants. The FBI included the results of that check in a report in May 1964. It appeared in the Warren Commission documents as Warren Commission exhibit 2985 (CE 2985).

(*2*) See ref. 1, CE 2985, p. 6.
(*3*) Id. at p. 7.
(*4*) Staff interview of Marie Tippit Thomas, Dec. 8, 1977, House Select Committee on Assassinations, p. 1 (JFK Doc. No. 003988).
(*5*) Id. at p. 2.
(*6*) Id. at p. 1.
(*7*) Ibid.
(*8*) See ref. 1, CE 1974.

INVESTIGATION OF THE ASSASSINATION OF PRESIDENT JOHN F. KENNEDY

APPENDIX TO HEARINGS

BEFORE THE

SELECT COMMITTEE ON ASSASSINATIONS

OF THE

U.S. HOUSE OF REPRESENTATIVES

NINETY-FIFTH CONGRESS

SECOND SESSION

VOLUME X

ANTI-CASTRO ACTIVITIES AND ORGANIZATIONS
LEE HARVEY OSWALD IN NEW ORLEANS

CIA PLOTS AGAINST CASTRO

ROSE CHERAMIE

MARCH 1979

Printed for the use of the Select Committee on Assassinations

U.S. GOVERNMENT PRINTING OFFICE
43-944
WASHINGTON : 1979

For sale by the Superintendent of Documents, U.S. Government Printing Office
Washington, D.C. 20402
Stock No. 052-070-04981-2

INVESTIGATION OF THE ASSASSINATION
OF PRESIDENT JOHN F. KENN

I. THE INGREDIENTS OF AN ANTI-CASTRO CUBAN CONSPIRACY

(9)   Was the John F. Kennedy assassination a conspiracy involving anti-Castro Cuban exiles? The committee found that it was not easy to answer that question years after the event, for two reasons. First, the Warren Commission decided not to investigate further the issue despite the urging of staff counsel involved with that evidence and the apparent fact that the anti-Castro Cuban exiles had the means, motivation, and opportunity to be involved in the assassination.

(10)   In addition, the area of possible Cuban exile involvement was one in which the Warren Commission was not provided with an adequate investigative background. According to the Senate Select Committee on Intelligence:

> (11)   Despite knowledge of Oswald's apparent interest in pro-Castro and anti-Castro activities and top level awareness of certain CIA assassination plots, the FBI . . . made no special investigative effort into questions of possible Cuban Government or Cuban exile involvement in the assassination independent of the Oswald investigation. There is no indication that the FBI or the CIA directed the interviewing of Cuban sources or of sources within the Cuban exile community. (1)

(12)   Nevertheless, even from the paucity of evidence that was available to them in 1964, two staff attorneys for the Warren Commission speculated that Lee Harvey Oswald, despite his public posture as a Castro sympathizer, was actually an agent of anti-Castro exiles. Pressing for further investigation of that possibility, Assistant Counsel William Coleman and W. David Slawson wrote a memorandum to the Commission stating:

> (13)   The evidence here could lead to an anti-Castro involvement in the assassination on some sort of basis as this: Oswald could have become known to the Cubans as being strongly pro-Castro. He made no secret of his sympathies, and so the anti-Castro Cubans must have realized that law enforcement authorities were also aware of Oswald's feelings and that, therefore, if he got into trouble, the public would also learn of them . . . Second, someone in the anti-Castro organization might have been keen enough to sense that Oswald had a penchant for violence . . . On these facts, it is possible that some sort of deception was used to encourage Oswald to kill the President when he came to Dallas . . . The motive of this would, of course, be the expectation that after the President was killed Oswald would be caught or at least his identity ascertained, the law enforcement authorities and the public would then blame the assassination on

(5)

the Castro government and a call for its forceful overthrow
would be irresistible. . . .(2)

(14) It is important in considering the possibility of anti-Castro
Cuban involvement in the Kennedy assassination to recall the political and emotional conditions that affected the Cuban exile communities in Miami, New Orleans, and Dallas while Kennedy was
President.

THE BACKGROUND: THE REGIME OF FIDEL CASTRO RUZ

(15) If it can be said to have a beginning, the anti-Castro Cuban
exile movement was seeded in the early morning hours of New Year's
Day 1959 when a DC-4 lifted from the fog-shrouded Camp Columbia
airfield in Havana.(3) Aboard the plane was Fulgencio Batista, the
military dictator of Cuba for the previous 6 years.(4) Batista was
fleeing the country, his regime long beset by forces from within and
without, now crumbling under pressure from rebel forces sweeping
down from the mountains. When dawn came, the bells tolled in
Havana and, 600 miles away, Fidel Castro Ruz began his triumphal
march to the capital.(5) For seven days Castro and his 26th of July
Movement rebels moved down Cuba's Central Highway while thousands cheered and threw flowers in their path. (6) Castro finally
arrived in Havana on January 8 and characteristically gave a speech.
Clad in his green fatigue uniform while three white doves, which
someone had dramatically released, circled above him, Castro boldly
proclaimed: "There is no longer an enemy!"(7)

(16) That was not true, of course, and he knew it. A hard core of
Batistianos had fled the country early, many long before their leader,
and were already concocting counter-revolutionary plots from their
refuges in the United States, the Dominican Republic and elsewhere.(8)

(17) And it was not very long after Castro took power that a sense
of betrayal began to grow among those who had once been his strongest
supporters.(9) As each day went by it became more apparent that
Castro's revolution was, as one chronicler noted, "leading inexorably
toward an institutionalized dictatorship in which individuals were
contemptuously shorn of their rights and dissenters were met with
charges of treasonable conduct, counterrevolutionary activity or
worse." (10) Then, too, there was a large number of public executions.
Within 2 weeks of his reign, Castro shot 150 ex-Batista officials.(11)
Within 3 months, there were at least 506 executions.(12)

(18) The disillusionment for many Cubans deepened when it became
obvious that the form of Castro's rule was turning toward communism
and that Castro's attitude toward the United States was engendering a
hostile relationship. The publishing of Castro's Agrarian Reform Law
in May 1959, was a significant sign.(13) It was far more radical than
had been expected and was obviously designed to strip both Cuban and
American-owned sugar firms of their immensely valuable cane
lands.(14) A few weeks later the chief of Castro's air force. Maj. Pedro
Diaz-Lanz, resigned, charging "* * * there was Communist influence
in the armed forces and Government."(15) Then, when Castro's own
hand-picked president, Manuel Urrutia. announced at a press conference that he rejected the support of the Communists and said "I believe
that any real Cuban revolutionary should reject it openly," Castro

immediately forced him to resign and accused him of actions "bordering on treason." (16)

(19)   And so, after the broken pledges of free elections and a free press, the mass trials and executions, the assumption of unlimited power and the bellicose threats against the United States, it slowly became apparent to many Cubans that Fidel Castro was not the political savior they had expected. (17)

(20)   Then, on October 19, 1959, there occurred an incident which precipitated the formation of the first organized anti-Castro opposition within Cuba. Maj. Huber Matos, one of Castro's highest ranking officers and considered by most Cubans to be one of the key heroes of the revolution, resigned from the Army in protest against the increasing favoritism shown to known Communists. (18) The next day Matos was arrested, charged with treason, subsequently tried and sentenced to 20 years in prison. Shortly afterward, Castro himself called a secret meeting of the National Agrarian Reform Institute managers at which ·he outlined a plan to communize Cuba within 3 years. (19) There the suspicions of Dr. Manuel Artime, the manager in Oriente Province, were confirmed. "I realized," Artime later said, "that I was a democratic infiltrator in a Communist government." (20)

(21)   Artime returned to Oriente and began organizing students and peasants to fight against Castro and communism. By early November each province in Cuba had an element of Artime's new underground movement. It was called the Movimiento de Recuperación Revolucionaria (MRR). It was the first anti-Castro action group originating from within Castro's own ranks. (21)

(22)   By the summer of 1960, it had become obvious both within and outside of Cuba that the foundation for an eventual confrontation between Castro and anti-Castro forces had been laid. The Eisenhower administration had canceled the Cuban sugar quota. (22) Soviet first deputy chairman, Anastas Mikoyan had visited Havana and Raul Castro had gone to Moscow. (23) Ernesto "Che" Guevara had proclaimed publicly that the revolution was on the road set by Marx, and Allen Dulles of the Central Intelligence Agency had said in a speech that communism had perverted Castro's revolution. (24) By then, Castro had seized more than $700 million in U.S. property within Cuba. (25)

(23)   On March 17, 1960. President Eisenhower authorized the CIA to organize, train and equip Cuban refugees as a guerrilla force to overthrow Castro. (26) Soon it became common knowledge within Cuba that a liberation army was being formed and that a political structure in exile had been created. (27) As the flight from Cuba increased in size and fervor, the exile community in the United States grew in spirit and confidence. One historian captured the special characteristics of the new arrivals:

> They were new types of refugees. Instead of a home, they were seeking temporary asylum. They found it along the sandy beaches and curving coastline of Florida. They arrived by the thousands, in small fishing boats, in planes, chartered or stolen, and crowded into Miami. Along the boulevards, under the palms, and in hotel lobbies, they gathered and plotted their counterrevolution. Miami began to take on the air of a Cuban city. Even its voice was changing. Stores and cafes began advertising in Spanish and English * * *. Everyone talked of home only 100 miles away. And every-

one talked about the great liberation army being formed in
the secret camps somewhere far away. (*28*)

(24) By April 1961, the more than 100,000 Cubans who had fled
Castro's revolution lived in anticipation of its overthrow. They had
been buoyed in that hope by public pronouncements of support from
the U.S. Government. In his state of the Union address, President
Kennedy had spoken of "the Communist base established 90 miles
from the United States," and said that "* * * Communist domination in this hemisphere can never be negotiated."(*29*) In addition, the
Cuban exiles had been organized, directed and almost totally funded
by agencies of the U.S. Government, principally the CIA. (*30*)

(25) From an historical perspective, in light of its later radical
change, the attitude of the Cuban exiles toward the U.S. Government
prior to the Bay of Pigs is especially significant. Author Haynes
Johnson who, in writing a history of the invasion, collaborated with
the top Cuban leaders, including brigade civilian chief Manuel Artime, described that attitude in detail:

> From the beginning, the Cuban counterrevolutionists viewed
> their new American friends with blind trust. Artime was no
> exception. He, and later virtually all of the Cubans involved,
> believed so much in the Americans—or wanted so desperately
> to believe—that they never questioned what was happening
> or expressed doubts about the plans. Looking back on it,
> they agree now that their naivete was partly genuine and
> partly reluctance to turn down any offer of help in liberat-
> ing their country. In fact, they had little choice; there was no
> other place to turn. Some, of course, were driven by other
> motives: political power and personal ambition were in-
> volved. Even more important was the traditional Cuban at-
> titude toward America and Americans. To Cubans the
> United States was more than the colossus of the north, for
> the two countries were bound closely by attitudes, by history,
> by geography and by economics. The United States was great
> and powerful, the master not only of the hemisphere but
> perhaps of the world, and it was Cuba's friend. One really
> didn't question such a belief. It was a fact; everyone knew
> it. And the mysterious, anonymous, ubiquitous American
> agents who dealt with the Cubans managed to strengthen that
> belief. (*31*)

(26) This "blind trust" by the Cuban exiles in the U.S. Government prior to the Bay of Pigs was specifically noted by the military
commander of the 2506 Brigade, José (Pepe) Pérez San Román:

"Most of the Cubans were there," he said,

> because they knew the whole operation was going to be con-
> ducted by the Americans, not by me or anyone else. They did
> not trust me or anyone else. They just trusted the Americans.
> So they were going to fight because the United States was
> backing them. (*32*)

(27) The debacle at the Bay of Pigs was not only a military tragedy
for the anti-Castro Cuban exiles but also a painful shattering of their
confidence in the U.S. Government. The exile leaders claimed that
the failure of the invasion was a result of the lack of promised air

support, and for that they directly blamed President Kennedy.(*33*) Particularly galling to them was Kennedy's public declaration to Soviet Premier Khrushchev at the height of the invasion, when the Brigade was being slaughtered in the swamps of Bahia de Cochinos: ". . . I repeat now that the United States intends no armed intervention in Cuba."(*34*)

(28)   Even those exile leaders who were willing to rationalize the extent of Kennedy's responsibility were dissuaded when Kennedy himself admitted the blame. Cuban Revolutionary Council leader Manuel Antonio de Varona, in his executive session testimony before the committee, told of the President gathering the Council members together at the White House when it became clear that the invasion was a disaster. Varona recalled:

> We were not charging Mr. Kennedy with anything; we just wanted to clarify. We knew that he didn't have any direct knowledge of the problem, and we knew that he was not in charge of the military effects directly. Nevertheless, President Kennedy, to finish the talks, told us he was the one—the only one responsible.(*35*)

A few days after that meeting, the White House issued a public statement declaring that President Kennedy assumed "sole responsibility" for the U.S. role in the action against Cuba.(*36*)

(29)   The acceptance of responsibility did not cut the bitter disappointment the Cuban exiles felt toward the U.S. Government and President Kennedy. Much later, captured and imprisoned by Castro, Brigade Commander San Román revealed the depth of his reaction at the failure of the invasion: "I hated the United States," he said, "and I felt that I had been betrayed. Every day it became worse and then I was getting madder and madder and I wanted to get a rifle and come and fight against the U.S."(*37*)

(30)   Prominent Cuban attorney Mario Lazo wrote a book caustically titled Dagger in the Heart.(*38*) Lazo wrote:

> The Bay of Pigs defeat was wholly self-inflicted in Washington. Kennedy told the truth when he publicly accepted responsibility . . . The heroism of the beleaguered Cuban Brigade had been rewarded by betrayal, defeat, death for many of them, long and cruel imprisonment for the rest. The Cuban people and the Latin American nations, bound to Cuba by thousands of subtle ties of race and culture, were left with feelings of astonishment and disillusionment, and in many cases despair. They had always admired the United States as strong, rich, generous—but where was its sense of honor and the capacity of its leaders?
>
> The mistake of the Cuban fighters for liberation was that they thought too highly of the United States. They believed to the end that it would not let them down. But it did . . .(*39*)

(31)   President Kennedy was well aware of the bitter legacy left him by the Bay of Pigs debacle. It is not now possible to document the changes in Kennedy's personal attitude brought about by the military defeat, but the firming of U.S. policy toward Cuba and the massive infusion of U.S. aid to clandestine anti-Castro operations in the wake of the Bay of Pigs was editorially characterized by Taylor

Branch and George Crile in Harper's magazine as "the Kennedy vendetta."(40).

(32) What can be documented is the pattern of U.S. policy between the period of the Bay of Pigs failure in April 1961 and the Cuban missile crisis in October 1962. That pattern, replete with both overt and covert maneuvers, had a significant effect on the reshaping of Cuban exile attitudes and, when it was abruptly reversed, could have provided the motivation for involvement in the assassination of President Kennedy.

(33) In retrospect, the period between the Bay of Pigs and the Cuban missile crisis can be considered the high-water mark of anti-Castro activity, almost every manifestation of the U.S. policy providing a reassurance of support of the Cuban exile cause. As a matter of fact, only a few days after the Bay of Pigs invasion, President Kennedy delivered a particularly hard-line address before the American Society of Newspaper Editors on the implications of communism in Cuba. "Cuba must not be abandoned to the Communists," he declared. In appealing for support from Latin America, he indicated that the United States would expect more from the nations of the hemisphere with regard to Cuba and asserted that the United States would not allow the doctrine of nonintervention to hinder its policy. Said Kennedy, "... our restraint is not inexhaustible." and spoke of Cuba in the context of the "new and deeper struggle."(41)

(34) When Castro, in a May Day speech, declared Cuba to be a socialist nation, the State Department retorted that Cuba was a full-fledged member of the Communist bloc.(42)

(35) Another U.S. response was the establishment of the Alliance for Progress, after years of relatively little attention to Latin America's economic and social needs.(43) President Kennedy gave the Alliance concept a memorable launching in a speech in March, 1961 when he called for vigorous promotion of social and economic development in Latin America through democratic means and, at the same time, pledged substantial financial and political support.(44)

(36) While the campaign to broaden its Cuban policy base was being pursued, the United States was proceeding on another course. In one of the first unilateral efforts to isolate Cuba from its allies, the United States in September 1961 announced it would stop assistance to any country that assisted Cuba. In December, Kennedy extended the denial of Cuba's sugar quota through the first half of 1962.(45)

(37) Meanwhile, the secret policy aimed at removing Castro through assassination continued as FBI chief J. Edgar Hoover informed Attorney General Robert Kennedy in May that the CIA had used the Mafia in "clandestine efforts" against Castro.(46) In that month, poison pills to be used in a plot to kill Castro were passed to a Cuban exile in Miami by a Mafia figure.(47) In November 1961, Operation Mongoose, designed to enlist 2,000 Cuban exiles and dissidents inside Cuba to overthrow Castro, was initiated.(48)

(38) Although the bitter aftertaste of the Bay of Pigs invasion lingered in the Cuban exile community, those who remained active in the fight against Castro came to realize that these subsequent actions of the Kennedy administration were manifestations of its determination to reverse the defeat. What Kennedy had euphemistically termed "a new and deeper struggle" became, in actuality, a secret war:

* * * the new President apparently perceived the defeat as an affront to his pride. Within a matter of weeks he committed the United States to a secret war against Cuba that eventually required the services of several thousand men and cost as much as $100 million a year * * * Kennedy entrusted its direction to the CIA, which * * * conducted an operation that could be described either as a large-scale vendetta or a small crusade. (*49*)

(39)   The fact that the agency of the U.S. Government the anti-Castro exiles had dealt most with and relied on prior to the Bay of Pigs became, after the invasion failure, the controlling force of the "secret war" was another indication of the Cuban exiles that the Kennedy administration was, indeed, still sincere about overthrowing Castro.

Within a year of the Bay of Pigs, the CIA curiously and inexplicably began to grow, to branch out, to gather more and more responsibility for the "Cuban problem." The company was given authority to help monitor Cuba's wireless traffic; to observe its weather; to follow the Castro government's purchases abroad and its currency transactions; to move extraordinary numbers of clandestine field operatives in and out of Cuba; to acquire a support fleet of ships and aircraft in order to facilitate these secret agent movements; to advise, train, and help reorganize the police and security establishments of Latin countries which felt threatened by Castro guerrilla politics; to take a hand in U-2 overflights and sea-air Elint (Electronic Intelligence) operations aimed at tracing Cuban coastal defense communications on special devices; to pump * * * vast sums into political operations thought to be helpful in containing Castro * * *. (*50*)

(40)   The nerve center of the United States "new and deeper struggle" against Castro was established in the heartland of exile activity, Miami. There, on a secluded, heavily wooded 1,571-acre tract that was part of the University of Miami's south campus, the CIA set up a front operation, an electronics firm called Zenith Technological Services. (*51*) Its code name was JM/WAVE and it soon became the largest CIA installation anywhere in the world outside of its headquarters in Langley, Va. (*52*)
(41)   The JM/WAVE station had, at the height of its activities in 1962, a staff of more than 300 Americans, mostly case officers. (*53*) Each case officer employed from 4 to 10 Cuban "principal agents" who, in turn, would each be responsible for between 10 and 30 regular agents. (*54*) In addition, the CIA set up 54 front corporations—boat shops, real estate firms, detective agencies, travel companies, gun shops—to provide ostensible employment for the case officers and agents operating outside of JM/WAVE headquarters. (*55*) It also maintained hundreds of pieces of real estate, from small apartments to palatial homes, as "safe houses" in which to hold secret meetings. (*56*) As a result of its JM/WAVE operation, the CIA became one of Florida's largest employers. (*57*)
(42)   It was the JM/WAVE station that monitored, more or less controlled, and in most cases funded the anti-Castro groups. (*58*) It was

responsible for the great upsurge in anti-Castro activity and the lifted spirits of the Cuban exiles as American arms and weapons flowed freely through the training camps and guerrilla bases spotted around south Florida.(59) Anti-Castro raiding parties that left from small secret islands in the Florida Keys were given the "green light" by agents of the JM/WAVE station.(60) The result of it all was that there grew in the Cuban exile community a renewed confidence in the U.S. Government's sincerity and loyalty to its cause.

(43)   Then came the Cuban missile crisis. The more fervent Cuban exiles were initially elated by the possibility that the crisis might provoke a final showdown with Castro.(61) For several months there had been increasing pressure on President Kennedy to take strong measures against the buildup of the Soviet presence in Cuba, which was becoming daily more blatant. In a report issued at the end of March 1962, the State Department said that Cuba had received from the Soviet Union $100 million in military aid for the training of Cuban pilots in Czechoslovakia and that the Soviet Union also had provided from 50 to 75 Mig fighters as well as tons of modern weapons for Cuba's ground forces.(62) Fortifying the Cuban exile's hope for action was the fact that the increasing amounts of Soviet weapons moving into Cuba became the dominant issue in the news in the succeeding months, leading to congressional calls for action and a series of hard-line responses from President Kennedy.(63) In September, Kennedy declared that the United States would use "whatever means may be necessary" to prevent Cuba from exporting "its aggressive purposes by force or threat of force" against "any part of the Western Hemisphere."(64)

(44)   The fervent hope of the Cuban exiles—that the Cuban missile crisis would ultimately result in the United States smashing the Castro regime—was shattered by the manner in which President Kennedy resolved the crisis. Cuba itself was relegated to a minor role as tough negotiations took place between the United States and the Soviet Union, specifically through communication between President Kennedy and Premier Khrushchev.(65) The crisis ended, when President Kennedy announced that all IL–28 bombers were being withdrawn by the Soviets and progress was being made on the withdrawal of offensive missiles and other weapons from Cuba. In return, Kennedy gave the Soviets and the Cubans a "no invasion" pledge.(66)

(45)   If Kennedy's actions at the Bay of Pigs first raised doubts in the minds of the Cuban exiles about the President's sincerity and determination to bring about the fall of Castro, his handling of the missile crisis confirmed those doubts. Kennedy's agreement with Khrushchev was termed "a violation" of the pledge he had made 3 days after the Bay of Pigs invasion that the United States would never abandon Cuba to communism.(67) Wrote one prominent exile: "For the friendly Cuban people, allies of the United States, and for hundreds of thousands of exiles eager to stake their lives to liberate their native land, it was a soul-shattering blow."(68)

(46)   The bitterness of the anti-Castro exiles was exacerbated by the actions the U.S. Government took to implement the President's "no invasion" pledge. Suddenly there was a crackdown on the very training camps and guerrilla bases which had been originally established and funded by the United States and the exile raids which once had the

Government's "green light" were now promptly disavowed and condemned.

(47) On March 31, 1963, a group of anti-Castro raiders were arrested by British police at a training site in the Bahamas. (69) The U.S. State Department admitted it had given the British the information about the existence of the camp. (70) That same night another exile raiding boat was seized in Miami Harbor. (71) On April 3, the Soviet Union charged that the United States "encourages and bears full responsibility" for two recent attacks on Soviet ships in Cuban ports by anti-Castro exile commandos. (72) The United States responded that it was "taking every step necessary to insure that such attacks are not launched, manned or equipped from U.S. territory." (73) On April 5, the Coast Guard announced it was throwing more planes, ships, and men into its efforts to police the straits of Florida against anti-Castro raiders. (74) As a result of the crackdown, Cuban exile sources declared that their movement to rid their homeland of communism had been dealt "a crippling blow" and that they had lost a vital supply link with anti-Castro fighters inside Cuba.

(48) There were numerous other indications of the U.S. crackdown on anti-Castro activity following the missile crisis. The Customs Service raided what had long been a secret training camp in the Florida Keys and arrested the anti-Castro force in training there. (75) The FBI seized a major cache of explosives at an anti-Castro camp in Louisiana. (76) Just weeks later, the U.S. Coast Guard in cooperation with the British Navy captured another group of Cuban exiles in the Bahamas. (77) In September, the Federal Aviation Administration issued "strong warnings" to six American civilian pilots who had been flying raids over Cuba. (78) Shortly afterward, the Secret Service arrested a prominent exile leader for conspiring to counterfeit Cuban currency destined for rebel forces inside Cuba. (79) In October, the Coast Guard seized 4 exile ships and arrested 22 anti-Castro raiders who claimed they were moving their operations out of the United States. (80)

(49) The feeling of betrayal by the Cuban exiles was given reinforcement by prominent sympathizers outside their community, as well as by Kennedy's political opponents. Capt. Eddie Rickenbacker, chairman of the Committee for the Monroe Doctrine, asserted: "The Kennedy administration has committed the final betrayal of Cuban hopes for freedom by its order to block the activities of exiled Cuban freedom fighters to liberate their nation from Communism." (81) Senator Barry Goldwater accused Kennedy of "doing everything in his power" to keep the flag of Cuban exiles "from ever flying over Cuba again." (82) Richard Nixon urged the end of what he called the "quarantine" of Cuban exiles. (83)

(50) Of course, the most strident reactions came from within the anti-Castro community itself. Following the U.S. Government's notification that it would discontinue its subsidy to the Cuban Revolutionary Council, its president, José Miró Cardona, announced his resignation from the council in protest against U.S. policy. (84) The Cuban exile leader accused President Kennedy of "breaking promises and agreements" to support another invasion of Cuba. (85) Miró Cardona said the change in American policy reflected the fact that Kennedy had become "the victim of a master play by the Russians." (86)

(51) The extent of the deterioration of relationships between the Cuban exiles and the Kennedy administration is indicated in the State Department's reply to Miró Cardona's charges. It labeled them "a gross distortion of recent history."(87)

(52) Against the pattern of U.S. crackdown on Cuban exile activity during this period, however, emerges a countergrain of incidents that may have some bearing on an examination of the Kennedy assassination. These incidents involve some extremely significant Cuban exile raids and anti-Castro operations which took place, despite the crackdown, between the time of the missile crisis and the assassination of the President. In fact, in the midst of the missile crisis, one of the most active Cuban groups, Alpha 66, announced that it made a successful raid on the Cuban port city of Isabela de Sagua, killing about 20 defenders, including Russians.(88) On October 15, the same group sank a Cuban patrol boat.(89) On October 31, the day after the blockade was lifted, it struck again.(90) Immediately after the crisis ended in November, a spokesman for the group pledged new raids.(91)

(53) During this period, other anti-Castro groups also remained active. In April, a group calling itself the Cuban Freedom Fighters reported bombing an oil refinery outside Havana.(92) In May, the Cuban Government confirmed that anti-Castro rebels had carried out a "pirate" raid on a militia camp near Havana despite U.S. promises "to take measures to prevent such attacks."(93) Later that month, the anti-Castro Internal Front of Revolutionary Unity reported it had formed a military junta in Cuba to serve as "provisional government of Cuba in arms." Shortly afterwards, a group of returning Cuban exile raiders claimed they had blown up a Cuban refinery, sank a gunboat and killed "many" of Castro's soldiers.(94) It is not known exactly how many incidents took place during this period, but in April 1963 one anti-Castro fighter asserted that, by then, the U.S. Government knew of 11 raids on Cuba since the missile crisis and did nothing.(95)

(54) One analyst, reviewing that period of United States-Cuban relations, noted: "The U.S. Government's policy toward the exiles was equivocal and inconsistent * * *" (96)

(55) It cannot be determined to what extent, if any, the military activities of the anti-Castro exile groups were sanctioned or supported by the Kennedy administration or by the CIA or both. At a press conference in May 1963, in response to a question as to whether or not the United States was giving aid to exiles, President Kennedy was evasive: "We may well be * * * well, none that I am familiar with * * * I don't think as of today that we are." (97) And it is known that by June 1963, the U.S. Government was supporting at least one Cuban exile group, Jure. under what was termed an "autonomous operations" concept.(98)

(56) In retrospect. this much is clear: With or without U.S. Government support and whether or not in blatant defiance of Kennedy administration policy, there were a number of anti-Castro action groups which were determined to continue—and, in fact, did continue—their operations. The resignation of Miró Cardona actually split the Cuban Revolutionary Council down the middle and precipitated a bitter dispute among the exile factions. (99) The more moderate contended that without U.S. support there was little hope of ousting Castro and that the exiles should concentrate their efforts in mounting political pressure to reverse Washington's shift in policy. (100) Other exile

groups announced their determination to continue the war against Castro and, if necessary, to violently resist curtailment of their paramilitary activities in the Kennedy administration. (*101*) In New Orleans, for instance, Carlos Bringuier, the local leader of the Cuban Student Directorate (DRE) who, coincidentally, would later have a contact with Lee Harvey Oswald, proclaimed, in the wake of the Miró Cardona resignation, that his group "would continue efforts to liberate Cuba despite action by the United States to stop raids originating from U.S. soil." (*102*)

(57) The seeds of defiance of the Kennedy administration may have been planted with the exiles even prior to the Bay of Pigs invasion. In his history of the invasion, Haynes Johnson revealed that shortly before the invasion, "Frank Bender," the CIA director of the invasion preparations, assembled the exile leaders together at the CIA's Guatemala training camp:

> It was now early in April and Artime was in the camp as the civilian representative of the Revolutionary Council. Frank called Pepe (San Roman) and (Erneido) Oliva again. This time he had startling information. There were forces in the administration trying to block the invasion, and Frank might be ordered to stop it. If he received such an order, he said he would secretly inform Pepe and Oliva. Pepe remembers Frank's next words this way:
>
> "If this happens you come here and make some kind of show, as if you were putting us, the advisers, in prison, and you go ahead with the program as we have talked about it, and we will give you the whole plan, even if we are your prisoners." * * * Frank then laughed and said: "In the end we will win." (*103*)

(58) That, then, is the context in which the committee approached the question of whether or not the John F. Kennedy assassination was a conspiracy involving anti-Castro Cuban exiles. It also considered the testimony of the CIA's chief of its Miami JM/WAVE station in 1963, who noted " 'assassination' was part of the ambience of that time." (*104*)

(59) This section of this staff report details the evidence developed in the committee's examination of some of the most active anti-Castro exile groups and their key leaders. These groups were specifically selected from the more than 100 exile organizations in existence at the time of the Kennedy assassination. (*105*) Their selection was the result of both independent field investigation by the committee and the committee's examination of the files and records maintained by those Federal and local agencies monitoring Cuban exile activity at the time. These agencies included local police departments, the FBI, the CIA, the Bureau of Narcotics and Dangerous Drugs (now the DEA), the Customs Service, the Immigration and Naturalization Service, and the Department of Defense.

(60) The groups selected can be termed the "action groups." These were the ones most active on both the military and propaganda fronts, the ones that not only talked about anti-Castro operations, but actually planned and carried out infiltrations and raids into Cuba, conducted Castro assassination attempts, were involved in a multiplicity of arms dealings and had the most vociferous and aggressive leaders. These

were also the groups and individuals who took the brunt of the Kennedy administration's crackdown on anti-Castro operations when it came after the Cuban missile crisis. These were the ones who, in the end, were most bitter at President Kennedy, the ones who felt the most betrayed. Finally, these were the groups and individuals who had the means and motivation to be involved in the assassination of the President.

(61) The committee, however, found no specific evidence that any anti-Castro group or individual was involved in Kennedy's assassination. It did appear, however, that there were indications of association between Lee Harvey Oswald and individuals connected to at least some of the groups.

Submitted by:

GAETON J. FONZI,
Investigator.

REFERENCES

(1) "The Investigation of the Assassination of President John F. Kennedy: Performance of the Intelligence Agencies," Book V, Final Report, Senate Select Committee To Study Governmental Operations With Respect To Intelligence Activities, 94th Congress, 2d sess., Apr. 23, 1976, Washington, D.C.: U.S. Government Printing Office, 1976, p. 4 (Senate Report 94–755), (hereinafter Intelligence Committee Report, Book V).

(2) Memorandum of William T. Coleman, Jr. and W. David Slawson to Warren Commission, pp. 110–111, House Select Committee on Assassinations (J. F. K. Document 013105).

(3) "The Longest Night," Miami Herald, Tropic, Dec. 28, 1975, p. 7.

(4) Ibid.

(5) Haynes Johnson, "The Bay of Pigs" (Norton, 1964), p. 17 (hereinafter cited Johnson, "Bay of Pigs").

(6) Ibid.

(7) Id. at p. 18.

(8) "U.S. Seizes Batista Backer in Miami," New York Times, Apr. 9, 1961, p. 4.

(9) See ref. 5, Johnson, "Bay of Pigs," p. 23.

(10) Paul Bethel, "The Losers" (Arlington House, 1969), p. 102.

(11) "A Selected Chronology on Cuba and Castro, Mar. 10, 1952–Oct. 22, 1962," Congressional Research Service, Library of Congress, p. 6 (J. F. K. Document 013100) (hereinafter cited "A Selected Chronology on Cuba and Castro").

(12) Ibid.

(13) Mario Lazo, "Dagger in the Heart" (Funk & Wagnalls, 1968), p. 186 (hereinafter cited Lazo, "Dagger").

(14) Ibid.

(15) See ref. 11, "A Selected Chronology on Cuba and Castro," p. 7.

(16) Ibid.

(17) See ref. 5, Johnson, "Bay of Pigs," p. 23.

(18) Ibid.

(19) Ibid.

(20) Id. at p. 24.

(21) Ibid.

(22) See ref. 11, "A Selected Chronology on Cuba and Castro," Jan. 26, 1960, p. 9.

(23) Ibid.

(24) See ref. 5, Johnson, "Bay of Pigs," p. 18.

(25) Ibid.

(26) Id. at p. 28.

(27) Id. at p. 19.

(28) Ibid.

(29) "U.S.-Cuba Relations, 1959–1964: An Analysis," Congressional Research Service, Library of Congress, House Select Committee on Assassinations (J. F. K. Document 011478.) (hereinafter cited "United States-Cuba Relations.")

(30) See ref. 5, Johnson "Bay of Pigs," pp. 23–31.

(31) Id. at p. 27.

(32) Id. at p. 76.

ROSE CHERAMIE

(1)   According to accounts of assassinations researchers, a woman known as Rose Cheramie, a heroin addict and prostitute with a long history of arrests, was found on November 20, 1963, lying on the road near Eunice, La., bruised and disoriented.(*1*) She was taken to the Louisiana State Hospital in Jackson, La., to recover from her injuries and what appeared to be narcotics withdrawal.(*2*) Cheramie reportedly told the attending physician that President Kennedy was going to be killed during his forthcoming visit to Dallas.(*3*) The doctor did not pay much attention to the ravings of a patient going "cold turkey" until after the President was assassinated 2 days later.(*4*) State police were called in and Cheramie was questioned at length.(*5*) She reportedly told police officers she had been a stripper in Jack Ruby's night club and was transporting a quantity of heroin from Florida to Houston at Ruby's insistence when she quarreled with two men also participating in the dope run.(*6*) Cheramie said the men pushed her out of a moving vehicle and left her for dead.(*7*) After the assassination, Cheramie maintained Ruby and Lee Harvey Oswald had known each other well.(*8*) She said she had seen Oswald at Ruby's night club and claimed Oswald and Ruby had been homosexual partners.(*9*)

(2)   Ironically, the circumstances of Rose Cheramie's death are strikingly similar to the circumstances surrounding her original involvement in the assassination investigation. Cheramie died of injuries received from an automobile accident on a strip of highway near Big Sandy, Tex., in the early morning of September 4, 1965.(*10*) The driver stated Cheramie had been lying in the roadway and although he attempted to avoid hitting her, he ran over the top of her skull, causing fatal injuries.(*11*) An investigation into the accident and the possibility of a relationship between the victim and the driver produced no evidence of foul play.(*12*) The case was closed.(*13*)

(3)   Although Cheramie's allegations were eventually discounted, her death 2 years later prompted renewed speculation about her story. It was noted, for example, that over 50 individuals who had been associated with the investigation of the Kennedy assassination had died within 3 years of that event.(*14*) The deaths, by natural or other causes, were labeled "mysterious" by Warren Commission critics and the news media.(*15*) The skeptics claim that the laws of probability would show the number of deaths is so unlikely as to be highly suspect.(*16*) As detailed elsewhere, the committee studied such claims and determined they were erroneous.(*17*) Nevertheless, allegations involving Rose Cheramie, often counted among the "mysterious" deaths, was of particular interest to the committee, since it indicated a possible association of Lee Harvey Oswald and Jack Ruby; an association of these individuals with members of organized crime; and possible connection between Cheramie's confinement at the State Hospital in Jackson, La.

and Oswald's search for employment there in the summer of 1963.

(4)   The committee set out to obtain a full account of the Cheramie allegations and determine whether her statements could be at all corroborated. The committee interviewed and deposed pertinent witnesses. Files from U.S. Customs and the FBI were requested. Information developed during the investigation by New Orleans District Attorney Jim Garrison was examined. Records of Cheramie's hospitalization at the East Louisiana State Hospital were studied.

(5)   Hospital records indicate Melba Christine Marcades, alias Rose Cheramie, was brought to the State Hospital in Jackson, La. by police from Eunice on November 21, 1963 and officially admitted at 6 a.m.(18) She was originally from Houston, Tex., where her mother still lived. (19) She was approximately 34 years old in 1963, had used many aliases throughout her lifetime and had lived many years in Louisiana and Texas.(20)

(6)   According to the clinical notes, the deputy accompanying Cheramie said the patient had been "picked up on [the] side of [the] road and had been given something by the coroner."(21) The coroner in Eunice was contacted by doctors at the hospital and he told them Cheramie had been coherent when he spoke with her at 10:30 p.m., November 20, but he did administer a sedative.(22) He further indicated that Cheramie was a 9-year mainlining heroin addict, whose last injection had been around 2 p.m., November 20.(23) The doctors noted that Cheramie's condition upon initial examination indicated heroin withdrawal and clinical shock.(24)

(7)   Relevant to Cheramie's credibility was an assessment of her mental state. From November 22 to November 24, Cheramie required close attention and medication.(25) On November 25 she was transferred to the ward.(26) On November 27 she was released to Louisiana State Police Lieutenant Fruge.(27)

(8)   The hospital records gave no reference as to alleged statements made by Cheramie or why she was released to Lieutenant Fruge on November 27, 1963. These records do indicate Cheramie had been hospitalized for alcoholism and narcotics addiction on other occasions, including commitment to the same hospital in March 1961 by the criminal court of New Orleans.(28) During this stay, the woman was diagnosed as ". . . without psychosis. However, because of her previous record of drug addiction she may have a mild integrative and pleasure defect."(29) Her record would show she has "intervals of very good behavior" but at other times she "presents episodically psychopathic behavior" indicative in her history of drug and alcohol abuse, prostitution, arrest on numerous, if minor, charges.(30)

(9)   The committee interviewed one of the doctors on staff at East Louisiana State Hospital who had seen Cheramie during her stay there at the time of the Kennedy assassination.(31) The doctor corroborated aspects of the Cheramie allegations. Dr. Victor Weiss verified that he was employed as a resident physician at the hospital in 1963.(32) He recalled that on Monday, November 25, 1963, he was asked by another physician, Dr. Bowers, to see a patient who had been committed November 20 or 21.(33) Dr. Bowers allegedly told Weiss that the patient, Rose Cheramie, had stated before the assassination that President Kennedy was going to be killed.(34) Weiss questioned Cheramie about

her statements.(*35*) She told him she had worked for Jack Ruby. She did not have any specific details of a particular assassination plot against Kennedy, but had stated the "word in the underworld" was that Kennedy would be assassinated.(*36*) She further stated that she had been traveling from Florida to her home in Texas when the man traveling with her threw her from the automobile in which they were riding.(*37*)

(10)   Francis Fruge, a lieutenant with the Louisiana State Police in 1963, was the police officer who first came to Cheramie's assistance on November 20, 1963, had her committed to the State Hospital, and later released her into his custody following the assassination to investigate her allegations.(*38*) As such, he provided an account further detailing her allegations and the official response to her allegations.

(11)   Fruge was deposed by the committee on April 18, 1978. (*39*) He told the committee he was called on November 20, 1963 by an administrator at a private hospital in Eunice, La. that a female accident victim had been taken there for treatment.(*40*) She had been treated for minor abrasions, and although she appeared to be under the influence of drugs since she had "no financial basis" she was to be released.(*41*) Fruge did what he normally did in such instances. As the woman required no further medical attention, he put her in a jail cell to sober up.(*42*) This arrangement did not last long. The woman began to display severe symptoms of withdrawal.(*43*) Fruge said he called a doctor, who sedated Cheramie and Fruge transported Cheramie to the State hospital in Jackson, La.(*44*)

(12)   Fruge said that during the "1 to 2 hour" ride to Jackson, he asked Cheramie some "routine" questions.(*45*) Fruge told the committee:

> She related to me that she was coming from Florida to Dallas with two men who were Italians or resembled Italians. They had stopped at this lounge . . . and they'd had a few drinks and had gotten into an argument or something. The manager of the lounge threw her out and she got on the road and hitchhiked to catch a ride, and this is when she got hit by a vehicle.(*46*)

Fruge said the lounge was a house of prostitution called the Silver Slipper.(*47*) Fruge asked Cheramie what she was going to do in Dallas: "She said she was going to, number one, pick up some money, pick up her baby, and to kill Kennedy."(*48*) Fruge claimed during these intervals that Cheramie related the story she appeared to be quite lucid. (*49*) Fruge had Cheramie admitted to the hospital late on November 20.(*50*)

(13)   On November 22, when he heard the President had been assassinated, Fruge said he immediately called the hospital and told them not to release Cheramie until he had spoken to her.(*51*) The hospital administrators assented but said Fruge would have to wait until the following Monday before Cheramie would be well enough to speak to anyone.(*52*) Fruge waited. Under questioning, Cheramie told Fruge that the two men traveling with her from Miami were going to Dallas to kill the President.(*53*) For her part, Cheramie was to obtain $8,000 from an unidentified source in Dallas and proceed to Houston with the two men to complete a drug deal.(*54*) Cheramie was also supposed to

pick up her little boy from friends who had been looking after him. (*55*)
(14) Cheramie further supplied detailed accounts of the arrangement for the drug transaction in Houston. (*56*) She said reservations
had been made at the Rice Hotel in Houston. (*57*) The trio was to meet
a seaman who was bringing in 8 kilos of heroin to Galveston by
boat. (*58*) Cheramie had the name of the seaman and the boat he
was arriving on. (*59*) Once the deal was completed, the trio would
proceed to Mexico. (*60*)

(15) Fruge told the committee that he repeated Cheramie's story to
his supervisors and asked for instructions. (*61*) He was told to follow
up on it. (*62*) Fruge promptly took Cheramie into custody—as indicated in hospital records—and set out to check her story. (*63*) He
contacted the chief customs agent in Galveston who reportedly verified
the scheduled docking of the boat and the name of the seaman. (*64*)
Fruge believed the customs agent was also able to verify the name of
the man in Dallas who was holding Cheramie's son. (*65*) Fruge recalled
that the customs agent had tailed the seaman as he disembarked from
the boat, but then lost the man's trail. (*70*) Customs closed the case. (*71*)

(16) Fruge had also hoped to corroborate other statements made by
Cheramie. During a flight from Houston, according to Fruge,
Cheramie noticed a newspaper with headlines indicating investigators
had not been able to establish a relationship between Jack Ruby and
Lee Harvey Oswald. (*72*) Cheramie laughed at the headline, Fruge
said. (*73*) Cheramie told him she had worked for Ruby, or "Pinky,"
as she knew him, at his night club in Dallas and claimed Ruby and
Oswald "had been shacking up for years. (*74*) Fruge said he called
Capt. Will Fritz of the Dallas Police Department with this informa-
tion. (*75*) Fritz answered, he wasn't interested. (*76*) Fritz and the
Louisiana State Police dropped the investigation into the matter. (*77*)

(17) Four years later, however, investigators from the office of
District Attorney Garrison in New Orleans contacted Fruge. (*78*)
Fruge went on detail to Garrison's office to assist in the investiga-
tion into the Kennedy assassination. (*79*)

(18) During the course of the New Orleans D.A.'s investigation
Fruge was able to pursue leads in the Cheramie case that he had not
checked out in the original investigation. Although there appeared
to be different versions as to how Cheramie ended up by the side of
the road, and the number and identity of her companions, Fruge
attempted to corroborate the version she had given him. Fruge spoke
with the owner of the Silver Slipper Lounge. (*80*) The bar owner, a
Mr. Mac Manual since deceased, told Fruge that Cheramie had come
in with two men who the owner knew as pimps engaged in the business
of hauling prostitutes in from Florida. (*81*) When Cheramie became
intoxicated and rowdy, one of the men "slapped her around" and threw
her outside. (*82*)

(19) Fruge claims that he showed the owner of the bar a "stack" of
photographs and mug shots to identify. (*83*) According to Fruge, the
barowner chose the photos of a Cuban exile, Sergio Arcacha Smith,
and another Cuban Fruge believed to be named Osanto. (*84*) Arcacha
Smith was known to Kennedy assassination investigators as an anti-
Castro Cuban refugee who had been active in 1961 as the head of the
New Orleans Cuban Revolutionary Front. (*85*) At that time, he befriended anti-Castro activist and commercial pilot David Ferrie, who

was named and dismissed as a suspect in the Kennedy assassination within days of the President's death.(86) Ferrie and Arcacha Smith were also believed to have had ties with New Orleans organized crime figure Carlos Marcello.(87) Arcacha Smith moved from the New Orleans area in 1962 to go to Miami and later to settle in Houston.(88) The weekend following the assassination, Ferrie took a trip to Houston and Galveston for a little "rest and relaxation," while police searched New Orleans for him after receiving a tip he had been involved in the assassination.(89) The committee has found credible evidence indicating Ferrie and Oswald were seen together in August 1963 in the town of Clinton, La., 13 miles from the hospital in Jackson where Cheramie was treated and where Oswald reportedly sought employment. Allegations regarding Arcacha Smith and Ferrie and the committee's investigation are set forth in detail elsewhere in the Report. (90) Clearly, evidence of a link between Cheramie and Arcacha Smith would be highly significant, Arcacha Smith, however, denied any knowledge of Cheramie and her allegations. Other avenues of corroboration of Fruge's identification of Cheramie's traveling companion as Sergio Arcacha Smith and further substantiation of Cheramie's allegations remained elusive.

(20)   U.S. Customs was unable to locate documents and reports related to its involvement in the Cheramie investigation although such involvement was not denied.(91) Nor could customs officials locate those agents named by Fruge as having participated in the original investigation, as they had since left the employ of the agency.(92)

(21)   Since the FBI had never been notified by the Louisiana State Police and U.S. Customs of their interest in Cheramie, the FBI file did not have any reference to the Cheramie allegations of November 1963.(93) FBI files did give reference to the investigation of a tip from Melba Mercades, actually Rose Cheramie, in Ardmore, Okla. that she was en route to Dallas to deliver $2,600 worth of heroin to a man in Oak Cliff, Tex.(94) She was then to proceed to Galveston, Tex., to pick up a load of narcotics from a seaman on board a ship destined for Galveston in the next few days.(95) She gave "detailed descriptions as to individuals, names, places, and amounts distributed."(96) Investigations were conducted by narcotics bureaus in Oklahoma and Texas and her information was found to be "erroneous in all respects."(97)

(22)   A similar tale was told in 1965: FBI agents investigated a tip from Rozella Clinkscales, alias Melba Marcades, alias Rose Cheramie.(98) Like the stories told in 1963, Cheramie-Clinkscales claimed individuals associated with the syndicate were running prostitution rings in several southern cities such as Houston and Galveston, Tex., Oklahoma City, Okla. and Montgomery, Ala. by transporting hookers, including Cheramie-Clinkscales, from town to town. (99) Furthermore, she claimed she had information about a heroin deal operating from a New Orleans ship.(100) A call to the Coast Guard verified an ongoing narcotics investigation of the ship.(101) Other allegations made by Cheramie-Clinkscales could not be verified. Further investigation into Cheramie-Clinkscales revealed she had apparently previously furnished the FBI false information concerning her involvement in prostitution and narcotics matters and that she had been confined to a mental institution in Norman, Okla. on three

occasions. (*102*) FBI agents decided to pursue the case no further. (*103*) The FBI indicated agents did not know of the death of their informant on September 4, 1965, occurring just 1 month after she had contacted the FBI. Louisiana State Police investigating Cheramie's fatal accident also apparently did not know of the FBI's interest in her.

Submitted by,

PATRICIA ORR, *Researcher.*

REFERENCES

occasions. (*102*) FBI agents decided to pursue the case no further. (*103*) The FBI indicated agents did not know of the death of their informant on September 4, 1965, occurring just 1 month after she had contacted the FBI. Louisiana State Police investigating Cheramie's fatal accident also apparently did not know of the FBI's interest in her.

Submitted by,

PATRICIA ORR, *Researcher.*

REFERENCES

(*1*) "The Bizarre Deaths Following JFK's Murder," *Argosy.* March 1977, Vol. 384, No. 8, p. 52 (JFK Document No. 002559).
(*2*) Ibid.
(*3*) Ibid.
(*4*) Ibid.
(*5*) Ibid.
(*6*) Ibid.
(*7*) Ibid.
(*8*) Ibid.
(*9*) Ibid.
(*10*) Louisiana State Police Memo, from Lt. Francis Fruge, Parish of St. Landry, April 4, 1967, in (JFK Document No. 013520).
(*11*) Ibid.
(*12*) Ibid.
(*13*) Ibid.
(*14*) "The Bizarre Deaths . . ." See FN No. 1.
(*15*) Ibid.
(*16*) Ibid.
(*17*) See Anti-Castro Cuban section of the Staff Reports.
(*18*) East Louisiana State Hospital, Jackson, La., records for Melba Christine Marcades AKA Rose Cheramie (JFK Document No. 006097).
(*19*) Ibid.
(*20*) Ibid. Note: FBI records list Cheramie's (Marcades) birthdate as October 14, 1932, in Dallas, Tex. (See FBI file No. 166–1640 in JFK Document No. 012979).
(*21*) Ibid.
(*22*) Ibid.
(*23*) Ibid.
(*24*) Ibid.
(*25*) Ibid.
(*26*) Ibid.
(*27*) Ibid.
(*28*) Ibid.
(*29*) Ibid.
(*30*) Ibid.
(*31*) HSCA Contact Report, July 5, 1978, Bob Buras (with Dr. Victor Weiss), (JFK Document No. 009699).
(*32*) Ibid.
(*33*) Ibid.
(*34*) Ibid.
(*35*) Ibid.
(*36*) Ibid.
(*37*) Ibid.
(*38*) HSCA Contact Report, April 7, 1978, Bob Buras (with Mr. Francis Louis Fruge), p. 1 (JFK Document No. 014141).
(*39*) HSCA Deposition of Francis Louis Fruge, April 18, 1978 (JFK Document No. 014570).
(*40*) Id. at p. 4–5.
(*41*) Id. at p. 5.
(*42*) Ibid.
(*43*) Id. at p. 6.
(*44*) Ibid.
(*45*) Id. at p. 8.
(*46*) Ibid.
(*47*) Id. at p. 9.

INVESTIGATION OF THE ASSASSINATION OF PRESIDENT JOHN F. KENNEDY

APPENDIX TO HEARINGS

BEFORE THE

SELECT COMMITTEE ON ASSASSINATIONS

OF THE

U.S. HOUSE OF REPRESENTATIVES

NINETY-FIFTH CONGRESS

SECOND SESSION

VOLUME VIII

ACOUSTICS, POLYGRAPH, HANDWRITING, AND FINGERPRINT REPORTS

MARCH 1979

Printed for the use of the Select Committee on Assassinations

U.S. GOVERNMENT PRINTING OFFICE

46-120 O   WASHINGTON : 1979

For sale by the Superintendent of Documents, U.S. Government Printing Office
Washington, D.C. 20402

Stock No. 052-070-04979-1

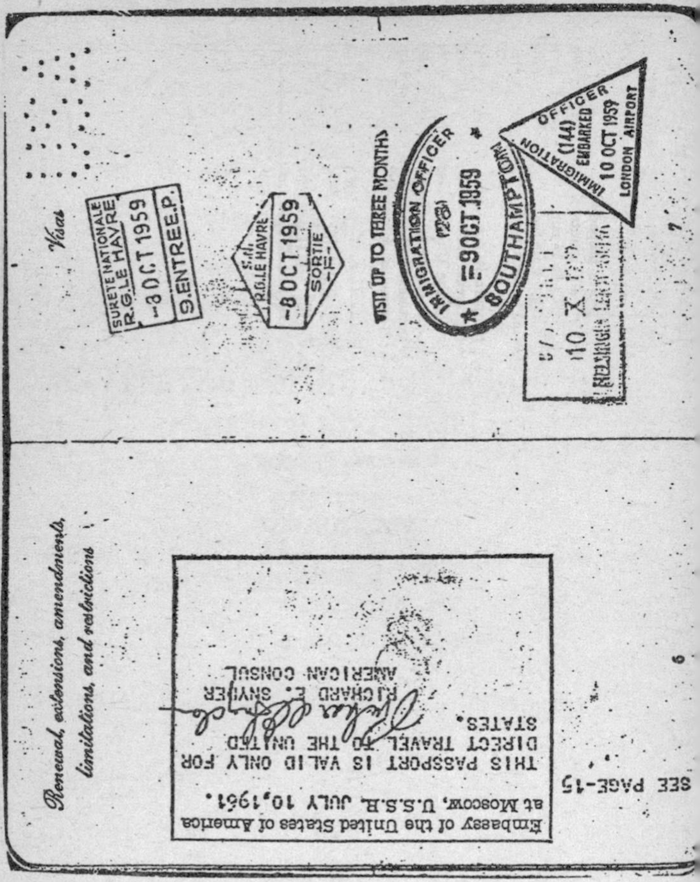

Visas

SURETE NATIONALE
R.G. LE HAVRE
-3 OCT 1959
Ø.ENTREE.P.

S.N.
R.G. LE HAVRE
-8 OCT 1959
SORTIE

VISIT UP TO THREE MONTHS

IMMIGRATION OFFICER
1281
=9 OCT 1959
SOUTHAMPTON

IMMIGRATION OFFICER
(144)
EMBARKED
10 OCT 1959
LONDON AIRPORT

10 X 1959

Renewal, extensions, amendments,
limitations, and restrictions.

Embassy of the United States of America
at Moscow, U.S.S.R., JULY 10, 1961.
THIS PASSPORT IS VALID ONLY FOR
DIRECT TRAVEL TO THE UNITED
STATES.
RICHARD E. SNYDER
AMERICAN CONSUL

SEE PAGE-15

Lee Harvey Oswald's Passport

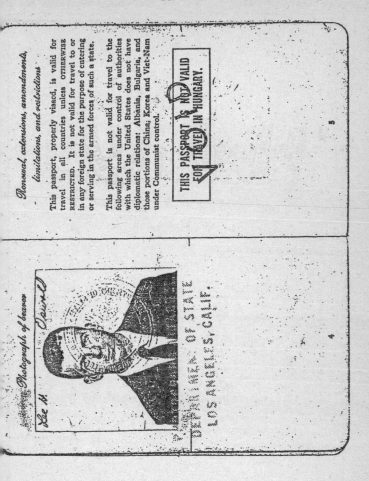

Renewal, extensions, amendments, limitations, and restrictions

This passport, properly visaed, is valid for travel in all countries unless OTHERWISE RESTRICTED. It is not valid for travel to or in any foreign state for the purpose of entering or serving in the armed forces of such a state.

This passport is not valid for travel to the following areas under control of authorities with which the United States does not have diplomatic relations: Albania, Bulgaria, and those portions of China, Korea and Viet-Nam under Communist control.

THIS PASSPORT IS NOT VALID FOR TRAVEL IN HUNGARY.

5

Photograph of bearer

See it

DEPARTMENT OF STATE
LOS ANGELES, CALIF.

4

REPORT

OF THE

SELECT COMMITTEE ON ASSASSINATIONS
U.S. HOUSE OF REPRESENTATIVES

NINETY-FIFTH CONGRESS

SECOND SESSION

FINDINGS AND RECOMMENDATIONS

MARCH 29, 1979.—Committed to the Committee of the Whole House
on the State of the Union and ordered to be printed

U.S. GOVERNMENT PRINTING OFFICE

43–112 O   WASHINGTON : 1979

While noting the deficiencies in the CIA assassination investigation, the committee was impressed with certain overseas capabilities of the CIA in 1963. The Agency had, for example, comprehensive coverage of anti-Castro Cuban groups that, in turn, had extensive information sources in and out of Cuba.(*200*) Thus, while it was flawed in certain specific respects, the committee concluded that the CIA assassination investigation could, in fact, be relied on—with only limited reservations—as a general indicator of possible Cuban involvement. That investigation found no evidence of Cuban complicity.

(i) Summary of the findings

While the committee did not take Castro's denials at face value, it found persuasive reasons to conclude that the Cuban Government was not involved in the Kennedy assassination. First, by 1963 there were prospects for repairing the hostility that had marked relations between the two countries since Castro had come to power. Second, the risk of retaliation that Cuba would have incurred by conspiring in the assassination of an American President must have canceled out other considerations that might have argued for that act. President Castro's description of the idea as "insane" is appropriate. And there was no evidence indicating an insane or grossly reckless lack of judgment on the part of the Cuban Government. Third, the CIA had both the motive to develop evidence of Cuban involvement and access to at least substantial, if incomplete, information bearing on relevant aspects of it, had such involvement existed. Its absence, therefore, must be weighed in the balance. Finally, the Cuban Government's cooperation with this committee in the investigation must be a factor in any judgment. In conclusion, the committee found, on the basis of the evidence available to it, that the Cuban Government was not involved in the assassination of President Kennedy.

3. THE COMMITTEE BELIEVES, ON THE BASIS OF THE EVIDENCE AVAILABLE TO IT, THAT ANTI-CASTRO CUBAN GROUPS, AS GROUPS, WERE NOT INVOLVED IN THE ASSASSINATION OF PRESIDENT KENNEDY, BUT THAT THE AVAILABLE EVIDENCE DOES NOT PRECLUDE THE POSSIBILITY THAT INDIVIDUAL MEMBERS MAY HAVE BEEN INVOLVED

The committee investigated possible involvement in the assassination by a number of anti-Castro Cuban groups and individual activists for two primary reasons:

First, they had the motive, based on what they considered President Kennedy's betrayal of their cause, the liberation of Cuba from the Castro regime; the means, since they were trained and practiced in violent acts, the result of the guerrilla warfare they were waging against Castro; and the opportunity, whenever the President, as he did from time to time, appeared at public gatherings, as in Dallas on November 22, 1963.

Second, the committee's investigation revealed that certain associations of Lee Harvey Oswald were or may have been with anti-Castro activists.

The committee, therefore, paid close attention to the activities of anti-Castro Cubans—in Miami, where most of them were concentrated and their organizations were headquartered,(*1*) and in New Orleans

130

and Dallas, where Oswald, while living in these cities in the months preceding the assassination, reportedly was in contact with anti-Castro activists. (2)

The Warren Commission did not, of course, ignore Oswald's ties to anti-Castroites. From the evidence that was available in 1964, two Warren Commission staff attorneys, W. David Slawson and William Coleman, went so far as to speculate that Oswald, despite his public posture as a Castro sympathizer, might actually have been an agent of anti-Castro exiles. (3) Indeed, pressing for further investigation of the possibility, they wrote a memorandum which read in part:

> The evidence here could lead to an anti-Castro involvement in the assassination on some sort of basis as this: Oswald could have become known to the Cubans as being strongly pro-Castro. He made no secret of his sympathies, so the anti-Castro Cubans must have realized that law enforcement authorities were also aware of Oswald's feelings and that, therefore, if he got into trouble, the public would also learn of them * * * Second, someone in the anti-Castro organization might have been keen enough to sense that Oswald had a penchant for violence * * * On these facts, it is possible that some sort of deception was used to encourage Oswald to kill the President when he came to Dallas * * * The motive of this would, of course, be the expectation that after the President was killed, Oswald would be caught or at least his identity ascertained, the law enforcement authorities and the public would blame the assassination on the Castro government and a call for its forceful overthrow would be irresistible * * *. (4)

While it is seemingly in contradiction of Oswald's personal character and known public posture, the committee seriously considered, therefore, the possibility of an anti-Castro conspiracy in the assassination (perhaps with Oswald unaware of its true nature). It is appropriate to begin that consideration with an examination of the history of United States-Cuban relations from the perspective of the anti-Castro movement, beginning with the victorious end of the revolution on January 1, 1959. (5)

(a) The anti-Castro Cuban perspective

The anti-Castro movement began not long after Fidel Castro assumed control of Cuba. (6) At first, the Cuban people cheered the revolution and its leader for the defeat of the dictatorial Batista regime, but it was not long before many former supporters found reason to condemn the new premier's policies and politics. (7) Many Cubans were deeply disillusioned when it became apparent that the Castro government was renouncing the country's long affiliation with the United States and moving closer to the Soviet Union. (8) As Castro's preference for Marxism became evident, underground opposition movements were born. (9) They survived for a time within Cuba, but as the effectiveness of Castro's militia system was recognized, they retreated to the exile communities of Miami and other cities in the United States. (10)

The U.S. Government was responsive to the efforts of exiles to remove a Communist threat from the Caribbean, only 90 miles from the

Florida coast, and to recapture business investments lost to the nationalization of industry in Cuba. (11) An official, yet covert, program to train and equip exiles determined to overthrow Castro was sanctioned by President Eisenhower and his successor, President Kennedy, and carried out by the American intelligence agencies, particularly the Central Intelligence Agency. (12) The Cuban exiles, dependent on the United States for arms and logistical support, had little choice but to put their trust in Washington. (13)

Their trust collapsed, however, at the Bay of Pigs on April 17, 1961, when an exile invasion of Cuba was annihilated by Castro's troops. (14) The failure of American airpower to support the landing shattered the confidence of the anti-Castro Cubans in the U.S. Government. (15) They blamed President Kennedy, and he publicly accepted responsibility for the defeat. (16)

President Kennedy's readiness to take the blame for the Bay of Pigs served to intensify the anger of the exiles. (17) In executive session before the committee, Manuel Antonio Varona, who in 1961 was the head of the united exile organization, the Revolutionary Democratic Front, told of a tense and emotional encounter with the President at the White House, as hope for the invasion was fading. (18) "We were not charging Mr. Kennedy with anything," Varona testified. (19) "We knew he was not in charge of the military efforts directly. Nevertheless, President Kennedy told us he was the one—the only one responsible." (20)

A noted Cuban attorney, Mario Lazo, summed up Cuban feeling toward President Kennedy in his book, "Dagger in the Heart":

> The Bay of Pigs was wholly self-inflicted in Washington. Kennedy told the truth when he publicly accepted responsibility * * * The heroism of the beleaguered Cuban Brigade had been rewarded by betrayal, defeat, death for many of them, long and cruel imprisonment for the rest. The Cuban people * * * had always admired the United States as strong, rich, generous—but where was its sense of honor and the capacity of its leaders? (21)

President Kennedy was well aware of the bitter legacy of the Bay of Pigs debacle. Far from abandoning the Cuban exiles, he set out to convince them of his loyalty to their cause. One of the most emotionally charged events of his relationship with the Cuban exiles occurred on December 29, 1962, at the Orange Bowl in Miami. (22) He had come to welcome the survivors of the invasion force, Brigade 2506, the 1,200 men who had been ransomed from Cuba after almost 20 months in prison. (23) The President was presented with the brigade flag in a dramatic and tumultuous scene. (24)

The euphoria was false and misleading. Although the Cuban exiles cheered President Kennedy that day, there also coursed through the crowd a bitter resentment among some who felt they were witnessing a display of political hypocrisy. Later, it would be claimed that the brigade feeling against President Kennedy was so strong that the presentation nearly did not take place, and it would be alleged (incorrectly, as it turned out) that the brigade flag given to Kennedy was actually a replica. (25)

It is not possible to know fully how the Bay of Pigs defeat changed President Kennedy's attitude toward Cuba, but when journalists Taylor Branch and George Crile wrote in Harper's Magazine about a massive infusion of U.S. aid to clandestine anti-Castro operations in the wake of the Bay of Pigs, they titled their article, "The Kennedy Vendetta."*(26)* What is known is that the period between the Bay of Pigs and the Cuban missile crisis in October 1962 can be characterized as the high point of anti-Castro activity.*(27)* Miami, the center of the exile community, became a busy staging ground for armed infiltrations Cuba.*(28)* While not every raid was supported or even known about in advance by Government agencies, the United States played a key role in monitoring, directing and supporting the anti-Castro Cubans.*(29)* Although this effort was cloaked in secrecy, most Cubans in the exile community knew what was happening and who was supporting the operations.*(30)*

(1) *The missile crisis and its aftermath.*—At the time of the missile crisis in October 1962, the Cuban exiles were initially elated at the prospect of U.S. military action that might topple the Castro regime.*(31)* In the end, it seemed to the world that President Kennedy had the best of the confrontation with Castro and Soviet leader Nikita Khrushchev by demanding, and getting, the withdrawal of offensive missiles and bombers from Cuba. From the exiles' perspective, however, they had been compromised, since as part of the bargain, President Kennedy made a pledge not to invade Cuba.[20] *(32)*

Anti-Castro forces in the United States were all the more embittered in the spring of 1963 when the Federal Government closed down many of their training camps and guerrilla bases.*(34)* In cases where government raids intercepted the illegal arms transfers, weapons were confiscated and arrests were made.*(35)* Some anti-Castro operations did continue, however, right up to the time of the assassination, though the committee found that U.S. backing had by that time been reduced.*(36)*

(2) *Attitude of anti-Castro Cubans toward Kennedy.*—President Kennedy's popularity among the Cuban exiles had plunged deeply by 1963. Their bitterness is illustrated in a tape recording of a meeting of anti-Castro Cubans and right-wing Americans in the Dallas suburb of Farmer's Branch on October 1, 1963.*(37)* In it, a Cuban identified as Nestor Castellanos vehemently criticized the United States and blamed President Kennedy for the U.S. Government's policy of "non-interference" with respect to the Cuban issue.*(38)* Holding a copy of the September 26 edition of the Dallas Morning News, featuring a front-page account of the President's planned trip to Texas in November, Castellanos vented his hostility without restraint:

CASTELLANOS. * * * we're waiting for Kennedy the 22d, buddy. We're going to see him in one way or the other. We're going to give him the works when he gets in Dallas. Mr. good ol' Kennedy. I wouldn't even call him President Kennedy. He stinks.

[20] The United States never actually signed the pledge, since it was conditioned on United Nations inspection of the weapons withdrawal that Castro would not honor. The fine point of signing the pledge was of little importance to the Cuban exiles, however, who could point out later that no invasion did, in fact, occur.*(33)*

QUESTIONER. Are you insinuating that since this downfall came through the leader there [Castro in Cuba], that this might come to us * * *?

CASTELLANOS. Yes ma'am, your present leader. He's the one who is doing everything right now to help the United States to become Communist.[21] (*39*)

(b) *The committee investigation*

The committee initiated its investigation by identifying the most violent and frustrated anti-Castro groups and their leaders from among the more than 100 Cuban exile organizations in existence in November 1963.(*40*) These groups included Alpha 66, the Cuban Revolutionary Junta (JURE), Commandos L, the Directorio Revolucionario Estudiantil (DRE), the Cuban Revolutionary Council (CRC) which included the Frente Revolucionario Democratico (FRD), the Junta del Gobierno de Cuba en el Exilio (JGCE), the 30th of November, the International Penetration Forces (InterPen), the Revolutionary Recovery Movement (MRR), and the Ejercito Invasor Cubano (EIC).(*41*) Their selection evolved both from the committee's independent field investigation and the examination of the files and records maintained by the Federal and local agencies then monitoring Cuban exile activity. These agencies included local police departments, the FBI, the CIA, the Bureau of Narcotics and Dangerous Drugs (now the Drug Enforcement Administration, or DEA), the Customs Service, the Immigration and Naturalization Service and the Department of Defense.(*42*)

The groups that received the committee's attention were "action groups"—those most involved in military actions and propaganda campaigns. Unlike most others, they did not merely talk about anti-Castro operations, they actually carried out infiltrations into Cuba, planned, and sometimes attempted, Castro's assassination, and shipped arms into Cuba. These were also the groups whose leaders felt most betrayed by U.S. policy toward Cuba and by the President; they were also those whose operations were frustrated by American law enforcement efforts after the missile crisis. .

(1) *Homer S. Echevarria.*—For the most part the committee found that the anti-Castro Cuban leaders were more vociferous than potentially violent in their tirades against the President. Nevertheless, it was unable to conclude with certainty that all of the threats were benign. For example, one that the committee found particularly disturbing—especially so, since it was not thoroughly looked into in the 1963–64 investigation—came to the attention of the Secret Service within days of the President's death, prompting the Acting Special Agent-in-Charge of the Chicago field office to write an urgent memorandum indicating he had received reliable information of "a group in the Chicago area who [sic] may have a connection with the J. F. K. assassination."(*43*) The memorandum was based on a tip from an informant who reported a conversation on November 21, 1963, with a Cuban activist named Homer S. Echevarria.(*44*) They were discussing an illegal arms sale, and Echevarria was quoted as saying his group now

---

[21] The committee uncovered no evidence that linked Castellanos to the assassination. His speech is quoted to illustrate the depth of feeling that existed in the Cuban exile community in 1963.

had "plenty of money" and that his backers would proceed "as soon as we take care of Kennedy."(45)

Following the initial memorandum, the Secret Service instructed its informant to continue his association with Echevarria and notified the Chicago FBI field office.(46) It learned that Echevarria might have been a member of the 30th of November anti-Castro organization, that he was associated with Juan Francisco Blanco-Fernandez, military director of the DRE, and that the arms deal was being financed through one Paulino Sierra Martinez by hoodlum elements in Chicago and elsewhere.(47)

Although the Secret Service recommended further investigation, the FBI initially took the position that the Echevarria case "was primarily a protection matter and that the continued investigation would be left to the U.S. Secret Service,"(48) and that the Cuban group in question was probably not involved in illegal activities.(49) The Secret Service initially was reluctant to accept this position, since it had developed evidence that illegal acts were, in fact, involved.(50) Then, on November 29, 1963, President Johnson created the Warren Commission and gave the FBI primary investigative responsibility in the assassination.(51) Based on its initial understanding that the President's order meant primary, not exclusive, investigative responsibility, the Secret Service continued its efforts;(52) but when the FBI made clear that it wanted the Secret Service to terminate its investigation,(53) it did so, turning over its files to the FBI.(54) The FBI, in turn, did not pursue the Echevarria case.(55)

While it was unable to substantiate the content of the informant's alleged conversations with Echevarria or any connection to the events in Dallas, the committee did establish that the original judgment of the Secret Service was correct, that the Echevarria case did warrant a thorough investigation. It found, for example, that the 30th of November group was backed financially by the Junta del Gobierno de Cuba en el Exilio (JGCE), a Chicago-based organization run by Paulino Sierra Martinez.(56) JGCE was a coalition of many of the more active anti-Castro groups that had been founded in April 1963; it was dissolved soon after the assassination.[22](57) Its purpose was to back the activities of the more militant groups, including Alpha 66 and the Student Directorate, or DRE, both of which had reportedly been in contact with Lee Harvey Oswald.(58) Much of JGCE's financial support, moreover, allegedly came from individuals connected to organized crime.(59)

As it surveyed the various anti-Castro organizations, the committee focused its interest on reported contacts with Oswald. Unless an association with the President's assassin could be established, it is doubtful that it could be shown that the anti-Castro groups were involved in the assassination. The Warren Commission, discounting the recommendations of Slawson and Coleman, had either regarded these contacts as insignificant or as probably not having been made or else was not aware of them.(60) The committee could not so easily dismiss them.

---

[22] The committee established—though it could make no judgment about there having been a connection—that many of the anti-Castro Cuban groups ceased their operations at about the time of President Kennedy's assassination. The Echevarria allegation is also discussed in section I D(1)(b) infra.

(2) *Antonio Veciana Blanch.*—The committee devoted a significant portion of its anti-Castro Cuban investigation to an alleged contact with Oswald that had been reported by Antonio Veciana Blanch, the founder of Alpha 66 which, throughout 1962 and most of 1963, was one of the most militant of the exile groups. (*61*) Its repeated hit-and-run attacks had drawn public criticism from President Kennedy in the spring of 1963, to which Veciana replied, "We are going to attack again and again."

Veciana claimed to have had the active support of the CIA, and in 1976 he reported to a Senate investigator that from 1960 to 1973 his adviser, whom he believed to be a representative of the CIA, was known to him as Maurice Bishop. (*62*) Veciana stated that over their 13-year association, he and Bishop met on over 100 occasions and that Bishop actually planned many Alpha 66 operations. (*63*) He also said that he knew the man only as Maurice Bishop and that all of their contacts were initiated by Bishop. (*64*)

· Veciana said that Bishop had guided him in planning assassination attempts of Castro in Havana in 1961 and in Chile in 1971; that Bishop had directed him to organize Alpha 66 in 1962; and that Bishop, on ending their relationship in 1973, had paid him $253,000 in cash for his services over the years. (*65*) Veciana also revealed that at one meeting with Bishop in Dallas in late August or early September 1963, a third party at their meeting was a man he later recognized as Lee Harvey Oswald. (*66*)

Veciana also indicated to the committee that subsequent to the assassination, he had been contacted by Bishop, who was aware that Veciana had a relative in Cuban intelligence in Mexico. (*67*) Bishop, according to Veciana, offered to pay Veciana's relative a large sum of money if he would say that it was he and his wife who had met with Oswald in Mexico City. (*68*) Veciana said he had agreed to contact his relative, but he had been unable to do so. (*69*)

The committee pursued the details of Veciana's story, particularly the alleged meeting with Oswald. It conducted numerous file reviews and interviews with associates and former associates of Veciana, to try to confirm the existence of a Maurice Bishop or otherwise assess Veciana's credibility. On a trip to Cuba, the committee interviewed Veciana's relative, the Cuban intelligence agent.

While the committee was unable to find corroboration for the contacts with Bishop, it did substantiate other statements by Veciana. For example, he did organize an attempted assassination of Castro in Havana in 1961, (*70*) and he probably did participate in another plot against Castro in Chile in 1971. (*71*) That Veciana was the principal organizer of the militant Alpha 66 organization was a matter of record. (*72*)

The committee went to great lengths in its unsuccessful effort to substantiate the existence of Bishop and his alleged relationship with Oswald. It reviewed CIA files, but they showed no record of such an agent or employee. It circulated a sketch via the national news media, but no one responded with an identification. (*73*) It pursued a lead originating with the Senate investigation that a former chief of the CIA's Western Hemisphere Division of the Directorate of Operations bore a resemblance to the Bishop sketch. (*74*) The committee arranged for a chance meeting between Veciana and the CIA officer, who had since retired. (75) Veciana said he was not Bishop. (76) In an executive session of the committee, the retired officer testified under oath that he had never used the name Maurice Bishop, had never known anyone by that name and had never known Veciana. (77) Veciana, also before a committee executive session, testified the officer was not Bishop, although he bore a "physical similarity." 23 (78)

A former Director of the CIA, John McCone, and an agent who had participated in covert Cuban operations, each told the committee they recalled that a Maurice Bishop had been associated with the Agency, though neither could supply additional details. (80) Subsequently, McCone was interviewed by CIA personnel, and he told them that his original testimony to the committee had been in error. (81) The agent did confirm, however, even after a CIA reinterview, that he had seen the man known to him as Maurice Bishop three or four times at CIA headquarters in the early 1960's. (82) He did not know his organizational responsibilities, and he had not known him personally. (83) The agent also testified that he had been acquainted with the retired officer who had been chief of the Western Hemisphere Division and that he was not Bishop. (84)

The committee also requested files on Bishop from the FBI and Department of Defense, with negative results. (85) It did discover, however, that Army intelligence had an operational interest in Veciana as a source of information on Alpha 66 activities, and that Veciana complied, hoping to be supplied in return with funds and weapons. (86) Veciana acknowledged his contacts with the Army, but he stated that the only relationship those contacts had to Bishop was that he kept Bishop informed of them. (87)

The CIA's files reflected that the Agency had been in contact with Veciana three times during the early 1960's, but the Agency maintained it offered him no encouragement. (88) (The committee could discover only one piece of arguably contradictory evidence—a record of $500 in operational expenses, given to Veciana by a person with whom the CIA had maintained a longstanding operational relationship. (89)) The CIA further insisted that it did not at any time assign a case officer to Veciana.24 (90)

The committee was left with the task of evaluating Veciana's story, both with respect to the existence of Maurice Bishop and the alleged meeting with Oswald, by assessing Veciana's credibility. It found several reasons to believe that Veciana had been less than candid:

---

23 The committee suspected that Veciana was lying when he denied that the retired CIA officer was Bishop. The committee recognized that Veciana had an interest in renewing his anti-Castro operations that might have led him to protect the officer from exposure as Bishop so they could work together again. For his part, the retired officer aroused the committee's suspicion when he told the committee he did not recognize Veciana as the founder of Alpha 66, especially since the officer had once been deeply involved in Agency anti-Castro operations. Further, a former CIA case officer who was assigned from September 1960 to November 1962 to the JM/WAVE station in Miami told the committee that the retired officer had in fact used the alias, Maurice Bishop. The committee also interviewed a former assistant of the retired officer but he could not recall his former superior ever having used the name or having been referred to as Bishop. (79)

24 The committee found it probable that some agency of the United States assigned a case officer to Veciana, since he was the dominant figure in an extremely active anti-Castro organization. The committee established that the CIA assigned case officers to Cuban revolutionaries of less importance than Veciana, though it could not draw from that alone an inference of CIA deception of the committee concerning Veciana, since Bishop could well have been in the employ of one of the military intelligence agencies or even perhaps of some foreign power.

First, Veciana waited more than 10 years after the assassination to reveal his story.

Second, Veciana would not supply proof of the $253,000 payment from Bishop, claiming fear of the Internal Revenue Service.

Third, Veciana could not point to a single witness to his meetings with Bishop, much less with Oswald.

Fourth, Veciana did little to help the committee identify Bishop. In the absence of corroboration or independent substantiation, the committee could not, therefore, credit Veciana's story of having met with Lee Harvey Oswald.

(3) *Silvia Odio.*—The incident of reported contact between Oswald and anti-Castro Cubans that has gained the most attention over the years involved Silvia Odio, a member of the Cuban Revolutionary Junta, or JURE. (*91*) Mrs. Odio had not volunteered her information to the FBI. (*92*) The FBI initially contacted Mrs. Odio after hearing of a conversation she had had with her neighbor in which she described an encounter with Lee Harvey Oswald. (*93*) Subsequently, in testimony before the Warren Commission, she said that in late September 1963, three men came to her home in Dallas to ask for help in preparing a fundraising letter for JURE. (*94*) She stated that two of the men appeared to be Cubans, although they also had characteristics that she associated with Mexicans. (*95*) The two individuals, she remembered, indicated that their "war" names were "Leopoldo" and "Angelo." (*96*) The third man, an American, was introduced to her as "Leon Oswald," and she was told that he was very much interested in the anti-Castro Cuban cause. (*97*)

Mrs. Odio stated that the men told her that they had just come from New Orleans and that they were then about to leave on a trip. (*98*) The next day, one of the Cubans called her on the telephone and told her that it had been his idea to introduce the American into the underground "* * * because he is great, he is kind of nuts." (*99*) The Cuban also said that the American had been in the Marine Corps and was an excellent shot, and that the American had said that Cubans "* * * don't have any guts * * * because President Kennedy should have been assassinated after the Bay of Pigs, and some Cubans should have done that, because he was the one that was holding the freedom of Cuba actually." (*100*) Mrs. Odio claimed the American was Lee Harvey Oswald. (*101*)

Mrs. Odio's sister, who was in the apartment at the time of the visit by the three men and who stated that she saw them briefly in the hallway when answering the door, also believed that the American was Lee Harvey Oswald. (*102*) Mrs. Odio fixed the date of the alleged visit as being September 26 or 27. (*103*) She was positive that the visit occurred prior to October 1. (*104*)

The Warren Commission was persuaded that Oswald could not have been in Dallas on the dates given by Mrs. Odio. (*105*) Nevertheless, it requested the FBI to conduct further investigation into her allegation, and it acknowledged that the FBI had not completed its Odio investigation at the time its report was published in September 1964. (*106*)

How the Warren Commission treated the Odio incident is instructive. In the summer of 1964, the FBI was pressed to dig more deeply into the Odio allegation. (*107*) On July 24, chief counsel J. Lee Rankin, in a letter to FBI Director J. Edgar Hoover, noted, ". . . the Commission already possesses firm evidence that Lee Harvey Oswald was on a bus traveling from Houston, Tex., to Mexico City, Mexico, on virtually the entire day of September 26."(108) J. Wesley Liebeler, the Warren Commission assistant counsel who had taken Mrs. Odio's deposition, disagreed, however, that there was firm evidence of Oswald's bus trip to Mexico City.(109) In a memorandum to another Commission attorney, Howard Willens, on September 14, 1964, Liebeler objected to a section of the Warren Report in which it was stated there was strong evidence that Oswald was on a bus to Mexico on the date in question.(110) Liebeler argued, "There really is no evidence at all that [Oswald] left Houston on that bus."(111) Liebeler also argued that the conclusion that there was "persuasive" evidence that Oswald was not in Dallas on September 24, 1963, a day for which his travel was unaccounted, was "too strong."(112) Liebeler urged Willens to tone down the language of the report,(113) contending in his memorandum: "There are problems. Odio may well be right. The Commission will look bad if it turns out that she is."(114)

On August 23, 1964, Rankin again wrote to Hoover to say, "It is a matter of some importance to the Commission that Mrs. Odio's allegation either be proved or disproved."(115) Rankin asked that the FBI attempt to learn the identities of the three visitors by contacting members of anti-Castro groups active in the Dallas area, as well as leaders of the JURE organization.(116) He asked the FBI to check the possibility that Oswald had spent the night of September 24, in a hotel in New Orleans, after vacating his apartment.(117) Portions of this investigation, which were inconclusive in supporting the Warren Commission's contention that Mrs. Odio was mistaken, were not sent to Rankin until November 9,(118) at which time the final report already had been completed.(119)

The FBI did attempt to alleviate the "problems." In a report dated September 26, it reported the interview of Loran Eugene Hall who claimed he had been in Dallas in September 1963, accompanied by two men fitting the general description given by Silvia Odio, and that it was they who had visited her.(120) Oswald, Hall said, was not one of the men.(121) Within a week of Hall's statement, the other two men Hall said had accompanied him. Lawrence Howard and William Seymour, were interviewed.(122) They denied ever having met Silvia Odio.(123) Later, Hall himself retracted his statement about meeting with Mrs. Odio.(124)

Even though the Commission could not show conclusively that Oswald was not at the Odio apartment, and even though Loran Hall's story was an admitted fabrication, the Warren report published this explanation of the Odio incident:

> While the FBI had not yet completed its investigation into this matter at the time the report went to press, the Commission has concluded that Lee Harvey Oswald was not at Mrs. Odio's apartment in September 1963.(125)

Not satisfied with that conclusion, the committee conducted interviews with and took depositions from the principals—Silvia Odio,(126) members of her family,(127) and Dr. Burton Einspruch,

(*128*) her psychiatrist. (Mrs. Odio had contacted Dr. Einspruch for consultation about problems that could not be construed to affect her perception or credibility.) (*129*) The committee also set up a conference telephone call between Dr. Einspruch in Dallas and Silvia Odio in Miami, during which she related to him the visit of the three men. (*130*) Mrs. Odio and Dr. Einspruch concurred that she had told him of the nighttime meeting shortly after its occurrence, but prior to the President's assassination. (*131*)

Loran Hall testified before the committee in executive session on October 5, 1977; Howard and Seymour were interviewed. (*132*) The FBI agent who wrote up the Hall story also testified before the committee. (*133*) From a review of FBI files, the committee secured a list of persons who belonged to the Dallas Chapter of JURE, and the committee attempted to locate and interview these individuals. Additionally, staff investigators interviewed the leader of JURE, Manolo Ray, who was residing in Puerto Rico. (*134*)

.Further, the committee secured photographs of scores of pro-Castro and anti-Castro activists who might have fit the descriptions of the two individuals who, Mrs. Odio said, had visited her with Oswald. (*135*) The committee also used the resources of the CIA which conducted a check on all individuals who used the "war" names of "Leopoldo" and "Angelo", and the name "Leon," or had similar names. (*136*) An extensive search produced the names and photographs of three men who might possibly have been in Dallas in September 1963. (*137*) These photographs were shown to Mrs. Odio, but she was unable to identify them as the men she had seen. (*138*)

The committee was inclined to believe Silvia Odio. From the evidence provided in the sworn testimony of the witnesses, it appeared that three men did visit her apartment in Dallas prior to the Kennedy assassination and identified themselves as members of an anti-Castro organization. Based on a judgment of the credibility of Silvia and Annie Odio, one of these men at least looked like Lee Harvey Oswald and was introduced to Mrs. Odio as Leon Oswald.

The committee did not agree with the Warren Commission's conclusion that Oswald could not have been in Dallas at the requisite time. Nevertheless, the committee itself could reach no definite conclusion on the specific date of the visit. It could have been as early as September 24, the morning of which Oswald was seen in New Orleans, (*139*) but it was more likely on the 25th, 26th or 27th of September. If it was on these dates, then Oswald had to have had access to private transportation to have traveled through Dallas and still reached Mexico City when he did, judging from other evidence developed by both the Warren Commission and the committee. (*140*)

(c) Oswald and anti-Castro Cubans

The committee recognized that an association by Oswald with anti-Castro Cubans would pose problems for its evaluation of the assassin and what might have motivated him. In reviewing Oswald's life, the committee found his actions and values to have been those of a self-proclaimed Marxist who would be bound to favor the Castro regime in Cuba, or at least not advocate its overthrow. For this reason, it did not seem likely to the committee that Oswald would have allied himself with an anti-Castro group or individual activist for the sole purpose of furthering the anti-Castro cause. The committee recognized the possibility that Oswald might have established contacts with such groups or persons to implicate the anti-Castro movement in the assassination. Such an implication might have protected the Castro regime and other left-wing suspects, while resulting in an intensive investigation and possible neutralization of the opponents of Castro. It is also possible, despite his alleged remark about killing Kennedy, that Oswald had not yet contemplated the President's assassination at the time of the Odio incident, or if he did, that his assassination plan had no relation to his anti-Castro contacts, and that he was associating with anti-Castro activists for some other unrelated reason. A variety of speculations are possible, but the committee was forced to acknowledge frankly that, despite its efforts, it was unable to reach firm conclusions as to the meaning or significance of the Odio incident to the President's assassination.

(1) *Oswald in New Orleans.*—Another contact by Lee Harvey Oswald with anti-Castro Cuban activists that was not only documented, but also publicized at the time in the news media, occurred when he was living in New Orleans in the summer of 1963, an especially puzzling period in Oswald's life. His actions were blatantly pro-Castro, as he carried a one-man Fair Play for Cuba Committee crusade into the streets of a city whose Cuban population was predominantly anti-Castro. Yet Oswald's known and alleged associations even at this time included Cubans who were of an anti-Castro persuasion and their anti-Communist American supporters.

New Orleans was Oswald's home town; he was born there on October 18, 1939.(*141*) In April 1963, shortly after the Walker shooting, he moved back, having lived in Fort Worth and Dallas since his return from the Soviet Union the previous June.(*142*) He spent the first 2 weeks job hunting, staying with the Murrets, Lillian and Charles, or "Dutz," as he was called, the sister and brother-in-law of Oswald's mother, Marguerite.(*143*) After being hired by the Reily Coffee Co. as a maintenance man, he sent for his wife Marina and their baby daughter, who were still in Dallas, and they moved into an apartment on Magazine Street.(*144*)

In May, Oswald wrote to Vincent T. Lee, national director of the Fair Play for Cuba Committee, expressing a desire to open an FPCC chapter in New Orleans and requesting literature to distribute.(*145*) He also had handouts printed, some of which were stamped "L. H. Oswald, 4907 Magazine Street," others with the alias, "A. J. Hidell, P.O. Box 30016," still others listing the FPCC address as 544 Camp Street.(*146*)

In letters written earlier that summer and spring to the FPCC headquarters in New York, Oswald had indicated that he intended to rent an office.(*147*) In one letter he mentioned that he had acquired a space but had been told to vacate 3 days later because the building was to be remodeled. The Warren Commission failed to discover any record of Oswald's having rented an office at 544 Camp and concluded he had fabricated the story.(*149*)

In investigating Oswald after the assassination, the Secret Service learned that the New Orleans chapter of the Cuban Revolutionary

Council (CRC), an anti-Castro organization, had occupied an office at 544 Camp Street for about 6 months during 1961–62. (150) At that time, Sergio Arcacha Smith was the official CRC delegate for the New Orleans area. (151) Since the CRC had vacated the building 15 months before Oswald arrived in New Orleans, the Warren Commission concluded that there was no connection with Oswald. (152) Nevertheless, the riddle of 544 Camp Street persisted over the years.

Oswald lost his job at the Reily Coffee Co. in July, and his efforts to find another were futile. (153) Through the rest of the summer, he filed claims at the unemployment office. (154)

On August 5, Oswald initiated contact with Carlos Bringuier, a delegate of the Directorio Revolucionario Estudiantil (DRE). (155) According to his testimony before the Warren Commission, Bringuier was the only registered member of the group in New Orleans. (156) Bringuier also said he had two friends at the time, Celso Hernandez and Miguel Cruz, who were also active in the anti-Castro cause. (157) Oswald reportedly told Bringuier that he wished to join the DRE, offering money and assistance to train guerrillas. (158) Bringuier, fearful of an infiltration attempt by Castro sympathizers or the FBI, told Oswald to deal directly with DRE headquarters in Miami. (159) The next day, Oswald returned to Bringuier's store and left a copy of a Marine training manual with Rolando Pelaez, Bringuier's brother-in-law. (160)

On August 9, Bringuier learned that a man was carrying a pro-Castro sign and handing out literature on Canal Street. (161) Carrying his own anti-Castro sign, Bringuier, along with Hernandez and Cruz, set out to demonstrate against the pro-Castro sympathizer. (162) Bringuier recognized Oswald and began shouting that he was a traitor and a Communist. (163) A scuffle ensued, and police arrested all participants. (164) Oswald spent the night in jail. (165) On August 12, he pleaded guilty to disturbing the peace and was fined $10. (166) The anti-Castro Cubans were not charged. (167)

During the incident with Bringuier, Oswald also encountered Frank Bartes, the New Orleans delegate of the CRC from 1962–64. (168) After Bringuier and Oswald were arrested in the street scuffle, Bartes appeared in court with Bringuier. (169) According to Bartes, the news media surrounded Oswald for a statement after the hearing. (170) Bartes then engaged in an argument with the media and Oswald because the Cubans were not being given an opportunity to present their anti-Castro views. (171)

On August 16, Oswald was again seen distributing pro-Castro literature. (172) A friend of Bringuier, Carlos Quiroga, brought one of Oswald's leaflets to Bringuier and volunteered to visit Oswald and feign interest in the FPCC in order to determine Oswald's motives. (173) Quiroga met with Oswald for about an hour. (174) He learned that Oswald had a Russian wife and spoke Russian himself. Oswald gave Quiroga an application for membership in the FPCC chapter, but Quiroga noted he did not seem intent on actually enlisting members. (175)

Oswald's campaign received newspaper, television, and radio coverage. (176) William Stuckey, a reporter for radio station WDSU who had been following the FPCC, interviewed Oswald on August 17 and proposed a television debate between Oswald and Bringuier, to be held on August 21.(*177*) Bringuier issued a press release immediately after the debate, urging the citizens of New Orleans to write their Congressmen demanding a congressional investigation of Lee Harvey Oswald.(*178*)

Oswald largely passed out of sight from August 21 until September 17, the day he applied for a tourist card to Mexico.(*179*) He is known to have written letters to left-wing political organizations, and he and Marina visited the Murrets on Labor Day.(*180*) Marina said her husband spent his free time reading books and practicing with his rifle.(*181*)

(2) *Oswald in Clinton, La.*—While reports of some Oswald contacts with anti-Castro Cubans were known at the time of the 1964 investigation, allegations of additional Cuba-related associations surfaced in subsequent years. As an example, Oswald reportedly appeared in August–September 1963 in Clinton, La., where a voting rights demonstration was in progress. The reports of Oswald in Clinton were not, as far as the committee could determine, available to the Warren Commission, although one witness said he notified the FBI when he recognized Oswald from news photographs right after the assassination.[25](*182*) In fact, the Clinton sightings did not publicly surface until 1967, when they were introduced as evidence in the assassination investigation being conducted by New Orleans District Attorney Jim Garrison.(*184*) In that investigation, one suspect, David W. Ferrie, a staunch anti-Castro partisan, died within days of having been named by Garrison; the other, Clay L. Shaw, was acquitted in 1969.(*185*) Aware that Garrison had been fairly criticized for questionable tactics, the committee proceeded cautiously, making sure to determine on its own the credibility of information coming from his probe. The committee found that the Clinton witnesses were credible and significant. They each were interviewed or deposed, or appeared before the committee in executive session. While there were points that could be raised to call into question their credibility, it was the judgment of the committee that they were telling the truth as they knew it.

There were six Clinton witnesses, among them a State representative, a deputy sheriff and a registrar of voters.(*186*) By synthesizing the testimony of all of them, since they each contributed to the overall account, the committee was able to piece together the following sequence of events:

Clinton, La., about 130 miles from New Orleans, is the county seat of East Feliciana Parish. In the late summer of 1963 it was targeted by the Congress of Racial Equality for a voting rights campaign.(*187*) Oswald first showed up in nearby Jackson, La., seeking employment at East Louisiana State Hospital, a mental institution.(*188*) Apparently on advice that his job would depend on his becoming a registered voter, Oswald went to Clinton for that purpose (although the committee could find no record that he was successful.(*189*)

In addition to the physical descriptions they gave that matched that of Oswald, other observations of the witnesses tended to substanti-

---

[25] Reeves Morgan, a member of the Louisiana Legislature, testified he was called back by the FBI a few days later and asked what Oswald had been wearing. He said he was not contacted again. The FBI had no record of Morgan's call. (*183*)

ate their belief that he was, in fact, the man they saw. For example, he referred to himself as "Oswald," and he produced his Marine Corps discharge papers as identification. (*190*) Some of the witnesses said that Oswald was accompanied by two older men whom they identified as Ferrie and Shaw. (*191*) If the witnesses were not only truthful but accurate as well in their accounts, they established an association of an undetermined nature between Ferrie, Shaw and Oswald less than 3 months before the assassination.

(3) *David Ferrie.*—The Clinton witnesses were not the only ones who linked Oswald to Ferrie. On November 23, the day after the assassination, Jack S. Martin, a part-time private detective and police informant, told the office of the New Orleans District Attorney that a former Eastern Airlines pilot named David Ferrie might have aided Oswald in the assassination. (*192*) Martin had known Ferrie for over 2 years, beginning when he and Ferrie had performed some investigative work on a case involving an illegitimate religious order in Louisville, Ky. (*193*) Martin advised Assistant New Orleans District Attorney Herman Kohlman that he suspected Ferrie might have known Oswald for some time and that Ferrie might have once been Oswald's superior officer in a New Orleans unit of the Civil Air Patrol. (*194*) Martin made further allegations to the FBI on November 25. (*195*) He indicated he thought he once saw a photograph of Oswald and other CAP members when he visited Ferrie's home and that Ferrie might have assisted Oswald in purchasing a foreign firearm. (*196*) Martin also informed the FBI that Ferrie had a history of arrests and that Ferrie was an amateur hypnotist, possibly capable of hypnotizing Oswald. (*197*)

The committee reviewed Ferrie's background. He had been fired by Eastern Airlines, (*198*) and in litigation over the dismissal, which continued through August 1963, he was counseled by a New Orleans attorney named G. Wray Gill. (*199*) Ferrie later stated that in March 1962, he and Gill made an agreement whereby Gill would represent Ferrie in his dismissal dispute in return for Ferrie's work as an investigator on other cases. (*200*) One of these cases involved deportation proceedings against Carlos Marcello, the head of the organized crime network in Louisiana and a client of Gill.[26] (*201*) Ferrie also said he had entered into a similar agreement with Guy Banister, a former FBI agent (Special Agent-in-Charge in Chicago) who had opened a private detective agency in New Orleans. (*203*)

(4) *544 Camp Street.*—Banister's firm occupied an office in 1963 in the Newman Building at 531 Lafayette Street. (*204*) Another entrance to the building was at 544 Camp Street, the address Oswald had stamped on his Fair Play for Cuba Committee handouts. (*205*) During the summer of 1963, Ferrie frequented 544 Camp Street regularly as a result of his working relationship with Banister. (*206*)

Another occupant of the Newman Building was the Cuban Revolutionary Council, whose chief New Orleans delegate until 1962 was Ser-

[26] The committee learned that Ferrie's associations with Marcello might have begun earlier. An unconfirmed U.S. Border Patrol report indicated that in February 1962, Ferrie piloted an airplane that returned Marcello to the United States following his ouster from the country by Federal agents in April 1961, as part of the Kennedy administration's crackdown on organized crime. Marcello denied to the committee in executive session that Ferrie flew him out of Latin America, saying that he flew commercial airlines. Records do not exist that can confirm or refute this contention. (*202*)

gio Arcacha Smith.(*207*) He was replaced by Luis Rabel who, in turn, was succeeded by Frank Bartes.(*208*) The committee interviewed or deposed all three CRC New Orleans delegates.(*209*) Arcacha said he never encountered Oswald and that he left New Orleans when he was relieved of his CRC position in early 1962.(*210*) Rabel said he held the post from January to October 1962, but that he likewise never knew or saw Oswald and that the only time he went to the Newman Building was to remove some office materials that Arcacha had left there. (*211*) Bartes said the only time he was in contact with Oswald was in their courtroom confrontation, that he ran the CRC chapter from an office in his home and that he never visited an office at either 544 Camp Street or 531 Lafayette Street.(*212*)

The committee, on the other hand, developed information that, in 1961, Banister, Ferrie, and Arcacha were working together in the anti-Castro cause. Banister, a fervent anti-Communist, was helping to establish Friends of Democratic Cuba as an adjunct to the New Orleans CRC chapter run by Arcacha in an office in the Newman Building.(*213*) Banister was also conducting background investigations of CRC members for Arcacha.(*214*) Ferrie, also strongly anti-Communist and anti-Castro, was associated with Arcacha (and probably Banister) in anti-Castro activism.(*215*)

On November 22, 1963, Ferrie had been in a Federal courtroom in New Orleans in connection with legal proceedings against Carlos Marcello.[27](*216*) That night he drove, with two young friends, to Houston, Tex., then to Galveston on Saturday, November 23, and back to New Orleans on Sunday.(*218*) Before reaching New Orleans, he learned from a telephone conversation with G. Wray Gill that Martin had implicated him in the assassination.(*219*) Gill also told Ferrie about the rumors that he and Oswald had served together in the CAP and that Oswald supposedly had Ferrie's library card in his possession when he was arrested in Dallas.(*220*) When he got to his residence, Ferrie did not go in, but sent in his place one of his companions on the trip, Alvin Beauboeuf.(*221*) Beauboeuf and Ferrie's roommate, Layton Martens, were detained by officers from the district attorney's office.(*222*) Ferrie drove to Hammond, La., and spent the night with a friend.(*223*)

On Monday, November 25, Ferrie turned himself in to the district attorney's office where he was arrested on suspicion of being involved in the assassination.(*224*) In subsequent interviews with New Orleans authorities, the FBI and the Secret Service, Ferrie denied ever having known Oswald or having ever been involved in the assassination. (*225*) He stated that in the days preceding November 22, he had been working intensively for Gill on the Marcello case.(*226*) Ferrie said he was in New Orleans on the morning of November 22, at which time Marcello was acquitted in Federal court of citizenship falsification. (*227*) He stated that he took the weekend trip to Texas for relaxation.(*228*) Ferrie acknowledged knowing Jack Martin, stating that Martin resented him for forcibly removing him from Gill's office earlier that year.(*229*)

---

[27] With Ferrie's employer, G. Wray Gill. as his counsel. Marcello was successfully resisting an attempt by the Government to have him legally deported or convicted of a crime. (*217*)

The FBI and Secret Service investigation into the possibility that Ferrie and Oswald had been associated ended a few days later.(230) A Secret Service report concluded that the information provided by Jack Martin that Ferrie had been associated with Oswald and had trained him to fire a rifle was "without foundation."(231) The Secret Service report went on to state that on November 26, 1963, the FBI had informed the Secret Service that Martin had admitted that his information was a "figment of his imagination." [28](232) The investigation of Ferrie was subsequently closed for lack of evidence against him.(234)

(5) *A committee analysis of Oswald in New Orleans.*—The Warren Commission had attempted to reconstruct a daily chronology of Oswald's activities in New Orleans during the summer of 1963, and the committee used it, as well as information arising from critics and the Garrison investigation, to select events and contacts that merited closer analysis. Among these were Oswald's confrontation with Carlos Bringuier and with Frank Bartes, his reported activities in Clinton, La., and his ties, if any, to Guy Banister, David Ferrie, Sergio Arcacha Smith and others who frequented the office building at 544 Camp Street.

The committee deposed Carlos Bringuier and interviewed or deposed several of his associates.(235) It concluded that there had been no relationship between Oswald and Bringuier and the DRE with the exception of the confrontation over Oswald's distribution of pro-Castro literature. The committee was not able to determine why Oswald approached the anti-Castro Cubans, but it tended to concur with Bringuier and others in their belief that Oswald was seeking to infiltrate their ranks and obtain information about their activities.

As noted, the committee believed the Clinton witnesses to be telling the truth as they knew it. It was, therefore, inclined to believe that Oswald was in Clinton, La., in late August, early September 1963, and that he was in the company of David Ferrie, if not Clay Shaw. The committee was puzzled by Oswald's apparent association with Ferrie, a person whose anti-Castro sentiments were so distant from those of Oswald, the Fair Play for Cuba Committee campaigner. But the relationship with Ferrie may have been significant for more than its anti-Castro aspect, in light of Ferrie's connection with G. Wray Gill and Carlos Marcello.

The committee also found that there was at least a possibility that Oswald and Guy Banister were acquainted. The following facts were considered:

The 544 Camp Street address stamped on Oswald's FPCC handouts was that of the building where Banister had his office;

Ross Banister told the committee that his brother had seen Oswald handing out FPCC literature during the summer of 1963; (236) and

Banister's secretary, Delphine Roberts, told the committee she saw Oswald in Banister's office on several occasions, the first being

---

[28] It appeared to the committee that the FBI overstated Martin's recantation in its information to the Secret Service. Martin had cautioned the FBI that he had no evidence to support his suspicions but that he believed they merited investigation.(233)

when he was interviewed for a job during the summer of 1963.[29] (237)

The committee learned that Banister left extensive files when he died in 1964. (238) Later that year, they were purchased by the Louisiana State Police from Banister's widow. (239) According to Joseph Cambre of the State police, Oswald's name was not the subject of any file, but it was included in a file for the Fair Play for Cuba Committee. (240) Cambre said the FPCC file contained newspaper clippings and a transcript of a radio program on which Oswald had appeared. (241) The committee was not able to review Banister's files, since they had been destroyed pursuant to an order of the superintendent of Louisiana State Police that all files not part of the public record or pertinent to ongoing criminal investigations be burned. (242)

Additional evidence that Oswald may have been associated or acquainted with Ferrie and Banister was provided by the testimony of Adrian Alba, proprietor of the Crescent City Garage which was next door to the Reily Coffee Co. where Oswald had worked for a couple of months in 1963. (The garage and the coffee company were both located less than a block from 544 Camp Street.) Although Alba's testimony on some points was questionable, he undoubtedly did know Oswald who frequently visited his garage, and the committee found no reason to question his statement that he had often seen Oswald in Mancuso's Restaurant on the first floor of 544 Camp. (243) Ferrie and Banister also were frequent customers at Mancuso's. (244)

(6) *Summary of the evidence.*—In sum, the committee did not believe that an anti-Castro organization was involved in a conspiracy to assassinate President Kennedy. Even though the committee's investigation did reveal that in 1964 the FBI failed to pursue intelligence reports of possible anti-Castro involvement as vigorously as it might have, the committee found it significant that it discovered no information in U.S. intelligence agency files that would implicate anti-Castroites. Contact between the intelligence community and the anti-Castro movement was close, so it is logical to suppose that some trace of group involvement would have been detected had it existed.

The committee also thought it significant that it received no information from the Cuban Government that would implicate anti-Castroites. The Cubans had dependable information sources in the exile communities in Miami, New Orleans, Dallas and other U.S. cities, so there is high probability that Cuban intelligence would have been aware of any group involvement by the exiles. Following the assassination, the Cuban Government would have had the highest incentive to report participation by anti-Castroites, had it existed to its knowledge, since it would have dispelled suspicions of pro-Castro Cuban involvement. The committee was impressed with the cooperation it received from the Cuban Government, and while it acknowledged this cooperation might not have been forthcoming in 1964, it concluded that, had such information existed in 1978, it would have been supplied by Cuban officials.

On the other hand, the committee noted that it was unable to preclude from its investigation the possibility that individuals with anti-

---

[29] The committee did not credit the Roberts' testimony standing alone. It came late in the investigation and without corroboration or independent substantiation, and much of Roberts' other testimony lacked credibility.

Castro leanings might have been involved in the assassination. The committee candidly acknowledged, for example, that it could not explain Oswald's associations—nor at this late date fully determine their extent—with anti-Castro Cubans. The committee remained convinced that since Oswald consistently demonstrated a left-wing Marxist ideology, he would not have supported the anti-Castro movement. At the same time, the committee noted that Oswald's possible association with Ferrie might be distinguishable, since it could not be simply termed an anti-Castro association. Ferrie and Oswald may have had a personal friendship unrelated to Cuban activities. Ferrie was not Cuban, and though he actively supported the anti-Castro cause, he had other interests. For one, he was employed by Carlos Marcello as an investigator.(245) (It has been alleged that Ferrie operated a service station in 1964, the franchise for which was reportedly paid by Marcello.) (246) The committee concluded, therefore, that Oswald's most significant apparent anti-Castro association, that with David Ferrie, might in fact not have been related to the Cuban issue.

In the end, the committee concluded that the evidence was sufficient to support the conclusion that anti-Castro Cuban groups, as groups, were not involved in the assassination, but it could not preclude the possibility that individual members may have been involved.

4. THE COMMITTEE BELIEVES, ON THE BASIS OF THE EVIDENCE AVAILABLE TO IT, THAT THE NATIONAL SYNDICATE OF ORGANIZED CRIME, AS A GROUP, WAS NOT INVOLVED IN THE ASSASSINATION OF PRESIDENT KENNEDY, BUT THAT THE AVAILABLE EVIDENCE DOES NOT PRECLUDE THE POSSIBILITY THAT INDIVIDUAL MEMBERS MAY HAVE BEEN INVOLVED

Lee Harvey Oswald was fatally shot by Jack Ruby at 11:21 a.m. on Sunday, November 24, 1963, less than 48 hours after President Kennedy was assassinated. While many Americans were prepared to believe that Oswald had acted alone in shooting the President, they found their credulity strained when they were asked to accept a conclusion that Ruby, too, had not acted as part of a plot. As the Warren Commission observed,

> * * * almost immediately speculation arose that Ruby had acted on behalf of members of a conspiracy who had planned the killing of President Kennedy and wanted to silence Oswald.(1).

The implications of the murder of Oswald are crucial to an understanding of the assassination itself. Several of the logical possibilities should be made explicit:

Oswald was a member of a conspiracy, and he was killed by Ruby, also a conspirator, so that he would not reveal the plot.

Oswald was a member of a conspiracy, yet Ruby acted alone, as he explained, for personal reasons.

Oswald was not a member of a conspiracy as far as Ruby knew, but his murder was an act planned by Ruby and others to take justice into their own hands.

94TH CONGRESS }
2d Session }

SENATE

{ REPORT
{ No. 94-755

SUPPLEMENTARY DETAILED STAFF REPORTS ON INTELLIGENCE ACTIVITIES AND THE RIGHTS OF AMERICANS

BOOK III

FINAL REPORT

OF THE

SELECT COMMITTEE
TO STUDY GOVERNMENTAL OPERATIONS

WITH RESPECT TO

INTELLIGENCE ACTIVITIES

UNITED STATES SENATE

APRIL 23 (under authority of the order of APRIL 14), 1976

U.S. GOVERNMENT PRINTING OFFICE
69-984 O   WASHINGTON : 1976

ants to take advantage of ideological splits in an organization dates
back to the first COINTELPRO. The originating CUPSA document
refers to the use of informants to capitalize on the discussion within
the Party following Khrushchev's denunciation of Stalin.[182]

Informants were also used to widen rifts in other organizations.
For instance, an informant was instructed to imply that the head of
one faction of the SDS was using group funds for his drug habit,
and that a second leader embezzled funds at another school. The field
office reported that "as a result of actions taken by this informant,
there have been fist fights and acts of name calling at several of the
recent SDS meetings." In addition, members of one faction "have
made early morning telephone calls" to other SDS members and "have
threatened them and attempted to discourage them from attending
SDS meetings." [183]

In another case, an informant was used to "raise the question"
among his associates that an unmarried, 30-year old group leader
"may be either a bisexual or a homosexual." The field office believed
that the question would "rapidly become a rumor" and "could have
serious results concerning the ability and effectiveness of [the target's]
leadership." [184]

5. Fictitious Organizations

There are basically three kinds of "notional" or fictitious organizations. All three were used in COINTELPRO attempts to factionalize.

The first kind of "notional" was the organization whose members
were all Bureau informants. Because of the Committee's agreement
with the Bureau not to reveal the identities of informants, the only
example which can be discussed publicly is a proposal which, although
approved, was never implemented. That proposal involved setting up
a chapter of the W.E.B. DuBois Club in a Southern city which would
be composed entirely of Bureau informants and fictitious persons.
The initial purpose of the chapter was to cause the CPUSA expense by
sending organizers into the area, cause the Party to fund Bureau
coverage of out-of-town CP meetings by paying the informants'
expenses, and receive literature and instructions. Later, the chapter
was to begin to engage in deviation from the Party line so that it
would be expelled from the main organization "and then they could
claim to be the victim of a Stalinist type purge." It was anticipated
that the entire operation would take no more than 18 months.[185]

The second kind of "notional" was the fictitious organization with
some unsuspecting (non-informant) members. For example, Bureau
informants set up a Klan organization intended to attract membership away from the United Klans of America. The Bureau paid the
informant's personal expenses in setting up the new organization,
which had, at its height, 250 members.[186]

The third type of "notional" was the wholly fictitious organization,
with no actual members, which was used as a pseudonym for mailing

---

[182] Memorandum from FBI Headquarters to New York Field Office, 9/6/56.
[183] Memorandum from Los Angeles Field Office to FBI Headquarters, 12/12/68,
p. 2.
[184] Memorandum from San Diego Field Office to FBI Headquarters, 2/2/70.
[185] Memorandum from New York Field Office to FBI Headquarters, 7/9/64.
[186] Memorandum from C. D. Brennan to W. C. Sullivan, 8/28/67.

letters or pamphlets. For instance, the Bureau sent out newsletters from something called "The Committee for Expansion of Socialist Thought in America," which attacked the CPUSA from the "Marxist right" for at least two years.[187]

6. Labeling Targets As Informants

The "snitch jacket" technique—neutralizing a target by labeling him a "snitch" or informant, so that he would no longer be trusted—was used in all COINTELPROs. The methods utilized ranged from having an authentic informant start a rumor about the target member,[188] to anonymous letters or phone calls,[189] to faked informants' reports.[190]

When the technique was used against a member of a nonviolent group, the result was often alienation from the group. For example, a San Diego man was targeted because he was active in draft counseling at the city's Message Information Center. He had, coincidentally, been present at the arrest of a Selective Service violator, and had been at a "crash pad" just prior to the arrest of a second violator. The Bureau used a real informant to suggest at a Center meeting that it was "strange" that the two men had been arrested by federal agents shortly after the target became aware of their locations. The field office reported that the target had been "completely ostracized by members of the Message Information Center and all of the other individuals throughout the area . . . associated with this and/or related groups." [191]

In another case, a local police officer was used to "jacket" the head of the Student Mobilization Committee at the University of South Carolina. The police officer picked up two members of the Committee on the pretext of interviewing them concerning narcotics. By pre-arranged signal, he had his radio operator call him with the message, "[name of target] just called. Wants you to contact her. Said you have her number." [192] No results were reported.

The "snitch jacket" is a particularly nasty technique even when used in peaceful groups. It gains an added dimension of danger when it is used—as, indeed, it was—in groups known to have murdered informers.[193]

For instance, a Black Panther leader was arrested by the local police with four other members of the BPP. The others were released, but the leader remained in custody. Headquarters authorized the field office to circulate the rumor that the leader "is the last to be released" because "he is cooperating with and has made a deal with the Los Angeles Police Department to furnish them information concerning the BPP."

[187] Memorandum from F. J. Baumgardner to W. C. Sullivan, 1/5/65.
[188] Memorandum from FBI Headquarters to San Diego Field Office, 2/14/69.
[189] Memorandum from FBI Headquarters to Jackson Field Office. 11/15/68.
[190] Memorandum from FBI Headquarters to New York Field Office, 2/9/60.
[191] Memorandum from San Diego Field Office to FBI Headquarters, 2/17/69; memorandum from FBI Headquarters to San Diego Field Office, 3/6/69; memorandum from San Diego Field Office to FBI Headquarters 4/30/69.
[192] Memorandum from San Diego Field Office to FBI Headquarters, 1/31/69; memorandum from FBI Headquarters to San Diego Field Office, 2/14/69.
[193] One Bureau document stated that the Black Panther Party "has murdered two members it suspected of being police informants." (Memorandum from FBI Headquarters to Cincinnati Field Office, 2/18/71.)

REPORT

OF THE

SELECT COMMITTEE ON ASSASSINATIONS U.S. HOUSE OF REPRESENTATIVES

NINETY-FIFTH CONGRESS

SECOND SESSION

FINDINGS AND RECOMMENDATIONS

MARCH 29, 1979.—Committed to the Committee of the Whole House on the State of the Union and ordered to be printed

---

U.S. GOVERNMENT PRINTING OFFICE

43-112 O   WASHINGTON : 1979

An analysis by the committee revealed that the Kennedy administration brought about the strongest effort against organized crime that had ever been coordinated by the Federal Government.(164) John and Robert Kennedy brought to their respective positions as President and Attorney General an unprecedented familiarity with the threat of organized crime—and a commitment to prosecute its leaders—based on their service as member and chief counsel respectively of the McClellan Committee during its extensive investigation of labor racketeering in the late 1950's.(165) A review of the electronic surveillance conducted by the FBI from 1961 to 1964 demonstrated that members of La Cosa Nostra, as well as other organized crime figures, were quite cognizant of the stepped-up effort against them, and they placed responsibility for it directly upon President Kennedy and Attorney General Kennedy.(166)

During this period, the FBI had comprehensive electronic coverage of the major underworld figures, particularly those who comprised the commission.[8](167) The committee had access to and analyzed the product of this electronic coverage; it reviewed literally thousands of pages of electronic surveillance logs that revealed the innermost workings of organized crime in the United States.(168) The committee saw in stark terms a record of murder, violence, bribery, corruption, and an untold variety of other crimes.(169) Uniquely among congressional committees, and in contrast to the Warren Commission, the committee became familiar with the nature and scope of organized crime in the years before and after the Kennedy assassination, using as its evidence the words of the participants themselves.

An analysis of the work of the Justice Department before and after the tenure of Robert Kennedy as Attorney General also led to the conclusion that organized crime directly benefited substantially from the changes in Government policy that occurred after the assassination. (170) That organized crime had the motive, opportunity and means to kill the President cannot be questioned.(171) Whether it did so is another matter.

In its investigation of the decisionmaking process and dynamics of organized crime murders and intrasyndicate assassinations during the early 1960's, the committee noted the extraordinary web of insulation, secrecy, and complex machinations that frequently surrounded organized crime leaders who ordered such acts.(172) In testimony before the Senate on September 25, 1963, 2 months before his brother's assassination, Attorney General Kennedy spoke of the Government's continuing difficulty in solving murders carried out by organized crime elements, particularly those ordered by members of the La Cosa Nostra commission. Attorney General Kennedy testified that:

> * * * because the members of the Commission, the top members, or even their chief lieutenants, have insulated themselves from the crime itself, if they want to have somebody knocked off, for instance, the top man will speak to somebody who will speak to somebody else who will speak to somebody else and order it. The man who actually does the gun work, who might

---

[8] The ruling council of 9 to 12 Mafia leaders who collectively rule the national crime syndicate.

get paid $250, or $500, depending on how important it is, perhaps nothing at all, he does not know who ordered it. To trace that back is virtually impossible. (*173*)

The committee studied the Kennedy assassination in terms of the traditional forms of violence used by organized crime and the historic pattern of underworld slayings. While the murder of the President's accused assassin did in fact fit the traditional pattern—a shadowy man with demonstrable organized crime connections shoots down a crucial witness—the method of the President's assassination did not resemble the standard syndicate killing. (*174*) A person like Oswald—young, active in controversial political causes, apparently not subject to the internal discipline of a criminal organization—would appear to be the least likely candidate for the role of Mafia hit man, especially in such an important murder. Gunmen used in organized crime killings have traditionally been selected with utmost deliberation and care, the most important considerations being loyalty and a willingness to remain silent if apprehended. These are qualities best guaranteed by past participation in criminal activities. (*175*)

There are, however, other factors to be weighed in evaluating the method of possible operation in the assassination of President Kennedy. While the involvement of a gunman like Oswald does not readily suggest organized crime involvement, any underworld attempt to assassinate the President would in all likelihood have dictated the use of some kind of cover, a shielding or disguise. (*176*) The committee made the reasonable assumption that an assassination of a President by organized crime could not be allowed to appear to be what it was.

Traditional organized crime murders are generally committed through the use of killers who make no effort to hide the fact that organized crime was responsible for such murders or "hits." (*177*) While syndicate-authorized hits are usually executed in such a way that identification of the killers is not at all likely, the slayings are nonetheless committed in what is commonly referred to as the "gangland style." (*178*) Indeed, an intrinsic characteristic of the typical mob execution is that it serves as a self-apparent message, with the authorities and the public readily perceiving the nature of the crime as well as the general identity of the group or gang that carried it out. (*179*)

The execution of a political leader—most particularly a President—would hardly be a typical mob execution and might well necessitate a different method of operation. The overriding consideration in such an extraordinary crime would be the avoidance of any appearance of organized crime complicity. (*180*)

In its investigation, the committee noted three cases, for the purposes of illustration, in which the methodology employed by syndicate figures was designed to insulate and disguise the involvement of organized crime. (*181*) These did not fit the typical pattern of mob killings, as the assassination of a President would not. (*182*) While the atypical cases did not involve political leaders, two of the three were attacks on figures in the public eye. (*183*)

In the first case, the acid blinding of investigative reporter Victor Riesel in April 1956, organized crime figures in New York used a complex series of go-betweens to hire a petty thief and burglar to commit the act. (*184*) Thus, the assailant did not know who had actually authorized the crime for which he had been recruited. (*185*) The use of such an individual was regarded as unprecedented, as he had not been associated with the syndicate, was a known drug user, and outwardly appeared to be unreliable. (*186*) Weeks later, Riesel's assailant was slain by individuals who had recruited him in the plot. (*187*)

The second case, the fatal shooting of a well-known businessman, Sol Landie, in Kansas City, Mo., on November 22, 1970, involved the recruitment, through several intermediaries, of four young Black men by members of the local La Cosa Nostra family. (*188*) Landie had served as a witness in a Federal investigation of gambling activities directed by Kansas City organized crime leader Nicholas Civella. The men recruited for the murder did not know who had ultimately ordered the killing, were not part of the Kansas City syndicate, and had received instructions through intermediaries to make it appear that robbery was the motive for the murder. (*189*) All of the assailants and two of the intermediaries were ultimately convicted.

The third case, the shooting of New York underworld leader Joseph Columbo before a crowd of 65,000 people in June 1971, was carried out by a young Black man with a petty criminal record, a nondescript loner who appeared to be alien to the organized crime group that had recruited him through various go-betweens. (*190*) The gunman was shot to death immediately after the shooting of Columbo, a murder still designated as unsolved. (*191*) (Seriously wounded by a shot to the head, Columbo lingered for years in a semiconscious state before he died in 1978.)

The committee found that these three cases, each of which is an exception to the general rule of organized crime executions, had identifiable similarities. (*192*) Each case was solved, in that the identity of the perpetrator of the immediate act became known. (*193*) In two of the cases, the assailant was himself murdered soon after the crime. (*194*) In each case, the person who wanted the crime accomplished recruited the person or persons who made the attack through more than one intermediary. (*195*) In each case, the person suspected of inspiring the violence was a member of, or connected to, La Cosa Nostra. (*196*) In each case, the person or persons hired were not professional killers, and they were not part of organized criminal groups. (*197*) In each case, the persons recruited to carry out the acts could be characterized as dupes or tools who were being used in a conspiracy they were not fully aware of. (*198*) In each case, the intent was to insulate the organized crime connection, with a particular requirement for disguising the true identity of the conspirators, and to place the blame on generally nondescript individuals. (*199*) These exceptions to the general rule of organized crime violence made it impossible for the committee to preclude, on the basis of an analysis of the method of the assassination, that President Kennedy was killed by elements of organized crime. (*200*)

In its investigation into the possibility that organized crime elements were involved in the President's murder, the committee examined various internal and external factors that bear on whether organized crime leaders would have considered, planned and executed an assassination conspiracy. (201) The committee examined the decisionmaking process that would have been involved in such a conspiracy, and two primary propositions emerged. (202) The first related to whether the national crime syndicate would have authorized and formulated a conspiracy with the formal consent of the commission, the ruling council of Mafia leaders. (203) The second related to whether an individual organized crime leader, or possibly a small combination of leaders, might have conspired to assassinate the President through unilateral action, that is, without the involvement of the leadership of the national syndicate. (204)

The most significant evidence that organized crime as an institution or group was not involved in the assassination of President Kennedy was contained in the electronic surveillance of syndicate leaders conducted by the FBI in the early 1960's. (205) As the President's Crime Commission noted in 1967, and as this committee found through its review of the FBI surveillance, there was a distinct hierarchy and structure to organized crime. (206) Decisions of national importance were generally made by the national commission, or at least they depended on the approval of the commission members. (207) In 1963, the following syndicate leaders served as members of the commission: Vito Genovese, Joseph Bonanno, Carlo Gambino, and Thomas Lucchese of New York City; Stefano Magaddino of Buffalo; Sam Giancana of Chicago; Joseph Zerilli of Detroit; Angelo Bruno of Philadelphia and Raymond Patriarca of Providence. (208) The committee's review of the surveillance transcripts and logs, detailing the private conversations of the commission members and their associates, revealed that there were extensive and heated discussions about the serious difficulties the Kennedy administration's crackdown on organized crime was causing. (209)

The bitterness and anger with which organized crime leaders viewed the Kennedy administration are readily apparent in the electronic surveillance transcripts, with such remarks being repeatedly made by commission members Genovese, Giancana, Bruno, Zerilli, Patriarca and Magaddino. (210) In one such conversation in May 1962, a New York Mafia member noted the intense Federal pressure upon the mob, and remarked, "Bob Kennedy won't stop today until he puts us all in jail all over the country. Until the commission meets and puts its foot down, things will be at a standstill." (211) Into 1963, the pressure was continuing to mount, as evidenced by a conversation in which commission member Magaddino bitterly cursed Attorney General Kennedy and commented on the Justice Department's increasing knowledge of the crime syndicate's inner workings, stating, "They know everything under the sun. They know who's back of it—they know there is a commission. We got to watch right now—and stay as quiet as possible." (212)

While the committee's examination of the electronic surveillance program revealed no shortage of such conversations during that period, the committee found no evidence in the conversations of the formulation of any specific plan to assassinate the President. (213) Nevertheless, that organized crime figures did discuss possible violent courses of action against either the President or his brother, Attorney General Robert F. Kennedy—as well as the possible repercussions of such action—can be starkly seen in the transcripts. (214)

One such discussion bears quoting at length. It is a conversation between commission member Angelo Bruno of Philadelphia and an associate, Willie Weisburg, on February 8, 1962. (215) In the discussion, in response to Weisburg's heated suggestion that Attorney General Kennedy should be murdered, Bruno cautioned that Kennedy might be followed by an even worse Attorney General:

> WEISBURG. See what Kennedy done. With Kennedy, a guy should take a knife, like all them other guys, and stab and kill the [obsenity], where he is now. Somebody should kill the [obscenity], I mean it. This is true. Honest to God. It's about time to go. But I tell you something. I hope I get a week's notice, I'll kill. Right in the [obscenity] in the White House. Somebody's got to get rid of this [obscenity].
>
> BRUNO. Look, Willie, do you see there was a king, do you understand. And he found out that everybody was saying that he was a bad king. This is an old Italian story. So, he figured. Let me go talk to the old woman. She knows everything. So he went to the old wise woman. So he says to her: "I came here because I want your opinion." He says: "Do you think I'm a bad king?" She says: "No, I think you are a good king." He says: "Well how come everybody says I'm a bad king?" She says: "Because they are stupid. They don't know." He says: "Well how come, why do you say I'm a good king?" "Well," she said, "I knew your great grandfather. He was a bad king. I knew your grandfather. He was worse. I knew your father. He was worse than them. You, you are worse than them, but your son, if you die, your son is going to be worse than you. So its better to be with you." [All laugh.] So Brownell—former Attorney General—was bad. He was no [obscenity] good. He was this and that.
>
> WEISBURG. Do you know what this man is going to do? He ain't going to leave nobody alone.
>
> BRUNO. I know he ain't. But you see, everybody in there was bad. The other guy was good because the other guy was worse. Do you understand? Brownell came. He was no good. He was worse than the guy before.
>
> WEISBURG. Not like this one.
>
> BRUNO. Not like this one. This one is worse. Right? If something happens to this guy * * * [laughs]. (216)

While Angelo Bruno had hoped to wait out his troubles, believing that things might get better for him as time went by, such was not to be the case during the Kennedy administration. The electronic surveillance transcripts disclosed that by mid 1963, Bruno was privately making plans to shut down his syndicate operations and leave America, an unprecedented response by a commission member to Federal law enforcement pressure. (217)

Another member of the mob commission, Stefano Magaddino, voiced similar anger toward the President during that same period. (218) In October 1963, in response to a Mafia family member's remark that President Kennedy "should drop dead," Magaddino exploded, "They should kill the whole family, the mother and father too. When he talks he talks like a mad dog, he says, my brother the Attorney General."*(219)*

The committee concluded that had the national crime syndicate, as a group, been involved in a conspiracy to kill the President, some trace of the plot would have been picked up by the FBI surveillance of the commission.*(220)* Consequently, finding no evidence in the electronic surveillance transcripts of a specific intention or actual plan by commission members to have the President assassinated, the committee believed it was unlikely that it existed. The electronic surveillance transcripts included extensive conversations during secret meetings of various syndicate leaders, set forth many of their most closely guarded thoughts and actions, and detailed their involvement in a variety of other criminal acts, including murder.*(221)* Given the far-reaching possible consequences of an assassination plot by the commission, the committee found that such a conspiracy would have been the subject of serious discussion by members of the commission, and that no matter how guarded such discussions might have been, some trace of them would have emerged from the surveillance coverage.*(222)* It was possible to conclude, therefore, that it is unlikely that the national crime syndicate as a group, acting under the leadership of the commission, participated in the assassination of President Kennedy.*(223)*

While there was an absence of evidence in the electronic surveillance materials of commission participation in the President's murder, there was no shortage of evidence of the elation and relief of various commission members over his death.*(224)* The surveillance transcripts contain numerous crude and obscene comments by organized crime leaders, their lieutenants, associates and families regarding the assassination of President Kennedy.*(225)* The transcripts also reveal an awareness by some mob leaders that the authorities might be watching their reactions.*(226)* On November 25, 1963, in response to a lieutenant's remark that Oswald "was an anarchist * * * a Marxist Communist," Giancana exclaimed, "He was a marksman who knew how to shoot."*(227)* On November 29, 1963, Magaddino cautioned his associates not to joke openly about the President's murder, stating, "You can be sure that the police spies will be watching carefully to see what we think and say about this."*(228)* Several weeks later, during a discussion between Bruno and his lieutenants, one participant remarked of the late President, "It is too bad his brother Bobby was not in that car too."*(229)*

While the committee found it unlikely that the national crime syndicate was involved in the assassination, it recognized the possibility that a particular organized crime leader or a small combination of leaders, acting unilaterally, might have formulated an assassination conspiracy without the consent of the commission.*(230)*

In its investigation of the national crime syndicate, the committee noted factors that could have led an organized crime leader who was considering an assassination to withold it from the national commission.*(231)* The committee's analysis of the national commission disclosed that it was splintered by dissension and enmity in 1963. Rivalry between two blocks of syndicate families had resulted in a partial paralysis of the commission's functions.*(232)*

One significant reason for the disarray was, of course, the pressure being exerted by Federal law enforcement agencies.(233) In the fall of 1963, Attorney General Kennedy noted,

> * * * in the past 2 years, at least three carefully planned commission meetings had to be called off because the leaders learned that we had uncovered their well-concealed plans and meeting places.

The Government's effort got an unprecedented boost from the willingness of Joseph Valachi, a member of the "family" of commission member Vito Genovese of New York, to testify about the internal structure and activities of the crime syndicate, a development described by Attorney General Kennedy as "the greatest intelligence breakthrough" in the history of the Federal program against organized crime.(234) While it was not until August 1963 that Valachi's identity as a Federal witness became public, the surveillance transcripts disclose that syndicate leaders were aware as early as the spring of 1963 that Valachi was cooperating with the Justice Department.(235) The transcripts disclose that the discovery that Valachi had become a Federal informant aroused widespread suspicion and fear over the possibility of other leaks and informants within the upper echelons of the syndicate.(236) The televised Senate testimony by Valachi led to considerable doubt by syndicate leaders in other parts of the country as to the security of commission proceedings, with Genovese rapidly losing influence as a result of Valachi's actions.(237)

The greatest source of internal disruption within the commission related to the discovery in early 1963 of a secret plan by commission member Joseph Bonanno to assassinate fellow members Carlo Gambino and Thomas Lucchese.(238) Bonanno's assassination plan, aimed at an eventual takeover of the commission leadership, was discovered after one of the gunmen Bonanno had enlisted, Joseph Columbo, informed on him to the commission.(239) The Bonanno conspiracy, an unheard-of violation of commission rules, led to a long series of acrimonious deliberations that lasted until early 1964.(240) Bonanno refused to submit to the judgment of the commission, and his colleagues were sharply divided over how to deal with his betrayal, Gambino recommending that Bonanno be handled with caution, and Giancana urging that he be murdered.(241)

The committee concluded, based on the state of disruption within the commission and the questions that had arisen as to the sanctity of commission proceedings, that an individual organized crime leader who was planning an assassination conspiracy against President Kennedy might well have avoided making the plan known to the commission or seeking approval for it from commission members.(242) Such a course of unilateral action seemed to the committee to have been particularly possible in the case of powerful organized crime leaders who were well established, with firm control over their jurisdictions.(243)

The committee noted a significant precedent for such a unilateral course of action. In 1957, Vito Genovese engineered the assassination of Albert Anastasia, then perhaps the most feared Mafia boss in the country.(244) Six months earlier, Genovese's men had shot and wounded Frank Costello, who once was regarded as the single most influential

organized crime leader.(245) Both the Anastasia assassination and
the Costello assault were carried out without the knowledge or consent
of the national commission.(246) Genovese did, however, obtain
approval for the crimes after the fact.(247) It was an extraordinary
sequence of events that Attorney General Kennedy noted in September
1963, when he stated that Genovese "* * * wanted Commission approval
for these acts—which he has received." The Genovese plot against
Anastasia and Costello and the ex post facto commission approval
were integral events in the rise to dominance of organized crime figures
for the years that followed. It directly led to the assemblage of national
syndicate leaders at the Apalachin conference 3 weeks after the Anastasia murder, and to the rise of Carlo Gambino to a position of pre-
eminence in La Costa Nostra.(248)

(5) *Analysis of the 1963-64 investigation.*—In its investigation, the
committee learned that fears of the possibility that organized crime
was behind the assassination were more common among Government
officials at the time than has been generally recognized. Both Attorney
General Kennedy and President Johnson privately voiced suspicion
about underworld complicity.(249) The Attorney General requested
that any relevant information be forwarded directly to him, and there
was expectation at the time that the recently created Warren Commission would actively investigate the possibility of underworld
involvement.(250)

The committee found, however, that the Warren Commission conducted only a limited pursuit of the possibility of organized crime
complicity.(251) As has been noted, moreover, the Warren Commission's interest in organized crime was directed exclusively at Jack
Ruby, and it did not involve any investigation of the national crime
syndicate in general, or individual leaders in particular.(252) This
was confirmed to the committee by J. Lee Rankin, the Commission's
general counsel, and by Burt W. Griffin, the staff counsel who conducted the Ruby investigation.(253) Griffin testified before the committee that "* * * the possibility that someone associated with the
underworld would have wanted to assassinate the President * * *
[was] not seriously explored" by the Warren Commission.(254)

The committee similarly learned from testimony and documentation that the FBI's investigation of the President's assassination was
also severely limited in the area of possible organized crime involvement. While the committee found that the Bureau was uniquely equipped, with the Special Investigative Division having been formed 2
years earlier specifically to investigate organized crime, the specialists
and agents of that Division did not play a significant role in the assassination investigation.(255) Former Assistant FBI Director Courtney
Evans, who headed the Special Investigative Division, told the committee that the officials who directed the investigation never consulted
him or asked for any participation by his Division.(256) Evans
recalled, "I know they sure didn't come to me. We had no part in that
that I can recall."(257) Al Staffeld, a former FBI official who super-
vised the day-to-day operations of the Special Investigative Division,
told the committee that if the FBI's organized crime specialists had
been asked to participate, "We would have gone at it in every damn
way possible."(258)

Ironically, the Bureau's own electronic surveillance transcripts revealed to the committee a conversation between Sam Giancana and a lieutenant, Charles English, regarding the FBI's role in investigating President Kennedy's assassination. *(259)* In the December 3, 1963 conversation, English told Giancana: "I will tell you something, in another 2 months from now, the FBI will be like it was 5 years ago. They won't be around no more. They say the FBI will get it (the investigation of the President's assassination). They're gonna start running down Fair Play for Cuba, Fair Play for Matsu. They call that more detrimental to the country than us guys." *(260)*

The committee found that the quality and scope of the investigation into the possibility of an organized crime conspiracy in the President's assassination by the Warren Commission and the FBI was not sufficient to uncover one had it existed. The committee also found that it was possible, based on an analysis of motive, means and opportunity, that an individual organized crime leader, or a small combination of leaders, might have participated in a conspiracy to assassinate President Kennedy. The committee's extensive investigation led it to conclude that the most likely family bosses of organized crime to have participated in such a unilateral assassination plan were Carlos Marcello and Santos Trafficante. *(261)* While other family bosses on the commission were subjected to considerable coverage in the electronic surveillance program, such coverage was never applied to Marcello and almost never to Trafficante. *(262)*

(6) *Carlos Marcello.*—The commitee found that Marcello had the motive, means and opportunity to have President John F. Kennedy assassinated, *(263)* though it was unable to establish direct evidence of Marcello's complicity.

In its investigation of Marcello, the committee identified the presence of one critical evidentiary element that was lacking with the other organized crime figures examined by the committee: credible associations relating both Lee Harvey Oswald and Jack Ruby to figures having a relationship, albeit tenuous, with Marcello's crime family or organization. *(264)* At the same time, the committee explicitly cautioned: association is the first step in conspiracy; it is not identical to it, and while associations may legitimately give rise to suspicions, a careful distinction must always be drawn between suspicions suspected and facts found.

As the long-time La Cosa Nostra leader in an area that is based in New Orleans but extends throughout Louisiana and Texas, Marcello was one of the prime targets of Justice Department efforts during the Kennedy administration. *(265)* He had, in fact, been temporarily removed from the country for a time in 1961 through deportation proceedings personally expedited by Attorney General Kennedy. *(266)* In his appearance before the committee in executive session, Marcello exhibited an intense dislike for Robert Kennedy because of these actions, claiming that he had been illegally "kidnaped" by Government agents during the deportation. *(267)*

While the Warren Commission devoted extensive attention to Oswald's background and activities, the committee uncovered significant details of his exposure to and contacts with figures associated with the underworld of New Orleans that apparently had escaped the Commission.(268) One such relationship actually extended into Oswald's own family through his uncle, Charles "Dutz" Murret, a minor underworld gambling figure.(269) The committee discovered that Murret, who served as a surrogate father of sorts throughout much of Oswald's life in New Orleans, was in the 1940's and 1950's and possibly until his death in 1964 an associate of significant organized crime figures affiliated with the Marcello organization.(270)

The committee established that Oswald was familiar with his uncle's underworld activities and had discussed them with his wife, Marina, in 1963.(271) Additionally, the committee found that Oswald's mother, Marguerite Oswald, was acquainted with several men associated with lieutenants in the Marcello organization. One such acquaintance, who was also an associate of Dutz Murret, reportedly served as a personal aide or driver to Marcello at one time.(272) In another instance, the committee found that an individual connected to Dutz Murret, the person who arranged bail for Oswald following his arrest in August 1963 for a street disturbance, was an associate of two of Marcello's syndicate deputies. (One of the two, Nofio Pecora, as noted, also received a telephone call from Ruby on October 30, 1963, according to the committee's computer analysis of Ruby's phone records.)(273)

During the course of its investigation, the committee developed several areas of credible evidence and testimony indicating a possible association in New Orleans and elsewhere between Lee Harvey Oswald and David W. Ferrie, a private investigator and even, perhaps, a pilot for Marcello before and during 1963.(274) From the evidence available to the committee, the nature of the Oswald-Ferrie association remained largely a mystery. The committee established that Oswald and Ferrie apparently first came into contact with each other during Oswald's participation as a teenager in a Civil Air Patrol unit for which Ferrie served as an instructor, although Ferrie, when he was interviewed by the FBI after his detainment as a suspect in the assassination,(275) denied any past association with Oswald.

In interviews following the assassination, Ferrie stated that he may have spoken in an offhand manner of the desirability of having President Kennedy shot, but he denied wanting such a deed actually to be done.(276) Ferrie also admitted his association with Marcello and stated that he had been in personal contact with the syndicate leader in the fall of 1963. He noted that on the morning of the day of the President's death he was present with Marcello at a courthouse in New Orleans.(277) In his executive session testimony before the committee, Marcello acknowledged that Ferrie did work for his lawyer, G. Wray Gill, on his case, but Marcello denied that Ferrie worked for him or that their relationship was close.(278) Ferrie died in 1967 of a ruptured blood vessel at the base of the brain, shortly after he was named in the assassination investigation of New Orleans District Attorney Jim Garrison.

The committee also confirmed that the address, 544 Camp Street, that Oswald had printed on some Fair Play for Cuba Committee handouts in New Orleans, was the address of a small office building

where Ferrie was working on at least a part-time basis in 1963. (*279*)
The Warren Commission stated in its report that despite the Commission's probe into why Oswald used this return address on his literature, "investigation has indicated that neither the Fair Play for Cuba Committee nor Lee Oswald ever maintained an office at that address." (*280*)

The committee also established associations between Jack Ruby and several individuals affiliated with the underworld activities of Carlos Marcello. (*281*) Ruby was a personal acquaintance of Joseph Civello, the Marcello associate who allegedly headed organized crime activities in Dallas; he also knew other individuals who have been linked with organized crime, including a New Orleans nightclub figure, Harold Tannenbaum, with whom Ruby was considering going into partnership in the fall of 1963. (*282*) [9]

The committee examined a widely circulated published account that Marcello made some kind of threat on the life of President Kennedy in September 1962 at a meeting at his Churchill Farms estate outside New Orleans. (*284*) It was alleged that Marcello shouted an old Sicilian threat, "Livarsi na petra di la scarpa!" "Take the stone out of my shoe!" against the Kennedy brothers, stating that the President was going to be assassinated. He spoke of using a "nut" to carry out the murder. (*285*)

The committee established the origin of the story and identified the informant who claimed to have been present at the meeting during which Marcello made the threat. (*286*) The committee also learned that even though the FBI was aware of the informant's allegations over a year and half before they were published in 1969, and possessed additional information indicating that the informant may in fact have met with Marcello in the fall of 1962, a substantive investigation of the information was never conducted. (*287*) Director Hoover and other senior FBI officials were aware that FBI agents were initiating action to "discredit" the informant, without having conducted a significant investigation of his allegations. (*288*) Further, the committee discovered that the originating office relied on derogatory information from a prominent underworld figure in the ongoing effort to discredit the informant. (*289*) An internal memorandum to Hoover noted that another FBI source was taking action to discredit the informant, "in order that the Carlos Marcello incident would be deleted from the book" that first recounted the information. (*290*)

The committee determined that the informant who gave the account of the Marcello threat was in fact associated with various underworld figures, including at least one person well-acquainted with the Marcello organization. (*291*) The committee noted, however, that as a consequence of his underworld involvement, the informant had a questionable reputation for honesty and may not be a credible source of information. (*292*)

[9] Law enforcement files have long contained information suggesting that Joseph Campisi, a restaurant owner in Dallas, occupied a position in organized crime. The committee's investigation did not confirm or refute the allegation, but it did establish that Ruby visited Campisi's restaurant on the evening of November 21 and that Ruby was visited in jail after the shooting of Oswald by Campisi and his wife. Further, Campisi acknowledged a longstanding business and personal relationship with Marcello. (*283*)

The committee noted further that it is unlikely that an organized crime leader personally involved in an assassination plot would discuss it with anyone other than his closest lieutenants, although he might be willing to discuss it more freely prior to a serious decision to undertake such an act. In his executive session appearance before the committee, Marcello categorically denied any involvement in organized crime or the assassination of President Kennedy. Marcello also denied ever making any kind of threat against the President's life. (293)

As noted, Marcello was never the subject of electronic surveillance coverage by the FBI. The committee found that the Bureau did make two attempts to effect such surveillance during the early 1960's, but both attempts were unsuccessful. (294) Marcello's sophisticated security system and close-knit organizational structure may have been a factor in preventing such surveillance. [10] A former FBI official knowledgeable about the surveillance program told the committee, "That was our biggest gap * * *. With Marcello, you've got the one big exception in our work back then. There was just no way of penetrating that area. He was too smart." (296)

Any evaluation of Marcello's possible role in the assassination must take into consideration his unique stature within La Cosa Nostra. The FBI determined in the 1960's that because of Marcello's position as head of the New Orleans Mafia family (the oldest in the United States, having first entered the country in the 1880's), the Louisiana organized crime leader had been endowed with special powers and privileges not accorded to any other La Cosa Nostra members. (297) As the leader of "the first family" of the Mafia in America, according to FBI information, Marcello has been the recipient of the extraordinary privilege of conducting syndicate operations without having to seek the approval of the national commission. (298)

Finally, a caveat. Marcello's uniquely successful career in organized crime has been based to a large extent on a policy of prudence; he is not reckless. As with the case of the Soviet and Cuban Governments, a risk analysis indicated that he would be unlikely to undertake so dangerous a course of action as a Presidential assassination. Considering that record of prudence, and in the absence of direct evidence of involvement, it may be said that it is unlikely that Marcello was in fact involved in the assassination of the President. On the basis of the evidence available to it, and in the context of its duty to be cautious in its evaluation of the evidence, there is no other conclusion that the committee could reach. On the other hand, the evidence that he had the motive and the evidence of links through associates to both Oswald and Ruby, coupled with the failure of the 1963-64 investigation to explore adequately possible conspiratorial activity in the assassination, precluded a judgment by the committee that Marcello and his associates were not involved.

(7) *Santos Trafficante.*—The committee also concentrated its attention on Santos Trafficante, the La Cosa Nostra leader in Florida. The

---

[10] In addition Marcello was considered by his FBI case agent to be a legitimate businessman. which may account for the fact that the case agent was less than enthusiastic about pressing an investigation of the Louisiana Mafia leader. (295)

committee found that Trafficante, like Marcello, had the motive, means, and opportunity to assassinate President Kennedy.(*299*)

Trafficante was a key subject of the Justice Department crackdown on organized crime during the Kennedy administration, with his name being added to a list of the top 10 syndicate leaders targeted for investigation.(*300*) Ironically, Attorney General Kennedy's strong interest in having Trafficante prosecuted occurred during the same period in which CIA officials, unbeknown to the Attorney General, were using Trafficante's services in assassination plots against the Cuban chief of state, Fidel Castro. (*301*)

The committee found that Santos Trafficante's stature in the national syndicate of organized crime, notably the violent narcotics trade, and his role as the mob's chief liaison to criminal figures within the Cuban exile community, provided him with the capability of formulating an assassination conspiracy against President Kennedy. Trafficante had recruited Cuban nationals to help plan and execute the CIA's assignment to assassinate Castro. (The CIA gave the assignment to former FBI Agent Robert Maheu, who passed the contract along to Mafia figures Sam Giancana and John Roselli. They, in turn, enlisted Trafficante to have the intended assassination carried out.)(*302*)

In his testimony before the committee, Trafficante admitted participating in the unsuccessful CIA conspiracy to assassinate Castro, an admission indicating his willingness to participate in political murder. (*303*) Trafficante testified that he worked with the CIA out of a patriotic feeling for his country, an explanation the committee did not accept, at least not as his sole motivation.(*304*)

As noted, the committee established a possible connection between Trafficante and Jack Ruby in Cuba in 1959.(*305*) It determined there had been a close friendship between Ruby and Lewis McWillie, who, as a Havana gambler, worked in an area subject to the control of the Trafficante Mafia family.(*306*) Further, it assembled documentary evidence that Ruby made at least two, if not three or more, trips to Havana in 1959 when McWillie was involved in underworld gambling operations there.(*307*) Ruby may in fact have been serving as a courier for underworld gambling interests in Havana, probably for the purpose of transporting funds to a bank in Miami.(*308*)

The committee also found that Ruby had been connected with other Trafficante associates—R. D. Matthews, Jack Todd, and James Dolan—all of Dallas.(*309*)

Finally, the committee developed corroborating evidence that Ruby may have met with Trafficante at Trescornia prison in Cuba during one of his visits to Havana in 1959, as the CIA had learned but had discounted in 1964.(*310*) While the committee was not able to determine the purpose of the meeting, there was considerable evidence that it did take place.(*311*)

During the course of its investigation of Santos Trafficante, the committee examined an allegation that Trafficante had told a prominent Cuban exile, José Aleman, that President Kennedy was going to be assassinated.(*312*) According to Aleman, Trafficante made the statement in a private conversation with him that took place sometime in September 1962.(*313*) In an account of the alleged conversation published by the Washington Post in 1976, Aleman was quoted as stating that Trafficante had told him that President Kennedy was "going to be hit."(*314*) Aleman further stated, however, that it was his impression that Trafficante was not the specific individual who was allegedly planning the murder.(*315*) Aleman was quoted as having noted that Trafficante had spoken of Teamsters Union President James Hoffa during the same conversation, indicating that the President would "get what is coming to him" as a result of his administration's intense efforts to prosecute Hoffa.(*316*)

During an interview with the committee in March 1977, Aleman provided further details of his alleged discussion with Trafficante in September 1962.(*317*) Aleman stated that during the course of the discussion, Trafficante had made clear to him that he was not guessing that the President was going to be killed. Rather he did in fact know that such a crime was being planned.(*318*) In his committee interview, Aleman further stated that Trafficante had given him the distinct impression that Hoffa was to be principally involved in planning the Presidential murder.(*319*)

In September 1978, prior to his appearance before the committee in public session. Aleman reaffirmed his earlier account of the alleged September 1962 meeting with Trafficante. Nevertheless, shortly before his appearance in public session, Aleman informed the committee staff that he feared for his physical safety and was afraid of possible reprisal from Trafficante or his organization. In this testimony, Aleman changed his professed understanding of Trafficant's comments. Aleman repeated under oath that Trafficante had said Kennedy was "going to be hit," but he then stated it was his impression that Trafficante may have only meant the President was going to be hit by "a lot of Republican votes" in the 1964 election, not that he was going to be assassinated.(*320*)

Appearing before the committee in public session on September 28, 1978, Trafficante categorically denied ever having discussed any plan to assassinate President Kennedy.(*321*) Trafficante denied any foreknowledge of or participation in the President's murder. (*322*) While stating that he did in fact know Aleman and that he had met with him on more than one occasion in 1962, Trafficante denied Aleman's account of their alleged conversation about President Kennedy. and he denied ever having made a threatening remark against the President.(*323*)

The committee found it difficult to understand how Aleman could have misunderstood Trafficante during such a conversation, or why he would have fabricated such an account. Aleman appeared to be a reputable person, who did not seek to publicize his allegations, and he was well aware of the potential danger of making such allegations against a leader of La Costa Nostra. The committee noted, however, that Aleman's prior allegations and testimony before the committee had made him understandably fearful for his life.

The committee also did not fully understand why Aleman waited so many years before publicly disclosing the alleged incident. While he stated in 1976 that he had reported Trafficante's alleged remarks about the President to FBI agents in 1962 and 1963, the committee's review of Bureau reports on his contacts with FBI agents did not reveal a record of any such disclosure or comments at the time. (324) Additionally, the FBI agent who served as Aleman's contact during that period denied ever being told such information by Aleman.

Further, the committee found it difficult to comprehend why Trafficante, if he was planning or had personal knowledge of an assassination plot, would have revealed or hinted at such a sensitive matter to Aleman. It is possible that Trafficante may have been expressing a personal opinion, "The President ought to be hit," but it is unlikely in the context of their relationship that Trafficante would have revealed to Aleman the existence of a current plot to kill the President. As previously noted with respect to Carlos Marcello, to have attained his stature as the recognized organized crime leader of Florida for a number of years. Trafficante necessarily had to operate in a characteristically calculating and discreet manner. The relationship between Trafficante and Aleman, a business acquaintance, does not seem to have been close enough for Trafficante to have mentioned or alluded to such a murder plot. The committee thus doubted that Trafficante would have inadvertently mentioned such a plot. In sum, the committee believed there were substantial factors that called into question the validity of Aleman's account.

Nonetheless, as the electronic surveillance transcripts of Angelo Bruno, Stefano Magaddino and other top organized crime leaders make clear, there were in fact various underworld conversations in which the desirability of having the President assassinated was discussed. (325) There were private conversations in which assassination was mentioned, although not in a context that indicated such a crime had been specifically planned. (326) With this in mind, and in the absence of additional evidence with which to evaluate the Aleman account of Trafficante's alleged 1962 remarks, the committee concluded that the conversation, if it did occur as Aleman testified, probably occurred in such a circumscribed context.

As noted earlier, the committee's examination of the FBI's electronic surveillance program of the early 1960's disclosed that Santos Trafficante was the subject of minimal, in fact almost nonexistent, surveillance coverage. (327) During one conversation in 1963, overheard in a Miami restaurant, Trafficante had bitterly attacked the Kennedy administration's efforts against organized crime, making obscene comments about "Kennedy's right-hand man" who had recently coordinated various raids on Trafficante gambling establishments. (328) In the conversation, Trafficante stated that he was under immense pressure from Federal investigators, commenting, "I know when I'm beat, you understand?" (329) Nevertheless, it was not possible to draw conclusions about Trafficante's actions based on the electronic surveillance program since the coverage was so limited. Finally, as with Marcello, the committee noted that Trafficante's cautious character is inconsistent with his taking the risk of being involved in an assassination plot against the President. The committee found, in the context of its duty to be cautious in its evaluation of the evidence, that it is unlikely that Trafficante plotted to kill the President, although it could not rule out the possibility of such participation on the basis of available evidence.

(8) *James R. Hoffa.*—During the course of its investigation, the committee also examined a number of areas of information and allegations pertaining to James R. Hoffa and his Teamsters Union and underworld associates. The long and close relationship between Hoffa and powerful leaders of organized crime, his intense dislike of John and Robert Kennedy dating back to their role in the McClellan Senate investigation, together with his other criminal activities, led the committee to conclude that the former Teamsters Union president had the motive, means and opportunity for planning an assassination attempt upon the life of President John F. Kennedy.

The committee found that Hoffa and at least one of his Teamster lieutenants, Edward Partin, apparently did, in fact, discuss the planning of an assassination conspiracy against President Kennedy's brother, Attorney General Robert F. Kennedy, in July or August of 1962.(*330*) Hoffa's discussion about such an assassination plan first became known to the Federal Government in September 1962, when Partin informed authorities that he had recently participated in such a discussion with the Teamsters president.(*331*)

In October 1962, acting under the orders of Attorney General Kennedy, FBI Director Hoover authorized a detailed polygraph examination of Partin.(*332*) In the examination, the Bureau concluded that Partin had been truthful in recounting Hoffa's discussion of a proposed assassination plan.(*333*) Subsequently, the Justice Department developed further evidence supporting Partin's disclosures, indicating that Hoffa had spoken about the possibility of assassinating the President's brother on more than one occasion.(*334*)

In an interview with the committee, Partin reaffirmed the account of Hoffa's discussion of a possible assassination plan, and he stated that Hoffa had believed that having the Attorney General murdered would be the most effective way of ending the Federal Government's intense investigation of the Teamsters and organized crime.(*335*) Partin further told the committee that he suspected that Hoffa may have approached him about the assassination proposal because Hoffa believed him to be close to various figures in Carlos Marcello's syndicate organization.(*336*) Partin, a Baton Rouge Teamsters official with a criminal record, was then a leading Teamsters Union official in Louisiana. Partin was also a key Federal witness against Hoffa in the 1964 trial that led to Hoffa's eventual imprisonment.(*337*)

While the committee did not uncover evidence that the proposed Hoffa assassination plan ever went beyond its discussion, the committee noted the similarities between the plan discussed by Hoffa in 1962 and the actual events of November 22, 1963. While the committee was aware of the apparent absence of any finalized method or plan during the course of Hoffa's discussion about assassinating Attorney General Kennedy, he did discuss the possible use of a lone gunman equipped with a rifle with a telescopic sight,(*338*) the advisability of having the assassination committed somewhere in the South,(*339*) as well as the potential desirability of having Robert Kennedy shot while riding in a convertible.(*340*) While the similarities are present, the committee also noted that they were not so unusual as to point ineluctably in a particular direction. President Kennedy himself, in fact, noted that he was vulnerable to rifle fire before his Dallas trip. Nevertheless, references to Hoffa's discussion about having Kennedy assassinated while riding in a convertible were contained in several Justice Department memoranda received by the Attorney General and FBI Director Hoover in the fall of 1962. (341) Edward Partin told the committee that Hoffa believed that by having Kennedy shot as he rode in a convertible, the origin of the fatal shot or shots would be obscured. (342) The context of Hoffa's discussion with Partin about an assassination conspiracy further seemed to have been predicated upon the recruitment of an assassin without any identifiable connection to the Teamsters organization or Hoffa himself. (343) Hoffa also spoke of the alternative possibility of having the Attorney General assassinated through the use of some type of plastic explosives. (344)

The committee established that President Kennedy himself was notified of Hoffa's secret assassination discussion shortly after the Government learned of it. The personal journal of the late President's friend, Benjamin C. Bradlee, executive editor of the Washington Post, reflects that the President informed him in February 1963 of Hoffa's discussion about killing his brother. (345) Bradlee noted that President Kennedy mentioned that Hoffa had spoken of the desirability of having a silenced weapon used in such a plan. Bradlee noted that while he found such a Hoffa discussion hard to believe, "the President was obviously serious" about it. (346)

Partly as a result of their knowledge of Hoffa's discussion of assassination with Partin in 1962, various aides of the late President Kennedy voiced private suspicions about the possibility of Hoffa complicity in the President's assassination. (347) The committee learned that Attorney General Robert F. Kennedy and White House Chief of Staff Kenneth O'Donnell contacted several associates in the days immediately following the Dallas murder to discuss the possibility of Teamsters Union or organized crime involvement. (348)

As noted in the account of Ruby's telephone records, the committee confirmed the existence of several contacts between Ruby and associates of Hoffa during the period of October and November 1963. (349) including one Hoffa aide whom Robert Kennedy had once described as one of Hoffa's most violent lieutenants. (350) Those associates. Barney Baker, Irwin Weiner and Dusty Miller, stated that Ruby had been in touch with them for the sole purpose of seeking assistance in a nightclub labor dispute. (351)

The committee learned that Attorney General Kennedy and his aides arranged for the appointment of Charles Shaffer, a Justice Department attorney, to the Warren Commission staff in order that the possibility of Teamster involvement be watched. Shaffer confirmed to the committee that looking into Hoffa was one purpose of his appointment. (352)

Yet, partly as a result of the Commission's highly circumscribed approach to investigating possible underworld involvement, as well as limited staff resources, certain areas of possible information relating to Hoffa—such as the Ruby telephone calls—were not the subject of in-depth investigation. (353) Nevertheless, in a lengthy Commission memorandum prepared for the CIA in February 1964, the Teamsters Union had been listed first on a list of potential groups to be investigated in probing "ties between Ruby and others who might have been interested in the assassination of President Kennedy." (354)

During the course of its investigation, the committee noted the existence of other past relationships between Ruby and associates of Hoffa, apart from those disclosed by a review of the Ruby phone records. Two such figures were Paul Dorfman, the Chicago underworld figure who was instrumental in Hoffa's rise to power in the labor movement, and David Yaras, the reputed organized crime executioner whose relationship to Ruby dated back to their early days in Chicago. (*355*)

The committee also confirmed that another Teamsters official, Frank Chavez, had spoken to Hoffa about murdering Robert Kennedy in early 1967, shortly before Hoffa went to Federal prison. (*356*) During that incident, Hoffa reportedly sharply rebuked his aide, telling him that such a course of action was dangerous and should not be considered. (*357*)

In an interview with a newsman several weeks before his disappearance and presumed murder, Hoffa denied any involvement in the assassination of President Kennedy, and he disclaimed knowing anything about Jack Ruby or his motivations in the murder of Oswald. Hoffa also denied that he had ever discussed a plan to assassinate Robert Kennedy. (*358*)

As in the cases of Marcello and Trafficante, the committee stressed that it uncovered no direct evidence that Hoffa was involved in a plot on the President's life, much less the one that resulted in his death in Dallas in November 1963. In addition, and as opposed to the cases of Marcello and Trafficante, Hoffa was not a major leader of organized crime. Thus, his ability to guarantee that his associates would be killed if they turned Government informant may have been somewhat less assured. Indeed, much of the evidence tending to incriminate Hoffa was supplied by Edward Grady Partin, a Federal Government informant who was with Hoffa when the Teamster president was on trial in October 1962 in Tennessee for violating the Taft-Hartley Act.[11]

It may be strongly doubted, therefore, that Hoffa would have risked anything so dangerous as a plot against the President at a time that he knew he was under active investigation by the Department of Justice.[12]

Finally, a note on Hoffa's character. He was a man of strong emotions who hated the President and his brother, the Attorney General. He did not regret the President's death, and he said so publicly. Nevertheless, Hoffa was not a confirmed murderer, as were various organized crime leaders whose involvement the committee considered, and he cannot be placed in that category with them, even though he had extensive associations with them. Hoffa's associations with such organized crime leaders grew out of the nature of his union and the industry whose workers it represented. Organized crime and the violence of the labor movement were facts of life for Hoffa; they were part of the milieu in which he grew up and worked. But when he encountered the only specific plot against a Kennedy that came to the attention of the committee (the suggestion from Frank Chavez), he rejected it.

[11] Hoffa was in fact facing charges of trying to bribe the jury in his 1962 trial in Tennessee on November 22, 1963. The case was scheduled to go to trial in January 1964. Hoffa was ultimately convicted and sentenced to a prison term. Partin was the Government's chief witness against him.
[12] The committee found no evidence to indicate that Hoffa was under electronic surveillance.

The committee concluded, therefore, that the balance of the evidence argued that it was improbable that Hoffa had anything to do with the death of the President.

(c) Summary and analysis of the evidence

The committee also believed it appropriate to reflect on the general question of the possible complicity of organized crime members, such as Trafficante or Marcello, in the Kennedy assassination, and to try to put the evidence it had obtained in proper perspective.

The significance of the organized crime associations developed by the committee's investigation speaks for itself, but there are limitations that must be noted. That President Kennedy's assassin and the man who, in turn, murdered him can be tied to individuals connected to organized crime is important for one reason: for organized crime to have been involved in the assassination, it must have had access to Oswald or Ruby or both.

The evidence that has been presented by the committee demonstrates that Oswald did, in fact, have organized crime associations. Who he was and where he lived could have come to the attention of those in organized crime who had the motive and means to kill the President. Similarly, there is abundant evidence that Ruby was knowledgeable about and known to organized crime elements. Nevertheless, the committee felt compelled to stress that knowledge or availability through association falls considerably short of the sort of evidence that would be necessary to establish criminal responsibility for a conspiracy in the assassination. It is also considerably short of what a responsible congressional committee ought to have before it points a finger in a legislative context.

It must also be asked if it is likely that Oswald was, in fact, used by an individual such as Marcello or Trafficante in an organized crime plot. Here, Oswald's character comes into play. As the committee noted, it is not likely that Oswald was a hired killer; it is likely that his principal motivation in the assassination was political. Further, his politics have been shown to have been generally leftwing, as demonstrated by such aspects of his life as his avowed support of Fidel Castro. Yet the organized crime figures who had the motive and means to murder the President must be generally characterized as rightwing and anti-Castro. Knitting these two contradictory strands together posed a difficult problem. Either the assassination of President Kennedy was essentially an apolitical act undertaken by Oswald with full or partial knowledge of who he was working for—which would be hard to believe—or Oswald's organized crime contacts deceived him about their true identity and motivation, or else organized crime was not involved.

From an organized crime member's standpoint, the use of an assassin with political leanings inconsistent with his own would have enhanced his insulation from identification with the crime. Nevertheless, it would have made the conspiracy a more difficult undertaking, which raises questions about the likelihood that such a conspiracy occurred. The more complicated a plot becomes, the less likely it will work. Those who rationally set out to kill a king, it may be argued, first design a plot that will work. The Oswald plot did in fact work, at least for 15 years, but one must ask whether it would have looked workable 15 years ago. Oswald was an unstable individual. Shortly before the assassination, for example, he delivered a possibly threatening note to the Dallas FBI office. With his background, he would have been an immediate suspect in an assassination in Dallas, and those in contact with him would have known that. Conspirators could not have been assured that Oswald or his companion would be killed in Dealey Plaza; they could not be sure that they could silence them. The plot, because of Oswald's involvement, would hardly have seemed to be a low risk undertaking.

The committee weighed other factors in its assessment of Oswald, his act and possible co-conspirators. It must be acknowleged that he did, in the end, exhibit a high degree of brutal proficiency in firing the shot that ended the President's life, and that, as an ex-marine, that proficiency may have been expected. In the final analysis, it must be admitted that he accomplished what he set out to do.

Further, while Oswald exhibited a leftist political stance for a number of years, his activities and associations were by no means exclusively leftwing. His close friendship with George de Mohren-schildt, an oilman in Dallas with rightwing connections, is a case in point. Additionally, questions have been raised about the specific nature of Oswald's pro-Castro activities. It has been established that on at least one occasion in 1963, he offered his services for clandestine paramilitary actions against the Castro regime, though, as has been suggested, he may have merely been posing as an anti-Castro activist. That the evidence points to the possibility that Oswald was also associated in 1963 with David Ferrie, the Marcello operative who was openly and actively anti-Castro, is troubling, too. Finally, the only Cuba-related activities that have ever been established at 544 Camp Street, New Orleans, the address of an office building that Oswald stamped on some of his Fair Play for Cuba Committee handouts, were virulently anti-Castro in nature.

Thus, the committee was unable to resolve its doubts about Lee Harvey Oswald. While the search for additional information in order to reach an understanding of Oswald's actions has continued for 15 years, and while the committee developed significant new details about his possible organized crime associations, particularly in New Orleans, the President's assassin himself remains not fully understood. The committee developed new information about Oswald and Ruby, thus altering previous perceptions, but the assassin and the man who murdered him still appear against a backdrop of unexplained, or at least not fully explained, occurrences, associations and motivations.

The scientific evidence available to the committee indicated that it is probable that more than one person was involved in the President's murder. That fact compels acceptance. And it demands a re-examination of all that was thought to be true in the past. Further, the committee's investigation of Oswald and Ruby showed a variety of relationships that may have matured into an assassination conspiracy. Neither Oswald nor Ruby turned out to be "loners," as they had been painted in the 1964 investigation. Nevertheless, the committee frankly acknowledged that it was unable firmly to identify the other gunman or the nature and extent of the conspiracy.

Castro leanings might have been involved in the assassination. The committee candidly acknowledged, for example, that it could not explain Oswald's associations—nor at this late date fully determine their extent—with anti-Castro Cubans. The committee remained convinced that since Oswald consistently demonstrated a left-wing Marxist ideology, he would not have supported the anti-Castro movement. At the same time, the committee noted that Oswald's possible association with Ferrie might be distinguishable, since it could not be simply termed an anti-Castro association. Ferrie and Oswald may have had a personal friendship unrelated to Cuban activities. Ferrie was not Cuban, and though he actively supported the anti-Castro cause, he had other interests. For one, he was employed by Carlos Marcello as an investigator. (245) (It has been alleged that Ferrie operated a service station in 1964, the franchise for which was reportedly paid by Marcello.) (246) The committee concluded, therefore, that Oswald's most significant apparent anti-Castro association, that with David Ferrie, might in fact not have been related to the Cuban issue.

In the end, the committee concluded that the evidence was sufficient to support the conclusion that anti-Castro Cuban groups, as groups, were not involved in the assassination, but it could not preclude the possibility that individual members may have been involved.

4. THE COMMITTEE BELIEVES, ON THE BASIS OF THE EVIDENCE AVAILABLE TO IT, THAT THE NATIONAL SYNDICATE OF ORGANIZED CRIME, AS A GROUP, WAS NOT INVOLVED IN THE ASSASSINATION OF PRESIDENT KENNEDY, BUT THAT THE AVAILABLE EVIDENCE DOES NOT PRECLUDE THE POSSIBILITY THAT INDIVIDUAL MEMBERS MAY HAVE BEEN INVOLVED

Lee Harvey Oswald was fatally shot by Jack Ruby at 11:21 a.m. on Sunday, November 24, 1963, less than 48 hours after President Kennedy was assassinated. While many Americans were prepared to believe that Oswald had acted alone in shooting the President, they found their credulity strained when they were asked to accept a conclusion that Ruby, too, had not acted as part of a plot. As the Warren Commission observed,

* * * almost immediately speculation arose that Ruby had acted on behalf of members of a conspiracy who had planned the killing of President Kennedy and wanted to silence Oswald. (1).

The implications of the murder of Oswald are crucial to an understanding of the assassination itself. Several of the logical possibilities should be made explicit:

Oswald was a member of a conspiracy, and he was killed by Ruby, also a conspirator, so that he would not reveal the plot.

Oswald was a member of a conspiracy, yet Ruby acted alone, as he explained, for personal reasons.

Oswald was not a member of a conspiracy as far as Ruby knew, but his murder was an act planned by Ruby and others to take justice into their own hands.

Both Oswald and Ruby acted alone or with the assistance of only one or two confederates, but there was no wider conspiracy, one that extended beyond the immediate participants.

If it is determined that Ruby acted alone, it does not necessarily follow that there was no conspiracy to murder the President. But if Ruby was part of a sophisticated plot to murder Oswald, there would be troublesome implications with respect to the assassination of the President. While it is possible to develop an acceptable rationale of why a group might want to kill the President's accused assassin, even though its members were not in fact involved in the assassination, it is difficult to make the explanation sound convincing. There is a possibility, for example, that a Dallas citizen or groups of citizens planned the murder of Oswald by Ruby to revenge the murders of President Kennedy or Patrolman J. D. Tippit, or both. Nevertheless, the brief period of time between the two murders, during which the vengeful plotters would have had to formulate and execute Oswald's murder, would seem to indicate the improbability of such an explanation. A preexisting group might have taken action within 48 hours, but it is doubtful that a group could have planned and then carried out Oswald's murder in such a short period of time.

(a) The Warren Commission investigation

The Warren Commission looked at Ruby's conduct and associations from November 21 through November 24 to determine if they reflected a conspiratorial relationship with Oswald.(2) It found no "* * * grounds for believing that Ruby's killing of Oswald was part of a conspiracy."(3) It accepted as true his explanation that his conduct reflected "genuine shock and grief" and strong affection for President Kennedy and his family.(4) As for numerous phone contacts Ruby had with underworld figures in the weeks preceding the assassination, the Commission believed his explanation that they had to do with his troubles with the American Guild of Variety Artists, rather than reflecting any sinister associations that might have been related to the President's assassination.(5)

The Commission also found no evidence that Ruby and Oswald had ever been acquainted, although the Commission acknowledged that they both lived in the Oak Cliff section of Dallas, had post office boxes at the terminal annex, and had possible but tenuous third party links. These included Oswald's landlady, Earlene Roberts, whose sister, Bertha Cheek, had visited Ruby at his nightclub on November 18,(6) and a fellow boarder at Oswald's roominghouse, John Carter, who was friendly with a close friend and employee of Ruby, Wanda Killam.(7).

The Commission also looked to Ruby's ties to other individuals or groups that might have obviated the need for direct contact with Oswald near the time of the assassination. Ruby was found not to be linked to pro- or anti-Castro Cuban groups;(8) he was also found not to be linked to "illegal activities with members of the organized underworld."(9) The Commission noted that Ruby "disclaimed that he was associated with organized criminal activities," and it did not find reason to disbelieve him.(10) The evidence "fell short" of demonstrating that Ruby "was significantly affiliated with organized crime."(11) He was, at worst, "familiar, if not friendly" with some

149

criminal elements, but he was not a participant in "organized criminal activity."(*12*) Consequently, the Commission concluded that "the evidence does not establish a significant link between Ruby and organized crime."(*13*) And in its central conclusion about Jack Ruby, the Commission stated that its investigation had "yielded no evidence that Ruby conspired with anyone in planning or executing the killing of Lee Harvey Oswald."(*14*) For the Warren Commission, therefore, Ruby's killing of Oswald had no implications for Oswald's killing of the President.

(b) The committee investigation

Like the Warren Commission, the committee was deeply troubled by the circumstances surrounding the murder of the President's accused assassin. It, too, focused its attention on Jack Ruby, his family and his associates. Its investigation, however, was not limited to Ruby, Oswald and their immediate world. The committee's attention was also directed to organized crime and those major figures in it who might have been involved in a conspiracy to kill the President because of the Kennedy administration's unprecedented crackdown on them and their illicit activities.

(1) *Ruby and organized crime.*—The committee, as did the Warren Commission, recognized that a primary reason to suspect organized crime of possible involvement in the assassination was Ruby's killing of Oswald. For this reason, the committee undertook an extensive investigation of Ruby and his relatives, friends and associates to determine if there was evidence that Ruby was involved in crime, organized or otherwise, such as gambling and vice, and if such involvement might have been related to the murder of Oswald.

The evidence available to the committee indicated that Ruby was not a "member" of organized crime in Dallas or elsewhere, although it showed that he had a significant number of associations and direct and indirect contacts with underworld figures, a number of whom were connected to the most powerful La Cosa Nostra leaders. Additionally, Ruby had numerous associations with the Dallas criminal element.

The committee examined the circumstances of a well-known episode in organized crime history in which representatives of the Chicago Mafia attempted in, 1947, a move into Dallas, facilitated by the bribery of members of the Dallas sheriff's office.(*15*) The Kefauver committee of the U.S. Senate, during its extensive probe of organized crime in the early 1950's, termed this attempt by the Chicago syndicate to buy protection from the Dallas authorities an extraordinary event, one of the more brazen efforts made during that postwar period of criminal expansion.

In the years since the assassination, there had been allegations that Ruby was involved in organized crime's 1947 attempt to move into Dallas, perhaps as a frontman for the Chicago racketeers.(*16*) During discussions of the bribe offer, Dallas Sheriff Steve Guthrie secretly taped conversations in which the Chicago mob representative outlined plans for its Dallas operation.(*17*) They spoke of establishing a nightclub as a front for illegal gambling. It happens that Ruby moved from Chicago to Dallas in 1947 and began operating a number of nightclubs.(*18*) While the FBI and the Warren Commission were aware in 1964 of the alleged links between Ruby and those involved in the bribery attempt, a thorough investigation of the charges was not undertaken. (*19*)

The committee frankly realized that because this incident occurred 32 years in the past, it would be difficult, if not impossible, to answer all the allegations fully and finally. Nevertheless, the committee was able to develop substantial evidence from tape recordings made by the sheriff's office, detailed law enforcement documents and the testimony of knowledgeable witnesses.

As a result, the committee concluded that while Ruby and members of his family were acquainted with individuals who were involved in the incident, including Chicago gangsters who had moved to Dallas, and while Ruby may have wished to participate, there was no solid evidence that he was, in fact, part of the Chicago group. (*20*) There was also no evidence available that Ruby was to have been involved in the proposed gambling operation had the bribery attempt been successful, or that Ruby came to Dallas for that purpose. (*21*)

The committee found it reasonable to assume that had Ruby been involved in any significant way, he would probably have been referred to in either the tape recordings or the documentation relating to the incident, but a review of that available evidence failed to disclose any reference to Ruby. (*22*) The committee, however, was not able to interview former Sheriff Guthrie, the subject of the bribery attempt and the one witness who maintained to the FBI in 1963–64 that Ruby was significantly involved in the Chicago syndicate plan.[1] (*23*)

The committee also examined allegations that, even before the 1947 move to Dallas, Ruby had been personally acquainted with two professional killers for the organized crime syndicate in Chicago, David Yaras and Lenny Patrick. (*25*) The committee established that Ruby, Yaras and Patrick were in fact acquainted during Ruby's years in Chicago, particularly in the 1930's and 1940's. (*26*) Both Yaras and Patrick admitted, when questioned by the FBI in 1964, that they did know Ruby, but both said that they had not had any contact with him for 10 to 15 years. (*27*) Yaras and Patrick further maintained they had never been particularly close to Ruby, had never visited him in Dallas and had no knowledge of Ruby being connected to organized crime. (*28*) Indeed, the Warren Commission used Patrick's statement as a footnote citation in its report to support its conclusion that Ruby did not have significant syndicate associations. (*29*)

On the other hand, the committee established that Yaras and Patrick were, in fact, notorious gunmen, having been identified by law enforcement authorities as executioners for the Chicago mob (*30*) and closely associated with Sam Giancana, the organized crime leader in Chicago who was murdered in 1975. Yaras and Patrick are believed to have been responsible for numerous syndicate executions, including the murder of James Ragan, a gambling wire service owner. (*31*) The evidence implicating Yaras and Patrick in syndicate activities is unusually reliable. (*32*) Yaras, for example, was overheard in a 1962 electronic surveillance discussing various underworld murder con-

---

[1] With reference to Guthrie's claim that Ruby's name had been mentioned frequently in the discussions with Chicago underworld representatives, the committee's review of the tape recordings failed to disclose such references. Portions of the tapes were unintelligible and two entire recordings were discovered by investigators in 1964 to be missing, so the evidence was not conclusive. (*24*)

tracts he had carried out and one he had only recently been assigned. While the committee found no evidence that Ruby was associated with Yaras or Patrick during the 1950's or 1960's,(33) it concluded that Ruby had probably talked by telephone to Patrick during the summer of 1963.(34)

While Ruby apparently did not participate in the organized crime move to Dallas in 1947, he did establish himself as a Dallas nightclub operator around that time. His first club was the Silver Spur, which featured country and western entertainment. Then he operated the Sovereign, a private club that failed and was converted into the Carousel Club, a burlesque house with striptease acts. Ruby, an extroverted individual, acquired numerous friends and contacts in and around Dallas, some of whom had syndicate ties.

Included among Ruby's closest friends was Lewis McWillie. McWillie moved from Dallas to Cuba in 1958 and worked in gambling casinos in Havana until 1960.(35) In 1978, McWillie was employed in Las Vegas, and law enforcement files indicate he had business and personal ties to major organized crime figures, including Meyer Lansky and Santos Trafficante.(36)

Ruby traveled to Cuba on at least one occasion to visit McWillie. (37) McWillie testified to the committee that Ruby visited him only once in Cuba, and that it was a social visit.(38) The Warren Commission concluded this was the only trip Ruby took to Cuba,(39) despite documentation in the Commission's own files indicating Ruby made a second trip.(40)

Both Ruby and McWillie claimed that Ruby's visit to Cuba was at McWillie's invitation and lasted about a week in the late summer or early fall of 1959.(41) The committee, however, obtained tourist cards from the Cuban Government that show Ruby entered Cuba on August 8, 1959, left on September 11, reentered on September 12 and left again on September 13, 1959.(42) These documents supplement records the committee obtained from the Immigration and Naturalization Service (INS) indicating that Ruby left Cuba on September 11, 1959, traveling to Miami, returned to Cuba on September 12, and traveled on to New Orleans on September 13, 1959.(43) The Cuban Government could not state with certainty that the commercial airline flights indicated by the INS records were the only ones Ruby took during the period.(44)

Other records obtained by the committee indicate that Ruby was in Dallas at times during the August 8 to September 11, 1959, period.(45) He apparently visited his safe deposit box on August 21, met with FBI Agent Charles W. Flynn on August 31,[2] and returned to the safe deposit box on September 4.(47) Consequently, if the tourist card documentation, INS, FBI and bank records are all correct, Ruby had to have made at least three trips to Cuba. While the records appeared to be accurate, they were incomplete. The committee was unable to determine, for example, whether on the third trip, if it occurred, Ruby

---

[2] In March 1959, Ruby told the FBI he wished to assist the Bureau by supplying on a confidential basis criminal information that had come to his attention. Between April and October 1959, Ruby met with Agent Flynn eight times and gave him a small bit of information a'out thefts and related offenses. On November 6, 1959, Flynn wrote that Ruby's information had not been particularly helpful, that further attempts to develop Ruby as a PCI (potential criminal informant) would be fruitless and that the file on Ruby should be closed.(46)

traveled by commercial airline or some other means. Consequently, the committee could not rule out the possibility that Ruby made more trips during this period or at other times.

Based on the unusual nature of the 1-day trip to Miami from Havana on September 11–12 and the possibility of at least one additional trip to Cuba, the committee concluded that vacationing was probably not the purpose for traveling to Havana, despite Ruby's insistence to the Warren Commission that his one trip to Cuba in 1959 was a social visit. (48) The committee reached the judgment that Ruby most likely was serving as a courier for gambling interests when he traveled to Miami from Havana for 1 day, then returned to Cuba for a day, before flying to New Orleans. (49) This judgment is supported by the following:

> McWillie had made previous trips to Miami on behalf of the owners of the Tropicana, the casino for which he worked, to deposit funds; (50)

> McWillie placed a call to Meyer Panitz, a gambling associate in Miami, to inform him that Ruby was coming from Cuba, resulting in two meetings between Panitz and Ruby; (51)

> There was a continuing need for Havana casino operators to send their assets out of Cuba to protect them from seizure by the Castro government; (52) and

> The 1-day trip from Havana to Miami was not explained by Ruby, and his testimony to the Warren Commission about his travels to Cuba was contradictory. (53)

The committee also deemed it likely that Ruby at least met various organized crime figures in Cuba, possibly including some who had been detained by the Cuban government. (54) In fact, Ruby told the Warren Commission that he was later visited in Dallas by McWillie and a Havana casino owner and that they had discussed the gambling business in Cuba.[3] (55)

As noted by the Warren Commission, an exporter named Robert McKeown alleged that Ruby offered in 1959 to purchase a letter of introduction to Fidel Castro in hopes of securing the release of three individuals being held in a Cuban prison. (57) McKeown also claimed Ruby contacted him about a sale of jeeps to Cuba.[4] (58) If McKeown's allegations were accurate, they would support a judgment that Ruby's travels to Cuba were not merely for a vacation. (The committee was unable to confirm or refute McKeown's allegations. In his appearance before the committee in executive session, however, McKeown's story did not seem to be credible, based on the committee's assessment of his demeanor.) (61)

It has been charged that Ruby met with Santos Trafficante in Cuba sometime in 1959. (62) Trafficante, regarded as one of the Nation's most powerful organized crime figures, was to become a key participant in Castro assassination attempts by the Mafia and the CIA from 1960 to 1963. (63) The committee developed circumstantial evidence

---

[3] Earlier, though both he and McWillie denied it, Ruby apparently sent a coded message to McWillie in Havana, containing various sets of numerals, a communication Ruby transmitted to McWillie via McWillie's girlfriend. (56)

[4] Ruby denied this to the Warren Commission, stating he did not have sufficient contacts to obtain jeeps at the time. (59) The Warren Commission noted that Ruby "made preliminary inquiries, as a middleman" in regard to the possible sale of jeeps to Cuba, but stated that he "was merely pursuing a moneymaking opportunity." (60)

that makes a meeting between Ruby and Trafficante a distinct possibility,(64) but the evidence was not sufficient to form a final conclusion as to whether or not such a meeting took place.

While allegations of a Ruby link to Trafficante had previously been
raised, mainly due to McWillie's alleged close connections to the Mafia
leader, it was not until recent years that they received serious attention. Trafficante had long been recognized by law enforcement officials
as a leading member of the La Cosa Nostra, but he did not become
the object of significant public attention in connection with the assassination of the President until his participation in the assassination
plots against Castro was disclosed in 1975.

In 1976, in response to a freedom of information suit, the CIA de-
classified a State Department cablegram received from London on
November 28, 1963. It read:

> On 26 November 1963, a British Journalist named John
> Wilson, and also known as Wilson-Hudson, gave information
> to the American Embassy in London which indicated that
> an "American gangster-type named Ruby" visited Cuba
> around 1959. Wilson himself was working in Cuba at that
> time and was jailed by Castro before he was deported.
>
> In prison in Cuba, Wilson says he met an American gang-
> ster-gambler named Santos who could not return to the
> U.S.A. * * * Instead he preferred to live in relative luxury
> in a Cuban prison. While Santos was in prison, Wilson says,
> Santos was visited frequently by an American gangster type
> named Ruby.(65)

Several days after the CIA had received the information, the Agency
noted that there were reports that Wilson-Hudson was a "psychopath"
and unreliable. The Agency did not conduct an investigation of the
information, and the Warren Commission was apparently not informed of the cablegram. The former staff counsel who directed the
Commission's somewhat limited investigation of organized crime told
the committee that since the Commission was never told of the CIA's
use of the Mafia to try to assassinate Castro from 1960 to 1963, he was
not familiar with the name Santos Trafficante in 1964.(66)

The committee was unable to locate John Wilson-Hudson. (According to reports, he had died.) Nor was the committee able to obtain independent confirmation of the Wilson-Hudson allegation. The committee
was able, however, to develop corroborative information to the effect
that Wilson-Hudson was incarcerated at the same detention camp in
Cuba as Trafficante.(67)

On June 6, 1959, Trafficante and others who controlled extensive
gambling interests in Cuba were detained as part of a Castro government policy that would subsequently lead to the confiscation of all
underworld holdings in Cuba.(68) They were held in Trescornia, a
minimum security detention camp.(69) According to documentation
supplied by the Cuban Government, Trafficante was released from
Trescornia on August 18, 1959.(70) Tourist card documentation, also
obtained by the committee, as well as various Warren Commission
documents, indicate Ruby's first trip to Cuba began on August 8,
1959.(71) Thus, Ruby was in Cuba during part of the final days of
Trafficante's detention at Trescornia.(72)

McWillie testified before the committee that he had visited another detainee at Trescornia during that period, and he recalled possibly seeing Trafficante there. McWillie claimed, however, he did not say more than "hello" to him. (73) McWillie further testified it was during that period that Ruby visited him in Havana for about a week, and that Ruby tagged along with him during much of his stay. (74) Mc-Willie told the committee that Ruby could have gone with him to visit Trescornia, although he doubted that Ruby did so. (75) McWillie testified that he could not clearly recall much about Ruby's visit. (76)

Jose Verdacia Verdacia, a witness made available for a committee interview by the Cuban Government, was the warden at Trescornia in August 1959. (77) Verdacia told the committee that he could not recall the name John Wilson-Hudson, but he could remember a British journalist who had worked in Argentina, as had Wilson-Hudson, who was detained at Trescornia. (78)

In his own public testimony before the committee, Trafficante testified that he did not remember Ruby ever having visited him at Trescornia. Trafficante stated,

> There was no reason for this man to visit me. I have never seen this man before. I have never been to Dallas, I never had no contact with him. I don't see why he was going to come and visit me. (79)

Trafficante did, however, testify that he could recall an individual fitting British journalist John Wilson-Hudson's description, and he stated that the man was among those who were held in his section at Trescornia. (80)

The importance of a Ruby-Trafficante meeting in Trescornia should not be overemphasized. The most it would show would be a meeting, at that a brief one. No one has suggested that President Kennedy's assassination was planned at Trescornia in 1959. At the same time, a meeting or an association, even minor, between Ruby and Trafficante would not have been necessary for Ruby to have been used by Trafficante to murder Oswald. (81) Indeed, it is likely that such a direct contact would have been avoided by Trafficante if there had been a plan to execute either the President or the President's assassin, but, since no such plot could have been under consideration in 1959, there would not have been a particular necessity for Trafficante to avoid contact with Ruby in Cuba.

The committee investigated other aspects of Ruby's activities that might have shown an association with organized crime figures. An extensive computer analysis of his telephone toll records for the month prior to the President's assassination revealed that he either placed calls to or received calls from a number of individuals who may be fairly characterized as having been affiliated, directly or indirectly, with organized crime. (82) These included Irwin Weiner, a Chicago bondsman well-known as a frontman for organized crime and the Teamsters Union; (83) Robert "Barney" Baker, a lieutenant of James R. Hoffa and associate of several convicted organized crime executioners: (84) Nofio J. Pecora, a lieutenant of Carlos Marcello, the Mafia boss in Louisiana: (85) Harold Tannenbaum, a New Orleans French Quarter nightclub manager who lived in a trailer park owned by Pecora; (*86*) McWillie, the Havana gambler; (*87*) and Murray "Dusty" Miller, a Teamster deputy of Hoffa and associate of various underworld figures. (*88*) Additionally, the committee concluded that Ruby was also probably in telephonic contact with Mafia executioner Lenny Patrick sometime during the summer of 1963. (*89*) Although no such call was indicated in the available Ruby telephone records, Ruby's sister, Eva Grant, told the Warren Commission that Ruby had spoken more than once of having contacted Patrick by telephone during that period. (*90*)

The committee found that the evidence surrounding the calls was generally consistent—at least as to the times of their occurrence—with the explanation that they were for the purpose of seeking assistance in a labor dispute. (*91*) Ruby, as the operator of two nightclubs, the Carousel and the Vegas, had to deal with the American Guild of Variety Artists (AGVA), an entertainers union. (*92*) Ruby did in fact have a history of labor problems involving his striptease performers, and there was an ongoing dispute in the early 1960's regarding amateur performers in Dallas area nightclubs. (*93*) Testimony to the committee supported the conclusion that Ruby's phone calls were, by and large, related to his labor troubles. (*94*) In light of the identity of some of the individuals, however, the possibility of other matters being discussed could not be dismissed. (*95*)

In particular, the committee was not satisfied with the explanations of three individuals closely associated with organized crime who received telephone calls from Ruby in October or November 1963. (*96*)

Weiner, the Chicago bondsman, refused to discuss his call from Ruby on October 26, 1963, with the FBI in 1964, (*97*) and he told a reporter in 1978 that the call had nothing to do with labor problems. (*98*) In his executive session testimony before the committee, however, Weiner stated that he had lied to the reporter, and he claimed that he and Ruby had, in fact, discussed a labor dispute. (*99*) The committee was not satisfied with Weiner's explanation of his relationship with Ruby. Weiner suggested Ruby was seeking a bond necessary to obtain an injunction in his labor troubles, yet the committee could find no other creditable indication that Ruby contemplated seeking court relief, nor any other explanation for his having to go to Chicago for such a bond. (*100*)

Barney Baker told the FBI in 1964 that he had received only one telephone call from Ruby (on Nov. 7, 1963) during which he had curtly dismissed Ruby's plea for assistance in a nightclub labor dispute. (*101*) The committee established, however, that Baker received a second lengthy call from Ruby on November 8. (*102*) The committee found it hard to believe that Baker, who denied the conversation ever took place, could have forgotten it. (*103*)

The committee was also dissatisfied with the explanation of a call Ruby made on October 30, 1963, to the New Orleans trailer park office of Nofio J. Pecora, the long-time Marcello lieutenant. (*104*) Pecora told the committee that only he would have answered his phone and that he never spoke with Ruby or took a message from him. (*105*) The committee considered the possibility that the call was actually for Harold Tannenbaum, a mutual friend of Ruby and

Pecora who lived in the trailer park, although Pecora denied he would have relayed such a message. (106)

Additionally, the committee found it difficult to dismiss certain Ruby associations with the explanation that they were solely related to his labor problems. For example, James Henry Dolan, a Dallas AGVA representative, was reportedly an acquaintance of both Carlos Marcello and Santos Trafficante. (107) While Dolan worked with Ruby on labor matters, they were also allegedly associated in other dealings, including a strong-arm attempt to appropriate the proceeds of a one-night performance of a stage review at the Adolphus Hotel in Dallas called "Bottoms Up." (108) The FBI, moreover, has identified Dolan as an associate of Nofio Pecora. (109) The committee noted further that reported links between AGVA and organized crime figures have been the subject of Federal and State investigations that have been underway for years.[5] (110) The committee's difficulties in separating Ruby's AGVA contacts from his organized crime connections was, in large degree, based on the dual roles that many of his associates played.[6]

In assessing the significance of these Ruby contacts, the committee noted, first of all, that they should have been more thoroughly explored in 1964 when memories were clearer and related records (including, but not limited to, additional telephone toll records) were available. Further, while there may be persuasive arguments against the likelihood that the attack on Oswald would have been planned in advance on the telephone with an individual like Ruby, the pattern of contacts did show that individuals who had the motive to kill the President also had knowledge of a man who could be used to get access to Oswald in the custody of the Dallas police. In Ruby, they also had knowledge of a man who had exhibited a violent nature and who was in serious financial trouble. The calls, in short, established knowledge and possible availability, if not actual planning.

(2) *Ruby and the Dallas Police Department.*—The committee also investigated the relationship between Ruby and the Dallas Police Department to determine whether members of the department might have helped Ruby get access to Oswald for the purpose of shooting him. (111) Ruby had a friendly and somewhat unusual relationship with the Dallas Police Department, both collectively and with individual officers, but the committee found little evidence of any significant influence by Ruby within the force that permitted him to engage in illicit activities. (112) Nevertheless, Ruby's close relationship with one or more members of the police force may have been a factor in his entry to the police basement on November 24, 1963. (113)

Both the Warren Commission and a Dallas Police Department investigative unit concluded that Ruby entered the police basement on November 24, 1963, between 11:17 a.m., when he apparently sent a telegram, and 11:21, when he shot Oswald, via the building's Main Street ramp as a police vehicle was exiting, thereby fortuitously

---

[5] According to FBI records, AGVA has been used frequently by members of organized crime as a front for criminal activities.
[6] Although it was dissatisfied with the explanations it received for these calls, the committee also noted that the individuals called may have been reluctant to admit that Ruby was seeking their assistance in an illegal effort to settle his labor problems.

creating a momentary distraction.(*114*) The committee, however, found that Ruby probably did not come down the ramp,(*115*) and that his most likely route was an alleyway located next to the Dallas Municipal Building and a stairway leading to the basement garage of police headquarters.(*116*)

The conclusion reached by the Warren Commission that Ruby entered the police basement via the ramp was refuted by the eyewitness testimony of every witness in the relevant area, only Ruby himself excepted.(*117*) It was also difficult for the committee to reconcile the ramp route with the 55-second interval (derived from viewings of the video tapes of the Oswald murder) from the moment the police vehicle started up the ramp and the moment Ruby shot Oswald.(*118*) Ruby would have had to come down the ramp after the vehicle went up, leaving him less than 55 seconds to get down the ramp and kill Oswald. Even though the Warren Commission and the Dallas police investigative unit were aware of substantial testimony contradicting the ramp theory,(*119*) they arrived at their respective conclusions by relying heavily on Ruby's own assertions and what they perceived to be the absence of a plausible alternative route.(*120*)

The committee's conclusion that Ruby entered from the alley was supported by the fact that it was much less conspicuous than the alternatives,(*121*) by the lack of security in the garage area and along the entire route,(*122*) and by the testimony concerning the security of the doors along the alley and stairway route.(*123*) This route would also have accommodated the 4-minute interval from Ruby's departure from a Western Union office near police headquarters at 11:17 a.m. to the moment of the shooting at 11:21.(*124*)

Based on a review of the evidence, albeit circumstantial, the committee believed that Ruby's shooting of Oswald was not a spontaneous act, in that it involved at least some premeditation.(*125*) Similarly, the committee believed that it was less likely that Ruby entered the police basement without assistance, even though the assistance may have been provided with no knowledge of Ruby's intentions. The assistance may have been in the form of information about plans for Oswald's transfer or aid in entering the building or both.[7] (*126*)

The committee found several circumstances significant in its evaluation of Ruby's conduct. It considered in particular the selectively recalled and self-serving statements in Ruby's narration of the events of the entire November 22–24 weekend in arriving at its conclusions. (*127*) It also considered certain conditions and events. The committee was troubled by the apparently unlocked doors along the stairway route and the removal of security guards from the area of the garage nearest the stairway shortly before the shooting;(*128*) by a Saturday night telephone call from Ruby to his closest friend, Ralph Paul, in which Paul responded to something Ruby said by asking him if he was crazy;(*129*) and by the actions and statements of several Dallas police officers, particularly those present when Ruby was initially interrogated about the shooting of Oswald.(*130*)

---

[7] While the Warren Commission did not make reference to it in its report, Ruby refused in his first interviews with the FBI, Secret Service and the Dallas police to indicate how he entered the basement or whether anyone had assisted him. In later interviews, Ruby stated he had walked down the ramp.

There is also evidence that the Dallas Police Department withheld relevant information from the Warren Commission concerning Ruby's entry to the scene of the Oswald transfer.(*131*) For example, the fact that a polygraph test had been given to Sergeant Patrick Dean in 1964 was never revealed to the Commission, even though Dean was responsible for basement security and was the first person to whom Ruby explained how he had entered the basement.(*132*) Dean indicated to the committee that he had "failed" the test, but the committee was unable to locate a copy of the actual questions, responses and results.(*133*)

(3) *Other evidence relating to Ruby.*—The committee noted that other Ruby activities and movements during the period immediately following the assassination—on November 22 and 23—raised disturbing questions. For example, Ruby's first encounter with Oswald occurred over 36 hours before he shot him. Ruby was standing within a few feet of Oswald as he was being moved from one part of police headquarters to another just before midnight on November 22.(*134*) Ruby testified that he had no trouble entering the building, and the committee found no evidence contradicting his story. The committee was disturbed, however, by Ruby's easy access to headquarters and by his inconsistent accounts of his carrying a pistol. In an FBI interview on December 25, 1963, he said he had the pistol during the encounter with Oswald late in the evening of November 22. But when questioned about it by the Warren Commission, Ruby replied, "I will be honest with you. I lied about it. It isn't so, I didn't have a gun."(*135*) Finally, the committee was troubled by reported sightings of Ruby on Saturday, November 23, at Dallas police headquarters and at the county jail at a time when Oswald's transfer to the county facility had originally been scheduled. These sightings, along with the one on Friday night, could indicate that Ruby was pursuing Oswald's movements throughout the weekend.

The committee also questioned Ruby's self-professed motive for killing Oswald, his story to the Warren Commission and other authorities that he did it out of sorrow over the assassination and sympathy for the President's widow and children. Ruby consistently claimed there had been no other motive and that no one had influenced his act.(*136*) A handwritten note by Ruby, disclosed in 1967, however, exposed Ruby's explanation for the Oswald slaying as a fabricated legal ploy.(*137*) Addressed to his attorney, Joseph Tonahill, it told of advice Ruby had received from his first lawyer, Tom Howard, in 1963: "Joe, you should know this. Tom Howard told me to say that I shot Oswald so that Caroline and Mrs. Kennedy wouldn't have to come to Dallas to testify. OK?"(*138*)

The committee examined a report that Ruby was at Parkland Hospital shortly after the fatally wounded President had been brought there on November 22, 1963. Seth Kantor, a newsman then employed by Scripps-Howard who had known Ruby, later testified to the Warren Commission that he had run into him at Parkland and spoken with him briefly shortly before the President's death was announced.(*139*) While the Warren Commission concluded that Kantor was mistaken,(*140*) the committee determined he probably was not. The committee was impressed by the opinion of Burt W. Griffin, the

Warren Commission counsel who directed the Ruby investigation and wrote the Ruby section of the Warren report. Griffin told the committee he had come to believe, in light of evidence subsequently brought out, that the Commission's conclusion about Kantor's testimony was wrong.(141)

Subsequent to Ruby's apprehension, he was given a polygraph examination by the FBI in which he denied that he had been involved with any other person in killing Oswald, or had been involved in any way in the assassination of President Kennedy.(142) The Warren Commission stated it did not rely on this examination in drawing conclusions, although it did publish a transcript of the examination.(143) The FBI in 1964 also expressed dissatisfaction with the test,(144) based on the circumstances surrounding its administration. A panel of polygraph experts reviewed the examination for the committee and concluded that it was not validly conducted or interpreted.(145) Because there were numerous procedural errors made during the test, the committee's panel was unable to interpret the examination.(146)

Finally, the committee analyzed the finances of Ruby and of his family to determine if there was any evidence of financial profit from his killing of the accused assassin.(147) It was an analysis the Warren Commission could not perform so soon after the assassination.(148) Some financial records, including tax returns, could not be legally obtained by the committee without great difficulty, and others no longer existed.(149) Nevertheless, on the basis of the information that it did obtain, the committee uncovered no evidence that Ruby or members of his family profited from the killing of Oswald. (150) Particular allegations concerning the increased business and personal incomes of Ruby's brother Earl were investigated, but the committee found no link between Earl Ruby's finances and the Oswald slaying.(151) Earl Ruby did say he had been approached by the Chicago bondsman and associate of organized crime figures, Irwin Weiner, who made a business proposition to him in 1978, the day before Earl Ruby was to testify before the committee.(152) Earl Ruby said he declined the offer,(153) while Weiner denied to the committee he ever made it.(154) The committee was not able to resolve the difference between the two witnesses.

(4) *Involvement of organized crime.*—In contrast to the Warren Commission, the committee's investigation of the possible involvement of organized crime in the assassination was not limited to an examination of Jack Ruby. The committee also directed its attention to organized crime itself.

Organized crime is a term of many meanings. It can be used to refer to the crimes committed by organized criminal groups—gambling, narcotics, loan-sharking, theft and fencing, and the like.(155) It can also be used to refer to the criminal groups that commit those crimes.(156) Here, a distinction may be drawn between an organized crime enterprise that engages in providing illicit goods and services and an organized crime syndicate that regulates relations between individual enterprises—allocating territory, settling personal disputes, establishing gambling payoffs, etc.(157) Syndicates, too, are of different types. They may be metropolitan, regional, national or interna-

The committee regarded the incident of the note as a serious impeachment of Shanklin's and Hosty's credibility. It noted, however, that the note, if it contained threats in response to FBI contacts with Oswald's wife, would have been evidence tending to negate an informant relationship. The committee noted further the speculative nature of its findings about the note incident. Because the note had been destroyed, it was not possible to establish with confidence what its contents were.

(7) *Conclusion.*—In summary, although there have been many allegations of an Oswald-FBI informant relationship, there was no credible evidence that Oswald was ever an informant for the Bureau. Absent a relationship between Oswald and the FBI, grounds for suspicions of FBI complicity in the assassination become remote.

(c) *The Central Intelligence Agency* [1]

In 1964, the CIA advised the Warren Commission that the Agency had never had a relationship of any kind with Lee Harvey Oswald. Testifying before the Commission, CIA Director John A. McCone indicated that:

> Oswald was not an agent, employee, or informant of the Central Intelligence Agency. The Agency never contacted him, interviewed him, talked with him, or solicited any reports or information from him, or communicated with him directly or in any other manner * * * Oswald was never associated or connected directly or indirectly in any way whatsoever with the Agency.(1)

McCone's testimony was corroborated by Deputy Director Richard M. Helms.(2) The record reflects that once these assurances had been received, no further efforts were made by the Warren Commission to pursue the matter.

Recognizing the special difficulty in investigating a clandestine agency, the committee sought to resolve the issue of Oswald's alleged association with the CIA by conducting an inquiry that went beyond taking statements from two of the Agency's most senior officials. The more analytical approach used by the committee consisted of a series of steps:

First, an effort was made to identify circumstances in Oswald's life or in the way his case was handled by the CIA that possibly suggested an intelligence association.

Then, the committee undertook an intensive review of the pertinent files, including the CIA's 144-volume Oswald file and hundreds of others from the CIA, FBI, Department of State, Department of Defense and other agencies.

Based on these file reviews, a series of interviews, depositions and executive session hearings was conducted with both Agency and non-Agency witnesses. The contacts with present and former CIA personnel covered a broad range of individuals, including staff and division chiefs, clandestine case officers, area desk officers, research analysts, secretaries and clerical assistants. In total, more

[1] For a brief history of the CIA and description of its organisational structure, see Section I D 4 infra.

than 125 persons, including at least 50 present and former CIA employees, were questioned.[2]

The results of this investigation confirmed the Warren Commission testimony of McCone and Helms. There was no indication in Oswald's CIA file that he had ever had contact with the Agency. Finally, taken in their entirety, the items of circumstantial evidence that the committee had selected for investigation as possibly indicative of an intelligence association did not support the allegation that Oswald had an intelligence agency relationship.

This finding, however, must be placed in context, for the institutional characteristics—in terms of the Agency's strict compartmentalization and the complexity of its enormous filing system—that are designed to prevent penetration by foreign powers have the simultaneous effect of making congressional inquiry difficult. For example, CIA personnel testified to the committee that a review of Agency files would not always indicate whether an individual was affiliated with the Agency in any capacity.(3) Nor was there always an independent means of verifying that all materials requested from the Agency had, in fact, been provided. Accordingly, any finding that is essentially negative in nature—such as that Lee Harvey Oswald was neither associated with the CIA in any way, nor ever in contact with that institution—should explicitly acknowledge the possibility of oversight.

To the extent possible, however, the committee's investigation was designed to overcome the Agency's security-oriented institutional obstacles that potentially impede effective scrutiny of the CIA. The vast majority of CIA files made available to the committee were reviewed in undeleted form.(4) These files were evaluated both for their substantive content and for any potential procedural irregularities suggestive of possible editing or tampering. After review, the files were used as the basis for examination and cross-examination of present and former Agency employees. Each of the present and former Agency employees contacted by the committee was released from his secrecy oath by the CIA insofar as questions relevant to the committee's legislative mandate were concerned. Because of the number of Agency personnel who were interrogated,(5) it is highly probable that any significant inconsistencies between the files and witnesses' responses would have been discovered by the committee.

During the course of its investigation, the committee was given access by the CIA to information based on sensitive sources and methods that are protected by law from unauthorized disclosure. The committee noted that in some circumstances disclosure of such information in detail would necessarily reveal the sensitive sources and methods by which it was acquired. With respect to each item of such information, the committee carefully weighed the possible advancement of public understanding that might accrue from disclosure of the details of the information against the possible harm that might be done to the national interests and the dangers that might result to individuals. To

---

[2] The committee also attempted to identify CIA employees who may have had the motive, means and opportunity to assassinate President Kennedy. In this regard, no useful information was generated from selected file reviews. An effort was also made to locate a man identified as Maurice Bishop who was said to have been a CIA officer who had been seen in the company of Lee Harvey Oswald. The effort to find "Bishop" was likewise unsuccessful.

the extent required by the balancing process, sections of this report were written in a somewhat conclusionary manner in order to continue the protection of such classified information.

(1) *CIA personnel in the Soviet Russia Division.*[3]—Since Oswald spent time in the Soviet Union, a subject of special attention by the committee was the Russia-related activities of the CIA. In addition to obtaining testimony from former Directors McCone and Helms, the committee interviewed the chiefs of the Soviet Russia Division from 1959 to 1963. In each case, the committee received a categorical denial of any association of the CIA with Oswald.(6)

To investigate this matter further, the committee interviewed the persons who had been chiefs or deputy chiefs during 1959–62 of the three units within the Soviet Russia Division that were responsible respectively for clandestine activities, research in support of clandestine activities, and the American visitors program.[4] The heads of the clandestine activity section stated that during this period the CIA had few operatives in the Soviet Union and that Oswald was not one of them. Moreover, they stated that because of what they perceived to be his obvious instability, Oswald would never have met the Agency's standards for use in the field.[5] (7) The heads of the Soviet Russia Division's section that sought the cooperation of visitors to the Soviet Union informed the committee that they met with each person involved in their program and that Oswald was not one of them.(8) These officials also advised the committee that "clean-cut" collegiate types tended to be used in this program, and that Oswald did not meet this criterion.(9) Finally, the officers in charge of the Soviet Russia Division's research section in support of clandestine activities indicated that, had Oswald been contacted by the Agency, their section would probably have been informed, but that this, in fact, never occurred.(10)

(2) *CIA personnel abroad.*—Turning to particular allegations, the committee investigated the statement of former CIA employee James Wilcott, who testified in executive session that shortly after the assassination of President Kennedy he was advised by fellow employees at a CIA post abroad that Oswald was a CIA agent who had received financial disbursements under an assigned cryptonym.[6] (11) Wilcott explained that he had been employed by the CIA as a finance officer from 1957 until his resignation in 1966. In this capacity, he

---

[3] Classified analyses of these issues, written in undeleted form, are in the committee's files.

[4] The visitors program sought the cooperation, for limited purposes, of carefully selected persons traveling in the Soviet Union. For this unit, only the years 1959–61 were covered. Nevertheless, since every American traveler who was involved in this program was contacted before visiting the Soviet Union, the relevant year for Lee Harvey Oswald was 1959, the year he departed from the United States.

[5] One officer acknowledged the remote possibility that an individual could have been run by someone as part of a "vest pocket" (private or personal) operation without other Agency officials knowing about it. But even this possibility, as it applies to Oswald, was negated by the statement of the deputy chief of the Soviet Russia clandestine activities section. He commented that in 1963 he was involved in a review of every clandestine operation ever run in the Soviet Union, and Oswald was not involved in any of these cases.

[6] A cryptonym is a code designation for an agency project, program or activity or an organization, agency or individual (for whom a legal signature is not required) having a sensitive operational relationship with the agency. Cryptonyms are used in communications only to the extent necessary to protect sensitive information from disclosure to unauthorized persons. They are used (1) when disclosure of the true identity of persons, organizations or activities would be detrimental to the interest of the U.S. Government or to the persons, organizations or activities concerned; or (2) to prevent disclosure of a sensitive operational relationship with the agency.

served as a fiscal account assistant on the support staff at a post abroad from June 1960 to June 1964. In addition to his regular responsibilities, he had performed security duty on his off-hours in order to supplement his income. This put him in contact with other employees of the post who would come by the office and engage in informal conversations. On the day after President Kennedy's assassination, Wilcott claimed he was informed by a CIA case officer that Oswald was an agent. (12) He further testified that he was told that Oswald had been assigned a cryptonym and that Wilcott himself had unknowingly disbursed payments for Oswald's project. (13) Although Wilcott was unable to identify the specific case officer who had initially informed him of Oswald's agency relationship, he named several employees of the post abroad with whom he believed he had subsequently discussed the allegations. (14)

Wilcott advised the committee that after learning of the alleged Oswald connection to the CIA, he never rechecked official Agency disbursement records for evidence of the Oswald project. He explained that this was because at that time he viewed the information as mere shop talk and gave it little credence. (15) Neither did he report the allegations to any formal investigative bodies, as he considered the information hearsay. (16) Wilcott was unable to recall the agency cryptonym for the particular project in which Oswald had been involved, (17) nor was he familiar with the substance of that project. In this regard, however, because project funds were disbursed on a code basis, as a disbursement officer he would not have been apprised of the substantive aspects of projects.

In an attempt to investigate Wilcott's allegations, the committee interviewed several present and former CIA employees selected on the basis of the position each had held during the years 1954-64. Among the persons interviewed were individuals whose responsibilities covered a broad spectrum of areas in the post abroad, including the chief and deputy chief of station, as well as officers in finance, registry, the Soviet Branch and counterintelligence.

None of these individuals interviewed had ever seen any documents or heard any information indicating that Oswald was an agent. (18) This allegation was not known by any of them until it was published by critics of the Warren Commission in the late 1960's. (19) Some of the individuals, including a chief of counterintelligence in the Soviet Branch, expressed the belief that it was possible that Oswald had been recruited by the Soviet KGB during his military tour of duty overseas, as the CIA had identified a KGB program aimed at recruiting U.S. military personnel during the period Oswald was stationed there. (20) An intelligence analyst whom Wilcott had specifically named as having been involved in a conversation about the Oswald allegation told the committee that he was not in the post abroad at the time of the assassination. (21) A review of this individual's office of personnel file confirmed that, in fact, he had been transferred from the post abroad to the United States in 1962. (22)

The chief of the post abroad from 1961 to 1964 stated that had Oswald been used by the Agency he certainly would have learned about it. (23) Similarly, almost all those persons interviewed who worked in the Soviet Branch of that station indicated they would have known if Oswald had, in fact, been recruited by the CIA when he was overseas. (24) These persons expressed the opinion that, had Oswald been recruited without their knowledge, it would have been a rare exception contrary to the working policy and guidelines of the post abroad. (25)

Based on all the evidence, the committee concluded that Wilcott's allegation was not worthy of belief.

(3) *Oswald's CIA file.*—The CIA has long acknowledged that prior to the President's assassination, it had a personality file on Oswald, that is, a file that contained data about Oswald as an individual. This file, which in Agency terminology is referred to as a 201 file, was opened on December 9, 1960. (26) The Agency explained that 201 files are opened when a person is considered to be of potential intelligence or counterintelligence significance. (27) The opening of such a file is designed to serve the purpose of placing certain CIA information pertaining to that individual in one centralized records system. The 201 file is maintained in a folder belonging to the Directorate for Operations, the Agency component responsible for clandestine activities. (28)

The existence of a 201 file does not necessarily connote any actual relationship or contact with the CIA. For example, the Oswald file was opened, according to the Agency, because as an American defector, he was considered to be of continuing intelligence interest. (29) Oswald's file contained no indication that he had ever had a relationship with the CIA. Nevertheless, because the committee was aware of one instance (in an unrelated case) where an Agency officer had apparently contemplated the use of faked files with forged documents, (30) special attention was given to procedural questions that were occasioned by this file review.

(4) *Why the delay in opening Oswald's 201 file?*—A confidential State Department telegram dated October 31, 1959, sent from Moscow to Washington and forwarded to the CIA, reported that Oswald, a recently discharged Marine, had appeared at the U.S. Embassy in Moscow to renounce his American citizenship and "has offered Soviets any information he has acquired as [an] enlisted radar operator." (31) At least three other communications of a confidential nature that gave more detail on the Oswald case were sent to the CIA in about the same time period. (32) Agency officials questioned by the committee testified that the substance of the October 31, 1959, cable was sufficiently important to warrant the opening of a 201 file. (33) Oswald's file was not, however, opened until December 9, 1960. (34)

The committee requested that the CIA indicate where documents pertaining to Oswald had been disseminated internally and stored prior to the opening of his 201 file. The agency advised the committee that because document dissemination records of relatively low national security significance are retained for only a 5-year period, they were no longer in existence for the years 1959–63. (35)[a] Consequently, the Agency was unable to explain either when these documents had been received or by which component.

---

[a] None of these documents were classified higher than confidential.

An Agency memorandum, dated September 18, 1975, indicates that Oswald's file was opened on December 9, 1960, in response to the receipt of five documents: two from the FBI, two from the State Department and one from the Navy. (*36*) This explanation, however, is inconsistent with the presence in Oswald's file of four State Department documents dated in 1959 and a fifth dated May 25, 1960. It is, of course, possible that the September 18, 1975, memorandum is referring to State Department documents that were received by the Directorate for Plans [9] in October and November of 1960 and that the earlier State Department communications had been received by the CIA's Office of Security but not the Directorate for Plans. In the absence of dissemination records, however, the issue could not be resolved.

The September 18, 1975, memorandum also states that Oswald's file was opened on December 9, 1960, as a result of his " 'defection' to the U.S.S.R. on October 31, 1959 and renewed interest in Oswald brought about by his queries concerning possible reentry into the United States."(*37*) There is no indication, however, that Oswald expressed to any U.S. Government official an intention to return to the United States until mid-February 1961. (*38*) Finally, reference to the original form that was used to start a file on Oswald did not resolve this issue because the appropriate space that would normally indicate the "source document" that initiated the action referred to an Agency component rather than to a dated document.[10](*39*)

The committee was able to determine the basis for opening Oswald's file on December 9, 1960, by interviewing and then deposing the Agency employee who was directly responsible for initiating the opening action. This individual explained that the CIA had received a request from the State Department for information concerning American defectors. After compiling the requested information, she responded to the inquiry and then opened a 201 file on each defector involved. (*40*)

This statement was corroborated by review of a State Department letter which indicated that such a request, in fact, had been made of the CIA on October 25, 1960. Attached to the State Department letter was a list of known defectors; Oswald's name was on that list. The CIA responded to this request on November 21, 1960, by providing the requested information and adding two names to the State Department's original list. (*41*)

Significantly, the committee reviewed the files of 11 individuals on the original State Department list and determined that files were opened in December 1960 for each of the five (including Oswald) who did not have 201 files prior to receipt of the State Department inquiry. In each case, the slot for "source document" referred to an Agency component rather than to a dated document. (*42*)

Even so, this analysis only explained why a file on Oswald was finally opened; it did not explain the seemingly long delay in the opening of the file. To determine whether such a delayed opening was unusual, the committee reviewed the files of 13 of the 14 persons on the CIA's November 21, 1960, response to the State Department and

---

[9] The Directorate for Plans was the predecessor of the Directorate of Operations.
[10] The Agency indicated that it is customary to refer to a component when the opening action is taken on that component's authority.

of 16 other defectors (from an original list of 380) who were American-born, had defected during the years 1958–63, and who had returned to the United States during that same time period. Of 29 individuals whose files were reviewed, 8 had been the subject of 201 files prior to the time of their defection. In only 4 of the remaining 21 cases were 201 files opened at the time of defection. The files on the 17 other defectors were opened from 4 months to several years after the defection.(43) At the very least, the committee's review indicated that during 1958–63, the opening of a file years after a defection was not uncommon. In many cases, the opening was triggered by some event, independent of the defection, that had drawn attention to the individual involved.

(5) *Why was he carried as Lee Henry Oswald in his 201 file?*—Oswald's 201 file was opened under the name Lee Henry Oswald.(44) No Agency witness was able to explain why. All agency personnel, however, including the person who initiated the file opening, testified that this must have been occasioned innocently by bureaucratic error.(45) Moreover, the committee received substantial testimony to the effect that this error would not have prevented the misnamed file from being retrieved from the CIA's filing system during a routine name trace done under the name Lee Harvey Oswald.(46)

(6) *The meaning of "AG" under "Other Identification" in Oswald's 201 file.*—The form used to initiate the opening of a 201 file for Lee Harvey Oswald contains the designation AG in a box marked "Other Identification." Because this term was considered to be of potential significance in resolving the issue of Oswald's alleged Agency relationship, the CIA was asked to explain its meaning.

The Agency's response indicated that "AG" is the OI ("Other Identification") code meaning "actual or potential defectors to the East or the Sino/Soviet block including Cuba," and that anyone so described could have the OI code "AG." This code was reportedly added to Oswald's opening form because of the comment on the form that he had defected to the Soviet Union in 1959.(47)

An Agency official, who was a Directorate of Operations records expert and for many years one who had been involved in the CIA's investigation of the Kennedy assassination, gave the committee a somewhat different explanation of the circumstances surrounding the term "AG" and its placement on Oswald's opening form. This individual testified that "AG" was an example of a code used to aid in preparing computer listings of occupational groupings or intelligence affiliations. He explained that these codes always used two letters and that, in this case, the first letter "A" must have represented communism, while the second letter would represent some category within the Communist structure.(48)

His recollection was that at the time of the assassination, the "AG" code was not yet in existence because there were no provisions then in effect within the Agency for indexing American defectors. He recalled that it was only during the life of the Warren Commission that the CIA realized that its records system lacked provisions for indexing an individual such as Oswald. Consequently, the CIA revised its records manual to permit the indexing of American defectors and established a code for its computer system to be used for that category. Although this witness did not know when the notation "AG" was added to Oswald's opening sheet, he presumed that it must have been following the addition of the American defector code, thus placing the time somewhere in the middle of the Warren Commission's investigation. He explained that it was difficult to determine when any of the notations on the opening sheet had been made, since it was standard procedure to update the forms whenever necessary so that they were as reflective as possible of the available information.[11] (49)

Finally, this witness testified that the regulations regarding the use of this occupation and intelligence code specifically prohibited indicating that a particular person was either an employee of the Agency or someone who was used by the Agency. This prohibition was designed to prevent anyone from being able to produce any kind of categorical listing of CIA employees, contacts or connections. (50)

(7) *Why was Oswald's 201 file restricted?*—The form used to initiate the opening of Oswald's 201 file contains a notation indicating that the file was to be "restricted". (51) This indication was considered potentially significant because of the CIA's practice of restricting access to agents' files to persons on a "need-to-know" basis. Further investigation revealed, however, that restricting access to a file was not necessarily indicative of any relationship with the CIA.

The individual who actually placed the restriction on Oswald's file testified that this was done simply to allow her to remain aware of any developments that might have occurred with regard to the file. (52) The restriction achieved this purpose because any person seeking access to the file would first have to notify the restricting officer, at which time the officer would be apprised of any developments.

This testimony was confirmed by a CIA records expert who further testified that had the file been permanently charged to a particular desk or case officer, as well as restricted, the possibility of a relationship with the CIA would have been greater. (53) There is no indication on Oswald's form that it had been placed on permanent charge.

Finally, the committee reviewed the files of four other defectors that had been opened at the same time and by the same person as Oswald's, and determined that each of the files had been similarly restricted. Each of these other individuals was on the lists of defectors that had been exchanged by the CIA and State Department. None of the files pertaining to these other defectors had any evidence suggestive of a possible intelligence agency association.

(8) *Were 37 documents missing from Oswald's 201 file?*—In the course of reviewing Oswald's 201 file, the committee discovered an unsigned memorandum to the Chief of Counterintelligence, Research and Analysis, dated February 20, 1964, which stated that 37 documents were missing from Oswald's 201 file. (54) According to the memorandum, this statement was based on a comparison of a machine listing of documents officially recorded as being in the 201 file and those documents actually physically available in the file. (55) While the memorandum mentioned that such a machine listing was attached, no such attachment was found in the 201 file at the time of the committee's

review. The memorandum itself bears the classification "Secret Eyes Only" and was one of the documents that had been fully withheld from release under the Freedom of Information Act.(56)

In response to a committee inquiry, the CIA advised that, because Oswald's file had been so active during the course of the Warren Commission investigation, up-to-date machine listings were produced periodically. On this basis, the Agency stated that

> * * * it must be assumed that whoever was responsible for maintaining the Oswald file brought this file up-to-date by locating the 37 documents and placing them in the file.(57)

Because this response was incomplete, the author of the memorandum was deposed. He testified that once a document had been registered into a 201 file by the Agency's computer system, physical placement of the document in the file was not always necessary.(58) On this basis, he explained, the items listed in the memorandum were not missing but rather had either been routinely placed in a separate file because of their sensitivity or were being held by other individuals who needed them for analytical purposes.(59) He further stated that in the course of his custodianship of Oswald's file, he had requested perhaps as many as 100 computer listings on the contents of the Oswald file. While there had been many instances in which one or more documents had been charged out to someone, he stated that he had never discovered that any documents were actually missing.(60) According to his testimony, the 37 documents were, in fact, available, but they were not located in the file at the time.(61) The committee regarded this to be a plausible explanation.

(9) *Did the CIA maintain a dual filing system on Oswald?*—The committee was aware of the possibility that a dual filing system (one innocuous file and one that contained operational detail of a relationship with the CIA) could have been used to disguise a possible relationship between Oswald and the Agency. This awareness became a concern with the discovery that at least two Agency officers had contemplated the use of faked files and forged documents to protect the ZR Rifle project from disclosure.[12](62) The implications of this discovery in terms of the possibility that the Oswald file might also have been faked were disturbing to the committee.

In the Oswald case, two items were scrutinized because they were potentially indicative of a dual filing system. The first was a photograph of Oswald that had been taken in Minsk in 1961; the second was a copy of a letter that had been written to Oswald by his mother during his stay in the Soviet Union. At the time of President Kennedy's assassination, both of these items were in the CIA's possession, but neither was in Oswald's 201 file.

The photograph of Oswald taken in Minsk shows him posing with several other people. According to the CIA, the picture was found after the assassination as a result of a search of the Agency's graphics files for materials potentially relevant to Oswald's stay in the Soviet

---

[12] ZR Rifle was an executive action (assassination of foreign leader) program unrelated to the Oswald case. Former CIA Director Helms testified that the assassination aspect of ZR Rifle was never implemented and, in fact, was discontinued as soon as it was brought to his attention.(63)

Union.(64) The Agency advised that this photograph, as well as several others not related to Oswald, were routinely obtained in 1962 from some tourists by the CIA's Domestic Contacts Division, an Agency component that regularly sought information on a nonclandestine basis from Americans traveling abroad in Communist countries. (65)

Committee interviews with the tourists in question confirmed that the photograph, along with 159 other photographic slides, had routinely been made available to the Domestic Contacts Division. Neither tourist had heard of Oswald prior to the assassination or knew which photographs had been of interest to the Agency.(66)

CIA records indicate that only 5 of the 160 slides initially made available were retained.(67) Committee interviews with the two CIA employees who had handled the slides for the Domestic Contacts Division established that Oswald had not been identified at the time that these photographic materials were made available.(68) One of these employees stated that the Oswald picture had been retained because it depicted a Soviet Intourist guide; the other employee indicated that the picture had been kept because it showed a crane in the background.(69) Of these two employees, the one who worked at CIA headquarters (and therefore was in a position to know) indicated that the photograph of Oswald had not been discovered until a post-assassination search of the Minsk graphics file for materials pertaining to Oswald.(70)

Accordingly, this photograph was not evidence that the CIA maintained a dual filing system with respect to Oswald. The picture apparently was kept in a separate file until 1964, when Oswald was actually identified to be one of its subjects.

The committee's investigation of a copy of a letter to Oswald from his mother that was in the Agency's possession similarly did not show any evidence of a dual filing system. This letter, dated July 6, 1961, and sent by Marguerite Oswald, was intercepted as a result of a CIA program (71) known as HT-Lingual,[13] the purpose of which was to obtain intelligence and counterintelligence information from letters sent between the United States and Russia. Typically, intercepted letters and envelopes would be photographed and then returned to the mails.(72)

In response to a committee inquiry, the CIA explained that because of HT-Lingual's extreme sensitivity, all materials generated as a result of mail intercepts were stored in a separate project file that was maintained by the counterintelligence staff.(73) Consequently, such items were not placed in 201 files. This explanation was confirmed by the testimony of a senior officer from the counterintelligence staff who had jurisdiction over the HT-Lingual project files.[14](74)

(10) *Did Oswald ever participate in a CIA counterintelligence project?*—The committee's review of HT-Lingual files pertaining to

---

[13] The HT-Lingual program was no longer in effect in 1978. Prior to that time, it had been found to be illegal.

[14] Since Oswald was known to have sent or received more than 50 communications during his stay in the Soviet Union, the committee also questioned why the Agency ostensibly had just one letter in its possession directly related to Oswald. In essence, the Agency's response suggested that HT-Lingual only operated 4 days a week, and, even then, proceeded on a sampling basis.

the Oswald case [15] resulted in the discovery of reproductions of four
index cards, two with reference to Lee Harvey Oswald and two to
Marina Oswald, which were dated after the assassination of President
Kennedy. The pages containing the reproductions of these cards were
stamped "Secret Eyes Only." (75)

The first card regarding Lee Harvey Oswald, dated November 9,
1959, states that Oswald is a recent defector to the U.S.S.R. and a
former marine. It also bears the notation "CI/Project/RE" and
some handwritten notations.(76) The second card on Oswald places
him in Minsk. It contains background information on him and
states that he "reportedly expresses a desire for return to the United
States under certain conditions." This card is dated August 7, 1961,
and also bears the notation "Watch List." (77) These cards, particularly the reference to "CI/Project/RE," raised the question of
whether Oswald was, in fact, involved in some sort of counterintelligence project for the CIA.

The committee questioned former employees of the CIA who may
have had some knowledge pertaining to the HT-Lingual project in
general and these cards in particular. Some of these employees recognized the cards as relating to the HT-Lingual project, but were
unable to identify the meaning of the notation, "CI/Project/RE."(78)

One employee, however, testified that the "CI Project" was "simply
a name of convenience that was used to describe the HT-Lingual
project"; (79) another testified that "CI Project" was the name of the
component that ran the HT-Lingual project. This person also explained that "RE" represented the initials of a person who had been
a translator of foreign language documents and that the initials had
probably been placed there so that someone could come back to the
translator if a question arose concerning one of the documents.(80)
Another employee indicated that the "Watch List" notation on the
second card referred to persons who had been identified as being of
particular interest with respect to the mail intercept program.(81)

The committee requested the CIA to provide an explanation for
the terms "CI/Project/RE" and "Watch List" and for the handwritten notations appearing on the index cards. In addition, the committee
requested a description of criteria used in compiling a "Watch List."

With respect to the meaning of the notation "CI/Project/RE," the
CIA explained that there existed an office within the counterintelligence staff that was known as "CI/Project," a cover title that had been
used to hide the true nature of the office's functions. In fact, this office
was responsible for the exploitation of the material produced by the
HT-Lingual project. The Agency further explained that "RE" represented the initials of a former employee.(82)

In responding to a request for the criteria used in compiling a
"Watch List," the CIA referred to a section of the "Report to the President by the Commission on CIA Activities Within the United States,"
which states:

[15] Although the Agency had only one Oswald letter in its possession, the HT-Lingual
files were combed after the assassination for additional materials potentially related to him.
Approximately 30 pieces of correspondence that were considered potentially related to the
investigation of Oswald's case (even though not necessarily directly related to Oswald)
were discovered. None of these was ultimately judged by the CIA to be of any significance.
These materials, however, were stored in a separate Oswald HT-Lingual file.

Individuals or organizations of particular intelligence interest (one should also add counterintelligence interest) were specified in watch lists provided to the mail project by the counterintelligence staff, by other CIA components, and by the FBI. The total number of names on the Watch List varied, from time to time, but on the average, the list included approximately 300 names, including about 100 furnished by the FBI. The Watch List included the names of foreigners and of U.S. citizens.(83)

Thus, the full meaning of the notation is that on November 9, 1959, an employee whose initials were RE placed Oswald's name on the "Watch List" for the HT-Lingual project for the reason stated on the card—that Oswald was a recent defector to the U.S.S.R. and a former Marine.(84)

The response went on to state that the handwritten number, No. 7-305, which also appears on the first card, is a reference to the communication from the CI staff to the Office of Security expressing the CI staff's interest in seeing any mail to or from Oswald in the Soviet Union. Finally, the other handwritten notation, "N/R–RI, 20 Nov. 59" signifies that a name trace run through the central records register indicates that there was no record for Lee Oswald as of that date.[16](85)

The Agency's explanation of the meaning of the second card was that on August 7, 1961, the CIA staff officer who opened the Oswald 201 file requested that Oswald's name be placed on the "Watch List" because of Oswald's expressed desire to return to the United States, as stated on the card. The handwritten notation indicates, in this instance, that Oswald's name was deleted from the "Watch List" on May 28, 1962.(86)

With reference to the two cards on Marina Oswald, the Agency stated that her name was first placed on the "Watch List" on November 26, 1963, because she was the wife of Lee Harvey Oswald. The second card served the purpose of adding the name Marina Oswald Porter to the "Watch List" on June 29, 1965, after she had remarried. Both names were deleted from the list as of May 26, 1972.(87)

Thus the statements of former CIA employees were corroborated by the Agency's response regarding the explanation of the index cards in the CIA's HT-Lingual files pertaining to Oswald. The explanations attested that the references on the cards were not demonstrative of an Agency relationship with Oswald, but instead were examples of notations routinely used in connection with the HT-Lingual project.

(11) *Did the CIA ever debrief Oswald?*—The CIA has denied ever having had any contact with Oswald,(88) and its records are consistent with this position. Because the Agency has a Domestic Contacts Division that routinely attempts to solicit information on a nonclandestine basis from Americans traveling abroad,(89) the absence of any record indicating that Oswald, a returning defector who had worked in a Minsk radio factory, had been debriefed has been con-

---

[16] This, of course, is contrary to the Agency's record that indicates the receipt of a telegram concerning Oswald on Oct. 31, 1959, and of two telegrams from the Navy concerning him on Nov. 3 and 4, 1959.

sidered by Warren Commission critics to be either inherently unbelievable (that is, the record was destroyed) or indicative that Oswald had been contacted through other than routine Domestic Contact Division channels. (*90*)

After reviewing the Agency's records pertaining to this issue, the committee interviewed the former chief of an Agency component responsible for research related to clandestine operations within the Soviet Union. He had written a November 25, 1963, memorandum indicating that, upon Oswald's return from the Soviet Union, he had considered "the laying of interviews [on him] through the [Domestic Contacts Division] or other suitable channels." [17](*91*) The officer indicated that Oswald was considered suspect because the Soviets appeared to have been very solicitous of him. For this reason, a nonclandestine contact, either by the Domestic Contacts Division or other "suitable channels" such as the FBI or the Immigration and Naturalization Service, was considered. (*92*) The officer stated, however, that to his knowledge no contact with Oswald was ever made. Moreover, if a debriefing had occurred, the officer stated that he would have been informed. Finally, he said that Oswald was considered a potential lead, but only of marginal importance, and therefore the absence of a debriefing was not at all unusual. (*93*)

The committee interviewed five other Agency employees who were in a position to have discussed Oswald in 1962 with the author of this memorandum, including the person who replaced the author of the memorandum as chief of the research section. None of them could recall such a discussion. (*94*) Interviews with personnel from the Soviet Russia Division's clandestine operations section, the visitors program and the clandestine activity research section failed to result in any evidence suggesting that Oswald had been contacted at any time by the CIA. (*95*)

The author of the November 25, 1963, memorandum also informed the committee that the CIA maintained a large volume of information on the Minsk radio factory in which Oswald had worked. This information was stored in the Office of Research and Reports. (*96*)

Another former CIA employee, one who had worked in the Soviet branch of the Foreign Documents Division of the Directorate of Intelligence in 1962, advised the committee that he specifically recalled collecting intelligence regarding the Minsk radio plant. In fact, this individual claimed that during the summer of 1962, he reviewed a contact report from representatives of a CIA field office who had interviewed a former marine who had worked at the Minsk radio plant following his defection to the U.S.S.R. This defector, whom the employee believed may have been Oswald, had been living with his family in Minsk. (*97*)

The employee advised the committee that the contact report had been filed in a volume on the Minsk radio plant that should be retrievable from the Industrial Registry Branch, then a component of the Office of Central Reference. Accordingly, the committee requested that the CIA provide both the contact report and the volume of ma-

---

[17] The November 25, 1963 memorandum indicates that the possibility of an Oswald contact was discussed during the summer of 1960, but the author indicated that the conversation actually took place during the summer of 1962, shortly before his transfer to a new assignment. During the summer of 1960, the author was not on active assignment.

terials concerning the Minsk radio plant. A review by the committee of the documents in the volumes on the Minsk radio plant, however, failed to locate any such contact report.(98)

Since the Minsk radio plant seemed to be a logical subject of CIA concern, the committee theorized that questions about it would have been included in the debriefing of defectors. The committee therefor asked the Agency for a statement regarding its procedures for debriefing defectors. In response, the CIA stated that between 1958 and 1963 it had no procedure for systematically debriefing overseas travelers, including returning defectors. Instead, the Agency relied upon the FBI both to make such contacts and report any significant results.(99)

To investigate this question further, the committee reviewed the files of 22 other defectors to the Soviet Union (from an original list of 380) who were born in America and appeared to have returned to the United States between 1958 and 1963.[18] Of these 22 individuals, only 4 were interviewed at any time by the CIA. These four instances tended to involve particular intelligence or counterintelligence needs, but this was not always the case.(100)

Based on this file review, it appeared to the committee that, in fact, the CIA did not contact returning defectors in 1962 as a matter of standard operating procedure. For this reason, the absence of any Agency contact with Oswald on his return from the Soviet Union could not be considered unusual, particularly since the FBI did fulfill its jurisdictional obligation to conduct defector interviews.(101)

(12) *The Justice Department's failure to prosecute Oswald.*— When Oswald appeared at the U.S. Embassy on October 31, 1959, to renounce his American citizenship, he allegedly threatened to give the Soviets information he had acquired as a Marine Corps radar operator.(102) The committee sought to determine why the Justice Department did not prosecute Oswald on his return to the United States for his offer to divulge this kind of information.

A review of Oswald's correspondence with the American Embassy in Moscow indicates that on February 13, 1961, the embassy received a letter in which Oswald expressed a "desire to return to the United States if * * * some agreement [could be reached] concerning the dropping of any legal proceedings against [him]."(103) On February 28, 1961, the embassy sought guidance from the State Department concerning Oswald's potential liability to criminal prosecution.(104) The State Department, however, responded on April 13, 1961, that it was

> not in a position to advise Mr. Oswald whether upon his desired return to the United States he may be amenable to prosecution for any possible offenses committed in violation of the laws of the United States * * *.(105)

In May 1961, Oswald wrote the embassy demanding a "full guarantee" against the possibility of prosecution.(106) He visited with Embassy Consul Richard Snyder on July 16, 1961, and denied that he had ever given any information to the Soviets.(107) Snyder advised

---

[18] An effort was also made to review only the files of those who had defected between 1958 and 1963. Not all of the 22 defectors, however, met this criterion.

Oswald on an informal basis that, while no assurances could be given, the embassy did not perceive any basis for prosecuting him.(*108*)

There is no record that the State Department ever gave Oswald any assurances that he would not be prosecuted. Upon his return to the United States, Oswald was interviewed twice by the FBI. On each occasion, he denied ever having given information to the Soviet Union.(*109*)

In response to a committee request, the Department of Justice indicated that prosecution of Oswald was never considered because his file contained no evidence that he had ever revealed or offered to reveal national defense information to the Soviet Union.(*110*) In a subsequent response, the Department acknowledged the existence of some evidence that Oswald had offered information to the Soviet Union, but stated that there were, nevertheless, serious obstacles to a possible prosecution:

> It [the Department file] does contain a copy of an FBI memorandum, dated July 3, 1961, which is recorded as having been received in the Justice Department's Internal Security Division on December 10, 1963, which states that the files of the Office of Naval Intelligence contained a copy of a Department of State telegram, dated October 31, 1959, at Moscow. The telegram, which is summarized in the FBI report, quoted Oswald as having offered the Soviets any information he had acquired as a radar operator. The FBI report did not indicate that the information to which Oswald had access as a radar operator was classified.

> Oswald returned to the United States on June 13, 1962. He was interviewed by the FBI on June 26, 1962, at Fort Worth, Tex., at which time he denied furnishing any information to the Soviets concerning his Marine Corps experiences. He stated that he never gave the Soviets any information which would be used to the detriment of the United States.

> In sum, therefore, the only "evidence" that Oswald ever offered to furnish information to the Soviets is his own reported statement to an official at the U.S. Embassy in Moscow. That statement, of course, was contradicted by his denial to the FBI, upon his return to the United States, that he had ever made such an offer.

> In the prosecution of a criminal case, the Government cannot establish a prima facie case solely on a defendant's unsupported confession. The Government must introduce substantial independent evidence which would tend to establish the trustworthiness of the defendant's statement. See, *Opper* v. *United States* 348 U.S. 84 (1954).

> Accordingly, in the absence of any information that Oswald had offered to reveal classified information to the Soviets, and lacking corroboration of his statement that he had proferred information of any kind to the Russians, we did not consider his prosecution for violation of the espionage statutes, 18 U.S.C. 793, 794.(*111*)

Based upon this analysis, the committee could find no evidence that Oswald received favorable treatment from either the State Department or the Justice Department regarding the possibility of criminal prosecution.

(13) *Oswald's trip to Russia via Helsinki and his ability to obtain a visa in 2 days.*—Oswald's trip from London to Helsinki has been a point of controversy. His passport indicates he arrived in Finland on October 10, 1959. The Torni Hotel in Helsinki, however, had him registered as a guest on that date, although the only direct flight from London to Helsinki landed at 11:33 p.m., that day. According to a memorandum signed in 1964 by Richard Helms, "[i]f Oswald had taken this flight, he could not normally have cleared customs and landing formalities and reached the Torni Hotel downtown by 2400 (midnight) on the same day."(*112*) Further questions concerning this segment of Oswald's trip have been raised because he had been able to obtain a Soviet entry visa within only 2 days of having applied for it on October 12, 1959.(*113*) [19]

The committee was unable to determine the circumstances surrounding Oswald's trip from London to Helsinki. Louis Hopkins, the travel agent who arranged Oswald's initial transportation from the United States, stated that he did not know Oswald's ultimate destination at the time that Oswald booked his passage on the freighter *Marion Lykes*.(*114*) Consequently, Hopkins had nothing to do with the London-to-Helsinki leg of Oswald's trip. In fact, Hopkins stated that had he known Oswald's final destination, he would have suggested sailing on another ship that would have docked at a port more convenient to Russia.(*115*) Hopkins indicated that Oswald did not appear to be particularly well-informed about travel to Europe. The travel agent did not know whether Oswald had been referred to him by anyone.(*116*)

A request for any CIA and Department of Defense files on Louis Hopkins resulted in a negative response. The committee was unable to obtain any additional sources of information regarding Oswald's London-to-Helsinki trip.

The relative ease with which Oswald obtained his Soviet Union entry visa was more readily amenable to investigation. This issue is one that also had been of concern to the Warren Commission.(*117*) In a letter to the CIA dated May 25, 1964, J. Lee Rankin inquired about the apparent speed with which Oswald's Soviet visa had been issued. Rankin noted that he had recently spoken with Abraham Chayes, legal adviser to the State Department, who maintained that at the time Oswald received his visa to enter Russia from the Soviet Embassy in Helsinki, normally at least 1 week would elapse between the time of a tourist's application and the issuance of a visa. Rankin contended that if Chayes' assessment was accurate, then Oswald's ability to obtain his tourist visa in 2 days might have been significant.(*118*)

The CIA responded to Rankin's request for information on July 31, 1964. Helms wrote to Rankin that the Soviet Consulate in Helsinki

[19] Since Oswald arrived in Helsinki on October 10, 1959, which was a Saturday, it is assumed that his first opportunity to apply for a visa would have been on Monday, October 12.

was able to issue a transit visa (valid for 24 hours) to U.S. business-men within 5 minutes, but if a longer stay were intended, at least 1 week was needed to process a visa application and arrange lodging through Soviet Intourist.(119) A second communication from Helms to Rankin, dated September 14, 1964, added that during the 1964 tourist season, Soviet consulates in at least some Western European cities issued Soviet tourist visas in from 5 to 7 days.(120)

In an effort to resolve this issue, the committee reviewed classified information pertaining to Gregory Golub, who was the Soviet Consul in Helsinki when Oswald was issued his tourist visa. This review revealed that, in addition to his consular activities, Golub was suspected of having been an officer of the Soviet KGB. Two American Embassy dispatches concerning Golub were of particular significance with regard to the time necessary for issuance of visas to Americans for travel into the Soviet Union. The first dispatch recorded that Golub disclosed during a luncheon conversation that:

> Moscow had given him the authority to give Americans visas without prior approval from Moscow. He [Golub] stated that this would make his job much easier, and as long as he was convinced the American was "all right" he could give him a visa in a matter of minutes * * *.(121)

The second dispatch, dated October 9, 1959, 1 day prior to Oswald's arrival in Helsinki, illustrated that Golub did have the authority to issue visas without delay. The dispatch discussed a telephone contact between Golub and his consular counterpart at the American Embassy in Helsinki:

> * * * Since that evening [September 4, 1959] Golub has only phoned [the U.S. consul] once and this was on a business matter. Two Americans were in the Soviet Consulate at the time and were applying for Soviet visas thru Golub. They had previously been in the American consulate inquiring about the possibility of obtaining a Soviet visa in 1 or 2 days. [The U.S. Consul] advised them to go directly to Golub and make their request, which they did. Golub phoned [the U.S. Consul] to state that he would give them their visas as soon as they made advance Intourist reservations. When they did this, Golub immediately gave them their visas * * *.[20](122)

Thus, based upon these two factors, (1) Golub's authority to issue visas to Americans without prior approval from Moscow, and (2) a demonstration of this authority, as reported in an embassy dispatch approximately 1 month prior to Oswald's appearance at the Soviet Embassy, the committee found that the available evidence tends to support the conclusion that the issuance of Oswald's tourist visa within 2 days after his appearance at the Soviet Consulate was not indicative of an American intelligence agency connection.[21]

[20] Evidently Oswald had made arrangements with Intourist. On his arrival at the Moscow railroad station on October 16, he was met by an Intourist representative and taken to the Hotel Berlin where he registered as a student.(123)
[21] If anything, Oswald's ability to receive a Soviet entry visa so quickly was more indicative of a Soviet interest in him.

(14) *Oswald's contact with Americans in the Soviet Union.*—
Priscilla Johnson McMillan, author of "Marina and Lee," became a
subject of the committee's inquiry because she was one of two American
correspondents who had obtained an interview with Oswald during his
stay in Moscow in 1959. The committee sought to investigate an allegation that her interview with Oswald may have been arranged by the
CIA. (124)

John McVickar, a consul at the American Embassy, testified that he
had discussed Oswald's case with McMillan, and that he thought
"* * * she might help us in communicating with him and help him in
dealing with what appeared to be a very strong personal problem if
she were able to talk with him." (125) McVickar stated, however, that
he had never worked in any capacity for the CIA, nor did he believe
that McMillan had any such affiliation. (126) McVickar's State Department and CIA files were consistent with his testimony that he had
never been associated with the CIA.

McMillan gave the following testimony about the events surrounding her interview with Oswald. In November 1959, she had returned
from a visit to the United States where she covered the Camp David
summit meeting between President Eisenhower and Premier Khrushchev. On November 16, 1959, she went to the American Embassy to pick
up her mail for the first time since her return to the Soviet Union. The
mail pickup facility was in a foyer near the consular office. Consular
Officer John A. McVickar came out of this office and welcomed McMillan back to the Soviet Union. They exchanged a few words, and, as
she was leaving, McVickar commented that at her hotel was an American who was trying to defect to the Soviet Union. McVickar stated
that the American would not speak to "any of us," but he might speak
to McMillan because she was a woman. She recalled that as she
was leaving, McVickar told her to remember that she was an
American. (127)

McMillan proceeded to her hotel, found out the American's room
number, knocked on his door and asked him for an interview. The
American, Lee Harvey Oswald, did not ask her into the room, but he
did agree to talk to her in her room later that night. (128) No American Government official arranged the actual interview. McMillan met
with Oswald just once. She believed that McVickar called her on November 17, the day after the interview, and asked her to supper. That
evening they discussed the interview. McVickar indicated a general
concern about Oswald and believed that the attitude of another American consular official might have pushed Oswald further in the direction of defection. McVickar indicated a personal feeling that it would
be a sad thing for Oswald to defect in view of his age, but he did not
indicate that this was the U.S. Government's position. (129)

McMillan also testified that she had never worked for the CIA, nor
had she been connected with any other Federal Government agency
at the time of her interview with Oswald. (130) According to an affidavit that McMillan filed with the committee, her only employment
with the Federal Government was as a 30-day temporary
translator. (131)

Finally, McMillan testified that because of her background in Russian studies, she applied for a position with the CIA in 1952 as an

intelligence analyst. The application, however, was withdrawn. (*132*)
She acknowledged having been debriefed by an Agency employee in
1962 after returning from her third trip to the Soviet Union, but
explained that this contact was in some way related to the confiscation of her notes by Soviet officials. (*133*) [22]

The committee's review of CIA files pertaining to Ms. McMillan
corroborated her testimony. There was no indication in these files
suggesting that she had ever worked for the CIA. In fact, the Agency
did not even debrief her after her first two trips to the Soviet Union.
An interview with the former Agency official who had been deputy
chief and then chief of the visitors program during the years 1958 to
1961 similarly indicated that McMillan had not been used by the CIA
in the program. (*134*)

There was information in McMillan's file indicating that on occasion during the years 1962–65 she had provided cultural and literary
information to the CIA. None of this information was, however, suggestive in any way of a clandestine relationship. Accordingly, there
was no evidence that McMillan ever worked for the CIA or received
the Agency's assistance in obtaining an interview with Oswald. [23]

Richard E. Snyder was the consular official in the U.S. Embassy in
Moscow who handled the Oswald case. It was Snyder with whom Oswald had met in 1959 when he sought to renounce his American citizenship. (*135*) Two years later, when Oswald initiated his inquiries
about returning to the United States, Snyder again became involved
in the case. (*136*) Warren Commission critics have alleged that Snyder
was associated in some way with the CIA during his service in the
Moscow Embassy. (*137*)

In his committee deposition, Richard Snyder acknowledged that
for a 11-month period during 1949–50 he worked for the CIA while
he was on the waiting list for a foreign service appointment with the
State Department. (*138*) Snyder testified, however, that since resigning from the CIA in March 1950, he had had no contact with the CIA
other than a letter written in 1970 or 1971 inquiring about employment on a contractual basis. (*139*) [24]

The committee reviewed Snyder's files at the State Department,
Defense Department and the CIA. Both the State Department and
Defense Department files are consistent with his testimony. Snyder's
CIA file revealed that, at one time prior to 1974, it had been red
flagged and maintained on a segregated basis. The file contained a

[22] In her affidavit McMillan discussed the circumstances surrounding this encounter in
some detail: "In November 1962, I had a conversation with a man who identified himself
as a CIA employee * * * I agreed to see him in part because the confiscation of my papers
and notes had utterly altered my situation—I now had no hope of returning to the
U.S.S.R. and was free for the first time to write what I knew. I was preparing a series of
articles for The Reporter which would contain the same information about which [the
CIA employee] had expressed a desire to talk to me. Finally, during the latter part of my
1962 trip to the U.S.S.R., I had been under heavy surveillance and the KGB knew what
Soviet citizens I had seen. Many of those I had talked to for the Reporter articles were
Russian 'liberals' (anti-Stalin and pro-Khrushchev). What reprisals might befall those
whom I had interviewed I did not know, but since my notes were now part of the KGB
files, I felt that it might help them if the CIA knew that which the KGB already knew.
My meeting with—the CIA employee—which occurred at the Brattle Inn, Cambridge, was a
reversal of my usual effort to avoid contact with the CIA, and the subject matter was
confined to my impressions of the Soviet literary and cultural climate."
[23] Nor was there any basis, based on McMillan's testimony, CIA files or evidence provided by McMillan's publisher, Harper and Row, to support the allegation that the CIA
financed or was otherwise involved in publishing "Marina and Lee."
[24] Snyder also denied contact with any other intelligence service while active as a
foreign service officer.

routing indicator that stated that the file had been red flagged because of a "DCI [Director of Central Intelligence] statement and a matter of cover" concerning Snyder. (140)

In response to a committee inquiry, the CIA indicated that the DCI statement presumably refers to comments which former Director Richard Helms had made in 1964 concerning the Oswald case, when Helms was Deputy Director for Plans.[25] The CIA also stated that Snyder's file had been flagged at the request of DDO/CI (Directorate of Operations/Central Intelligence) to insure that all inquiries concerning Snyder would be referred to that office. The Agency was unable to explain the reference to "cover," because, according to its records, Snyder had never been assigned any cover while employed. Further, the Agency stated that "[t]here is no record in Snyder's official personnel file that he ever worked, directly or indirectly, in any capacity for the CIA after his resignation on 26 September 1950." (142)

The committee did not regard this explanation as satisfactory, especially since Snyder's 201 file indicated that for approximately 1 year during 1956–57 he had been used by an Agency case officer as a spotter at a university campus because of his access to others who might be going to the Soviet Union, nor was the Agency able to explain specifically why someone considered it necessary to red flag the Snyder file.

The remainder of the Snyder file, however, is consistent with his testimony before the committee concerning the absence of Agency contacts. In addition, the CIA personnel officer who handled Snyder's case in 1950 confirmed that Snyder had, in fact, terminated his employment with the CIA at that time. Moreover, he added that Snyder had gone to the State Department as a bona fide employee without any CIA ties. (143) This position was confirmed by a former State Department official who was familiar with State Department procedures regarding CIA employees. In addition, this individual stated that at no time from 1959 to 1963 did the CIA use the State Department's overseas consular positions as cover for CIA intelligence officers. (144)

The CIA's failure to explain adequately the red-flagging of Snyder's file was extremely troubling to the committee. Even so, based on Snyder's sworn testimony, the review of his file and the statements of his former personnel officer, a finding that he was in contact with Oswald on behalf of the CIA was not warranted.

Dr. Alexis H. Davison was the U.S. Embassy physician in Moscow from May 1961 to May 1963. In May 1963, the Soviet Union declared him persona non grata in connection with his alleged involvement in the Penkovsky case. (145) After the assassination of President Kennedy, it was discovered that the name of Dr. Davison's mother, Mrs. Hal Davison, and her Atlanta address were in Oswald's address book under the heading "Mother of U.S. Embassy Doctor." (146) In addition, it was determined that the flight that Oswald, his wife and child took from New York to Dallas on June 14, 1962, had stopped in Atlanta. (147) For this reason, it has been alleged that Dr. Davison was Oswald's intelligence contact in Moscow. (148)

---

[25] Responding to a newspaper allegation that Oswald had met with CIA representatives in Moscow, Richard Helms wrote a memorandum to the Warren Commission on March 18, 1964, in which he stated the "desire to state for the record that the allegation carried in this press report is utterly unfounded as far as the CIA is concerned." (141)

In a committee interview, Dr. Davison stated that he had been a physician in the U.S. Air Force and was stationed in Moscow as the U.S. Embassy physician from May 1961 to May 1963. In this capacity, it was his duty to perform physical examinations on all Soviet immigrants to the United States. He recalled that most of these immigrants were elderly, but he remembers two young women, one who was a mathematics teacher from the south of Russia and one who was married to an American. The individual who was married to the American was frightened by the prospect of going to the United States. She stated that she was going to Texas with her husband. Davison told her that if she and her husband traveled through Atlanta on their way to Texas, his mother, a native-born Russian, would be happy to see her. He gave his mother's name and address in Atlanta to the woman's husband, who was "scruffy looking." This was not an unusual thing to do, since his family had always very hospitable to Russians who visited Atlanta. In retrospect, he assumed that he gave his mother's name and address to either Lee or Marina Oswald, but he was uncertain about this. (149)

After the assassination of President Kennedy, Davison was interviewed first by a Secret Service agent and later by an FBI agent in connection with the entry of his mother's name and address in Oswald's address book. The FBI agent also interviewed Davison's mother, Natalia Alekseevna Davison. Davison indicated that the Secret Service and the FBI were the only Government agencies to interview him about his contact with the Oswalds. (150)

Davison stated that in connection with his assignment as U.S. Embassy physician in Moscow, he had received some superficial intelligence training. This training mainly involved lectures on Soviet life and instructions on remembering and reporting Soviet names and military activities. (151)

Davison admitted his involvement in the Penkovsky spy case. During his tour of duty in Moscow, Davison was asked by an Embassy employee, whose name he no longer remembered, to observe a certain lamppost on his daily route between his apartment and the Embassy and to be alert for a signal by telephone. Davison agreed. According to his instructions, if he ever saw a black chalk mark on the lamppost, or if he ever received a telephone call in which the caller blew into the receiver three times, he was to notify a person whose name he also no longer remembered. He was told nothing else about the operation. Davison performed his role for approximately 1 year. On just one occasion, toward the end of his stay in the Soviet Union, he observed the mark on the lamppost and his wife received the telephone signal. As instructed, he reported these happenings. Shortly thereafter, the Soviets reported that they had broken the Penkovsky spying operation. The Soviets declared Davison persona non grata just after he left Moscow, his tour of duty having ended. He did not recall any intelligence debriefings on the Penkovsky case. (152)

Davison denied under oath participating in any other intelligence work during his tour in Moscow. (153) The deputy chief of the CIA's Soviet Russia clandestine activities section from 1960 to 1962 confirmed Davison's position, characterizing his involvement in the Penkovsky case as a "one shot" deal. (154) In addition, a review of Davison's CIA and Department of Defense files showed them to be consistent with his committee testimony.

Accordingly, there was insufficient evidence for concluding that Dr. Davison was an intelligence contact for Oswald in Moscow.

(15) *Alleged intelligence contacts after Oswald returned from Russia.*—George de Mohrenschildt was an enigmatic man—a geologist-businessman who befriended Oswald in Texas in 1962, (*155*) thus causing considerable speculation based on the contrasting backgrounds of the two men. De Mohrenschildt, who committed suicide in 1977, was sophisticated and well educated, a man who moved easily among wealthy Texas oilmen and a circle of white Russians in Dallas, many of whom were avowed conservatives. Oswald, because of his background and his Marxist ideological positions, was shunned by most of the people de Mohrenschildt counted among his friends.

In his Warren Commission testimony, de Mohrenschildt stated that he believed he had discussed Oswald with J. Walton Moore, whom he described as "a Government man—either FBI or Central Intelligence." (*156*) He said that Moore was known as the head of the FBI in Dallas, and that Moore had interviewed him in 1957 when he returned from a trip to Yugoslavia. (*157*) De Mohrenschildt indicated that he had asked Moore and Fort Worth attorney Max Clark about Oswald, to reassure himself that it was "safe" for the de Mohrenschildts to assist him and was told by one of these persons, "The guy seems to be OK." (*158*) This admitted association with J. Walton Moore, an employee of the CIA, gave rise to the question of whether de Mohrenschildt had contacted Oswald on behalf of the CIA. (*159*)

In 1963, J. Walton Moore was employed by the CIA in Dallas in the Domestic Contacts Division. (*160*) According to Moore's CIA personnel file, he had been assigned to the division in 1948. During the period April 1, 1963, to March 31, 1964, he was an overt CIA employee assigned to contact persons traveling abroad for the purpose of eliciting information they might obtain. He was not part of a covert or clandestine operation.

In an Agency memorandum dated April 13, 1977, contained in de Mohrenschildt's CIA file, Moore set forth facts to counter a claim that had been recently made by a Dallas television station that Oswald had been employed by the CIA and that Moore had known him. In that memorandum, Moore was quoted as saying that, according to his records, the last time he had talked with de Mohrenschildt was in the fall of 1961. Moore said that he had no recollection of any conversation with de Mohrenschildt concerning Oswald. The memorandum also said that Moore recalled only two occasions when he had met de Mohrenschildt—first, in the spring of 1958, to discuss a mutual interest in China; and then in the fall of 1961, when de Mohrenschildt and his wife showed films of their Latin American walking trip. (*161*)

Other documents in de Mohrenschildt's CIA file, however, indicated more contact with Moore than was stated in the 1977 memorandum. In a memorandum dated May 1, 1964, submitted to the Acting Chief of the Domestic Contacts Division of the CIA, Moore stated that he had known de Mohrenschildt and his wife since 1957, at which time Moore obtained biographical data on de Mohrenschildt following his trip to Yugoslavia for the International Cooperation Administration. Moore also wrote in that 1964 memorandum that he had seen de Mohrenschildt several times in 1958 and 1959. De Mohrenschildt's CIA file contained several reports submitted by de Mohrenschildt to the CIA on topics concerning Yugoslavia.(*162*)

De Mohrenschildt testified before the Warren Commission that he had never been in any respect an intelligence agent.(*163*) Further, the committee's interview with Moore and its review of the CIA's Moore and de Mohrenschildt files showed no evidence that de Mohrenschildt had ever been an American intelligence agent. (In this regard, the committee noted that during 1959–63, upon returning from trips abroad, as many as 25,000 Americans annually provided information to the CIA's Domestic Contacts Division on a nonclandestine basis.(*164*) Such acts of cooperation should not be confused with an actual Agency relationship).[26]

Prior to visiting Mexico in September 1963, Oswald applied in New Orleans for a Mexican tourist card. The tourist card immediately preceding his in numerical sequence was issued on September 17, 1963, (*167*) to William G. Gaudet, a newspaper editor. Two days later, Gaudet departed on a 3- or 4-week trip to Mexico and other Latin American countries.(*168*) This happened to coincide with Oswald's visit to Mexico City between September 27, 1963, and October 3, 1963.(*169*) After the assassination, Gaudet advised the FBI during an interview that he had once been employed by the CIA.(*170*) Speculation about Gaudet's possible relationship with Oswald arose when it was discovered that the Warren Commission Report contained a list, provided by the Mexican Government, purporting to include all individuals who had been issued Mexican tourist cards at the same time as Oswald, a list that omitted Gaudet's name.(*171*)

In a committee deposition, Gaudet testified that his contact with the CIA was primarily as a source of information (obtained during his trips abroad). In addition, he explained that he occasionally performed errands for the Agency.(*172*) Gaudet stated that his last contact with the CIA was in 1969, although the relationship had never been formally terminated.(*173*)

The committee reviewed Gaudet's CIA file but found neither any record reflecting a contact between him and the Agency after 1961, nor any indication that he had "performed errands" for the CIA. A memorandum, dated January 23, 1976, also indicated the absence of any further contact after this time:

> The Domestic Collections Division (DCD) has an inactive file on William George Gaudet, former editor and publisher of the Latin American Report. The file shows that Gaudet was a source of the New Orleans DCD (Domestic Contacts Division) Resident Office from 1948 to 1955 during which period he provided foreign intelligence information on Latin American political and economic conditions resulting from his extensive travel in South and Central America in pursuit

---

[26] De Mohrenschildt's file also contains a reference to an occasion when he may have been involved in arranging a meeting between a Haitian bank officer and a CIA or Department of Defense official.(*165*) The Department of Defense official, when interviewed by the committee, stated that the meeting was arranged by Department of Defense officials and that de Mohrenschildt's presence (in the company of his wife) was unanticipated. (*166*) The committee did not regard this incident as evidence of a CIA relationship.

of journalistic interests. The file further indicates that Gaudet was a casual contact of the New Orleans Office between 1955 and 1961 when, at various times, he furnished fragmentary intelligence. (*174*)

Gaudet said he could not recall whether his trip to Mexico and other Latin American countries in 1963 involved any intelligence-related activity. (*175*) He was able to testify, however, that during that trip he did not encounter Oswald, whom he had previously observed on occasion at the New Orleans Trade Mart. (*176*) [27] Gaudet stated that he was unaware at the time his Mexican tourist card was issued that it immediately preceded Oswald's, and he could not recall having seen Oswald on that day. (*177*) Finally, Gaudet said he did not have any information concerning the omission of his name from the list published in the Warren Commission Report. (*178*)

Based upon this evidence, the committee did not find a basis for concluding that Gaudet had contacted Oswald on behalf of the CIA. Although there was a conflict between Gaudet's testimony and his CIA file concerning the duration of his Agency contacts as well as the performance of errands, there was no indication from his file or testimony that Gaudet's cooperation involved clandestine activity. Again, it should be stressed that the Domestic Contacts Division, which was the Agency component that was in touch with Gaudet, was not involved in clandestine operations.

(16) *Alleged intelligence implications of Oswald's military service.*—The committee reviewed Oswald's military records because of allegations that he had received intelligence training and had participated in intelligence operations during his term of Marine service. (*179*) Particular attention was given to the charges that Oswald's early discharge from the corps was designed to serve as a cover for an intelligence assignment and that his records reflected neither his true security clearance nor a substantial period of service in Taiwan. These allegations were considered relevant to the question of whether Oswald had been performing intelligence assignments for military intelligence, as well as to the issue of Oswald's possible association with the CIA.

Oswald's Marine Corps records bear no indication that he ever received any intelligence training or performed any intelligence assignments during his term of service. As a Marine serving in Atsugi, Japan, Oswald had a security clearance of confidential, but never received a higher classification. (*180*) In his Warren Commission testimony, John E. Donovan, the officer who had been in charge of Oswald's crew at the El Toro Marine base in California, stated that all personnel working in the radar center were required to have a minimum security clearance of secret. (*181*) Thus, the allegation has been made that the security clearance of confidential in Oswald's records is inaccurate. The committee, however, reviewed files belonging to four enlisted men who had worked with Oswald either in Japan or California and found that each of them had a security clearance of confidential. (*182*) [28]

---

[27] Gaudet testified that he had never met Oswald, although he had known of him prior to the assassination because Oswald had distributed literature near his office. Gaudet also stated that on one occasion he observed Oswald speaking to Guy Bannister on a street corner.

[28] John E. Donovan, Oswald's commanding officer, did have a security clearance of secret.

It has been stated that Oswald claimed to have served in Taiwan. *(183)* The committee's review of his military records, including unit diaries that were not previously studied by the Warren Commission, indicated, however, that he had not spent substantial time, if any, in Taiwan. These records show that, except for a 3½ month period of service in the Philippines, Oswald served in Japan from September 12, 1957, until November 2, 1958. *(184)* Although Department of Defense records do indicate that MAG (Marine Air Group) 11, Oswald's unit, was deployed to Taiwan on September 16, 1958, and remained in that area until April 1959, an examination of the MAG 11 unit diaries indicated that Oswald was assigned at that time to a rear echelon unit. *(185)* The term rear echelon does not, on its face, preclude service with the main unit in Taiwan, but the Department of Defense has specifically stated that "Oswald did not sail from Yokosuka, Japan on September 16, 1958. He remained aboard NAS Atsugi as part of the MAG–11 rear echelon." [29] *(186)*

Oswald's records also reflect that on October 6, 1958, he was transferred within MAG 11 to a Headquarters and Maintenance Squadron subunit in Atsugi, Japan. *(187)* He reportedly spent the next week in the Atsugi Station Hospital. *(188)* On November 2, 1958, Oswald left Japan for duty in the United States. *(189)*

Accordingly, based upon a direct examination of Oswald's unit diaries, as well as his own military records, it does not appear that he had spent any time in Taiwan. This finding is contrary to that of the Warren Commission that Oswald arrived with his unit in Taiwan on September 30, 1958, and remained there somewhat less than a week, *(190)* but the Commission's analysis apparently was made without access to the unit diaries of MAG 11. [30]

Moreover, even if Oswald, in fact, did make the trip with his unit to Taiwan, it is clear that any such service there was not for a substantial time. The unit arrived at Atsugi on September 30, 1958, and by November 2, 1958, Oswald had left from Japan to complete his tour of duty in the United States. *(192)*

Finally, with one exception, the circumstances surrounding Oswald's rapid discharge from the military do not appear to have been unusual. Oswald was obligated to serve on active duty until December 7, 1959, but on August 17 he applied for a hardship discharge to support his mother. About 2 weeks later the application was approved. *(193)* [31]

It appeared that Oswald's hardship discharge application was processed so expeditiously because it was accompanied by all of the necessary documentation. In response to a committee inquiry, the Department of Defense stated that "... to a large extent, the time involved in processing hardship discharge applications depended on how well the individual member had prepared the documentation needed for

---

[29] This is contrary to statements attributed to Lieutenant Charles R. Rhodes by Edward J. Epstein in his book, "The Secret World of Lee Harvey Oswald." Rhodes maintains, according to Epstein, that Oswald did make the trip with the main unit but was sent back to Japan on October 6, 1958.

[30] Similarly, a message sent on November 4, 1959, from the Chief of Naval Operations concerning Oswald, which states that he had "served with Marine Air Control Squadrons in Japan and Taiwan," *(191)* may have been issued without checking unit diaries which indicated that Oswald had not been so deployed.

[31] By September 4, 1959, Oswald had been informed that he would be discharged on September 11, 1959. *(194)* This explains why he was able to tell passport officials on that day that he expected to depart the United States for Europe on September 21, 1959.

consideration of his or her case."(*195*) A review of Oswald's case indicates that his initial hardship discharge application was accompanied by all of the requisite documentation. Oswald had met the preliminary requirements of having made a voluntary contribution to the hardship dependent (his mother) and of applying for a dependent's quarters allotment [32] to alleviate the hardship.(*196*) Even though all of the supporting affidavits for the quarters allotment had not been submitted at the time that the hardship discharge application was filed, the endorsements on the application indicated that the reviewing officers were aware that both the requisite voluntary contribution and the application for a quarters allotment had been made.(*197*) Moreover, that application was accompanied by two letters and two affidavits attesting to Marguerite Oswald's inability to support herself.(*198*)

Documents provided to the committee by the American Red Cross indicate that Oswald had sought its assistance and therefore was probably well advised on the requisite documentation to support his claim.(*199*) Indeed, Red Cross officials interviewed Marguerite Oswald and concluded that she "could not be considered employable from an emotional standpoint."(*200*) The Fort Worth Red Cross office indicated a quarters allotment was necessary for Marguerite Oswald, rather than a hardship discharge for Lee, and assisted her in the preparation of the necessary application documents.(*201*) Nevertheless, Oswald informed the Red Cross office in El Toro, Calif., where he was then stationed, that he desired to apply for a hardship discharge. (*202*)

The unusual aspect of Oswald's discharge application was that, technically, his requisite application for a quarters allowance for his mother should have been disallowed because Marguerite's dependency affidavit stated that Oswald had not contributed any money to her during the preceding year.(*203*) Even so, the first officer to review Oswald's application noted in his endorsement, dated August 19, 1959, that "[a] genuine hardship exists in this case, and in my opinion approval of the 'Q' [quarters] allotment will not sufficiently alleviate this situation."(*204*) This quotation suggests the possibility that applications for quarters allotments and hardship discharges are considered independently of one another. In addition, six other officers endorsed Oswald's application.(*205*) The committee was able to contact three of the seven endorsing officers (one had died); two had no memory of the event,(*206*) and one could not recall any details.(*207*) The committee considered their absence of memory to be indicative of the Oswald case having been handled in a routine manner.

Based on this evidence, the committee was not able to discern any unusual discrepancies or features in Oswald's military record.

(*17*) *Oswald's military intelligence file.*—On November 22, 1963, soon after the assassination, Lieutenant Colonel Robert E. Jones, operations officer of the U.S. Army's 112th Military Intelligence Group (MIG), Fort Sam Houston, San Antonio, Tex., contacted the FBI offices in San Antonio and Dallas and gave those offices detailed information concerning Oswald and A. J. Hidell, Oswald's alleged alias. (*208*) This information suggested the existence of a military intelli-

---

[32] A dependent's quarters allotment is one that is jointly paid to the dependent by the serviceman and the service.

222

gence file on Oswald and raised the possibility that he had intelligence associations of some kind. (209)

The committee's investigation revealed that military intelligence officials had opened a file on Oswald because he was perceived as a possible counterintelligence threat. Robert E. Jones testified before the committee that in June 1963 he had been serving as operations officer of the 112th Military Intelligence Group at Fort Sam Houston, Tex.[33] Under the group's control were seven regions encompassing five States: Texas. Louisiana. Arkansas, New Mexico and Oklahoma. Jones was directly responsible for counterintelligence operations, background investigations, domestic intelligence and any special operations in this five-State area. (210) He believed that Oswald first came to his attention in mid-1963 through information provided to the 112th MIG by the New Orleans Police Department to the effect that Oswald had been arrested there in connection with Fair Play for Cuba Committee activities. (211) As a result of this information, the 112th Military Intelligence Group took an interest in Oswald as a possible counterintelligence threat. (212) It collected information from local agencies and the military central records facility, and opened a file under the names Lee Harvey Oswald and A. J. Hidell. (213) Placed in this file were documents and newspaper articles on such topics as Oswald's defection to the Soviet Union, his travels there, his marriage to a Russian national, his return to the United States, and his pro-Cuba activities in New Orleans. (214)

Jones related that on November 22. 1963. while in his quarters at Fort Sam Houston, he heard about the assassination of President Kennedy. (215) Returning immediately to his office, he contacted MIG personnel in Dallas and instructed them to intensify their liaisons with Federal. State and local agencies and to report back any information obtained. Early that afternoon, he received a telephone call from Dallas advising that an A. J. Hidell had been arrested or had come to the attention of law enforcement authorities. Jones checked the MIG indexes, which indicated that there was a file on Lee Harvey Oswald, also known by the name A. J. Hidell. (216) Pulling the file, he telephoned the local FBI office in San Antonio to notify the FBI that he had some information. (217) He soon was in telephone contact with the Dallas FBI office. to which he summarized the documents in the file. He believed that one person with whom he spoke was FBI Special-Agent-in-Charge J. Gordon Shanklin. He may have talked with the Dallas FBI office more than one time that day. (218)

Jones testified that his last activity with regard to the Kennedy assassination was to write an "after action" report that summarized the actions he had taken, the people he had notified and the times of notification. (219) In addition. Jones believed that this "after action" report included information obtained from reports filed by the 8 to 12 military intelligence agents who performed liaison functions with the Secret Service in Dallas on the day of the assassination. (220) This "after action" report was then maintained in the Oswald file. (221) Jones did not contact, nor was he contacted by, any other law enforce-

---

[33] Questions had been raised about the contents of some FBI communications on November 22. 1963, that reflected information allegedly provided by military intelligence. In his testimony, Jones clarified several points and corrected several errors in these communications.

ment or intelligence agencies concerning information that he could provide on Oswald.(*222*) To Jones' knowledge, neither the FBI nor any law enforcement agency ever requested a copy of the military intelligence file on Oswald.(*223*) To his surprise, neither the FBI, Secret Service, CIA nor Warren Commission ever interviewed him.(*224*) No one ever directed him to withhold any information; on the other hand, he never came forward and offered anyone further information relevant to the assassination investigation because he "felt that the information that [he] had provided was sufficient and . . . a matter of record. . . ."(*225*)

The committee found Jones' testimony to be credible. His statements concerning the contents of the Oswald file were consistent with FBI communications that were generated as a result of the information that he initially provided. Access to Oswald's military intelligence file, which the Department of Defense never gave to the Warren Commission, was not possible because the Department of Defense had destroyed the file as part of a general program aimed at eliminating all of its files pertaining to nonmilitary personnel. In response to a committee inquiry, the Department of Defense gave the following explanation for the file's destruction:

1. Dossier AB 652876, Oswald, Lee Harvey, was identified for deletion from IRR (Intelligence Records and Reports) holdings on Julian date 73060 (1 March 1973) as stamped on the microfilmed dossier cover. It is not possible to determine the actual date when physical destruction was accomplished, but is credibly surmised that the destruction was accomplished within a period not greater than 60 days following the identification for deletion. Evidence such as the type of deletion record available, the individual clerk involved in the identification, and the projects in progress at the time of deletion, all indicate the dossier deletion resulted from the implementation of a Department of the Army, Adjutant General letter dated 1 June 1971, subject: Acquisition of Information Concerning Persons and Organizations not Affiliated with the Department of Defense (DOD) (Incl 1). Basically, the letter called for the elimination of files on non-DOD affiliated persons and organizations.

2. It is not possible to determine who accomplished the actual physical destruction of the dossier. The individual identifying the dossier for deletion can be determined from the clerk number appearing on the available deletion record. The number indicates that Lyndall E. Harp was the identifying clerk. Harp was an employee of the IRR from 1969 until late 1973, at which time she transferred to the Defense Investigative Service, Fort Holabird, Md., where she is still a civil service employee. The individual ordering the destruction or deletion cannot be determined. However, available evidence indicates that the dossier was identified for deletion under a set of criteria applied by IRR clerks to all files. The basis for these criteria were [sic] established in the 1 June 1971 letter. There is no indication that the dossier was specifically identified for review or deletion. All evidence shows that the file was

reviewed as part of a generally applied program to eliminate any dossier concerning persons not affiliated with DOD.

3. The exact material contained in the dossier cannot be determined at this time. However, discussions with all available persons who recall seeing the dossier reveal that it most probably included: newspaper clippings relating to pro-Cuban activities of Oswald, several Federal Bureau of Investigation reports, and possibly some Army counterintelligence reports. None of the persons indicated that they remember any significant information in the dossier. It should be noted here that the Army was not asked to investigate the assassination. Consequently, any Army-derived information was turned over to the appropriate civil authority.

4. At the time of the destruction of the Oswald dossier, IRR was operating under the records disposal authority contained in the DOD Memorandum to Secretaries of the Military Departments, OASD(A), 9 February 1972, subject: Records Disposal Authority (Incl 2). The memorandum forwards National Archivist disposal criteria which is similar in nature to the requirements outlined in the 1 June 1971 instructions. It was not until 1975 that the Archivist changed the criteria to ensure non-destruction of investigative records that may be of historical value. (226)

Upon receipt of this information, the committee orally requested the destruction order relating to the file on Oswald. In a letter dated September 13, 1978, the General Counsel of the Department of the Army replied that no such order existed:

Army regulations do not require any type of specific order before intelligence files can be destroyed, and none was prepared in connection with the destruction of the Oswald file. As a rule, investigative information on persons not directly affiliated with the Defense Department can be retained in Army files only for short periods of time and in carefully regulated circumstances. The Oswald file was destroyed routinely in accordance with normal files management procedures, as are thousands of intelligence files annually. (227)

The committee found this "routine" destruction of the Oswald file extremely troublesome, especially when viewed in light of the Department of Defense's failure to make this file available to the Warren Commission. Despite the credibility of Jones' testimony, without access to this file, the question of Oswald's possible affiliation with military intelligence could not be fully resolved.

(18) *The Oswald photograph in Office of Naval Intelligence files.*— The Office of Naval Intelligence's (ONI) Oswald file contained a photograph of Oswald, taken at the approximate time of his Marine Corps induction. It was contained in an envelope that had on it the language "REC'D 14 November 1963" and "CIA 77978." (228) These markings raised the possibility that Oswald had been in some way associated with the CIA.

In response to a committee inquiry, the Department of Defense stated that the photograph had been obtained by ONI as a result of an October 4, 1963 CIA request for two copies of the most recent photographs of Oswald so that an attempt could be made to verify his reported presence in Mexico City. The requested copies, however, were not made available to the CIA until after the President's assassination.[34] Because of the absence of documentation, no explanation could be given for how or when the Office of Naval Intelligence received this particular photograph of Oswald. *(229)*

The committee's review of CIA cable traffic confirmed that cable No. 77978, dated October 24, 1963, was in fact a request for two copies of the Department of the Navy's most recent photograph of Lee Henry [sic] Oswald. Moreover, review of other cable traffic corroborated the Agency's desire to determine whether Lee Harvey Oswald had, in fact, been in Mexico City. *(230)*

The committee concluded, therefore, that the ONI photograph of Oswald bearing a reference to the CIA, was not evidence that Oswald was a CIA agent. Again, however, the destruction of the military file on Oswald prevented the committee from resolving the question of Oswald's possible affiliation with military intelligence.

(19) *Oswald in Mexico City.*—The committee also considered whether Oswald's activities in Mexico City in the fall of 1963 were indicative of a relationship between him and the CIA. This aspect of the committee's investigation involved a complete review both of alleged Oswald associates and of various CIA operations outside of the United States. *(231)*

The committee found no evidence of any relationship between Oswald and the CIA. Moreover, the Agency's investigative efforts prior to the assassination regarding Oswald's presence in Mexico City served to confirm the absence of any relationship with him. Specifically, when apprised of his possible presence in Mexico City, the Agency both initiated internal inquiries concerning his background and, once informed of his Soviet experience, notified other potentially interested Federal agencies of his possible contact with the Soviet Embassy in Mexico City. *(232)*

Conclusion

Based on the committee's entire investigation, it concluded that the Secret Service, FBI, and CIA were not involved in the assassination. The committee concluded that it is probable that the President was assassinated as a result of a conspiracy. Nothing in the committee's investigation pointed to official involvement in that conspiracy. While the committee frankly acknowledged that its investigation was not able to identify the members of the conspiracy besides Oswald, or the extent of the conspiracy, the committee believed that it did not include the Secret Service, Federal Bureau of Investigation, or Central Intelligence Agency.

---

[34] As noted, the military file on Oswald, presumably including the ONI photograph, was destroyed by the Department of Defense.